PHENOMENOLOGY AND PHILOSOPHY
OF MIND

Phenomenology and Philosophy of Mind

DAVID WOODRUFF SMITH
and
AMIE L. THOMASSON

CLARENDON PRESS · OXFORD

OXFORD
UNIVERSITY PRESS

Great Clarendon Street, Oxford OX2 6DP

Oxford University Press is a department of the University of Oxford.
It furthers the University's objective of excellence in research, scholarship,
and education by publishing worldwide in

Oxford New York

Auckland Cape Town Dar es Salaam Hong Kong Karachi
Kuala Lumpur Madrid Melbourne Mexico City Nairobi
New Delhi Shanghai Taipei Toronto

With offices in

Argentina Austria Brazil Chile Czech Republic France Greece
Guatemala Hungary Italy Japan Poland Portugal Singapore
South Korea Switzerland Thailand Turkey Ukraine Vietnam

Oxford is a registered trade mark of Oxford University Press
in the UK and in certain other countries

Published in the United States
by Oxford University Press Inc., New York

British Library Cataloguing in Publication Data

Data available

Library of Congress Cataloging in Publication Data

phenomenology and philosophy of mind / [edited by] David Woodruff Smith and Amie L.
Thomasson.
   p. cm.
   Includes bibliographical references and index.
1. Phenomenology. 2. Philosophy of mind. I. Smith, David Woodruff, 1944– II. Thomasson,
Amie L. (Amie Lynn), 1968–
   B829.5.P4531 2005
   128'.2—dc22   2005020148

Typeset by Newgen Imaging Systems (P) Ltd., Chennai, India
Printed in Great Britain
on acid-free paper by
Biddles Ltd., King's Lynn, Norfolk

ISBN 0–19–927244–1   978–0–19–927244–0
ISBN 0–19–927245–X (Pbk.)   978–0–19–927245–7 (Pbk.)

1 3 5 7 9 10 8 6 4 2

Acknowledgements

Portions of Paul Livingston's article appeared, in extended form, in chapter 5 of his book *Philosophical History and the Problem of Consciousness* (Cambridge University Press, 2004). This material is reprinted with the permission of Cambridge University Press.

Portions of Amie L. Thomasson's essay 'First Person Knowledge in Phenomenology' appeared in an earlier version as parts of 'Introspection and Phenomenological Method', *Phenomenology and the Cognitive Sciences*, 2/3 (2003), 239–54, © 2003 Kluwer Academic Publishers. That material appears here with kind permission of Kluwer Academic Publishers.

In the article by John Bickle and Ralph Ellis, Figure 3 is reprinted with permission from Figure 1 in Salzman et al. 1992, 2333, copyright 1992 by the Society for Neuroscience; Figure 4 is reprinted with permission from Figure 3 in Salzman et al. 1992, 2335, copyright 1992 by the Society for Neuroscience; and Figure 5 is reprinted with permission from Figure 1 in Britten and van Wezel, 1998, 60, copyright 1998 by Nature Publishing Group.

A much shorter version of the central sections of José Bermúdez's article was published as Bermúdez, J. L., 'The phenomenology of bodily awareness', *Theoria et Historia Scientiarum: International Journal for Interdisciplinary Studies* 7 (2004), 43–52. Material from that article is reproduced by kind permission of Tomasz Komendzinski and the Nicholas Copernicus University Press.

Contents

V. PERCEPTION, SENSATION, AND ACTION

Notes on Contributors

José Luis Bermúdez is Professor of Philosophy and Director of the Philosophy-Neuroscience-Psychology program at Washington University in St Louis. He is the author of *The Paradox of Self-Consciousness* (1998), *Thinking without Words* (2003), and *Philosophy of Psychology: A Contemporary Introduction* (2005).

John Bickle is Professor in the Department of Philosophy and in the Neuroscience Graduate Program at the University of Cincinnati. He is the author of *Psychoneural Reduction: The New Wave* (1998) and *Philosophy and Neuroscience: A Ruthlessly Reductive Account* (2003), and is co-author of *Understanding Scientific Reasoning*, 5th edn. (2005).

Johannes L. Brandl is Assistant Professor of Philosophy at the University of Salzburg. His recent publications are on Bolzano's theory of intuitions, on developmental issues in belief-ascriptions, on privileged access to the mind, and on the simplicity of perceptual experiences.

Clotilde Calabi is Associate Professor at the University of Milan. She is the author of *The Choosing Mind and the Judging Will: An Analysis of Attention* (1994), and *Passioni e ragioni. Un itinerario nella filosofia della psicologia* (Passions and Reasons. An Essay in the Philosophy of Psychology) (1996).

Taylor Carman is Associate Professor of Philosophy at Barnard College, Columbia University. He is author of *Heidegger's Analytic: Interpretation, Discourse, and Authenticity in 'Being and Time'* (2003) and coeditor of *The Cambridge Companion to Merleau-Ponty* (2004).

Ralph Ellis is Professor of Philosophy at Clark Atlanta University. He is the author of *An Ontology of Consciousness* (1986), *Theories of Criminal Justice* (1989), *Coherence and Verification in Ethics* (1992), *Questioning Consciousness* (1995), *Eros in a Narcissistic Culture* (1996), *Just Results: Ethical Foundations for Policy Analysis* (1998), and *The Caldron of Consciousness: Affect, Motivation, and Self-Organization* (2000).

Sean Dorrance Kelly is Assistant Professor of Philosophy at Princeton University. He is the author of *The Relevance of Phenomenology to the Philosophy of Language and Mind* (2000).

Paul Livingston is Assistant Professor of Philosophy at Villanova University. He is the author of *Philosophical History and the Problem of Consciousness* (2004).

Wayne M. Martin is Reader in Philosophy at the University of Essex. He is the author of *Idealism and Objectivity: Understanding Fichte's Jena Project* (1997) and *Theories of Judgment: Studies in the History of a Phenomeno-Logical Problem* (2005). He is the General Editor of *Inquiry: An Interdisciplinary Journal of Philosophy*.

Kay Mathiesen is Assistant Professor of Philosophy at Montclair State University. She has published articles on social ontology, collective action, and applied ethics.

Charles Siewert is Professor of Philosophy at the University of California at Riverside. He is author of *The Significance of Consciousness* (1998).

David Woodruff Smith is Professor of Philosophy at the University of California, Irvine. He is the author of *Mind World* (2004), *The Circle of Acquaintance* (1989), *Husserl and Intentionality* (1982, with Ronald McIntyre), and edited *The Cambridge Companion to Husserl* (1995, with Barry Smith).

Galen Strawson is Professor of Philosophy at the University of Reading and at City University of New York. He is the author of *Freedom and Belief* (1986), *The Secret Connexion (Realism, Causation, and David Hume)* (1989), and *Mental Reality* (1994).

Amie L. Thomasson is Associate Professor of Philosophy at the University of Miami. She is the author of *Fiction and Metaphysics* (1999).

Richard Tieszen is Professor of Philosophy at San Jose State University. He is the author of *Phenomenology, Logic and the Philosophy of Mathematics* (2005) and *Mathematical Intuition: Phenomenology and Mathematical Knowledge* (1989), and is co-editor of *Between Logic and Intuition: Essays in Honor of Charles Parsons* (2000).

Introduction

David Woodruff Smith and Amie L. Thomasson

Phenomenology and philosophy of mind can be defined either as disciplines or as historical traditions—they are both. As disciplines: phenomenology is the study of conscious experience as lived, as experienced from the first-person point of view, while philosophy of mind is the study of mind—states of belief, perception, action, etc.—focusing especially on the mind–body problem, how mental activities are related to brain activities. As traditions or literatures: phenomenology features the writings of Edmund Husserl, Martin Heidegger, Jean-Paul Sartre, Maurice Merleau-Ponty, Roman Ingarden, Aron Gurwitsch, and many others, while philosophy of mind includes the writings of Gilbert Ryle, David Armstrong, Hilary Putnam, Jerry Fodor, Daniel Dennett, John Searle, Paul Churchland and Patricia Smith Churchland, and many others. Historically, philosophy of mind has been considered part of the wider tradition called analytic philosophy, while phenomenology has been considered part of the wider tradition called continental philosophy. But all that is changing as we write, and the present volume is designed to express the change.

This volume involves both disciplinary and historical issues, and aims to integrate results and methods of the two disciplines in the interest of philosophy as a whole. There has been a long-standing assumption that—for historical, methodological, or doctrinal reasons—analytic philosophy of mind has little in common with the tradition of phenomenology that began with Brentano and was developed by Husserl and continued through such figures as Heidegger, Sartre, and Merleau-Ponty. This volume overturns that assumption by demonstrating how work in phenomenology may lead to progress on problems central to both classical phenomenology and contemporary philosophy of mind. Specifically, the essays gathered here (all written for the volume) bring ideas from classical phenomenology into the recent debates in philosophy of mind, and vice versa, in discussions of consciousness, intentionality, perception, action, self-knowledge, temporal awareness, holism about mental state contents, and the prospects for 'explaining' consciousness.

The assumption that phenomenology and analytic philosophy of mind form entirely separate traditions—with little dialogue between them possible or even desirable—is largely based on some pervasive misconceptions about the respective histories of phenomenology and philosophy of mind, as well as misconceptions about the basic goals, methods, and concepts of historical phenomenology. This introduction is designed to expose some of these misconceptions by reexamining the intertwined histories of the two traditions and clarifying the methods, goals, and central concepts of phenomenology in a way that can relieve us of the common misunderstandings. Once that work is done, the way will be cleared for the essays that follow to demonstrate the role of phenomenology (as an ongoing discipline) in the philosophy of mind (as on ongoing discipline).[1]

1. A BRIEF HISTORY OF PHILOSOPHY OF MIND

The canonical history of the philosophy of mind reads something like this:[2] In the eighteenth and nineteenth centuries, the study of the mind—in both rationalist and empiricist schools—was thought to proceed by introspection, not by the methods of external observation, experimentation, and theory-formation used in the natural sciences. But in the early twentieth century, at the point when philosophy and psychology were finally to diverge, the old 'introspectionist' approach to psychology was discredited. It was rejected by 'behaviorist' psychologists seeking to avoid guesswork about the mental states of human and animal subjects,[3] and by their philosophical counterparts adhering to the positivist view that propositions about mind or anything else can be meaningful only if publicly verifiable. If the scientific study of 'mind' was to survive at all, it had to be reconfigured as the study of something external, public, observable, and testable.

Initially, the obvious candidate for study was human behavior rather than 'inner' mental processes, and thus behaviorism came into prominence with psychologists like James Watson and B. F. Skinner. By the 1940s analytic philosophers were developing quasi-behaviorist analyses of language about mind, tying talk of mental states of sensation and belief to talk of behavior, this motif unfolding in Ludwig Wittgenstein, Gilbert Ryle, and Wilfrid Sellars. Though none were behaviorists proper, the air was laced with a certain suspicion of 'inner' mental states behind behavior and speech. Yet, as decades passed, the promised reductions of mind to behavior were not forthcoming. The elimination of the inner 'springs' of behavior seemed to have been a philosophical mistake, even if it had methodological benefits in psychology.

But what if mind were simply identified with brain? If the internal springs of action, in states of perception and thought and desire, were conceived not as distinct states of a Cartesian mind observable only by introspection, but as identical with physical states of the brain, then they too would be subject in principle to external observation

---

[1] Relations between phenomenology and philosophy of mind are the focus of two particularly relevant previous collections: Dreyfus (1982); Petitot et al. (1999). These two volumes concentrate on issues of cognitive science, at two periods in its recent history. The present volume aims to bring out conceptual and historical connections between phenomenology and analytic philosophy of mind broadly conceived (including but not exclusively focused on cognitive science).

[2] A nice synopsis of something like the canonical history may be found in Armstrong (1999: 3–7). An excellent sourcebook on philosophy of mind, congenial to the aims of the present volume, is Chalmers (2002). A wide-ranging collection of relevant work on consciousness in contemporary analytic philosophy of mind is Block et al. (1997).

[3] See, e.g., Watson (1914) and (1925), and Skinner (1938).

and scientific verification. Thus there arose, in the 1950s, the identity theory, proposed by U. T. Place, J. J. C. Smart, and David Armstrong as a way of reintroducing 'inner' mental states while retaining both public verifiability and a materialist ontology consistent with modern science. It was thus proposed, for example, that pain is simply identical with a certain process in the nervous system ('C-fiber stimulation', as the mock physiology put it).

However, when one-to-one correlations between types of neural states and types of mental states, such as belief and desire, were not forthcoming, heirs to the identity theory were developed. Taking root around 1970 in writings of Hilary Putnam and Jerry Fodor, functionalism identified mental state types with types of causal or computational function, rather than types of physical state defined, say, by structures of neurons. The computer model of information processing further encouraged a functionalist ontology, promoted by Daniel Dennett and others, proposing that mind is to brain as software is to hardware. Gradually, though, it became apparent that function alone does not capture the representational features of belief and desire, or the qualitative character of seeing yellow. The eliminativism developed by Paul Churchland and Patricia Smith Churchland then sought to eliminate the recalcitrant 'mental' states of common sense or 'folk' psychology in favor of neural network activity discovered by physical science alone.[4] These heirs to the identity theory are prominent on the stage of philosophy of mind today, seeking a theory of mind that is susceptible to empirical experimentation and committed only to a materialist ontology of physical-chemical-biological phenomena.

As a consequence of this path of development, contemporary philosophy of mind has been left with certain canonical problems and broad omissions. It is by now generally acknowledged that materialist views of mind at least have great difficulties in really explaining or understanding some of the philosophically most interesting features of mind, including the intentionality of many mental states, the nature and existence of sensory qualia, even the form and existence of consciousness itself.[5] Philosophers of mind such as Thomas Nagel and John Searle have argued for the irreducibly 'subjective' characters of consciousness and intentionality, while still seeking a naturalistic scientific metaphysics. Other traditional problems about consciousness also lie in waiting, involving, notably, the nature of time consciousness, whether or not sensation should be considered as exhibiting intentionality, and the possibility of collective consciousness. These features of mind don't seem susceptible to investigation by the natural scientific methods of public observation and testing (whether of behaviors, brain states, or causal roles), and so have been largely ignored by the mainstream materialist tradition, or treated in merely physiological or behavioral terms that seem to bypass the real philosophical issues. Thus, even in the view of its practitioners, contemporary philosophy of mind faces some great hurdles and leaves a lot of work to be

---

[4] Paul Feyerabend had proffered a view of eliminative materialism; the Churchlands pressed their case with details of neuroscience.

[5] Thus, e.g., Armstrong (1999: 6–7) lists consciousness, sensible qualities, and intentionality as the three most serious problems facing materialist views of mind. A detailed critique of contemporary naturalistic philosophy of mind, informed by phenomenology, is the introduction to Petitot et al. (1999).

done if it is to solve many of the central philosophical problems about the mental, including problems regarding intentionality, sensation, consciousness, and action—and if it is to provide the needed groundwork for addressing other philosophical problems dealing with action, artifacts, culture, and society.

2. THE HISTORY, CONCEPTS, AND METHODS OF PHENOMENOLOGY

The canonical history of philosophy of mind simply omits mention of phenomenology, on the assumption that the latter is part of a separate tradition of 'continental' philosophy, whose goals, methods, and doctrines are so completely separate from analytic philosophy of mind that the histories of the two traditions can be told in isolation. Phenomenology is well surveyed in its own right in many places.[6] But here we want to approach phenomenology in a context that includes philosophy of mind.

Phenomenology is often associated today with introspectionist psychology, the rejection of which marked the start of analytic philosophy of mind.[7] And so phenomenology is treated as justifiably ignored, and separated from philosophy of mind. But the idea that phenomenology is a hangover of an outmoded introspective approach to the mind is an unfortunate misconception that masks the history of the two traditions and misrepresents the goals and methods of phenomenology in a way that obscures its contribution to philosophy of mind.

The phenomenological approach to studying the mind was from the very start interwoven with the analytic tradition, as phenomenology grew out of Franz Brentano's response to John Stuart Mill, and Husserl's rejection of 'psychologistic' logic in Mill and other nineteenth-century authors.[8] In fact, Husserl's phenomenology influenced not only continental figures such as Heidegger, Sartre, and Merleau-Ponty, but also (less famously) central analytic figures including Rudolf Carnap, Gilbert Ryle, Wilfrid Sellars, and Hilary Putnam.[9] Most importantly, phenomenology sought a distinctively philosophical route to the study of the mind that avoids *both* the methods of introspectionist psychology *and* the methods of naturalistic psychology

---

[6] A brief overview of phenomenology, appropriate to our Introduction, is David Woodruff Smith (2003). A detailed survey of classical phenomenology is Moran (2000). Fundamentals of Husserlian phenomenology and its relation to philosophy of language, logic, and mind are laid out in Smith and McIntyre (1982). Barry Smith and David Woodruff Smith (1995) study key aspects of Husserl's philosophy in a broadly analytic style. A contemporary overview of transcendental phenomenology as a discipline is Sokolowski (2000).   [7] See Dennett (1987: 154, 157–8).

[8] See Dummett (1993–8).

[9] For discussion of the relationship between Husserl and Carnap see Friedman (1999). On the relation between Husserl and Ryle, see Livingston, this volume, and Thomasson (2002). Discussion of Sellars and Husserl may be found in Thomasson, this volume. For Husserl's influence on Putnam, see Putnam (1987), (1988), and (1981). There has also been at least an indirect influence on Jerry Fodor. Fodor's notion of a 'language of thought' develops a Lockean view detailed by Husserl, and Fodor's 'methodological solipsism' indirectly echoes Husserl's method of bracketing, as Carnap coined the term 'methodological solipsism' after hearing Husserl's lectures. (See Fodor (1982: 277–303).)

keyed to publicly observable physical phenomena—the methodology that has led to behaviorism, identity theories, functionalism, eliminativism, and their characteristic shortcomings.

On the standard story above, contemporary philosophy of mind emerged from the rejection of introspectionist psychology, the insistence on studying the mind via the methods of natural science, and the drive to preserve a materialist ontology consonant with the rest of natural science. But this line of theory was not the only reaction against the view that the mind was to be investigated by introspection of inner phenomena. In the late nineteenth century, before behaviorism of both psychological and philosophical varieties, before the Vienna Circle and its form of empiricism and positivism, and working already in a Viennese tradition of seeking exact and scientific philosophy, Franz Brentano sought to put psychology on a new path, notably in *Psychology from an Empirical Standpoint* (1874).[10] Brentano became dissatisfied with the idea that studying the mind is a matter of studying internal mental phenomena by a kind of inner observation, just as studying the physical world is a matter of studying physical phenomena by external observation. But Brentano did not try to collapse the two areas of study by basing the study of mental phenomena in external observation of physical phenomena such as behavior or brains. Instead, he sought a way to distinguish the method of study proper to the philosophical study of mind from that proper to empirical psychology (regardless of whether the empirical observations were 'internal' or 'external'). As a result, he distinguished what he called 'genetic' and 'descriptive' psychology.

For Brentano, 'genetic psychology' is the empirical study of mental phenomena, based in experimentation and statistical methods, from which we can search for laws and causal explanations. By contrast, Brentano held, 'descriptive psychology' or 'descriptive phenomenology' does not involve searching for laws of cause and effect, nor does it describe particular psychological episodes (whether by introspection or any other means). Instead, its purpose is to specify and classify the basic types of mental phenomena, determining their characteristics and essential interrelations. Thus, for example, rather than studying the causes of perceptions, emotions, etc. (whether through introspection, observation of behavior, investigation of brain states, or even, as Freud would soon propose, psychoanalysis), descriptive psychology would seek to answer such questions as: What is a perception, a judgment, an emotion, etc.? What is required for a particular emotion to be a case of regret? What is the characteristic relationship between emotion and judgment, or emotion and presentation? This sort of study involves the clarification of the very form of and relations among mental states of different types. And as such, Brentano argues,[11] descriptive psychology is prior to genetic psychology, since studying the causes of perception, memory, emotion, etc. presupposes understanding what it is for an event to be one of seeing, remembering, regretting, etc. This analysis of the basic types of mental functioning and their essential interrelations then comprises the distinctively *philosophical* approach to the mind, and provides a way of distinguishing it from the researches of empirical psychology.

---

[10] See Brentano (1874/1995) (1874/1982). Also see Barry Smith (1994: chs. 1, 2), for discussion of Brentano's influence on the development of philosophy in Vienna, including the Vienna Circle.

[11] Brentano (1982: 10).

Brentano's idea of descriptive psychology was then famously developed into his student Edmund Husserl's idea of phenomenology, first detailed in Husserl's *Logical Investigations* (1900–1). Husserl made a concerted effort to demonstrate that phenomenology does *not* involve an introspectionist recording of, for example, the feel of one's own mental states, repeatedly arguing that phenomenology does not rely on any kind of inner observation and is not subject to the kind of skepticism leveled against introspection-based psychologies.[12] Like Brentano before him, Husserl is clear that phenomenology is exclusively a matter of studying the general essences of experiences and relations among these, not a matter of empirical study of one's individual experiences, whether by 'internal' observation or any other means.[13] Like Brentano, he conceives of phenomenology as prior to empirical psychology, since it is concerned with analyzing and describing the 'intentional essences' of experiences of presentation, perception, judgment, imagination, etc., and thus with clarifying the essences or types of mental states that empirical psychologists must assume in their observations and experimentation.[14]

To give a certain authority or autonomy to phenomenology as distinct from empirical psychology and neuroscience—the cognitive sciences, in today's parlance—is not, however, to deny the latter's roles in understanding the mind. Nor is it to deny the relations of consciousness to its environment. Our conscious experience is dependent on what happens in our brains (see Bickle and Ellis, this volume). Furthermore, perception and action are intertwined with our bodies and are so experienced, as Husserl and Merleau-Ponty stressed (see Bermúdez, Siewert, and Carman, all in this volume). And our experience is further dependent, in different ways, on what happens around us in the world—on our personal histories, on social and political formations, on human history, and on the biological evolution of our species. But whatever gives rise to our conscious experience, the essences of our experiences of various types are there to be studied in their own right, and that is the point of the Brentano–Husserl conception of phenomenology as a discipline.

Nor is there anything mysterious about this study of 'essences'. The essences of experience types are understood through our *concepts* of experiences of different types. And so, to the extent that our concepts are accurate, we may study what is involved in the essence of, say, perceiving an external physical object, by asking what, according to the very concept of a perception of an external object, would be necessary for any experience to count as one of this type. Thus the phenomenological goal of studying the essential forms of and relations among different experience types has much in common with, and can be seen as leading into, the conceptual analysis of mental state types that characterizes at least one strain of analytic philosophy of mind.

In fact, Husserl's idea of a distinctively philosophical (phenomenological) approach to the mind—one based not on introspection, but rather on considering the essences and correlated concepts of mental states of various types—was the crucial historical influence on Gilbert Ryle's defense of conceptual analysis as the appropriate method of

---

[12] Husserl (1913/1962: §79, p. 204), known as *Ideas* I.
[13] Husserl (1900–1/2001: vol. ii, Investigation VI, Introduction, §1, p. 183).
[14] *Logical Investigations*, loc. cit., Volume II, Investigation VI, Introduction, §1, p. 183.

philosophy, and thereby also on Ryle's attempt to dissolve traditional problems with the concept of mind by rectifying the 'logic' of mental terms or concepts (see Livingston, this volume).[15] In *The Concept of Mind* (1949) Ryle prefers to speak in terms of analyzing mental concepts as used in ordinary discourse, rather than in the Husserlian idiom of intuiting and analyzing essences of lived experiences. Yet Ryle's method of studying the mind is based on the Brentano–Husserl view that the job of a *philosophy* of mind is the analysis of the general types of mental functioning, their intentionality, and their 'logical' status, structures, and interrelations, where such inquiry is independent of the studies of neurophysiology and psychology. Accordingly, Ryle writes that *The Concept of Mind* is an examination of various mental concepts, so that 'the book could be described as a sustained essay in phenomenology'.[16]

Unfortunately, given Ryle's going concern to reconfigure apparent talk about the mind in terms of talk about externally observable events, his book drew interest and has been remembered for the ways in which his proposed conceptual analyses could support logical behaviorism (a view of his work that he always rejected), rather than for its demonstration of a philosophical method of studying the mind distinct from both introspection and natural science—the point Ryle himself was most interested in. Nonetheless, *The Concept of Mind*, along with many of Ryle's essays,[17] remains as evidence of the linkage of the two traditions at hand, and joins Brentano and Husserl in charting the space for a distinctively philosophical kind of study of the mind. Indeed, the very term 'philosophy of mind' took root only in the wake of Ryle's influential book, and it was in reaction to that book that the identity theory was launched, leading into materialist, functionalist, and eliminativist ontologies of mind.

The word 'phenomenology' is often used in contemporary philosophy of mind to mean simply the qualitative or phenomenal character of an experience, that is, 'what it is like' to have an experience of a certain kind, primarily a sensation such as feeling pain or seeing red. While this concern with 'qualia' has led to some renewed interest in (or at least sympathy with) historical phenomenology, it is based in a double misrepresentation. First, the term as originally used by Brentano, Husserl, et al. is supposed to describe the *study* of experiences, not any part, quality, or aspect of experiences themselves (as noted by Strawson, this volume). Secondly, and even more crucially, historical phenomenology is not concerned exclusively or even primarily with studying the qualitative *sensuous* character of experience, as if that's all there is to the 'feel' of conscious experience. In fact, the widespread belief that this is what phenomenology is all about seems to derive from confusing classical phenomenology with the classical empiricist interest in mere seemings or sense-data. Instead, phenomenology—as a 'logic' of 'phenomena' of consciousness—sought to explicate what Husserl would call the essential 'logical' interrelations among experiences of different types (see Martin, this volume). Husserl uses 'logical' in a broad sense, covering not just essential relations and entailments among linguistic expressions based in logical form or syntax, but also

[15] See also Thomasson (2002).   [16] Ryle (1990: 188).

[17] See, e.g., 'Phenomenology', 'Phenomenology versus "The Concept of Mind"', 'Heidegger's "Sein und Zeit"', and 'Review of Martin Farber: "The Foundations of Phenomenology"', all reprinted in Ryle (1990: vol. i) and his 'The Theory of Meaning' and 'Ordinary Language' in Ryle (1990: vol. ii).

essential conceptual relations based in meanings. As a result, in the hands of Husserl and others, phenomenology is focused primarily on the intentional or, as Husserl often puts it, 'logical' form of experiences as *meaningful*. For it is only with regard to experiences considered as fully meaningful and intentional that one can examine the logical, conceptual interrelationships among forms of experience.[18]

Phenomenology as a discipline came of age in Husserl's 1900–1 opus *Logical Investigations*. There Husserl began with an idea of 'pure logic', defined as the theory of theories, studying ideal meanings, including propositions, their logical forms and logical relations, and their semantic representation of objects and states of affairs. This idea of logic led Husserl into a conception of phenomenology as the science of the essence of consciousness in general, studying especially intentionality and the role of meanings in representing objects of consciousness, and then into a phenomenological theory of knowledge.[19] For Husserl, the phenomenological theory of intentionality was thus a generalization of the logical theory of theories (or representational systems), studying meanings as ideal intentional contents of perception, judgment, imagination, emotion, etc. Phenomenology, in Husserl's hands, analyzes the forms and relations of intentional contents, including how they represent individuals, states of affairs, and events in the world. Indeed, today's concerns in philosophy of mind with the truth conditions or satisfaction conditions of contents of belief, perception, desire, etc.—adapting the notion of truth conditions from logical theory—fit smoothly into Husserl's original conception of phenomenology (see Smith, this volume).[20]

Husserl's idea of phenomenology developed hand-in-hand with his theory of intentionality. Brentano had revived the medieval notion of the mind's 'intentio' (aiming toward something), but it was Husserl who brought the concept of intentionality into a really sharp focus (along with Kasimir Twardowski and Alexius Meinong, fellow students of Brentano's). Husserl's innovation was to combine psychological theory (from Brentano) with logical theory (from Bernard Bolzano) into a bona fide theory of

[18] In fact, Husserl's conception of a 'logic' of mental states was influential not only on Ryle (and thereby on the philosophy of mind tradition), but also on the study of language and logic in analytic philosophy. In the late nineteenth century Gottlob Frege introduced new theories of logical form that transformed logic from Aristotelian syllogistic into modern quantifier-predicate logic. The new tools of logic were quickly put to work in philosophical analysis by Bertrand Russell and others. Then, in the 1920s and 1930s, amid the Vienna Circle movement, Rudolf Carnap's logical empiricism sought to use the new logical syntax to develop an ideal language that expresses our knowledge of the world based on sensory experiences, seeking to build up our public language about the world from our private language about sensation. In retrospect, Carnap turned logic through epistemology toward the study of mind: philosophy of logic led Carnap into theory of knowledge and therewith of mind. This turn was no accident, for Carnap had attended Husserl's lectures on phenomenology in 1924–5. In the 1930s and 1940s Alfred Tarski developed a semantic theory of truth, and the foundations of model-theoretic semantics. (See Tarski 1933/1983 and 1944/1952.) Tarski notes Husserl's conception of categories in *Logical Investigations*, central to Husserl's vision of 'pure logic'. And Tarski was occasionally schooled in what is called the Warsaw—Lvóv school of philosophy, founded by Kasimir Twardowski, who along with Husserl developed the act—content—object model of intentionality. And so, contrary to the prevailing view, logical theory, too, was intertwined with the roots of both analytic philosophy and phenomenology. (See Friedman (1999).)

[19] On the role of phenomenology in Husserl's overall philosophical system, see David Woodruff Smith (2002). On Husserl's theory of knowledge as grounded in phenomenology, see Willard (1984).   [20] Compare Searle (1983), and Perry (2001).

intentionality. Very briefly, Husserl's model of intentionality can be depicted in the structure:

subject—act—content → object.

Each experience or act of consciousness has a subject or ego ('I'), a content or meaning, and, if successful, an object toward which it is directed. The act is experienced by the subject, and is directed from the subject toward the object by way of the content. The content is a meaning (*Sinn* in Husserl's German), and meanings represent objects (individuals, states of affairs, etc.) in accordance with 'logical' or semantical laws, characterizing how various meanings are interrelated and how they represent various objects.[21]

As we have seen, the goal of phenomenology is not to record the 'feel' of one's own mental states, but rather to explicate the essential types and structures of conscious experience as lived (from the first-person perspective), thus the logical or conceptual relations among experience types, with the focus on the intentional or representational structure of experience. Accordingly, the methods of phenomenology do not rely on an introspective 'peering inwards' at one's passing stream of consciousness. Instead, Husserl proposes a new method, what he calls 'phenomenological reduction', the point of which is precisely to redirect our focus away from the entire empirical, natural world, including our real psychological experiences, and to refocus our study of the mind on the essences of conscious experience of various kinds, including especially their intentionality.[22] This method has been regularly misunderstood. Ironically, the method can be rather easily understood, by analogy with some familiar techniques of logical or linguistic analysis.

Although the method is explicated in different ways in different parts of Husserl's corpus, the fundamental idea of phenomenological reduction involves two steps detailed in *Ideas* I (1913). The first is a 'reductive' step that enables us to move from our ordinary world-oriented, world-representing experience to a philosophical description of its features *as* an experience. This is not an ontological reduction, but rather a methodological narrowing of focus, excluding from consideration certain empirical features of experience such as its relationship to the real, physical world. The second step is a generalizing or abstracting step that enables us to move from consideration of real, individual conscious experiences, to examining the general *types* or *essences* of the experiences involved.

Both stages famously involve 'bracketing', a kind of withholding of commitment. In the first stage, we bracket the 'thesis of the natural standpoint', viz., that the world around us (*Umwelt*) exists, the 'fact-world' of natural objects and other subjects and even numbers, so that we (globally) withhold commitment about the world represented in our experience.[23] By bracketing this thesis we can address our experience *as representing* things in the world in certain ways, rather than 'using' our experience so to

---

[21] This semantical model of intentionality is discussed in essays in Dreyfus (1982). The model is detailed, addressing historical precedents and relevant semantical theories, in Smith and McIntyre (1982). A partly differing interpretation of Husserlian intentionality theory is presented in Sokolowski (2000). [22] *Ideas* I, Introduction, p. 40; §79, p. 205.

[23] *Ideas* I, §§27–31.

represent things in the world. This move is similar to placing a piece of language in quotation marks, say, when we are mentioning what a witness said, rather than using those words to make an assertion ourselves; quotation thus enables us to address the meaningful content of a piece of language without committing ourselves to its truth. So understood, the first stage of phenomenological reduction involves not a pseudo-perceptual 'peering' at one's own experience, but rather a form of semantic ascent from world-representing experiences to talk or thought about the representational contents of these experiences. (See details in the articles by Smith and Thomasson, this volume. The term 'semantic ascent' is borrowed from W. V. Quine, whose concern was language.) The idea that knowledge of the contents of one's own mental states may be based in first-order world-directed experience, combined with a kind of conceptual transformation based in withholding commitment about the real nature of the world represented, has in turn been influential on contemporary 'outer aware-ness' views of self-knowledge developed by Sellars, Shoemaker, and Dretske (see Thomasson, this volume).

In the second stage of phenomenological reduction (sometimes called 'eidetic reduction'), we bracket the very existence of the experience addressed—considered as a real, occurrent experience—so that we can attend to the essence (or eidos) of the experience.[24] That is, we abstract the ideal essence from the concrete experience. Now, a crucial part of the essence of most experiences is their intentionality. As we turn to the structure of intentionality in an experience, we then turn to the content or meaning involved in the experience and its essential interrelations to other meanings ('logical' relations).[25] The essence and therewith the meaning of an experience remain to be studied whether or not there is any actual occurring experience. This way of avoiding reliance on any empirical claim about the existence of particular mental episodes enables us to discuss the *essences* of experiences of various types and the rela-tions among their meaning contents, rather than offering observational reports about the occurrence and content of various particular experiences. In this way Husserl pre-sents 'phenomenology as descriptive theory of the essence of pure experiences'.[26]

The later Husserl introduced a doctrine of 'transcendental idealism' that has vexed his interpreters ever since. For our purposes, we take Husserl to be a realist, not an ide-alist: the object of a veridical experience is something in the world, not in the mind. His transcendental idealism is then a theory about the role of meaning in the 'consti-tution' of objects: only through meanings are experiences directed toward certain objects. Alternatively put, we experience an object only 'as' such and such, and this mode of presentation is captured in the act's meaning. Husserl famously introduced the term 'noema' for this meaning, characterizing the noema or noematic meaning of

---

[24] *Ideas* I, §§69–75.

[25] *Ideas* I, §§88–90. Meanings and essences are distinct in kind: the essence or property of being an elm tree is distinct from the meaning or concept of an elm. For Husserl, the meaning 'elm' is part of the content of seeing or thinking about an elm, and the experience's being intentionally directed via that meaning is part of the essence of the experience. In the *Logical Investigations* Husserl had identified the intentional content or meaning in an act of consciousness with the act's species or essence of being directed in a certain way. Later, by the time of *Ideas* I, he distinguished these two types of ideal entities, introducing the Greek term 'noema' for the meaning (*Sinn*) of an act.

[26] *Ideas* I, §75. The phrase quoted is the title of that section.

an experience as the 'object-as-intended', somewhat as Kant spoke of 'phenomena' as 'things-as-they-appear'. The Kantian terminology may suggest, wrongly, that consciousness brings the world into existence, but that is not the point, on our reading of Husserl. In any case, interpretative issues aside, it is clear that neither the methods of his phenomenology nor its results for philosophy of mind involve one in any commitment to a metaphysical thesis of idealism.[27]

This brief sketch should be enough to make it clear that the phenomenological approach to the mind has been interwoven with the contemporary analytic 'philosophy of mind' tradition—despite common misconceptions in the histories of both philosophy of mind and phenomenology—and that its central methods and concepts are neither mysterious nor in conflict or competition with those of the empirical cognitive sciences. Yet it is not these historical facts in themselves that are of greatest interest, but rather the way in which the approach of the phenomenological tradition may help overcome some of the shortcomings of contemporary philosophy of mind. Work in the phenomenological tradition has long provided an alternative route to the study of the mind that avoids both introspectionism and collapsing the study of the mental into behavioral psychology or neuroscience. Indeed, the phenomenological approach to the mind was designed, in its very conception by Brentano, as complementary to, not in competition with, the results of empirical science—thus of neuroscience, empirical psychology, evolutionary biology, and the like (cf. Bickle and Ellis, this volume). Perhaps most importantly of all, the distinctively phenomenological approach to the mind has yielded a variety of detailed concrete analyses—notably, of consciousness, perception, intentionality, time-consciousness, and action—that can lead the way to reexamining current debates on these topics from a perspective unencumbered by some of the methodological and terminological commitments accrued by the analytic tradition's dedication to a publicly observable natural-scientific approach to the mind (see Strawson, this volume).

3. PHENOMENOLOGY AND PHILOSOPHY OF MIND IN THE ESSAYS TO FOLLOW

While some of the essays in this volume draw explicitly on historical work in phenomenology and others apply a phenomenological approach directly to contemporary problems or indicate the role of the phenomenological amid empirical studies, all help demonstrate the ways in which a phenomenological approach to the mind can both enrich and sharpen discussion in the philosophy of mind.

The essays below are divided into five parts. Those in Part I all contribute to understanding the place of phenomenology amidst other strands of work in philosophy of mind. Paul Livingston's essay reopens the history of philosophy of mind, especially functionalism, exhibiting its motivations and continuities with historical phenomenology, as both traditions seek to provide a logical/conceptual analysis of our mental terms and concepts. Understanding the commonalities between them helps bring to

---

[27] See the discussion of transcendental idealism in David Woodruff Smith (1995).

the fore the problems both approaches face in attempting to explain consciousness. Galen Strawson attempts to cut through the terminological accretions left behind by the tradition of analytic philosophy of mind, in its rush to explain features like intentionality, representation, and the like by separating them from experience and considering their application to non-conscious entities such as robots and thermometers. The terminological tangles that have resulted, he argues, have obscured some basic and obvious truths about the mind—for example, that there is cognitive experiential-qualitative content, and that intentionality is categorical, occurrent, and experiential—and have left the philosophy of mind mired in pseudo-disputes generated by bad terminological choices. Reaching back to a tradition of historical phenomenology, which preceded the later terminological tangles, may thus provide hope of a way out of contemporary pseudo-debates to rediscover certain natural and obvious views about the mental. In the final essay of this part Taylor Carman picks up a similar theme, arguing that eliminativisms like Dennett's are incoherent in denying the existence of qualitative sensory experience given the fallibility of our experience reports, for ultimately that means denying that there is anything about which we are fallible. As a result, we cannot coherently eliminate experience in favor of mere verbal judgments (Dennett's 'heterophenomenology'), and we must accept that we have some access to the structures and contents of our own experience, even if we are not infallible about them.

But what is the distinctively first-person access to experience supposed to be, which makes possible not only knowledge of our own mental states, but also a phenomenological approach to the mind? This is the central question behind the essays of Part II, which seek to draw out the possibility and distinctive characteristics of first-person knowledge, and its relation to the third-person knowledge characteristic of the neurosciences. David Woodruff Smith begins the section by explicating the sort of 'inner awareness' that forms the basis for phenomenological knowledge in a way that avoids the shortcomings of higher-order views. Properly understood, Smith argues, inner awareness in the phenomenological sense can provide a way to understand the characteristic privacy of inner awareness without making it incommunicable or beyond the reach of intersubjectively practiced phenomenology. Amie Thomasson, like Smith, insists that phenomenology is not based in any kind of inwardly directed observations of one's own mental states, by explicating and reinterpreting the central Husserlian method for phenomenology: the phenomenological reduction. Properly understood, Thomasson argues, phenomenological reduction is based in the idea that our knowledge of our own mental states is based not in introspective observation of them, but rather in our familiar outer observations of the world, combined with certain cognitive transformations initiated by bracketing assumptions about the world represented in our normal (outwardly directed) experience. So understood, phenomenological reduction does not rely on the viability of introspective approaches to the mind. More importantly, we can derive a new 'cognitive transformation' theory of self-knowledge based on Husserl's phenomenological reduction that may provide a viable contribution to contemporary debates about self-knowledge. Finally, John Bickle and Ralph Ellis bring issues about phenomenological methods and results into discourse with results of contemporary neuroscience. There is recent evidence that experiences very similar to those produced by normal sensation may be brought about by cortical microstimulation in the brain, and some have thought that this undermines claims to first-person phenomenological knowledge. But Bickle and Ellis argue that this latter reaction is based on confusing phenomenology with certain forms of folk psychology from which Husserl explicitly distinguished it. If we properly understand the goals and methods of phenomenology, they argue, we can see that not only is there no conflict between these results of neuroscience and phenomenology, but combining the two approaches may provide a useful route to address the hard problem of consciousness.

With the role and methods of phenomenology clarified, the essays of the later three parts apply some of the results of phenomenological work to other issues in contemporary philosophy of mind, beginning in Part III with the central issue of intentionality. Johannes Brandl begins by reaching back to consider Brentano's view that intentionality involves a relation between a subject and an immanent intentional or 'in-existent' object. This 'immanence' theory of intentionality, Brandl argues, is far more defensible than is commonly realized. Indeed, a contemporary version of the theory that takes the relevant immanent objects to be mental information bearers may be able to help explain the subjectivity of experience. Richard Tieszen addresses the largely ignored question of how we can account for intentional relations not just to concrete, perceived objects, but also to abstracta such as the objects studied in mathematics. Tieszen argues that, unlike many approaches to the mind, a Husserlian phenomenological account may offer the way to understand consciousness of abstract objects; indeed Gödel appealed to Husserl for just this purpose.

The three essays of Part IV examine three different senses in which there may be unities across different conscious experiences. First, Wayne Martin greatly clarifies the basic goals of phenomenology by reexamining Husserl's idea of phenomenology as a 'logic of consciousness'. Martin shows that taking this idea seriously presupposes conceiving of mental states not as atomistic, qualitative entities (as sense-data might be considered), but rather as intentional, meaningful states unified by internal relations among them. So understood, Husserl's ideal of phenomenology as a logic of consciousness may provide a distinctive approach to understanding consciousness as a cognitive and rule-governed domain that can present us with a world. Sean Kelly addresses the unities of conscious states as they unfold *over time*, asking how it is possible for us to experience (at a time) events that, like motion, must unfold over time. He brings the 'retention' view favored by Locke, Hume, and Husserl into dialogue with the 'specious present' view defended by James, Broad, and Dainton, arguing that the former has advantages that have long been overlooked by those steeped only in the 'analytic' tradition. In fact, Kelly argues, we can use Merleau-Ponty's descriptions of the phenomenology of indeterminate experience as the basis for giving more positive content to Husserl's 'retention' view, on the way to a more adequate understanding of the nature of time-consciousness. In the third essay of this part, Kay Mathiesen addresses the unities that may exist across experiences of different *individuals*, resulting in a 'collective consciousness'. While collective consciousness is often thought to play a role in the understanding of collective behavior and even in establishing conventions and a social world, how individuals may come to share in a collective consciousness is little understood. Mathiesen argues that we can make headway in this project by appealing to Husserl's idea of social 'subjectivities', although, to complete the task, we must also (as Alfred Schutz pointed out) supplement Husserl's story with an account of how social subjectivities may be constituted by the conscious acts of individuals.

Finally, the essays in Part V show how a phenomenological approach, and/or some results of classical phenomenology, may aid our understanding of the relation between perception, sensation, bodily awareness, and action. Clotilde Calabi reexamines the phenomenology of perception, arguing that normativity is involved even in perception, as perceivers exercise a faculty of attention that makes certain features show up as salient, and as providing reasons for action. In the second essay, Charles Siewert develops a new account of what is distinctive about sensory, as opposed to cognitive, intentionality. Building on ideas from Merleau-Ponty's *Phenomenology of Perception*, he argues that sensory intentionality is distinctive in being inseparably tied to our capacities for movement, indeed to our 'motor skills'. In the final essay, José Bermúdez similarly utilizes Merleau-Ponty's work on bodily awareness, combining it with recent research in scientific psychology on proprioception and motor control, to provide a new taxonomy of types and levels of bodily awareness, and to develop a better understanding of the difference between awareness of our own bodies and that of external objects.

While these essays address different topics using different aspects of phenomenology, they jointly provide models of how phenomenology may help us make progress in understanding the mind, complementing the work of psychology and neuroscience, and influencing, enriching, and occasionally providing a corrective to, dominant strains of analytic philosophy of mind. We hope that work like this can help lead to greater balance and progress in the philosophy of mind and phenomenology, as well as to a reassessment of the relationship between the two disciplines.

REFERENCES

Armstrong, David M. (1999) *The Mind-Body Problem: An Opinionated Introduction* (Boulder, Colo.: Westview).

Block, Ned, Flanagan, Owen, and Güzeldere, Güven (eds.) (1997) *The Nature of Consciousness: Philosophical Debates* (Cambridge, Mass.: MIT Press).

Brentano, Franz (1982) *Descriptive Psychology*, trans. and ed. Benito Müller (London: Routledge).

——(1874/1995) *Psychology from an Empirical Standpoint*, trans. Antos C. Rancurello, D. B. Terrell, and Linda L. McAlister (London: Routledge).

Chalmers, David J. (ed.) (2002) *Philosophy of Mind: Classical and Contemporary Readings* (Oxford and New York: Oxford University Press).

Dennett, Daniel (1987) *The Intentional Stance* (Cambridge, Mass.: MIT Press).

Dreyfus, Hubert L. (ed.) (1982) *Husserl, Intentionality and Cognitive Science* (Cambridge, Mass.: MIT Press).

Dummett, Michael (1993–8) *Origins of Analytic Philosophy* (Cambridge, Mass.: Harvard University Press).

Fodor, Jerry (1982) 'Methodological Solipsism considered as a Research Strategy in Cognitive Psychology', in Dreyfus (1982: 277–303).

Friedman, Michael (1999) *Reconsidering Logical Positivism* (Cambridge and New York: Cambridge University Press).

Husserl, Edmund (1913/1962) *Ideas: General Introduction to Pure Phenomenology*, trans. W. R. Boyce Gibson (New York: Collier). [known as *Ideas* I]

—— (1900/2001) *Logical Investigations*, Vols I–II, trans. J. N. Findlay (London and New York: Routledge).

—— (1990) *Collected Papers*, ii (Bristol: Thoemmes).

Moran, Dermot (2000) *Introduction to Phenomenology* (London and New York: Routledge).

Perry, John (2001) *Knowledge, Possibility and Consciousness* (Cambridge, Mass.: MIT Press).

Petitot, Jean, Varela, Francisco J., Pachoud, Bernard, and Roy, Jean-Michel (eds.) (1999) *Naturalizing Phenomenology: Issues in Contemporary Phenomenology and Cognitive Science* (Stanford: Stanford University Press; Cambridge and New York: Cambridge University Press).

Putnam, Hilary (1981) *Reason, Truth and History* (New York: Cambridge University Press).

—— (1983) *Representation and Reality* (Cambridge, Mass.: MIT Press).

—— (1987) *The Many Faces of Realism* (La Salle, Ill.: Open Court).

Ryle, Gilbert (1949) *The Concept of Mind* (Chicago: University of Chicago Press).

—— (1990) *Selected Papers*, 2 vols (Bristol: Thoemmes), 179–96.

Searle, John R. (1983) *Intentionality* (Cambridge and New York: Cambridge University Press).

Skinner, B. F. (1938) *The Behavior of Organisms* (New York: Appleton-Century-Crofts).

Smith, Barry (1994) *Austrian Philosophy: The Legacy of Franz Brentano* (Chicago: Open Court).

Smith, Barry and Smith, David Woodruff (eds.) (1995) *The Cambridge Companion to Husserl* (Cambridge and New York: Cambridge University Press).

Smith, David Woodruff (2003) 'Phenomenology', in *The Stanford Encyclopedia of Philosophy*, Winter 2003 edition, Edward N. Zalta, editors, http://plato.stanford.edu/archives/win 2003/entries/phenomenology.

—— (1995) 'Mind and Body', in Barry Smith and David Woodruff Smith (1995: 372–84).

—— (2002) 'What is "Logical" in Husserl's *Logical Investigations*? The Copenhagen Interpretation', in Dan Zahavi and Frederik Stjernfelt (eds.), *One Hundred Years of Phenomenology: Husserl's Logical Investigations Revisited* (Dordrecht and Boston: Kluwer Academic Publishers), 51–65.

Smith, David Woodruff and McIntyre, Ronald (1982) *Husserl and Intentionality* (Dordrecht and Boston: Reidel).

Sokolowski, Robert (2000) *Introduction to Phenomenology* (Cambridge and New York: Cambridge University Press).

Tarski, Alfred (1933/1983) 'The Concept of Truth in the Languages of the Deductive Sciences', in *Logic, Semantics, Metamathematics: Papers from 1923 to 1938*, ed. John Corcoran (Indianapolis: Hackett).

—— (1944/1952) 'The Semantic Conception of Truth', in Leonard Linsky (ed.), *Semantics and the Philosophy of Language* (Urbana: University of Illinois Press). Originally published in *Philosophy and Phenomenological Research* 4 (1944).

Thomasson, Amie L. (2002) 'Phenomenology and the Development of Analytic Philosophy', *Southern Journal of Philosophy* 40, Supplement (Proceedings of the 2001 Spindel Conference 'Origins: The Common Sources of the Analytic and Phenomenological Traditions'): 115–42.

Watson, J. B. (1914) *Behavior* (New York: H. Holt).

—— (1925) *Behaviorism* (New York: W. W. Norton).

Willard, Dallas (1984) *Logic and the Objectivity of Knowledge* (Athens, OH: Ohio University Press).

PART I

THE PLACE OF PHENOMENOLOGY IN PHILOSOPHY OF MIND

1

Functionalism and Logical Analysis

Paul Livingston

Abstract: Though it is most often deployed in service of naturalist and empirically sensitive explanatory projects, the functionalist theory of mind is essentially a formal theory, drawing its plausibility more from a sophisticated appreciation of the logic and conceptual grammar of terms of psychological description than from any empirical consideration. In this, the functionalist theory of mind exhibits significant methodological continuities with the tradition of phenomenology; but despite its successes, many philosophers believe that functionalism fails in that it leaves out any account of the central explanatory concept of phenomenology, the concept of immediate, subjective experience. In this essay, I analyze the history of the development of functionalism to make perspicuous some of the hidden structural features of the doctrine we know today. Functionalism emerges as a sophisticated response to problems of the meaning and reference of psychological terms left open by its predecessor theories. This shows that the question of the relationship of formally described functional states to empirically described physical states remains open and suggests a new way of viewing the source of functionalism's continued problems with explaining consciousness.

After more than thirty-five years of debate and discussion, versions of the functionalist theory of mind originating in the work of Hilary Putnam, Jerry Fodor, and David Lewis still remain the most popular positions among philosophers of mind on the nature of mental states and processes. Functionalism has enjoyed such popularity owing, at least in part, to its claim to offer a plausible and compelling description of the nature of the mental that is also consistent with an underlying physicalist or materialist ontology. Yet despite its continued popularity, many philosophers now think that functionalism leaves something out, in particular that functional explanations and analyses fail to account for consciousness, qualia, or phenomenal states of experience or awareness.[1] If the objection is correct, then functionalism fails in its inability to capture the central explanatory basis of phenomenological explanation: the phenomena of immediate, first-personal, subjective experience. The apparent failure is all the more striking in view of the close methodological parallels that exist between functionalism and phenomenology; for both projects depend centrally on a program of conceptual investigation of the definitional and explanatory interrelationships of our descriptions of experience and other

---

[1] See, e.g., Nagel (1974), Chalmers (1996), and Searle (1992).

psychological phenomena. A historical overview of the theoretical pressures that led to the development of functionalism shows that it was in fact problems about the logical form of immediate, subjective experience that led most centrally to its development, and that these problems continue to threaten the coherence of the functionalist theory. This, in turn, suggests that the contemporary problem of explaining consciousness is not a metaphysical or empirical one about the explanation of a particularly puzzling process, but a conceptual one about the logical structure of experience.

The resistance of consciousness to functionalist explanation can initially seem difficult to account for: why should *one* set of mental phenomena—those characterized by phenomenal or qualitative content—so stubbornly resist explanation in the functionalist terms that seem successful elsewhere? But historical investigation shows that the functionalist theory itself emerges from the philosophical pressure put on earlier theories—especially the identity theory of Place, Smart, and Feigl—by more general and recurrent problems with the explanation of the phenomena of subjective experience. For investigative projects in analytic philosophy, beginning with the 'meaning analysis' projects of the logical positivists, meaning has been intelligible as a matter of linguistic or logical structure, and the analysis of language as a matter of the description of this structure.[2] Over against the logical or grammatical structure of language, however, experience has consistently been characterized as immediate, nonrelational content, inaccessible to the structural explanations that the analysis of meaning can offer. Historically based attention to the consistency of this problematic sheds light on the underlying motivations and theoretical contours of various particular versions of the analytic project, and recommends a more explicit and methodologically sensitive discussion of the central question of the relationship of experience to meaning. In the light of historical investigation, the functionalist theory itself, I shall argue, emerges as a particularly sophisticated kind of conceptual analysis, continuous with phenomenology in its aim to give a broadly structural characterization of the logic or grammar of our concepts of psychological description and prediction. And both the underlying motivations for its development and the largest set of problems it continues to face emerge as consequences of the underlying and ongoing resistance of immediate, subjective experience or consciousness to such projects.

1

Functionalism first arose within the analytic tradition as a response to the then prevalent *identity theory* of mind, the theory that held that mental states, including sensations, mental images, and other phenomenal states, are (as a matter of empirical fact) identical with physical states of the brain. The identity theory of U. T. Place, J. J. C. Smart, and Herbert Feigl improved upon previous behavioristic analyses of mind in that it could construe reports of experience as genuinely referring to genuine inner items, albeit physical ones, rather than (as the logical behaviorist must) simply

---

[2] See my 'Structuralism and Content in the Protocol Sentence Debate', in Livingston (2004), for the origins of this way of thinking about meaning and experience.

taking them to replace more primitive bits of behavior.[3] But though the identity theory solved this decisive problem with the behaviorist's construal of the reference of reports of experience, it omitted any account of the relationship of the ordinary logic of psychological description and explanation—the logical structure of psychological terms, their roles in the prediction and explanation of behavior, and the criteria on the basis of which they are normally ascribed and deployed—to the logical structure of the neurophysiological description of physical states of the brain. Such an account would be needed in order for the identity theory to stand any chance of empirically earning the particular psychophysical identities that would justify its general claim, but such an account would also require all of the resources of a thoroughgoing conceptual investigation of the logical structure of psychology. Justifiably, philosophers wanted to know not only *that* mental states could be physical states, but also *how* they could be and *what* it would tell us if they were.

It was as a response to this question about the meaning of psychological and physical terms that the functionalist theory of mind began to emerge. In 1957, Hilary Putnam began to articulate a new way of looking at the relationship between psychological and physical terms, as this relationship might develop diachronically under the influence of the growth of empirical discovery. This provided the possibility, Putnam thought, for a new kind of defense of the identity theory. Key to the proposal was a distinction between meaning and reference: ordinary-language terms like 'blue sensation' could actually *refer* to brain states, even if there is no sense in which they *mean* the same as any neurophysiological description. When empirical progress reveals the underlying causes for a phenomenon, Putnam reasoned, it will often make sense to construe our language for discussing the phenomenon as referring to the underlying cause rather than the surface phenomenon. Thus, a term like 'polio' will initially be used to describe a characteristic set of symptoms; but when the underlying viral cause is recognized, it will make sense to hold that 'polio' is the underlying virus, and not simply the symptoms.[4] The relationship between mental states and brain states, Putnam reasoned, might share this structure. Future empirical discovery, if it made good on the identity theory's suggestion, would answer the semantic question about the identity theory by identifying the *actual* referents of our ordinary psychological discourse.

In the 1960 article 'Minds and Machines', Putnam further develops this account of the diachronic change in reference of psychological terms, tying it to a more explicit consideration of the success conditions for the identification of terms within a theory. Essential to Putnam's argument is the observation that, as scientific theories develop, terms are often used in new ways, not because they change their meanings, but because they take on new uses in the new contexts revealed by new pieces of theory. If theoretical identifications represent empirically justified extensions in the uses of terms without implying any great change in the underlying *meaning* of those terms, then the identity theorist can both admit that mental state/physical state identifications are today semantically abnormal and describe conditions under which the very same identifications could become normal and indeed necessary. The theoretical

---

[3] Smart (1959: 144).   [4] Putnam (1957: 100).

identification of mental states with physiological states, Putnam suggests, will begin to make sense when we understand not only how the two kinds of states are correlated, but also how physiological states themselves *cause* behavior. Were physical science capable of describing the causation of behavior by physiological states, the identification of physical states with mental states would subsequently have two theoretical advantages:

1. It would be possible...to derive from physical theory the classical laws (or low-level generalizations) of common-sense 'mentalistic' psychology, such as: 'People tend to avoid things with which they have had painful experiences'.

2. It would be possible to predict the cases (and they are legion) in which common-sense 'mentalistic' psychology fails.[5]

In contemplating the possibility of reducing psychological theory to physical law, Putnam had also begun to think about the logical structure of common-sense psychological description itself, as well as its relationship to the traditional philosophical problems of mind–body identity. This led him to the most historically significant suggestion of the paper: that a sufficiently complex computational machine with certain abilities of self-description and theory-building—for instance a machine of the abstract kind suggested by Turing a few years earlier—could serve as a rough analogue for a human's psychological organization; and that in so doing, it would develop strict analogues for *all* of the traditional philosophical problems about the relationship of mind–body identity:

In particular, if the machine has electronic 'sense organs' which enable it to 'scan' itself while it is in operation, it may formulate theories concerning its own structure and subject them to test. Suppose the machine is in a given state (say, 'state A') when, and only when, flip-flop 36 is on. Then this statement: 'I am in state A when, and only when, flip-flop 36 is on', may be one of the theoretical principles concerning its own structure accepted by the machine . . . Now all of the usual considerations for and against mind–body identification can be paralleled by considerations for and against saying that state A is in fact identical with flip-flop 36 being on.[6]

Given only the possibility that such a machine can issue reports of its abstract or computational states which do not immediately expose their relation to the *physical* states underlying them, such a machine would be justified in wondering, just as a person might, about the identities between the two kinds of states. The machine could have the same questions that a human might about whether identifying the two kinds of states would unify theory or eliminate unnecessary entities; it could even make the 'dualistic' argument that state A *could not be* identical with the state of having flip-flop 36 on because the one is, while the other is not, an 'immediately observable' or apprehensible state. The possibility of such concerns arises, in the case of the machine at least, from the distinction between two levels on which it might seek to describe itself: in terms of its abstract functional or logical states, on the one hand, and in terms of the underlying physical states that realize these, on the other.[7]

---

[5] Putnam (1960: 380).   [6] Putnam (1960: 363).   [7] Putnam (1960: 372).

Putnam notes that this situation gives the machine a strict analogue of the distinction between 'mental' and 'physical' as it usually operates in *our* discussions of the mind–brain question. The machine's directly apprehensible and self-evident *logical* states seem, to the machine at least, to be categorically different from its non-obvious and mostly unknown physical states. Putnam even suggests that the distinction between the two levels in the machine case parallels two approaches one can take toward human psychology: the logical-level description of the machine parallels classical psychology's intuitive description of human thoughts as impressions, ideas, and other rationally organized 'mental' states, whereas the physical-level description of the machine parallels the physicalist's description of human behavior in terms that connect it to base-level physical and chemical theories.[8] Just as in the case of human psychology, the logical-level description can be given entirely independently of the physical-level one; but also as in the case of human psychology, the physical-level description explains such deviations as may appear in the machine's behavior from the laws established by its logical-level description.

2

In a series of papers written over the early 1960s, Putnam would develop the analogy between minds and machines into a full-blown metaphysical description of mind, culminating in the decisive suggestion that our mental states simply *are* abstract states within our total functional organization. In the 1963 article 'Brains and Behavior' Putnam gave a new, and stronger, argument against the logical behaviorist identification of pains and other mental states with behaviors and behavioral dispositions. To show that there is no necessary logical link between mental states and behaviors, Putnam suggested the example of a race of people who, owing to restrictive social conventions, never describe or otherwise express their feelings of pain. These 'super-Spartans' would exhibit no pain behavior; yet it is, Putnam argued, still meaningful to say that they feel pain. For instance, it might well be possible to detect within them a distinctive neurological configuration similar to ours when we are in pain.[9] Given this, it would make sense to conclude that they are indeed in pain. Even if their neurological states were, in general, different from ours, we could still come to conclude that they are in states enough like ours in relevant respects to be called pains.

This argument's more explicit consideration of the relationship between behavioral evidence and empirical discovery gave Putnam new resources against the logical behaviorist, but still depended on the thought that mental states ultimately are brain states. Putnam still treats states like pains as the *causes* of the behaviors that express them, and he repeats the suggestion that the grammar of pain-ascriptions is controlled by behavioral criteria that function as 'symptoms' of an underlying structure. The Turing machine analogy makes no appearance in the article, and there is no suggestion that mental states like pains are in any sense functional or logical states distinct from underlying physical states.

[8] Putnam (1960: 372–3).   [9] Putnam (1963: 337).

The first impetus for Putnam's development of the Turing machine analogy into functionalism, and indeed much of the theoretical apparatus of functionalism itself, would come, instead, from the articulation of a new anti-reductionist description of psychological explanation by the young philosopher Jerry Fodor. In the 1964 article 'Explanations in Psychology', Fodor argues for the autonomy of psychological explanations from physicalist descriptions on the basis of an extended application of the functionalist model that Putnam had suggested in 1960. Arguing from assumptions strikingly unlike those of Putnam's original reductionist picture of the mental/physical relationship, Fodor suggests that the characterization of psychological states as functional states offers a reasonable model of both the logic of psychological theory and the relationship we can expect to find between it and lower-level physiological and physical descriptions.

Much of Fodor's argument for this depends on a sophisticated consideration of the structure of psychological explanation and prediction, on the basis of which he argues against an oversimple and naïve reductionist view of the relationship of such explanation and prediction to lower-level causal explanations. Psychological theory, Fodor argues, intends to explain and predict behavior; but it is misleading to suppose that this explanation and prediction can be reduced to terms any more basic or primitive than the terms of psychology themselves.[10] Even the simplest notions of psychological description, for instance the behaviorist notion of a 'response', resist reduction to a physicalistic description in terms purely of physical motions. For there is no way even to characterize the set of possible physical movements that can count as a simple behavioral response without using the psychological predicate that characterizes them all as the same 'response' to begin with. The psychological description in terms of responses is not elliptical for an underlying physicalist description, but an autonomous functional description in its own right.[11]

Even in the simple case of Skinnerian behaviorism, Fodor argues, the grammar of psychological explanation makes ineliminable use of terms that cannot be defined physicalistically; even if explanation on this level is partly causal, what is important in understanding its logic is not definitional reduction of psychological to physical predicates but a functional characterization of the relations of definition and causality *among* psychological terms and their referents.[12]

But what, exactly, is a 'functional' characterization, and what is the relationship between a 'functional' description and a straightforward causal description if one

---

[10] Fodor's doctrine thus has motivations that parallel, and somewhat overlap, those of Davidson's 'anomalous monism' about the mental, the view that although each (token) mental state is in fact identical with a token physical state, there are no strict psychophysical laws connecting the two types of states. The classic expression of this view is Davidson (1970), and the 'type-token' distinction suggested here would soon give philosophers a natural language in which to express and investigate the insight of functionalism.   [11] Fodor (1964: 168).

[12] A visible influence on Fodor's thinking here is Chomsky's (1959) review of Skinner's *Verbal Behavior*. In it, Chomsky argues that the Skinnerian notions of stimulus, response, and reinforcement, however well defined they may be in the context of particular experiments, resist extension to real-life behavior. Like Fodor, Chomsky argues that there is no helpful reduction of the Skinnerian notions to physicalistic terms. Fodor supplements this realization, however, with the suggestion that the Skinnerian notions *do* characterize the organism under consideration on an autonomous level of functional description.

does not reduce to the other? Picking up on Putnam's suggestion, Fodor argues that psychological explanation has two levels or 'phases.'[13] On the first phase, corresponding to classical psychology, mental states are characterized in irreducibly psychological terms according to their roles in producing behavior. Importantly, at this level of explanation, the explanatory use of descriptions of mental states requires no reference to the underlying physical mechanisms that correspond to or realize them:

It should be noticed that explanations afforded by phase one theories are not causal explanations, although a fully elaborated phase one theory claims to be able to predict behavior given sufficient information about current sensory stimulations. Phase one explanations purport to account for behaviour in terms of internal states, but they give no information whatever about the mechanisms underlying these states. That is, theory construction proceeds in terms of such functionally characterized notions as memories, motives, needs, drives, desires, strategies, beliefs, etc. with no reference to the physiological structures which may, in some sense, correspond to these concepts.[14]

By postulating intuitively described inner states like motives and memories, phase-one explanations, Fodor suggests, allow us to predict and explain behavior in a wide variety of situations; all that is required to formulate them is the observations we make of the behavior that people and other organisms produce in response to stimulations. Still, they give us no insight into underlying physiological mechanisms that are literally responsible for causing the behavior in question. For this we need a second phase of explanation, on which we specify the *mechanisms* that actually underlie our functionally defined phase-one states. Applying Putnam's machine analogy again, Fodor notes that any given functional-level explanation corresponds to *indefinitely many* mechanical-level explanations:

In a phase one explanation, we picture the organism as proceeding through a series of internal states that terminate in the production of observable behaviour. But we make no attempt to say what these states are states of: what internal mechanisms correspond to the functionally defined states we have invoked. Now, the set of mechanisms capable of realizing a series of such functionally defined states is indefinitely large. Only our ingenuity limits the number of mechanisms we could devise which, upon exposure to the relevant stimulations, would go through a sequence of internal states each functionally equivalent to a corresponding state of an organism and would then produce behaviour indistinguishable in relevant respects from the behaviour of the organism.[15]

The character of the relationship between mechanical-level explanations and functional-level ones has a number of significant consequences for the growth of psychological theory. First, Fodor suggests, mechanical-level explanations may help to suggest new functional-level ones; for instance, speculations about the neurology of memory might lead to new functional-level characterizations of memory in terms of familiar psychological notions. Second, mechanical-level explanations constrain functional-level ones; though each functional system has an indefinite number of mechanical realizations, any functional explanation that is *inconsistent* with the mechanical-level explanation of the same system can be dismissed.[16] Additionally, the one–many relationship between

---

[13] Fodor (1964: 171–4).   [14] Fodor (1964: 173–4).   [15] Fodor (1964: 174).
[16] Fodor (1964: 176).

functional-level and mechanical-level explanations implies a non-reductive picture of the relationship of mental to physical states. If psychological explanation really does have the two-phase structure of Fodor's account, then 'reductions,' if there are any such, from the mental to the physical are not mereological decompositions of higher-level entities into their lower-level parts. Instead, they correlate *functions* with *mechanisms*, explaining the functional role played by a mental state by referring to the mechanism enabling it to play that role.

Beginning with considerations of the logic of psychological theory and the unlikeli-hood of its reduction to physical theory, then, Fodor's article succeeded in defining 'ordinary' or classical psychology as the functional description of internal states of an organism, a description which, in each case, may correlate with any number of mechanical-level descriptions of the same organism couched in the language of neuro-science and physiology. This suggestion led Putnam to define and articulate, over the next five years, the thesis that a mind might simply *be* a system of functional states realized physically. In his articles defining and defending functionalism, Putnam sig-nificantly extended and developed Fodor's consideration of the logic of psychological explanation, and drew out its consequences for the philosophical question of the mind–body relation. These consequences would lead Putnam to move decisively beyond the identity theory, as well as to repudiate much of the semantic argument he had formerly deployed in its defense.

Putnam went on to define the functionalist theory of mind in three articles: 'Robots: Machines or Artificially Created Life?' (1964), 'The Mental Life of Some Machines' (1967), and 'The Nature of Mental States' (1967). In these articles, Putnam's arguments for functionalism fall into four main types.

First, there are arguments, akin to Fodor's, from *the logic of psychological terms*. Psychological terms, if they are definable at all, are only *inter*definable; there is no hope of 'unpacking' the definitions of psychological terms into behaviors or behavi-oral dispositions that are not themselves psychologically described.[17] This suggests that psychological descriptions do *not*, as the identity theory had held, covertly or elliptically refer to physical internal states, and indeed that the hope of defining a physicalist research program culminating in the identification of the physical referents of ordinary psychological description is largely misguided.

A second sort of Putnamian argument for functionalism grew from his earlier argu-ments against logical behaviorism, particularly the argument that there is no logically necessary link between behavior and mental states.[18] Because the functional states of a Turing machine need not necessarily correspond to or even be determinable on the basis of behavior, it is possible to construct a machine analogue of the 'super-Spartans', a machine which is often in a particular functional state but will not express that it is. Since formal rules govern the transitions between a Turing machine's logical states, it is possible to implement rule-governed 'preference-functions' for the Turing machine. These rules can govern the self-expression of the machine's states; so given an abnor-mal preference-function (for instance, one that places an infinitely high disvalue on

---

17   Putnam (1964: 391).
18   Putnam (1967a: 421–2); a similar argument is suggested at Putnam (1967b: 438–9).

expressing that it is in the state functionally defined as 'pain') the Turing machine could 'experience' functional states that it does not behaviorally express. Thus, functional states, like our mental states, need not be logically linked or interdefined with behavior. This recommends the functionalist account, and shows that it survives at least one of the objections that doomed logical behaviorism.

This shows the logical difference between functionalism and behaviorism; but a third sort of argument Putnam uses for functionalism actually suggests a surprising amount of commonality in philosophical motivation between the two theories. Even if functionalism allows that functional states—and hence mental states—need not be identifiable with or logical constructions from behavior, nevertheless the consideration that our *criteria* for the everyday ascription of mental states are largely behavioral provides an argument in favor of functionalism:

Turning now to the considerations *for* the functional-state theory, let us begin with the fact that we identify organisms as in pain, or hungry, or angry, or in heat, etc., on the basis of their *behavior*. But it is a truism that similarities in the behavior of two systems are at least a reason to suspect similarities in the functional organization of the two systems, and a much *weaker* reason to suspect similarities in the actual physical details. Moreover, we expect the various psychological states—at least the basic ones, such as hunger, thirst, aggression, etc.—to have more or less similar 'transition probabilities' (within wide and ill defined limits, to be sure) with each other and with behavior in the case of different species, because this is an artifact of the way in which we identify these states. Thus, we would not count an animal as *thirsty* if its 'unsatiated' behavior did not seem to be directed toward drinking and was not followed by 'satiation for liquid.' Thus any animal that we count as capable of these various states will at least *seem* to have a certain rough kind of functional organization.[19]

Even if mental states are not logically dependent on, or identifiable with, public behavior, it nevertheless remains a philosophically significant feature of the logic and grammar of our common-sense and classical psychological theories that we *ascribe* mental states on the basis of publicly observable behavior. Moreover, the connection between the observation of behavior and the ascription of a mental state is, as Putnam realizes, closer and tighter than the connection between evidence and theory. For as a matter of logical necessity (at least in an extended sense of that term), we will not ordinarily be prepared to *call* an organism 'thirsty,' 'hungry,' 'enraged,' etc., if it does not exhibit *any* of the behavior that is criterial for that particular ascription. Under normal circumstances, the proposition that Jones is angry, if he exhibits *none* of the usual behavioral signs of anger, will at least call for further clarification. As Putnam had earlier argued, the logical behaviorist takes this kind of logical connection between behavioral evidence and the determination of mental states to be stronger than it is, forgetting that there are, after all, *some* conceivable circumstances under which mental states might reasonably be ascribed in the absence of their usual behavioral symptoms. Still, its behavior is *prima facie* good evidence for an organism's having a particular functional organization; and many, if not all, functional states are primarily characterizable in virtue of their logical relationships to publicly observable behaviors.

[19] Putnam (1967b: 437).

Finally, the observation that functional states are partly characterized by their relationship to, and ascribed on the basis of, behavioral evidence suggests what is Putnam's most often cited and characteristic argument for functionalism, what has been called the 'multiple realization' argument.[20] It begins as an argument *against* the identity theory. The identity theorist, Putnam argues, is committed to the *identification* of a particular mental state, say pain, with a particular neurological or neurophysiological structure found in all and only those organisms that are currently feeling pain. Moreover, this identification, if the identity hypothesis has any explanatory force, must be at least nomologically necessary. Whatever state is to be identified with pain must exist, then, in mammalian and molluscan, human and extraterrestrial brains alike, and moreover must be correlated, as a matter of scientific law, with the behavioral manifestations of pain in all of these species. Of course, it is extremely unlikely that any such state exists. What all and only organisms that are in *pain* do share, though, is a certain *functional* state that can be characterized by its logical and causal interrelationships with other functional states (moving away from a particular stimulus, acting as one has acted when physically damaged in the past, etc.). Where the identity theory necessarily posits an underlying state that could hardly exist (or, anyway, be theoretically useful; we could, of course, refer to all the biologically distinct states that realize pain in various organisms as a single, wildly disjunctive state), the functional-state theory uses what we already know about the logical criteria on the basis of which mental states are ascribed and discussed to characterize them as functional states that *could* be held in common by a wide variety of possible organisms and systems.

The multiple realization argument has often been considered a decisive argument in favor of functionalism, but it is important to be clear about just what sort of argument it is. Even if the identity theory fails because it requires nomological connections between mental states and (possibly hugely disjunctive) brain states, the functional-state theory improves upon it in this respect only because the specification of a functional state has no particular consequences for the identity of the underlying physical states. The thought that a given functionally characterized system can be realized by any of an indefinite number of possible physical systems had been suggested in passing in Putnam's 1960 article, and Fodor had made it the basis of his anti-reductionist picture of the relationship of phase-one to phase-two psychological explanations. Following Fodor's suggestion, Putnam clearly thought of the one–many relationship between functional and physical descriptions as one of the most crucial recommendations of the functionalist program. Unlike the nomological identities required by the identity theory, the one–many structure of functionalist explanation allowed that the meaning of ordinary psychological descriptions does not depend, overtly or covertly, on their reference to esoteric neurological or physiological facts. On the level of functional explanation at least, the functional-state theory defines a much more plausible research program: rather than having to determine the underlying physical 'identities' of the entities invoked in our psychological explanations, we treat these entities as well-defined from the outset and simply attempt to characterize further their

---

[20] Its most usually cited version is Putnam (1967b: 436–7); compare Putnam (1964: 392–3) (quoted below) and Putnam (1969: 451).

functional roles, employing only such evidence as is available publicly and prior to the detailed investigations of the brain sciences.

The force of the multiple realization argument, then, does not arise as much from the failure of the identity theory to handle species-specific mental–physical correlations as from the ability of functionalism to define a program of psychological investigation which takes much greater and more sophisticated account of the evidentiary and causal logic of traditional psychological explanation. Were it only the first, defenders of the identity theory could simply respond, as Kim (1972) in fact did, that even if pain is realized in *various* ways in *various* different species, species-specific identity laws are enough to prove the identity theorist's case. Putnam resisted this position not because he thought it would be impossible to identify the species-specific physical 'correlates' of pain in each particular case, but because he thought such identification would have little relevance on the level of traditional psychological explanation and, accordingly, little to do with defining the *identity* of pain.

As Putnam began to define and articulate the view that mental states simply *are* functionally defined states, the one–many character of the functional-state/physical-realization relation became central to his thought about the metaphysical status of the mind, causing him to abandon some of the most important parts of his earlier picture of explanation and reduction. In fact, the thought that a functional description of the psychology of an organism has *no* consequences for the nature of its realization led Putnam to doubt physicalism itself. Since the functional-state hypothesis, as Putnam understood it in 1967, defines a mental state *simply* in terms of an abstract functional description, it has no consequences whatsoever for the nature of the medium realizing it. Functionally defined states are completely logically independent of their realizers. This gives the functionalist reason to doubt not only the identity theorist's 'definition' of mental states in terms of physical states but even materialism itself, as Putnam shows with another argument arising from the possibility of multiple realization:

Indeed, there could be a community of robots that did not all have the same physical constitution, but did all have the same psychology; and such robots could univocally say 'I have the sensation of red', 'you have the sensation of red', 'he has the sensation of red', even if the three robots referred to did not 'physically realize' the 'sensation of red' in the same way. Thus, the attributes having the 'sensation' of red and 'flip-flop 72 being on' are simply not identical in the case of the robots. If Materialism is taken to be the denial of the existence of 'nonphysical' attributes, then Materialism is false even for robots!   (pp. 392–3)

As Putnam remarks elsewhere, the functional-state theory is not even incompatible with dualism: even a nonphysical 'soul' could perfectly well 'implement' any given functional organization, as long as it has a number of logically distinct and temporally successive states. And even in the case of an actual, material Turing machine, its functionally defined states are logically distinct from, and not derivable from, *any* of its physical states or attributes. In this respect at least, they are genuinely 'non-physical', defining real and ascertainable attributes above and beyond the set of all of the machine's physical attributes and all of their logical consequences.

Putnam's goal in making these points against materialism, of course, was not to argue for dualism or some new account of the metaphysics of mind, but to suggest the emptiness, given the functionalist picture, of all traditional philosophical descriptions of the mind–body relation. As in the 1960 article, where Putnam had pointed out how analogues of *all* of the traditional philosophical positions on the mind–body problem would arise for a mechanistic Turing machine, his conclusion is not that functionalism recommends a new and interesting position, but that anyone seriously interested in the metaphysics of a functionally defined system like a Turing machine is wasting his or her time.

In sum, then, the functional-state identity theory, as developed by Fodor and Putnam through 1967, offered a theoretically innovative account of the mind–body relation that exhibited much greater sensitivity to the logic of psychological explanation than had its predecessors, abandoned the oversimple reductionism of previous versions of physicalism, and at least suggested that traditional pictures of the mind–body relation should be foregone or radically overhauled. Its respect for the criteria ordinarily employed in psychological description allowed it to characterize ordinary talk about mental states as straightforwardly meaningful, without involving it in the semantic contortions suggested by Putnam's original investigation of diachronic theory change and the logic of theoretical claims of identity. But while the multiple realization argument allowed the liberation of autonomous psychological description from the demand of physicalistic reduction, it also left deeply unclear the metaphysical nature of the relationship between physically and functionally defined systems. This led to the admitted possibility that functionalism might not be 'materialist' after all, as well as to the reality that functionalist description failed to define any program lending insight into the physical and physiological causation of behavior.

Functionalism earned its plausibility from its closeness to the logic of ordinary and classical psychological explanation. But, at least as it stood so far, it bought this closeness at the price of the kind of metaphysical specificity that would have been needed to fundamentally clarify the relationship of philosophical description of mental states to empirical discovery of their physical correlates. Methodologically, it rewrote what was common to the traditional analytic project of logical analysis of mental states and the phenomenological project of formal analysis in an idiom that avoided the excesses of logical behaviorism, but in so doing lost the empirical-mindedness of the identity theory. Despite years of concerted thought on the part of functionalists and their predecessors, the semantic and conceptual analysis of the logic of mental states still threatened to float free of any clear application to the newly developing cognitive sciences of mind and brain.

3

Though functionalism is often taken to be a naturalist theory inviting a purely physicalist ontology, the historical overview shows that its chief methodological motivation was a practice of logical analysis or clarification that is in fact far removed from empirical work. Attention to functionalism's method of logically analyzing our terms of mentalistic description therefore suggests its closeness to the central methods of the phenomenological tradition's conceptual and logical analysis of the structure of experience. Phenomenology's analysis of experience is *logical* in that it is grounded in ideal, formal structures of meaning; and it is *conceptual* in that it depends crucially on reasoning about the definitional and explanatory interrelationships among our concepts of experience, the same concepts whose logical interrelationships Putnam and Fodor sought to capture with the idea of a functional state description. The substantial historical and conceptual continuity between functionalism and phenomenology in this respect casts light on hidden features of functionalism's conceptual structure, and suggests a new way of viewing the contemporary problem of the recalcitrance of conscious experience to functionalist description.

Throughout the development of his phenomenological project, Husserl looked to analyses of the formal structure and meaning of our psychological concepts to underwrite the explanation of the nature of consciousness and the constitution of objects of awareness. Beginning in the *Logical Investigations*, he envisioned phenomenological investigation as the investigation of the ideal 'laws of essence' that characterize both the structure of our conscious experience and the structure of our concepts of it.[21] Phenomenology, as the investigation of the formal structure of experience, was to be grounded in 'pure logic', a universal system of rules governing the actual and possible combinations of objects, meanings, and phenomenal properties to comprise our experience of the world. Here, Husserl connected the project of phenomenological analysis, on the one hand, to the establishment of 'pure categories of meaning' that govern the semantic possibilities for using linguistic terms, and on the other to his vision of a pure phenomenology purged of empirical psychology by the logical purity of its terms of description.[22] In *Ideas I*, Husserl further expanded on the nature of phenomenology's investigation of laws of essence and their grounding in the ideal synthetic acts of the transcendental consciousness, suggesting at one point that the phenomenological investigation of transcendental constitution is essentially the investigation of a functionally defined structure.[23] In this work and elsewhere, Husserl argues that the formal, essential laws governing possible perceptual and cognitive structures as well as defining the ontology of material and other objects result from immediate, given experiences by way of a complicated process of formal abstraction. Indeed, since our access to empirical objects of perception and observation always depends upon their being given in intuition, every concrete act of perception involves the synthesis of unformed 'hyletic' or phenomenal data into a conceptually formed complex. It follows that the phenomenological analysis of the structure of experience is at the same time the formal analysis of our concepts of experience, and that the conceptual or logical interrelationships among these concepts are a main source of evidence for the analysis. Though the ideal laws of essence that govern the structure of experience are conceived as abstracted from both concrete experience and language, phenomenology's primary method of insight into them is logical-level reflection on the structure of the concepts with which we characterize it.[24]

---

[21] Husserl (1900).

[22] Husserl (1900); see, e.g., 'Prolegomena', section 67, and Investigation I, section 2.

[23] Husserl (1913), section 86.

[24] 'The objects which pure logic seeks to examine are, in the first instance, therefore given to it in grammatical clothing' (Husserl 1900, section I.2). See also *Ideas* I, section 11.

The continuities between phenomenology's logical investigations of experience and Putnam and Fodor's functionalism, moreover, are not only conceptual; for a significant line of historical influence on Putnam and Fodor's method also originates with Husserl's phenomenology. As early as the 1920s, logical empiricists like Carnap had sought the conceptual reduction of sentences involving psychological terms of description to logically prior terms describing immediate experience, citing Husserl's analysis of experience explicitly as an antecedent of their own project.[25] When it became clear to these philosophers that they could not give a unified description of the structure of propositions describing immediate experience itself, they suggested instead the analysis of psychological descriptions into logically prior descriptions of behavior, yielding the project of 'logical behaviorism.'[26] In the late 1940s, Gilbert Ryle's *The Concept of Mind* propounded an influential program for the investigation and clarification of our ordinary concepts of mentality. Though Ryle's main aim was to dispel the sources of the Cartesian dualist's theory of mind as a non-physical entity causally connected to the purely physical, mechanistic body, he also described his own work of 'conceptual geography' as a 'sustained essay in phenomenology' aiming to reveal the logical categories of our ordinary language of psychological description.[27] As we have seen, Putnam and Fodor essentially drew upon the logical behaviorist method of analysis of mentalistic terms in their own development of functionalism, even while repudiating the suggestion of any possibility of reducing the reference of these terms to patterns of behavior. In making use of this practice, they consistently applied much the same method of conceptual or logical analysis that Husserl had made the central methodological innovation of phenomenology. Putnam's central thought that a conceptual analysis of our concepts of experience and mentalistic explanation could yield a purely structural, functional description of the mind, abstracted from the particular mechanical operation of any specific mind or brain, was thus already a central component of Husserl's project. This basic phenomenological thought would continue to guide the development of functionalism, subsuming its appeal to a level of formal description of minds largely independent of, and only problematically related to, the level of physical and causal description of the brain.

Its continuities with phenomenology cast light, as well, on another important aspect of the conceptual structure of functionalism. As we have seen, much of the supposed advantage of functionalism over logical behaviorism rested on its ability to capture the results of the *empirical* investigation of the mind and brain and thereby ensure the possibility of a purely naturalistic method and a physicalist picture of the world. This at first seems to stand in stark contrast with the method of phenomenology; for Husserl famously and strenuously opposed any 'naturalization' of phenomenology's inquiry into essence, holding that it could be no part of pure phenomenology to invite or depend on empirical results.[28] But historical reflection on the development of functionalism shows that this difference is in fact more apparent than real. For throughout its development, the main source of evidence for

---

[25] Carnap (1928).   [26] See, e.g., Carnap (1931) and Hempel (1935).
[27] Ryle (1949); Ryle (1962: 188).   [28] See, e.g., Husserl (1911).

functionalism was non-empirical reflection on the structure of our concepts, a kind of reflection which is equally at home in phenomenology and in logical analysis. As we have seen, this conceptual work sat, initially at least, in some tension with functionalism's claim to be a thoroughly empirical theory; despite prognostications to the contrary, it was not clear how a functional description funded by the logical interrelationships of concepts could fit with a physical-level description of our physiological states. The tension reflects many of Husserl's own concerns about the prospects of providing a naturalistic basis for phenomenology, concerns, in particular, that no natural or empirical basis could preserve the necessity and *a priori* character of the phenomenological laws of essence and meaning. Though the subsequent development of the analytic tradition witnessed the widespread denial of any principled analytic/synthetic distinction, and accordingly of the kind of necessity that had formerly been thought to accrue to the results of pure conceptual analysis, the underlying methodological tension between conceptual description and empirical discovery remained unresolved. This tension, as we have seen, continued to affect the coherence of the theory of functionalism; and although it would be superficially healed on the level of doctrine a few years later, its effects continue to problematize functionalism's account of experience even today.

Of course, missing from functionalism's explicit theoretical vocabulary was any analogue to phenomenology's central appeal to subjective experience or intuition as the foundation and ground for all of our intentional acts and processes of cognition. For Husserl, the analysis of our concepts of experience could only be the analysis of structures founded on a basis of immediate, lived experience and abstracted from it; without this basis, no theory of mind or indeed of reality could be considered complete. Functionalism's chief divergence from phenomenology might, then, seem to consist in its apparent refusal to characterize subjective experience *itself* independently of our conceptualization of it; and this might easily be thought responsible for functionalism's apparent inability to provide an explanation of consciousness. But as the historical overview shows, concerns about the nature of subjective experience in fact played a central role in the development of functionalism, and decisively influenced its theoretical shape. It was, after all, the inability of logical behaviorism to explain our use of language referring directly to experience that most centrally inspired Putnam to reject it; and it was the problem of the meaningfulness and reference of our descriptions of experience that led him to propose the notion of a functional-state description as an alternative. In its very structure, therefore, functionalism retains a determinative concern with the nature of subjectivity and the special problems of theorizing it by means of conceptual, structural, or broadly logical analysis. If these underlying problems indeed explain functionalism's apparent inadequacy for explaining consciousness, then it seems likely that they arise equally, and as prominently, for phenomenology's parallel project. For both projects, the nature of immediate, unconceptualized experience poses a continuing problem for forms of explanation that are inherently conceptual and structural in nature. The underlying problem can be concealed, but not removed, by the foundationalist rhetoric of a basis of conceptual thought in subjective experience; Husserl's project, as much as Putnam and Fodor's, remains open to the same underlying tension.

4

In 1965, in a brief and crisply argued *Journal of Philosophy* article, David Lewis pro-posed a philosophical innovation that, when added to the functional-state theory as Putnam had defined it, completed the theory from a logical (if not a chronological) point of view, effectively ended the further metaphysical speculation that might other-wise have been engendered by the unclarity of Putnam's account, and defined much more specifically the kind of relationship between philosophical analysis and empir-ical discovery that could be expected on a functionalist theory. Despite its functionalist motivation, Lewis called his article 'An Argument for the Identity Theory'. But its cen-tral innovation was essentially a semantic one: that mental states, and in particular 'experiences', are *defined* by their *causal roles*, their pattern of typical causes and effects. With this innovation, Lewis made it possible to maintain that the functional roles definitive, according to functionalism, of mental states are *at the same time* causal roles, and therefore that the place of a mental state in our ordinary and classical psy-chological descriptions adverts to, and locates it in the total theory by means of, the *same* properties and features that locate it in the total causal web of physicalistically described nature.

If the suggestion is accepted, the logical analysis of the grammar of the ordinary description of mental states will henceforth be an *integral part* of the empirical analysis of the underlying physical states, for the semantic features of mental-state terms will mirror the causal roles in virtue of which their bearers can be identified with physical states. What had seemed to be purely 'logical', 'grammatical', or 'phenomenological' analysis will then have a new richness of empirical relevance; the structure of the tradi-tional philosophical investigation of the relational logic of mental states will be mir-rored as the empirical investigation of the causal relations of functionally defined states. Methodologically, the innovation of Lewis' account would add to Putnam's functionalism the most philosophically compelling features of Smart's physicalism: its explanatory and metaphysical economy, its sensitivity to the possible philosophical relevance of new discoveries in the reductive brain sciences, and its congeniality to an uncompromisingly physicalist picture of the world with no suggestion of esoteric non-physical or mental facts, properties, or entities.

Together, Lewis' arguments for his suggestion recommend a position that recogniz-ably combines the two distinct levels of analysis that Fodor had originally suggested: experiences are defined, Lewis suggests, as causal roles, and particular physical states, as a matter of contingent fact, are the *occupiers* of those causal roles. Experiences are defined, and spoken of, as the patterns of what causes them and what they cause, but it is ultimately particular physical states of the brain that are doing the causing. Thus, the contingent identities of the identity theory fit right alongside the analytic or near-analytic analyses of functional description; one side of the account constrains the other in that only something that really can do the causal work of a particular experi-ence is a candidate for contingent, species-specific identity with that experience.[29]

---

[29] Lewis (1969).

In 1968, David Armstrong would make much the same suggestion the centerpiece of his influential *A Materialist Theory of Mind*. Like Lewis, Armstrong aims to defend a sophisticated version of Smart's identity theory. But he argues that the identity theorist's identification of mental states with brain states ought to be augmented with specific analyses of our mental concepts much like the analyses suggested by logical behaviorists. The two strands of theory can be joined, Armstrong suggests, by recognizing that 'the concept of a mental state is primarily the concept of a state of the person apt for bringing about a certain sort of behaviour' (p. 82). On Armstrong's suggestion, then, mental states are identified in terms of the types of behavior that, under ordinary or appropriate circumstances, they normally cause.[30] As on Lewis' view, this allows the proponent of the identity theory to accept much of the logical behaviorist's analyses of mental concepts into behavioral facts, without denying that the objects of mental concepts are brain states:

I have emphasized that the argument put forward for a Materialist theory of mind involves two steps. In the first place, it is argued that a mental state is a state of a person apt for the bringing about of behaviour of a certain sort. This is intended to be a piece of logical analysis. In the second place, it is argued on general scientific grounds that this inner cause is, as a matter of fact, the brain. (p. 116)

To motivate the first component of the argument, Armstrong goes on to offer logical analyses of the concepts of willing, knowledge, perception, and mental images into the kinds of behavioral and public facts apt to cause them and be caused by them.[31]

With the Lewis/Armstrong suggestion, logical-level functional analysis and empirical-level discovery of psychophysical identities fall cleanly into their relative places in a comprehensive program of jointly functional and causal analysis. In addition to defining a realistic research program combining logical and causal analysis, moreover, the suggestion effectively quells any remaining doubts about the extent of functionalism's compatibility with physicalism. If the relationship between functionally defined states and their physical realizers is the relationship between a causal role and its occupant, then ontologically we need not countenance anything more than objects and causally interrelated events. From this perspective, there is no danger that functionally defined states, because *logically* distinct from their physical realizers, will be in any interesting or relevant sense 'non-physical' or represent any obstacle to a materialist description of the world. But at the same time, Lewis' suggestion, because it depends only on the

---

[30] Armstrong (1968: 83).

[31] It is worth noting, though, one slight difference of emphasis between Armstrong's and Lewis' ways of putting the point. Lewis draws more clearly than Armstrong does the distinction between causal roles and their contingent occupiers. This allows him to envision a program comprising two clearly distinct levels of analysis: first, the logical description of causal roles, and second, the empirical identification of their occupiers. Armstrong, by contrast, does not draw the role/occupier distinction and therefore often seems to consider the causal relationship between a physicalistically described brain state and a mental state to be logically on a par with the causal relationships among mental states. Although this leads to a less well-defined distinction between the two components of the suggested analysis, it also allows Armstrong's analysis more room to exploit the suggestion that the logic of many of our concepts of mental phenomena—for instance the concepts of sensation—already implies that they are caused by internal brain states, even before empirical results are available to verify this implication.

physical explicability *in principle* of every physical event, does not obviously demand or imply the oversimple reductionist picture of psychological explanation that Fodor had originally resisted. The relationship between a causal role and its contingent occupier, unlike the compositional relationship between a macro-level object or process and its micro-level constituents, is plausibly a relationship characterized by some degree of explanatory autonomy. Because various structures may accomplish one and the same causal role, the explicability in principle of each physical event does not demand, on this picture, that there be, in general, any univocal or nomological relationship of explanatory reduction between an experience and the physical state with which it is (contingently) identical.[32]

Much of the subsequent discussion of functionalism over the last thirty-five years can be traced to issues left open in the final configuration comprised of the combination of Putnam's functional-state theory and Lewis' suggestion. But functionalism has encountered its greatest obstacles in its description of the nature of *consciousness*. In 1972, together with Ned Block, Fodor first expressed cautious doubts about the ability of functionalist description to explain subjective, phenomenal, or conscious states, and in recent years these doubts have grown into a widespread position of resistance among philosophers who doubt that a functionalist explanation of consciousness can be correct.[33] This situation cannot be viewed without a certain level of historical irony, in that for Putnam and Lewis alike it was the facility of functionalism in describing the nature of subjective states like pains and other experiences that first, and most primarily, recommended it as a systematic description of the mind. Here, as at other moments in the history of twentieth-century thought about consciousness, what began as a systematic way of capturing the logic of the terms with which we describe experience became a structural pattern of explanation that seemed to deny the unstructured immediacy of experience itself. The very virtue that had originally recommended the functionalist theory over logical behaviorism—its ability to make reference to genuine inner states—involved functionalism in a complete structuralist explanation of these states that seems inadequate to capturing their immediacy, intuitiveness, and spontaneity.

5

Historically viewed, Lewis' suggestion saved (or prevented) Putnam's functional-state theory from inaugurating what might otherwise have become a far-reaching investigation, inspired by the special question of the relationship of physical to functional states, of the metaphysical relationship of minds to machines, rules to causes, and the logic of psychology to the logic of physics. By showing how functional analysis could at the same time be causal analysis, Lewis allowed the analytic program of logical analysis to continue in a new—and newly empirically respectable—form, while

---

[32] For more on the logic of Lewis' suggestion for the nature of theoretical identifications and comments on its relation to Putnam's developing account, see Lewis (1972).

[33] See Block and Fodor (1972).

guaranteeing the amenability of functionalist description to the prevailing physicalist picture of explanation and ontology. In this respect, Lewis' suggestion ameliorated the fundamental unclarity of Putnam and Fodor's unaugmented picture on the relationship of functionally defined states to their physically defined realizers. But viewed historically, his suggestion has something of the character of a solution by fiat, a pragmatic suggestion that allowed philosophical discussion to continue in an empirical domain but left many outstanding, and important, philosophical issues internal to its doctrine unresolved. Despite the physicalism of Lewis' account, the underlying suggestion that experiences are defined by their causal roles improves little, as Lewis himself recognizes, over the logical behaviorist's claim that mental states are logical constructions from publicly observable behaviors or dispositions to behave.[34]

Methodologically, then, the historical investigation reveals functionalism as a hybrid doctrine, born of the competing demands of conceptual, logical, and phenomenological analysis, on the one hand, and allowance for specialized empirical discovery, on the other. But the most philosophically significant suggestions made by a perspicuous representation of the history of the development of functionalism concern its relationship to consciousness. The historical overview reveals that the functionalist description of the mind arises primarily from logical-level attention to the explanatory structure of psychological theory and description. Whatever their causal implications, functionalist analyses of particular mental states often remain essentially semantic or conceptual analyses, characterized by a descriptive and explanatory logic largely independent of the logic of causal description. This suggests that the origin of the problem of functionalizing consciousness may *not* lie in some special feature or property of conscious states in their causal interrelationships with other physical events. Instead, the underlying problem may arise from the special *logical* features of conscious states that make them uncongenial to functional-level description. If this is the case, then the specially problematic features of consciousness are not special 'properties' of consciousness as an empirical phenomenon, but logical and conceptual features of the relationship of our descriptions of consciousness to our descriptions of other kinds of mental states and physical events.

Recognition of the substantial continuity between functionalism and earlier projects of logical, phenomenological and conceptual analysis allows the underlying problem with the explanation of consciousness to emerge in its full generality. In the light of historical interpretation, the complaint that consciousness resists functionalist explanation emerges as one instance of a more general and perennial phenomenon: the resistance of subjective experience to broadly *structuralist* practices of conceptual and logical analysis. Consistently throughout the history of twentieth-century attempts to theorize the mind, the structural form of conceptual or logical analyses of our concepts of experience has seemed to run counter to the demands of accounting for the immediacy of experience itself. This tension, the present investigation suggests, points to a deep and unresolved problem about the relationship of conceptual structure

---

[34] Lewis writes: 'Yet the principle that experiences are defined by their causal roles is itself behaviorist in origin, in that it inherits the behaviorist discovery that the (ostensibly) causal connections between an experience and its typical occasions and manifestations somehow contain a component of analytic necessity' (pp. 20–1).

to the immediate matter or content of subjective experience, a problem that vexes every systematic attempt to define or characterize experience in formal or structural terms. Phenomenology's 'ideal laws of essence' are themselves defined structurally by attending to the logical connections among our concepts of experience; in this respect, the form and method of the analytic tradition's logical analyses of our psychological concepts incur, despite phenomenology's central appeal to subjective experience, much the same tension. Against the backdrop of the deep tension, revealed by the historical analysis, between experience and structural and conceptual forms of explanation, the characteristic Husserlian appeal to an abstractive foundation of our concepts in immediate, unconceptualized experience emerges as deeply problematic.

In this way, the historical investigation of the development of functionalism clarifies one kind of parallel between the characteristic methods of analytic philosophy and one of the chief projects of the continental tradition. The parallel suggests that the problems about the nature and adequacy of our concepts of experience that led to the development of functionalism are substantially continuous with the problems that led Husserl increasingly to distance himself, in his last work, from any foundational appeal to conscious experience, preferring to speak of the foundation of theoretical practice in the untheorized everyday 'life-world'.[35] Much the same set of problems, moreover, presumably underwrote the tendency of Husserl's phenomenological successors, Maurice Merleau-Ponty and Martin Heidegger, to move away from Husserl's characteristic appeal to immediate experience and subjectivity as the foundation for all abstract conceptualization, and toward versions of the phenomenological project that no longer rely on individual experience or subjectivity as a theoretical basis.

More generally, identifying the real underlying form of the problem of explaining consciousness allows us to perceive the problem's true significance for our ongoing attempts to understand our own nature. For the recurrent problem with the explanation of consciousness is an enduring problem about the relationship of subjective experience to forms of explanation and analysis that are otherwise comprehensive. Viewed in the general light that the historical investigation makes possible, the problem with consciousness that both led to the development of functionalism and continues to trouble it is just the problem of our own relationship to structural forms of formal and scientific explanation. These forms of explanation—logical, structural, and causal—subsume a great amount of knowledge within a single, unified framework of objectivity. The protest against the functionalization of consciousness manifests the underlying thought that subjectivity itself cannot be captured within this structure, that our immediate experience systematically resists inclusion in its web. With this clarified, the complaint of contemporary philosophers who hold that consciousness resists functional explanation can emerge as the protest that it is: a protest, in the name of the distinctiveness of our own inmost nature, against the inclusion of this nature within an abstracted, total picture of the world in terms of its logical, conceptual, or causal structure. Against this totalizing picture, the complaint gestures toward the immediacy and irreducibility of subjective experience; but the historical investigation provides the beginning of the conceptual resources needed to identify

---

[35] Husserl (1937).

the complaint's genuine ground, rather, as the logical nature of the subject, a nature whose logical peculiarity will constantly tempt us to describe it, even as it continues to resist any such description.

REFERENCES

Armstrong, D. M. (1968) *A Materialist Theory of the Mind* (London: Routledge & Kegan Paul).

Block, N. and Fodor, J. A. [1972] (1980) 'What Psychological States are Not', Ned Block (ed.), *Readings in the Philosophy of Psychology*, vol. 1 (Cambridge, MA: Harvard University Press), 237–50.

Brandt, R. and Kim J. (1967) 'The Logic of the Identity Theory', *Journal of Philosophy* 64/17: 515–37.

Carnap, R. [1928] (1967) *The Logical Structure of the World*, trans. Rolf A. George (Berkeley: University of California Press).

—— [1931] (1959) 'Psychology in Physical Language', in A. J. Ayer (ed.), *Logical Positivism* (New York: The Free Press).

Chalmers, D. (1996) *The Conscious Mind* (New York: Oxford University Press).

Chomsky, N. [1959] (1980) A review of B. F. Skinner's *Verbal Behavior*, in Ned Block (ed.), *Readings in the Philosophy of Psychology*, vol. 1 (Cambridge, Mass: Harvard University Press), 48–63.

Davidson, D. (1963) 'Actions, Reasons, and Causes', *Journal of Philosophy* 60/23: 685–700.

—— [1970] (1980) 'Mental Events', in Ned Block (ed.), *Readings in the Philosophy of Psychology*, vol. 1 (Cambridge, Mass.: Harvard University Press), 107–19.

Fodor, J. A. (1964) 'Explanations in Psychology', in Max Black (ed.), *Philosophy in America* (Ithaca: Cornell University Press).

—— (1968) *Psychological Explanation: An Introduction to the Philosophy of Psychology* (New York: Random House).

—— [1974] (1980) 'Special Sciences, or the Disunity of Science as a Working Hypothesis', in Ned Block (ed.), *Readings in the Philosophy of Psychology*, vol. 1 (Cambridge, Mass.: Harvard University Press), 120–33.

Hempel, C. G. [1935] (1980) 'The Logical Analysis of Psychology', reprinted, with revisions, in Ned Block (ed.), *Readings in the Philosophy of Psychology*, vol. 1 (Cambridge, Mass.: Harvard University Press), 14–23.

Husserl, E. [1900] (1977) *Logical Investigations*, trans. J. N. Findlay (London: Routledge & Kegan Paul).

—— [1911] (1981) 'Philosophy as a Rigorous Science', in Q. Lauer, (ed.), *Phenomenology and the Crisis of Philosophy* (New York: Harper & Row).

—— [1913] (1983) *Ideas Pertaining to a Pure Phenomenology and to a Phenomenological Philosophy, First Book*, trans. F. Kersten (The Hague: Martinus Nijhoff Publishers).

—— [1937] (1970) *The Crisis of European Sciences and Transcendental Phenomenology*, trans. D. Carr (Evanston, Ill.: Northwestern University Press).

Kim, J. [1972] (1980) 'Physicalism and the Multiple Realizability of Mental States', in Ned Block (ed.), *Readings in the Philosophy of Psychology*, vol. 1 (Cambridge, Mass.: Harvard University Press), 234–6.

Lewis, D. K. (1966) 'An Argument for the Identity Theory', *Journal of Philosophy* 63/1: 17–25.

—— [1969] (1980) 'Review of Putnam' in Ned Block (ed.), *Readings in the Philosophy of Psychology*, vol. 1 (Cambridge, Mass.: Harvard University Press), 232–3.

Lewis, D. K. (1972) 'Psychophysical and Theoretical Identifications', *Australasian Journal of Philosophy* 50: 249–58.

Livingston, P. (2004) *Philosophical History and the Problem of Consciousness* (Cambridge: Cambridge University Press).

Nagel, T. [1974] (1997) 'What is it like to be a Bat?' in N. Block, O. Flanagan, and G. Guzeldere (eds.), *The Nature of Consciousness: Philosophical Debates* (Cambridge, Mass.: MIT Press).

Oppenheim, P. and Putnam, H. (1958) 'Unity of Science as a Working Hypothesis', in Herbert Feigl, Michael Scriven, and Grover Maxwell (eds.), *Minnesota Studies in the Philosophy of Science, Vol. 2* (Minneapolis: University of Minnesota Press).

Putnam, Hilary (1957) 'Psychological Concepts, Explication, and Ordinary Language', *Journal of Philosophy* 54: 94–9.

—— [1960] (1975) 'Minds and Machines', in Putnam (1975: 362–85).

—— [1963] (1975) 'Brains and Behavior', in Putnam (1975: 325–41).

—— [1964] (1975) 'Robots: Machines or Artificially Created Life?', in Putnam (1975: 386–407).

—— [1967a] (1975) 'The Mental Life of Some Machines', in Putnam (1975: 408–28).

—— [1967b] (1975) 'The Nature of Mental States', in Putnam (1975: 429–40).

—— [1969] (1975) 'Logical Positivism and the Philosophy of Mind', in Putnam (1975: 441–51).

—— [1973] (1975) 'Philosophy and our Mental Life', in Putnam (1975: 291–303).

—— (1975) *Mind, Language, and Reality: Philosophical Papers,* vol. 2 (Cambridge: Cambridge University Press).

Ryle, G. (1949) *The Concept of Mind* (Chicago: University of Chicago Press).

Ryle, G. [1962] (1971) 'Phenomenology versus *The Concept of Mind*', in *Collected Papers, Vvolume 1: Critical Essays* (Bristol: Thoemmes).

Searle, J. (1992) *The Rediscovery of the Mind* (Cambridge, Mass.: MIT Press).

Smart, J. J. C. (1959) 'Sensations and Brain Processes', *Philosophical Review* 68: 141–56.

2

Intentionality and Experience: Terminological Preliminaries

Galen Strawson

Abstract: Most of the current discussion of intentionality in analytic philosophy is a terminological squabble that thinks it is a substantive debate. This essay glosses 'naturalism', 'physicalism', 'intentionality', 'aboutness', 'mental', 'content', 'mental content', 'representational content', and so on in ways that may seem unorthodox but shouldn't; it points out that dispositions like belief dispositions cannot—metaphysically cannot—be (mentally) contentful entities; it argues dutifully for the existence of things that obviously exist—not only conscious experience, but also, more specifically, *cognitive* conscious experience as opposed to sensory experience. Then it puts the case for saying that [1] the only truly intentional entities are conscious experiential episodes. It argues that although one can with Humpty Dumpty use words like 'mental' and 'intentional' as one likes, there is in the end no tenable ground between [1] and [2] full-blown Dennettian behaviourism/instrumentalism/anti-realism about the mind—as Dennett himself agrees. To accept [2], however, is to have completely lost touch with reality.

1. INTRODUCTION

The current discussion of intentionality in analytic philosophy presents as an important substantive debate. I think it is little more than a terminological squabble. I can't offer a full case for this here, but I want to make some terminological proposals—some very unfashionable—that may help us to see more clearly what is going on.

The claim that the current disagreements are largely terminological is a substantive claim that would be rejected by nearly all participants in the debate. To underwrite it, I think, would be to see what it is to naturalize intentionality and to see that there is no particular philosophical difficulty in it. So it should be worth trying to make a start. If I seem to wander, I hope you will be patient.

Most of the key terms in analytic philosophy of mind have been put through the mangle and no longer have any clear agreed use. I will try to say what I mean by certain words by using other words that don't require me to say what I mean by them.

Sometimes, though, it will be impossible for me to avoid using a mangled word in trying to say what I mean by another mangled word before I have had a chance to say what I mean by the first one. It will be like Otto Neurath's boat. Sometimes you have to stand on one part to rebuild another part before standing on the other part to rebuild the first, or even jump between them as you go along.

2. 'NATURALISM', 'PHYSICALISM', 'EXPERIENCE'

Most present-day philosophers of mind favour *naturalism* and *physicalism*. They want a naturalistic account of mind and take it that it must be a materialist or physicalist account. In this essay I'm going to assume that they are right, and that 'naturalist(ic)' can always be replaced by 'physicalist' when the mind is in question, and vice versa. I will use one or the other term *au choix*.[1]

So naturalism is physicalism, and physicalism is a view about the actual universe, the view that every real, concrete phenomenon in the universe is . . . physical! What is it for something to be physical? An interesting question, if only because the only thing we know for certain to be physical, given that physicalism is true, is conscious experience, for conscious experience is the only thing we know for certain to exist.

Many think that a naturalistic account of mind faces two central problems: conscious experience and intentionality. The alleged problem of conscious experience is that it exists. I will use the noun 'experience' (in its non-count-noun form) to refer to it, together with the adjective 'experiential', taking it that experience is by definition conscious.[2] More precisely, I will use 'experience' and 'experiential' to refer specifically and only to the *experiential qualitative character* of conscious mental phenomena, to the phenomenon of experiential 'what-it's-likeness'; and I will use 'EQ' as short for 'experiential qualitative'.[3]

Experience is not in fact a problem for naturalism, for one thing is certain. You're not a serious physicalist, you're not a real or realistic physicalist, if you deny the existence of the natural phenomenon whose existence is more certain than the existence of anything else: experience, experiential 'what-it's-likeness', feeling, sensation, explicit conscious thought as we have it at almost every waking moment. This is where we start from. There is nothing more certain in philosophy and life. Real physicalism can have nothing to do with *physicSalism*, the view that the nature or essence of all concrete reality can in principle be fully captured in the terms of (human) physics.[4] If you think that physicalism can be physicSalism you must suppose that the terms of physics can fully capture the nature or essence of experience. But this is obviously—provably—false.[5] The only alternative is to deny the existence of experience altogether. But this is the Great Silliness: the silliest claim ever made in the whole history of philosophy.[6]

---

[1] I take 'materialist' and 'physicalist' to be equivalent and use 'physicalist'.

[2] The count-noun form of 'experience' remains available for talking of experiences (plural) as things that have non-experiential being as well as experiential being.

[3] I qualify 'qualitative' by 'experiential' because every intrinsic or non-relational property of a thing contributes to its qualitative character, and experiences also have non-experiential being— hence non-experiential qualitative character—according to standard physicalism.

[4] See e.g. Dennett (1991b: 40).   [5] See e.g. Strawson (1994) (henceforth *MR*), §3.6.

[6] See e.g. Strawson (2003) and (forthcoming).

A major terminological obstacle here is that there is a venerable tradition of using 'mental' (where the mental either is or includes the experiential) and 'physical' as mutually exclusive terms. This traditional opposition is fine if you are, say, Descartes, but it is not available to serious physicalists. Why not? Because they hold that everything concrete is physical and must acknowledge the existence of experience, the most certain concretely existing thing there is. It follows that they must hold that the mental/experiential is physical. They cannot therefore oppose the terms 'mental' and 'physical' and must instead use 'mental' and 'non-mental', or 'experiential and non-experiential'.[7]

I choose to use 'experience' instead of 'consciousness' because although 'consciousness' is perfectly adequate for philosophical purposes it has been very heavily mangled. It has been forced through the terminological looking glass by philosophers like Dennett who use it to mean precisely something that involves no consciousness.[8] I will mark this by saying that Dennett uses the word 'consciousness' to mean consciousness[LG], where the 'LG' stands for 'looking-glass'. Dennett looking-glasses the term 'consciousness', where to looking-glass a term is to use a term in such a way that whatever one means by it, it excludes what the term means.

To looking-glass a term is not the same as using a term to mean both what it means and also something that it does not mean. I will call this *starring*: to use the term 'mental' so that it covers essentially non-mental phenomena as well as mental phenomena is really to use the term 'mental*'. The difference between looking-glassing and starring is the difference between using 'gold' to mean pizza ('gold[LG]') and using it to mean gold and pizza ('gold*'). The cases that concern us in philosophy are less frivolous, although not always less bizarre. (There are many other possibilities, e.g. using 'animal'—'animal*'—to mean animals and and statues of animals; or just mammals; or mammals and statues of mammals; and so on.)

I'm not saying that attaching asterisks to terms is a bad thing in philosophy; it's often very helpful. I'm just using the verb 'star' in this essay to mark a bad thing. I'm not any sort of linguistic prescriptivist, and I'm not against terminological innovation. Words in human language soak similarities and metaphorical extensions into themselves with extraordinary ease, and although the facility with which we accept such extensions can cause havoc in philosophy it is one of our greatest cognitive gifts.

3. 'INTENTIONALITY', 'ABOUTNESS'

The second supposed problem for naturalism, the problem of *intentionality*, is posed by the fact that natural entities like human beings and dogs can have something in mind, can be aware of something, mentally in touch with something, cognizant of something in thought or feeling or perception. We can think about things. We can

---

[7] Hume is clear about this in his *Dialogues Concerning Natural Religion*, and Russell gives a dramatic statement of the serious physicalist's position: 'We know nothing about the intrinsic quality of physical events except when these are mental events that we directly experience'; 'as regards the world in general, both physical and mental, everything that we know of its intrinsic character is derived from the mental side' (1956: 153, 1927a: 402; Russell's use of 'intrinsic' is misleading and too strong as it stands—see Strawson 2003).   [8] See e.g. Dennett (2001).

target, hit, refer to, mean, intend an object, present or absent, concrete or not, in thought.

I will call this 'concrete intentionality', for it is intentionality considered as a concretely existing phenomenon, i.e. as something correctly attributed to concrete (states of or occurrences in) entities like ourselves and dogs, rather than intentionality considered as a property of entities like propositions that are not concrete entities ('abstract intentionality'). Since I am only concerned with concrete intentionality in this essay, I will simply call it 'intentionality'.

Many present-day philosophers quickly start talking about experienceless entities like robots and pictures, computers and books, when they talk about intentionality, claiming that such things can be in intentional states or 'have' intentionality even if they are not mental beings.[9] This is extremely startling to those unfamiliar with the current debate, but the link is made as follows. First, we naturally say that such experienceless or non-mental entities are *about* or *of* things, or are in states that are about or of things. Second, it has come to seem natural to say that the problem of intentionality is nothing other than the problem of how natural phenomena can be about things or of things.[10] Intentionality is thus equated with aboutness-or-ofness, which I will call *aboutness* for short, and the conclusion that non-mental entities can have intentionality follows immediately.[11]

I think, though, that this terminological equation leads to many unnecessary difficulties. Everyone can agree that intentionality entails aboutness $[I \rightarrow A]$ but the converse $[A \rightarrow I]$ requires reflection. It seems to me that one can either accept $[A \rightarrow I]$ and be tight with aboutness, or reject it and be generous with aboutness. My choice in this essay is to reject $[A \rightarrow I]$ and be generous with aboutness, in line with everyday talk (elsewhere I consider accepting it and being tight with aboutness). What I think one cannot wisely do—it is a terminological matter—is accept that aboutness entails intentionality and be generous with aboutness, and hence also with intentionality. But this is today a very popular choice.

Here, then, we reach a terminological parting of the ways. Some think it obvious that only mental entities or states or events in mental entities can be intentional or have intentionality; others are prepared to ascribe intentionality—*intentionality*, no less—to things that no ordinary person wishes to call mental.[12] I take intentionality to be an essentially mental and indeed essentially experiential (conscious) phenomenon. This is terminologically unorthodox in present-day analytic philosophy, and I adopt it not so much because it's simply correct in the English that I speak but because I think it offers the best way to put things when trying to get a clear general view of the phenomenon of intentionality and, more broadly, the phenomenon of one thing's being about another.

---

[9] I am going to assume that all robots and computers are experienceless for the purposes of discussion.

[10] 'About', unlike 'of', tends to imply an essentially discursive form of representation, but I won't make anything of this.

[11] Harman (1998: 602) holds that grass needing water is an intentional phenomenon.

[12] My use of 'mental' here is meant to be that of ordinary thought, but it is also Neurathian because 'mental' has been looking-glassed and starred in all sorts of ways; see §5.

I accept that it will be seen as a terminological *choice* in the current terminological pandemonium. Fine, so long as it is clearly understood that I'm not denying the reality of any of the phenomena that have led philosophers to say that non-experiential and even non-mental (ordinary understanding of the word—see §5) entities can be intentional entities or have intentionality. I'm quite sure I don't disagree with these philosophers on any relevant matter of fact.

4. NO DISPOSITIONS ARE INTENTIONAL

One obvious consequence of the decision to define intentionality as essentially experiential is that dispositional phenomena like belief dispositions are not properly counted as intentional phenomena. Since all experiential phenomena are occurrent phenomena, only occurrent phenomena can be intentional phenomena, properly speaking.[13]

Some analytic philosophers may feel that it isn't worth reading any further. Terminological habits are as powerful as any in human life and there is no way of talking more deeply engrained in the analytic-philosophy community than the one that allows that dispositional states can be contentful intentional states.

This is a very striking fact, for it takes only a very little reflection to see that a *disposition* (e.g. the disposition to answer Yes if intending to speak truly when asked if grass is green) is just not the kind of thing that can possibly be contentful in the way that it needs to be if it is to be an intentional thing. This is plainly so even if it can be identified as the disposition it is only by reference to the content *grass is green*. To think that a disposition is, metaphysically, the kind of entity that can be contentful in itself is a bit like thinking that an object's disposition to cause red-experience in human beings is itself something red, in the ordinary naïve understanding of the term 'red'; or that if an object has a fragile disposition, then it already in some sense contains or involves actual breaking.[14]

Obviously many ways of talking that are unacceptable taken strictly are fine as *façons de parler*; the long-known danger is that *façons de parler* turn into metaphysical systems. Much of the recent history of analytic philosophy of mind could be written as the story of what happened when intentionality was allowed to exist without experience (consciousness)—the story of how far philosophers were prepared to go in their uses of words like 'mental', 'mind', 'think', 'understand', and so on, in order to accommodate

---

[13] I will take beliefs to be essentially dispositional phenomena, although I think one can talk of conscious beliefs, meaning conscious assenting entertainings of believed propositions.

[14] Even if one thinks that the *categorical ground* of the red disposition is itself red-experience red, one can't coherently think this of the *disposition* to cause red-experience; and no one, I think, will want to turn to the (non-experiential, neural) categorical ground of the belief disposition to provide a truly, intrinsically mentally contentful *grass-is-green* item.

There are of course important differences (e.g. causal differences) between belief dispositions and colour and fragility dispositions; and setting them out takes one straight to the heart of a great instability in the standard analytic-philosophical account of mental dispositions like beliefs. I cannot discuss this here, and do so in *Intentionality!* Briefly, Dennettian anti-realism about belief dispositions as items with content turns out to be the only reasonable view. And this is all to the good, on my view, for Dennettian anti-realism amounts to a rejection of the idea of mental dispositions as entities with content.

the chain reaction set off by this particular terminological decision. Another connected part of the story is about what happened when it became common to talk in a strongly reificatory way about mental states as if they were things in us, rather than things—states—we are in. The combination was lethal.

5. 'MENTAL'/'NON-MENTAL'

I will return to states in §9. Here it must be said that it's not much use invoking the mental/non-mental distinction as I have been doing, because the word 'mental'—along with every other key word—has been chewed up beyond all recognition in the last fifty years.[15] It would be nice to be able to say that we have at least one firm grip on it, in the current confusion, because experience is an intrinsically and essentially mental phenomenon whose essential nature (or, at the very least, part of whose essential nature) we apprehend just in having it.[16] And of course we do. But even this has been flatly denied—it has even been *held to be false as a matter of meaning*—in the theoretico-terminological bedlam induced by behaviourism and its various offspring. 'Mental' has been starred, if not looking-glassed, in every imaginable way.

Sometimes I think the only thing to do is to abandon the mental/non-mental distinction and fall back on the very clear and indisputably real experiential/non-experiential distinction; or else collapse the two distinctions together, and say with Descartes that experiential phenomena are the only truly mental phenomena, the only irreducibly mental phenomena; or rather, and more specifically, that experiential phenomena are the only truly *mentally contentful* phenomena.

I think this last suggestion is rather a good one, and I will take it further in §8 and §10. For now, consider a thesis about 'mental' that seems hugely natural to many although we have got to the (terminological) point where others think it absurd. According to this thesis a mental episode, and *a fortiori* an intentional episode, can occur only in a being that is capable of experience. One could call this the *Only In An Experiential Being* thesis.

A question arises about what could justify it—it is a remarkable fact that it is open to the charge of complete arbitrariness in the current terminological environment—but I shall not try to answer it here.

It doesn't really need a justification, of course. It's just a fact about what the word 'mental' means. Some, though, think that the Only In An Experiential Being thesis is an obsolete intuition, frozen into the conventional meaning of the word 'mental', from which we must liberate ourselves.

Hmm. Sometimes our terms do change their meaning, and in a valuable way, but there's no profound paradigm shift occurring here, no new discovery or insight calling

---

[15] Obviously this is normal and perhaps inevitable in philosophy, and probably it is not always a bad thing.

[16] This apprehension is a matter of direct acquaintance, it is 'non-thetic' in the phenomenologists' terms, i.e. it does not involve any explicit taking of one's experience as the object of one's thought, although we can also do this.

out for certification in a radically new way of talking. I have felt the pull of this use of 'mental', as have many, but reflection in a cool hour finds little more than a war of words that has deluded itself into thinking that it is a substantive debate.

Many think that developments in Artificial Intelligence oblige us to admit that the realm of the mental, and of mental beings, is larger than we used to think, but the opposite view is at least as plausible: what developments in AI show is that the realm of the distinctively mental is actually smaller than we used to think, since so many of the abilities or properties that we used to take to be distinctively mental can now be seen to be possessed by things that are experienceless, and are not mental beings at all. On this view, developments in AI do not lead to the realization that mentality has nothing essentially to do with experience. Instead they confirm the Cartesian-naturalist view that the only thing that is distinctively and essentially mental—or at least (more narrowly) mentally *contentful*—is, precisely, experience.[17]

I need to put the case for this view—this terminological proposal. I will do so in §§8 and 10. First I need to say something about cognitive phenomenology, cognitive experience.

6. COGNITIVE EXPERIENCE

Recent philosophy has insisted on separating the notion of cognitive or conceptual mental content sharply from the notion of experience (there are, in the long wake of the British empiricists, real and fictional, some very good reasons for doing so). But this has had one very unfortunate consequence. It has become hard for many philosophers to hold onto the evident fact that there is such a thing as *cognitive experience* as well as sensation-mood-emotion-image-feeling experience, which I'll simply call *sensory experience* for short.[18] The existence of cognitive experience has been well argued for in recent years[19] and it is increasingly regaining acceptance, but it is still doubted by many and it is worth proving its existence because it is central to the problem of intentionality.

Proof 1. Life would be fabulously boring if this were not so. Life is not fabulously boring.

Proof 2. Many things which are not utterly mysterious would be utterly mysterious. We would, for example, have no explanation of why you are gripped by a talk, say, other than that you are fascinated by the sounds the speaker makes considered as merely auditory phenomena. It is no reply to say that the talk is objectively fascinating and that the qualitative character of your experience has nothing to do with it, for your distinguished neighbour in the audience—who has three heads and makes Mr Spock seem as impassive as Maria Callas—understands the talk as well as you and does not know what you are talking about when you say you are fascinated.

---

[17] This is to express things in overtly substantive, metaphysical terms, but the stand-off is really terminological. The two sides can agree on all the facts however much they fuss about the words. See *MR*, ch. 11.

[18] I am not concerned in any way with the current debate about 'non-conceptual content', and I'm taking the notion of sensory or non-cognitive experience for granted.

[19] See e.g. Ayers (1991: 1.277–88), Siewert (1998), Loar (2003), Pitt (2005).

The same goes for books, *mutatis mutandis*. It goes for anything whatever that goes beyond sensory experience, interoceptive or exteroceptive—cricket, ant-watching, dominoes, and so on. Here, however, I am particularly interested in the cognitive experience involved in comprehendingly entertaining propositions in reading, listening, or thinking, and I am going to limit my attention to this.

These two proofs are indirect in as much as they draw attention to a reaction that presupposes the existence of cognitive experience. I will leave them without further comment although many may not be convinced. It can take time to appreciate the point, given the current philosophical climate and the robust externalism of ordinary talk. (If you say 'It's the content that arouses my interest, not my cognitive experience!' I reply 'Of course it is'.)

Proof 3 is more direct. Consider the phenomenon of your understanding this very sentence and the next. Clearly this understanding—it is going on right now—is part of the character of your experience, part of the experiential character, the EQ character, of the current course of your experience.[20] Your experience would have been very different if the words had been 'The objection to the Realist Regularity theory of causation is accordingly very simple. It is that the theory is utterly implausible in asserting categorically that there is no reason in the nature of things for the regularity of the world.' And the difference wouldn't have been merely visual—a matter of the difference in the shapes and order of the letters on the page, the overall Gestalt of the sentences' appearance, and so on.[21] It is the meaning of the sentences—and now of this very sentence—that is playing the dominant part in determining the overall EQ character of this particular stretch of the course of your experience, although you may also be aware of page, print, sunshine, birdsong, and so on, and although the meaning would be more effortlessly to the fore, experientially, if you were not currently engaged in this particular exercise of self-inspection.

A little less introspectively: consider (experience) the difference, for you, between my saying 'I'm reading *War and Peace*' and my saying 'barath abalori trafalon'. In both cases you experience sounds, but in the first case you experience something more: you have understanding-experience, cognitive experience.[22]

Why isn't this point universally acknowledged? *Have you had only sensory experience for the last two minutes?* One problem is that there has been a terminological lock-in. When analytic philosophers talk generally about what I call 'EQ content'—when they talk generally of the 'subjective character' of experience, or 'what-it's-likeness', or 'qualitative character', or 'phenomenology' in the current

---

[20] This is loosely put, for strictly speaking it is the *experience* of understanding a particular sentence, the experience *as of* understanding a particular sentence, not the understanding itself, that has cognitive EQ content. *Mis*understanding the sentence equally involves cognitive experience, experience as of understanding (see *MR*: 6–7). Usually, of course, understanding-experience tracks actual understanding very well.

[21] Visual and quasi-auditory if we include the rapid silent imaging of the sound of the words that most experience when reading; audio-somatosensori-visual if we include visceral reactions to words; and so on.

[22] I call it 'cognitive phenomenology' (in Strawson 1986: e.g. pp. 30, 55, 70, 96, 107–9), and 'understanding-experience' and 'meaning-experience' (in *MR* 5–13).

deviant use of the term[23]—they standardly have only *sensory* EQ content, in mind, and the mistake has already been made. For this terminological habit simply forbids expression of the idea that there may be non-sensory or *cognitive* EQ content.

One doesn't have to be Husserl to be astounded by this terminological folly, and the metaphysical folly that it entrains—the denial of the existence of cognitive experience—as one negotiates the unceasing richness of everyday experience. It beggars belief. It amounts to an outright denial of the existence of almost all our actual experience, or rather of fundamental features of almost all (perhaps all) our experience. And yet it is terminological orthodoxy in present-day analytic philosophy of mind.

How did this happen? It was, perhaps, an unfortunate by-blow of the correct but excessively violent rejection, in the twentieth century, of the 'image theory of thinking' or 'picture theory of thinking' seemingly favoured, in various degrees, by the British empiricists and others. But rejecting the picture theory of thinking didn't require denying the existence of cognitive experience. On the contrary. Liberation from the picture-theory idea that cognitive experience centrally and constitutively involves sensory experience, and is indeed (somehow or other) a kind of internal sensory experience, is a necessary first step towards a decent account of what cognitive experience is. Schopenhauer certainly didn't reject the existence of cognitive experience when he refuted the picture theory of thinking in 1819 in terms that no one has improved on:

While another person is speaking, do we at once translate his speech into pictures of the imagination that instantaneously flash upon us and are arranged, linked, formed, and coloured according to the words that stream forth, and to their grammatical inflexions? What a tumult there would be in our heads while we listened to a speech or read a book! This is not what happens at all. The meaning of the speech is immediately grasped, accurately and clearly apprehended, without as a rule any conceptions of fancy being mixed up with it.[24]

When it comes to EQ content, then, when it comes to *the strictly qualitative character of experience*, which is wholly what it is considered entirely independently of its causes there is *cognitive* EQ content as well as sensory or non-cognitive EQ content. There is cognitive experience. Its existence is obvious to unprejudiced reflection, but some philosophers have denied it fiercely and, it must be said, rather scornfully.

It can seem difficult to get a decent theoretical grip on it. It is, for one thing, hard to pin down the contribution to the character of your current experience that is being made now by the content of this very sentence in such a way as to be able to take it as the object of reflective thought. (It is far easier to do this in the case of the phenomenological character of an experience of yellow, let the 'transparentists' say what they will.) In fact, when it comes to the attempt to figure to oneself the phenomenological character of understanding a sentence like 'Consider your hearing and understanding of this very sentence and the next' it seems that all one can really do is rethink the sentence as a whole, comprehendingly; and the trouble with doing this is that it seems to leave one with no mental room to stand back in such a way as to be able to take the

---

[23] It is incorrect first because 'phenomenology' is the study of experience, not experience itself, second because when it is used to mean experience itself it is used too narrowly to mean only sensory content.   [24] (1819/1969: 39).

phenomenological character of one's understanding of the sentence, redelivered to one by this rethinking, as the principal object of one's attention: one's mind is taken up with the sense of the thought in such a way that it is very hard to think about the experience of having the thought.[25]

This is, as it were, a merely practical difficulty. It is I think a further point that there is in any case something fundamentally insubstantial, intangible, unpindownable, about the character of much cognitive experience, and that this is so even though cognitive experience can also and simultaneously have a character of great determinacy. Consider, for example, your experience of understanding this very sentence, uneventful as it is. Or the sentence 'This sentence has five words.' Determinate but insubstantial.[26]

I use quiet sentences to make the point, rather than sentences like 'A thousand bonobos hurtled past on bright green bicycles', simply because it helps to still the imagistic or emotional accompaniments of thought or understanding as far as possible. It is then easier to see that what is left is something completely different, something that is equally real and definite and rich although it can seem troublesomely intangible when one tries to reflect on it: the experience that is standardly involved in the mere comprehending of words, read, thought, or heard—right now—, where this comprehending is (once again) considered quite independently of any imagistic or emotional accompaniments. Cognitive experience, we may say, is a matter of whatever EQ content is involved in such episodes after one has subtracted any non-cognitive EQ content trappings or accompaniments that such episodes may have.

I think we have no choice but to grant that our capacity for cognitive experience is a distinct naturally evolved *experiential modality* that is, whatever its origins, fundamentally different from all the sensory experiential modalities (at least as we currently understand them). This is a radical claim in the current context of discussion of experience or consciousness, especially given all the input from psychology and neuro-psychology, which very strongly constrains people to think that all experience *must* be somehow sensory.[27]

We also have to think through very clearly the initially difficult fact that cognitive EQ content is, in itself, purely a matter of experiential qualitative character, wholly what it is considered entirely independently of its causes. We may have to dwell on the point, work on it, especially if we have been trained up as analytic philosophers at any time in the last fifty years. Try now to imagine life without cognitive experience being part of the (experiential) qualitative character of experience. Consider yourself reading this now and try to convince yourself that all that is going on is sensory experience (accompanied by non-experiential changes in your dispositional set).

One of the difficulties that philosophers have with the idea of cognitive EQ content may derive from the fact that they fail to distinguish it sharply from cognitive content as currently understood. So let it be said: *cognitive EQ content is not the same thing as*

[25] Compare the 'transparency' or 'diaphanousness' of ordinary visual experience stressed, exaggerated, and regularly theoretically abused by 'representationalists'.

[26] When I talked inaccurately of the 'diaphaneity' of cognitive experience in *MR* (see e.g. 182–3), I meant only this gauziness, insubstantiality, intangibility.

[27] The best philosophizing psychologists, like Antonio Damasio and Jeffrey Gray, seem to accept this view. I think they underestimate evolution.

cognitive content. Cognitive content as we now understand it is not an EQ matter at all. The cognitive content of a thought-episode is (necessarily) *semantically evaluable*—assessable as true or false, accurate or inaccurate; the cognitive EQ content of the thought-episode is in itself no more semantically evaluable than sensory EQ content considered entirely independently of its causes. The cognitive EQ content of one's 'Twin-Earth' Twin's thoughts and experiences is by hypothesis identical to one's own in every respect although the cognitive content of one's Twin's thoughts and experiences is quite different. The same goes for one's 'Brain-in-a-Vat' Twin, and, for good measure, one's 'Instant' Twin who has just now popped flukishly into being. (Note that identity of cognitive *EQ* content across Twins must be conceded even by philosophers who claim that Instant-Twins don't really have thoughts—cognitive content—at all.)

Recognition of the existence of cognitive EQ content brings immediate relief to those who find it impossible to accept the popular idea that one fails to think a thought *at all* when one takes oneself to think that *a* is *F* in the case in which there is in fact no such thing as *a*. For in this case one can and must allow that there is a fully fledged thought-*experience*, with full cognitive *EQ* content, even if one wishes to say that there is no propositional content properly speaking, no 'Russellian' thought.[28]

Let me say it again: the cognitive EQ content of a thought is not the propositional content of the thought, which many nowadays simply call 'the content'.[29] It is that without which it cannot be true to say that the propositional content is being consciously entertained by someone (the comprehending entertaining of the content of a thought tends to be orders of magnitude faster than it is when it is no faster than the verbal spreading out of the thought in silent inner speech). We need to recognize it fully, now, in analytic philosophy of mind, because we have got into a sorry state without it.

—Philosophers' Twins are one thing, for their experience is identical by hypothesis, but I'm still confused, and one crucial question, it seems to me, is this: do two ordinary people thinking the same thought (entertaining the same cognitive content) necessarily have the same cognitive experience, the same cognitive EQ content? Suppose you and I both think 'The river is deep and wide'. Do we then have the same cognitive EQ content, according to you? Do we necessarily have the same cognitive EQ content?

This is a natural question and the answer is No, it would be hugely surprising if we had exactly the same cognitive EQ content, given that we're not Twins.

One way to put the point, perhaps, is to allow, strictly for purposes of discussion, that there is a sense in which we almost certainly don't have exactly the same river concept. This is like a key idea in 'conceptual role semantics', according to which we

---

[28] Perhaps cognitive EQ content is what you get when you give Kaplan's notion of character an explicitly experiential reading. I'm not sure. What I do know is that full and unqualified acknowledgement of the existence of cognitive EQ content, cognitive experience, is compatible with robust externalism.

[29] This is why most of my uses of 'content' are Neurathian—at least until the next section.

all have somewhat different river concepts because the concept RIVER[30] has different semantic or conceptual associations for us, sitting as it does in a different web of cognitive connections in each of us. One does not have to accept conceptual role semantics—I don't—in order to accept this as a helpful way of expressing how your and my *cognitive EQ content* can be different when we both think that the river is deep and wide. One can just as well be an outright Fodorian, a strong-as-you-like externalist about the (actual semantic) content of concepts.

The point can be put differently and perhaps better by saying that when we try to characterize the nature of cognitive EQ content we have to take account of what William James, talking of words, calls 'the halo, fringe or scheme in which we feel the words to lie'.[31] Or one might distinguish between the external and internal aspects of a concept considered as a mental particular—between RIVER$_I$ and RIVER$_E$ (GOLD$_I$ and GOLD$_E$), as it were. A huge and unnecessary debate in philosophy of mind has arisen from the fact that polarizing, adversarial philosophers have either stressed RIVER$_E$ at the expense of (or to the exclusion of) RIVER$_I$ or vice versa. And here the slippage between thinking of concepts as concrete mental particulars and thinking of them as abstract objects has much to answer for.

—But suppose you and I both focus furiously just on the cognitive content *The river is deep and wide*, or *All squares have four sides*. Won't we then have the same cognitive experience, perfectly focused as we are? Won't we *necessarily* have exactly the same cognitive EQ content? And isn't that a very implausible thing to have to say?

Yes to your second question, No to your first for the reasons already given. Necessary sameness of cognitive EQ content does not follow from perfect focusing, although the differences between us may indeed be small. The conceptual role semantics analogy is perhaps particularly helpful inasmuch as it introduces the possibility of difference right into the middle of the cognitive EQ content involved in thinking 'The river is deep and wide' by lodging it within the concepts deployed. On the face of it, the Jamesian fringe doesn't do this, but really the two analogies do the same thing, and it isn't hard to come up with others.

There is more to say, but this is enough for now. In conclusion, note that recognition of the existence of cognitive EQ content promises a complete and benign resolution of the conceptual role semantics debate, while at the same time explaining (socio-psychologically) the fact that it occurred. On the one hand, the existence of cognitive EQ content accounts naturally for the internalist (inscape) intuitions of those who favour conceptual role semantics. On the other hand, it allows all the externalist (outreach) Wittgensteinian and Fodorian intuitions to remain intact.

The debate between externalist and internalist construals of the notion of a concept has, in numerous forms, been one of the central topics of analytic philosophy at least

[30] 'The concept RIVER' is shorthand in so far as it is being questioned whether there is a single concept RIVER that we all possess. It stands for something like 'the concept that is, in any given one of us, the best candidate for being the concept RIVER on the assumption that there is only one river concept'.
[31] James (1890: i. 260). I am focusing for theoretical purposes on the conceptual aspect of the halo to the exclusion of the sensori-emotional aspect, although they are not disentanglable in everyday life.

since the 'incommunicability of content' debate of the 1920s and 1930s against which Wittgenstein reacted, and there have been correct—hence wholly reconcilable—intuitions on both sides. The debate is an almost constant presence in philosophy, in fact (it's only one step back to Frege...). But all we need to resolve it is a well-developed recognition of the existence of cognitive EQ content and of the difference between it and cognitive content as currently understood. With this in hand we don't have to have a psychologism versus anti-psychologism shoot out every time we consider the relations between thought, language, and reality. The intuitions of both sides can be fully preserved in the simple framework obtained by adding the notion of cognitive EQ content to the existing scheme of things.

By now it will be clear to many that the notion of cognitive EQ content is nothing new (it took me a while to see). It has been around in some form or other for as long as philosophers have grasped the tension between acknowledging thought to be the psychological phenomenon it is and taking full account of the fact that it allows us to think—and talk to each other—about reality. It is in Locke in all essentials; I am sure the scholastics had it clear; and so on into all the great past realms of philosophy.

7. 'CONTENT', 'REPRESENTATIONAL CONTENT', 'MENTAL CONTENT'

I'm continuing to ignore those—behaviourists, neo-behaviourists, functionalists, neo-functionalists, 'strong representationalists', and so on—who don't really believe in EQ content at all. These people do not need to be met with argument. They do however pose a practical problem, for many of them *pretend* that they believe in EQ content (sensory EQ content, that is). They star or looking-glass the standard terms for it—'phenomenology', 'qualia', 'consciousness', 'what-it's-likeness'—raising a great dust and then complaining that no one else can see. Many present-day 'representationalists', for example, say that experiences, e.g. perceptions, do have EQ content. ('Of course they do!', they say, 'Of course we don't deny this!') But then they go on to say that the EQ content of a perception P is really just its 'representational content'. And then it turns out that what they mean by the 'representational content' of P is typically something *wholly non-experiential*—a stickshift, a mountain, a hagfish, a moon; together with the functional role of P, its systemic causal role in the experiencer's mental economy, or some such.[32]

There is no clear defence against this terminological trick, because one can't move in the philosophy of mind without using terms that these philosophers immediately co-opt and turn inside out. My only resource is pleonasm: sometimes I will call EQ content 'real EQ content', because when the 'strong' representationalists (for example)

---

[32] See e.g. Dennett (2001), Dretske (1995), Lycan (1996). If P is an apprehension of someone else's feelings, Niobe's sorrow or Ivo's elation, then it will on the representationalists' terms have EQ content as (part of) its representational content. But in this case although P's content will be at least partly EQ content it will be nothing to do with P's own EQ content! (And the EQ content will be EQ content[LG].)

say that a perception of some non-experiential phenomenon does of course have EQ content they don't mean what they say; they mean that it has EQ content^{LG}, i.e. something wholly non-experiential: they looking-glass 'EQ content', even as their milder companions star it.

One finds the same terminological inversion with the expression 'representational content'. This expression has traditionally referred to properties that an entity like a mental occurrence has *considered completely independently of whatever it actually represents*. In the ordinary sense of 'representational content' a veridical perception and a qualitatively identical hallucination have exactly the same representational content, as do a portrait of X and a painting of an imaginary person that is qualitatively identical to the portrait of X. Their shared representational content is a matter of their indistinguishability as representational *vehicles*, their sameness of intrinsic EQ content as potential representations.[33] According to current terminological orthodoxy, by contrast, the representational content of an experience has *nothing* to do with its EQ content, nothing to do with its nature considered as a vehicle of representation in the above sense. The representational content of my experience of the moon is just the moon itself, the non-experiential, non-representational, non-mental entity the moon.[34] It is not, then, representational content; it is representational content^{LG}.

Confusing; though not, now, for those soaked in the new terminology, who have passed through the looking glass and may feel queasy at the idea that 'representational content' could mean anything other than what they have been conditioned to understand it to mean.

The confusion grows when philosophers go on to say that *all* mental content is representational content—by which they mean representational content^{LG}. For now the same terminological trick is turned: 'mental content', standardly shortened to 'content', is understood in such a way that the EQ content of a conscious mental episode M is no part of M's content—no part of M's mental content! All conscious mental episodes have EQ content by definition, but the present terminology has it that M's content is only what M is *of* or *about*, so that M has EQ content as part of its content only if M is of or about some EQ content or other that exists quite independently of M—Iphigenia's apprehension or Harry's feeling of peace. As for M's own EQ content, that can now be part of M's own content only in the vanishingly rare case in which M is about itself![35]

This looking-glassed—or at least heavily starred—use of the general phrase 'mental content' is now deeply entrenched. Many have grown so accustomed to it that they can no longer hear that there is anything wrong with it: it sounds to them obvious, accurate and unambiguous, just as 'gold' becomes an obvious, accurate, unambiguous

---

[33] Bear in mind that this intrinsic EQ content includes cognitive EQ content, e.g. the *taking what one is seeing to be an F* that is standardly built into seeing an F or hallucinating an F.

[34] Plus the experience's systemic functional role or some such: I will omit this qualification from now on.

[35] Is this possible? If M is about itself (*This very thought is puzzling*) then it is automatically about its own content in the representationalists' terms because it is itself its own content. But it is not at all clear that it can be about its own (real, non-looking-glassed) EQ content. It depends on the extent to which thought on the wing can be immediately self-aware (compare Strawson 1999: §X on the self-awareness of the thinking subject).

word for pizza for those who use it for long enough to mean pizza. It is for all that hopelessly counterintuitive in what it excludes.[36] For EQ content (real EQ content) is, evidently, mental content, given any remotely sensible use of the term 'mental content'.

I can imagine terminological contexts in which one might allow that what is now often called 'mental content' (stickshifts, hagfish, etc.) can indeed be called mental content; but the people who like to talk in this way would at least have to allow in return that EQ content is *also* mental content (in this case the term 'mental content' would be starred, not looking-glassed). And they won't, or many of them won't. So let me for the sake of clarity match them in terminological intransigence. The question is this. Given that (real) EQ content is obviously mental content, should 'mental content' also be taken to cover propositional/cognitive content, 'content' in the straitened externalist sense just described? And now, intransigently, I say No. When 'content' is understood in this way, *the content of a mental state or occurrence is not mental content*. Obviously. The opposition have looking-glassed 'mental content', rather than just starring it.

Does this sound strange? It shouldn't, for it is a straight consequence of standard externalism, and of all the overexcited statements of externalism that have led to this strange new way of talking.[37] For when the planet Mars, the very thing itself, is said to be (part of) the content of a mental state or occurrence M, in the externalist manner, it certainly does not follow, and is certainly not true, unless you are Berkeley (on one reading of him), that Mars, the thing itself, 150 million miles away from M, is itself a matter of mental content. So too for everything else we can perceive or think about that is not itself a mental phenomenon in the traditional sense. To think that the world-involving propositional content of a mental state or occurrence is itself mental content, i.e. something that is itself in some way mental in nature, is the very antithesis of externalism.[38] It's like thinking that the content of my bucket, these potatoes, is not just in the bucket, but partakes of buckethood in its intrinsic being by virtue of being in the bucket. Clearly one should not infer from 'A is the content of a B-ish container' to 'A is B-ish'.[39]

Chorus of voices saying of course they never meant anything like this. Of course—but concede the unclarity of the usage. So too for 'representation'. In the current idiom the content of a particular representation *R* of Mars—viz. Mars itself—is its

---

[36] How did this happen? It got a boost when 'externalism', a doctrine which, correctly understood, is accepted by all sensible people, including of course Descartes, went mad and metaphysical. Pyle (2003: ch. 5) gives a nice account of Arnauld's defence of the externalist Cartesian position against the terminologically slippery Malebranche.

[37] Overexcited: externalism is as old as thought and—as just remarked—fully Cartesian. Note that Descartes is also a representationalist, holding that pain, for example, is a perception of something, and hence intentional. Its defect, as a perception, is that it is not a very clear and distinct perception.

[38] Of course they reject the 'i.e.' clause, but to do that one has to Humpty-Dumpty around for a long time until it sounds OK.

[39] If this peculiar episode in the history of philosophy is remembered in the future, teachers of philosophy will have the same kind of task that they now have with Descartes when they explain to first-years that by 'objective' Descartes effectively means what we mean by 'subjective'.

representational content (it is representational content[LG]). What's more, many want to say that Mars is, in being the representational content of *R*, part of *R* itself. In the village I come from, however, a representation of something is wholly ontologically distinct from the thing it is a representation of (except in very rare cases). In the village I come from we always find that there is, on the one hand, the representation, a concrete particular thing, and, on the other hand, the thing represented, another particular concrete thing (putting aside 'abstract objects'). There is, certainly, a causal connection between representation and represented, in the case of a representation of a concrete entity; but this merely confirms the point, given that things that stand in causal relations are 'distinct existences'.

8. ALL MENTALLY CONTENTFUL PHENOMENA ARE EXPERIENTIAL PHENOMENA

Now for the sense in which all truly, genuinely, intrinsically, categorically[40] mentally contentful phenomena are experiential phenomena. I say 'the sense in which' because all I am going to do is to offer a way of putting things that certainly says something true when its terms are accepted even if many find its terms unacceptable.

In *The Mind Doesn't Work That Way* Jerry Fodor writes that:

our pretheoretical, 'folk' taxonomy of mental states conflates two quite different natural kinds: the intrinsically intentional ones, of which beliefs, desires, and the like are paradigms; and the intrinsically *conscious* ones, of which sensations, feelings, and the like are paradigms.

Fodor makes, here, a popular terminological choice about the word 'intentional'. Then, observing that some intentional states are conscious, he adds a footnote:

It is rather an embarrassment for cognitive science that any intentional mental states are conscious. 'Why aren't they all unconscious if so many of them are?' is a question that cognitive science seems to raise but not to answer. Since, however, I haven't got the slightest idea what the right answer is, I propose to ignore it.[41]

But if cognitive science raises Fodor's question then perhaps it also raises the complementary question: Why aren't they all conscious if so many of them are—all the tens of thousands of perceptions and conscious thoughts that fill every waking day? And perhaps the best answer to this question, all things considered, is that they are all conscious: that, strictly speaking, every genuinely intentional state is a conscious state.

This is my view—my terminological choice. It's hardly iconoclastic, for it is the view (terminology) of the vast majority of philosophers, from Aristotle to Avicenna to Brentano and Husserl and right up to the present-day community of philosophers excluding its analytic division. I really do think it is the best way to put things, once one has become clear about the existence and utter centrality to our lives of cognitive experience. It is true to say of you now—true without qualification—that you have

---

[40] Such words may be thought vague or vacuous or question-begging, but they have some useful force in contexts like the present one.   [41] Fodor 2000: 4–5, 106.

thousands of beliefs about things of which you are at present in no way conscious. Certainly. But it just doesn't follow that you are now in any truly or genuinely or intrinsically (etc.) contentful mental states that are about these things. And—outside today's terminological prison—it's utterly obvious that you aren't.

Why have we gone wrong? It is here, I think, that uncritical use of the expression 'mental state' has done most damage in the philosophy of mind, and this deserves a brief separate comment.

9. 'MENTAL STATES'

Many philosophers talk in a strongly reificatory way about mental states as if they were things in us, rather than things—states—we are in, and this (mixed in with the whole long behaviourist folly) has led many to find it natural to conceive of belief dispositions, preference dispositions, and so on as mentally contentful somethings that are 'in us' and are rightly thought of as intrinsically mentally contentful entities ('belief states', 'desire states') quite independently of the content of our present experience.[42] The use of plain count-noun forms like 'belief' and 'desire' for dispositional mental phenomena already leads us into metaphysical temptation (for we are weak, and these nouns do not have explicitly dispositional 'ility' endings). It dangerously smooths the way to the sense that a belief (for example) is somehow a categorical item rather than (or as well as) a disposition. The common use of 'belief' as a near synonym of 'proposition' makes things worse. It adds to the aura of categoricality and substantivality, for propositions are undoubtedly intrinsically contentful and non-dispositional entities, albeit abstract ones.

A proposition, however, is not a disposition. And a disposition is not a proposition. We know this, but there is leakage.

The point can be put concisely by saying that *to have a belief is not to be in any contentful mental state*. This sounds bizarre, given current terminological orthodoxy, although it sounded self-evident a hundred years ago; but to say that a person has a certain belief is simply to say that he is disposed in a certain way. It is, certainly, wholly natural to call this disposition a *mental* disposition, but to say that someone has a certain mental disposition, e.g. a belief disposition, is not to say that she is actually in any contentful mental state. To be in a state of dreamless sleep is not to be in any contentful mental state at all, although one has, asleep, tens of thousands of beliefs, preferences, and so on. And one must not (to repeat) think of one's mental dispositions as quasi-substantival intrinsically contentful somethings that are 'in' one. This is a case in which terminological choice kicks off metaphysical error.[43]

---

[42] This is well analysed by Helen Steward (1997, especially ch. 4). Recall from your pre-philosophical life how extraordinarily unnatural it is to use the phrase 'mental state' of beliefs and their like at all, rather than of states of anxiety, overexcitement and relaxation.

[43] Note that any supposed problems arising from the need to make a distinction between explicit and implicit beliefs vanish when the dispositional approach is taken seriously.

Some will think this obviously wrong. The phenomenon of linguistic conditioning is remarkable. It can make someone unable to see the duck-rabbit figure as anything other than a rabbit even in a context that makes it almost impossible to see it as anything other than a duck. I think it's not uncommon to have direct experience of this in a philosophical career, coming to see a possibility that one simply couldn't see—couldn't really see—before. It has happened to me.

Some will be as impatient as I used to be when others drew attention to the dangers of terminology. They will be confident that they can philosophize in their familiar idiom without being in any way misled; and it is true that a piece of terminology can work very well and introduce no distortion in many contexts even though there are other contexts in which it is disastrous. This is, in fact, a large part of the problem, because the contexts in which the use does no harm confer a false air of unrestricted legitimacy.

10. ALL MENTALLY CONTENTFUL PHENOMENA ARE EXPERIENTIAL PHENOMENA (CONT.)

So much for mental states. Here now is Louis, a representative human being, lying for our theoretical convenience in dreamless sleep during a thirty-second period of time t.[44] Consider the portion of reality that consists of Louis, which I call the *Louis-reality*—the *L-reality* for short (it is a rough notion, for as a physical being Louis is enmeshed in wide-reaching physical interactions, but it is serviceable and useful nonetheless). We truly ascribe beliefs, preferences and many other so-called 'propositional attitudes' to Louis as he lies there at t, and he undoubtedly has tens, hundreds of thousands of *dispositions* to behave in all sorts of ways, verbal and non-verbal, and to go into all sorts of states, mental and non-mental. Many, many disposition-ascribing *mental predicates* are true of Louis, true without qualification. Many propositional-content-citing predicates (e.g. 'believes that p', 'wants X to embrace Y', etc.) are true of him. Certainly. And yet there aren't really any truly mentally contentful entities in the L-reality during t, on the present view. Nor, therefore, are there any intentional phenomena.[45]

So what it is about Louis, lying there so dreamlessly at t, that makes it true to say that he believes that the sixth-century church of San Vitale is in Australia or that every even number greater than 2, except one, is the sum of two different prime numbers? What is it in the current L-reality that makes this true?[46] The standard naturalist physicalist answer is: a certain arrangement of neurons, call it N. By hypothesis N is not—does not constitute—a conscious, experiential state of Louis, nor is it any part of

---

[44] Here I draw on *MR* §6.6.

[45] I'm assuming for the purposes of argument that there aren't any other subjects of experience other than Louis in the L-reality. My 'micropsychism' (the view that some if not all of the ultimate constituents of reality have experiential being) commits me to saying that there are in fact other subjects of experience in the L-reality, but it is not relevant here.

[46] In the case of San Vitale a causal connection is also necessary, but it is not part of what is in the L-reality.

such a state. It is simply the neural categorical ground of one of Louis's mental dispositions. Is it nonetheless a genuinely mentally contentful, intentional entity, considered in its total intrinsic being, which is wholly non-experiential being? Surely not—whatever has caused it to exist as it does. Louis's brain has—by hypothesis—only non-experiential being at t, and we may therefore, in line with standard physicalism, take its nature at t to be wholly capturable, at least in principle, in the terms of neurophysiology and physics. Will these record any mental content, or intentionality at t, in their account of the being of N? Evidently not. They will tell us the bottom truth about why Louis is disposed to deny that San Vitale is in Italy, just as physics will tell us the bottom truth about why this calculator is disposed to display the numeral 49 when its keys are struck in a certain way; but they will not reveal anything intrinsically mentally contentful in Louis's brain at t, even while they reveal everything there is to Louis's brain at t. Certainly you won't get the required difference between Louis and the calculator without the Only In An Experiential Being thesis, and that alone won't be enough.

Take up your superpsychocerebroscope and aim it at Louis's brain during t. It has one switch with two positions. Switching to A reveals all experiential goings on, switching to B reveals all non-experiential goings on. You switch to A: nothing. You switch to B: all the unbelievably complex goings on accounted for in a perfected (non-experiential) physics. Question: when the psychoscope is switched to B, does it reveal any truly mentally contentful goings on (or entities) whose contents are what make the thousands of dispositional mental predicates that are true of Louis true of him? No, say I.

Imagine, in the spirit of the 'extended mind' hypothesis,[47] a prosthesis that gives you immediate mental access to a database on a memory storage device stitched in under your ribs. Thanks to this prosthesis, if someone asks you what the atomic numbers of platinum and mercury are, it comes immediately to your mind that they are 78 and 80 respectively, although you didn't know this before. Now the vast quantity of information on the device isn't intrinsically mentally contentful before you plug in. Does all of it become so immediately you plug in? It's hard to see how one could say No, on the view according to which dispositional phenomena can be intrinsically mentally contentful entities.

I think this is a serious problem for the whole idea that dispositional phenomena are intrinsically mentally contentful phenomena, even after one has put aside the (already decisive) point that dispositions just aren't the right kind of thing, metaphysically, to be intrinsically mentally contentful. Dreamless Louis was plugged in during t without him feeling a thing. Did a whole new realm of real, actually existing, concrete mental content come into existence at that moment? Surely not.

I don't say this because I doubt that the 'extended mind' hypothesis is any real help with seeing how things are in (mental) reality, although I do doubt this. What's relevant here is that the proponents of the extended mind thesis have anticipated this objection. They have seen that claiming that there is such a thing as *experienceless intentionality* will require one to agree that a whole new realm of concrete mental content leaps into being the moment we plug in the device, and they have accordingly—fatally—bitten the bullet.

---

[47] See Clark and Chalmers (1998), Clark (2001: ch. 8).

In some ways my view is close to Searle's. When there is no experience, he says, 'what is going on in the brain is neurophysiological processes [here he means non-experiential goings on] and consciousness [experience] and nothing more'.[48] There are no truly mentally contentful phenomena to be found when there is no experience. Nor, therefore, are there any truly intentional phenomena.

At certain points, however, Searle says that although belief dispositions are non-experiential they are nonetheless intrinsically intentional.[49] I deny this outright, but in the end we may differ only in emphasis, for he goes on to say that 'the ontology of mental states, at the time they are unconscious, consists entirely in the existence of purely neurophysiological phenomena',[50] and here again by 'purely neurophysiological phenomena' he means non-experiential phenomena, the point being that they are phenomena that cannot *really* be said to be intrinsically mentally contentful or genuinely intentional, considered in themselves, in their total physical being, any more than a CD of Shostakovich's 15th String Quartet can be said to be intrinsically musically contentful, considered in itself, in its total current physical being.

One's mental dispositions are no less than they are; but neural phenomena in the absence of experiential phenomena aren't intrinsically mentally contentful intentional phenomena any more than pits in a CD are intrinsically musically contentful. A perfect physical duplicate of a CD could come into existence by chance, or as a result of the impacts of random radio signals on a CD burner. So too, mutatis mutandis, for the non-experiential neural phenomena that ground a mental disposition.[51]

So the claim remains: all true, actual, mental content is, necessarily, (occurrent) experiential content, and there just isn't any in the L-reality during *t*. The intensely natural picture according to which it is just obvious that there is no mental content in the L-reality at *t* (I have put micropsychism aside) has become invisible to many present-day analytic philosophers, but from the perspective of this paper the view that there is mental content in the L-reality during *t* given Louis's mental dispositions is a bit like the view that there are intrinsically breakage-involving states or goings on actually present in a fragile but undisturbed object.

—But the view that there are intrinsically mentally contentful states inside the head of dreamless Louis isn't a philosophical concoction. Ordinary thought says the same, and philosophy should always treat ordinary thought with respect.

Yes. But, first, ordinary thought is not a good general guide to philosophical or scientific truth. Second, it won't help to appeal to it here. For even if it does endorse the view that there are intrinsically mentally contentful states in dreamless Louis, I am

[48] (1992: back cover).   [49] (1992: 158).

[50] (1992: 159). Note that the present proposal obviates Searle's need for what he calls the 'Connection Principle', which has trouble with Freud and raises puzzles about 'implicit' (never consciously entertained) beliefs.

[51] I discuss the CD analogy in *MR*, ch. 6, imagining a normal human brain permanently and irreversibly deprived of its capacity for consciousness but otherwise running normally. This brain has long been harnessed to a light-show-producing machine and produces spectacular displays. Does it contain beliefs, preferences and so on? Certainly there are plenty of true counterfactuals about what would happen if you placed it back in a normal human body.

quite sure that it does not endorse the standard philosophical view that *dispositions* are intrinsically mentally contentful phenomena. This point is hidden by the current terminology of analytic philosophy, because it takes over ordinary words like 'belief' and uses them for things it classifies as strictly dispositional phenomena (even as the word 'belief' creates a vague sense that beliefs are somehow categorical items). But in doing this it completely loses touch with ordinary thought, which takes it (it seems to me) that there are intrinsically mentally contentful phenomena in dreamless Louis only in so far as it pictures them non-dispositionally as little packets of intrinsic content laid up in the head and available for activation by consciousness. Ordinary thought pictures them as non-dispositional, categorically mentally contentful intentional entities (a bit like sentences in a book where a book is naively and wrongly conceived as intrinsically intentional). And when ordinary thought does consider mental dispositions, it does not think of them as mentally contentful at all. We say, for example, that Cordelia has a gentle disposition. But here we do not think that there is an actual gentleness *content*, a *contentful state of gentleness*, sitting there all the time in virtue of which it is true to say that Cordelia is a gentle person (or intelligent, or proud). And it seems to me that in so far as we talk of beliefs as dispositions, we should not treat them differently.

—Look, sometimes we move straight to action on the basis of our beliefs and preferences without any conscious contentful experiential episodes at all. We do A because we believe B and like C. This can be a straightforwardly true explanation of our action, as true as 'squares have four sides'. How can you possibly say that the B and C dispositions are not themselves intrinsically mentally contentful states, given that they have this causal and explanatory role?

No problem. I have no more reason to say this than I have to say that this glass's being fragile right now involves intrinsically breakage-involving goings on right now (even given the important differences between fragility dispositions and belief dispositions—see n. 14). In fact I not only think that the B-disposition and the C-disposition are definitely not intrinsically mentally contentful states. I also think that any *occurrent* but non-experiential episodes to which they give rise in leading to A, episodes that comfortable, familiar theory may seem to require us to think of as intrinsically mental-content-carrying, are not intrinsically mentally contentful, even though they, unlike dispositions, are not immediately ruled out for fundamental metaphysical reasons.

Here, perhaps, I am genuinely in conflict with ordinary thought. Perhaps I should allow that these occurrent non-experiential episodes can have aboutness, at least, given their causes, even though they can't be said to be intentional (because intentionality requires experience). Certainly I don't mind saying that they 'carry information'. In the long run, though, I think that if one allows true mental contentfulness to any non-experiential occurrences in the brain one will in the end have to allow that robots and pocket calculators can be in truly mentally contentful states in every sense in which we can. Nor will one be able to stop at pocket calculators. And that is a reductio.

You may retain some respect for the word 'mental' (many don't, and think it's deep not to) and try to exclude the robots and calculators by endorsing the Only In An Experiential Being thesis; but this thesis does nothing to help the metaphysically incoherent idea that *dispositions* are entities that can be intrinsically mentally contentful entities. The fact is that dispositional mental predicates can be wholly and straightforwardly true of Louis at *t* without there being any truly mentally contentful phenomena in the L-reality; just as 'fragile' can be true of an object without there being any actual breaking going on in that object.

Can we meet in the middle? You concede to me that dispositions cannot be truly mentally contentful, that only occurrent phenomena can. Then you return to the point that there are plenty of occurrent phenomena to be found connecting the B and C dispositions and the occurrence of A in such a way that A is appropriate given the nature of the B and C dispositions, and ask me to concede in return that non-experiential (sub-experiential) occurrent states as well as experiential states can be mentally contentful.[52] 'The null hypothesis', you say,

is that there isn't (that is, needn't be) any difference between a robot thinking 'it's raining' and me thinking 'it's raining'. I think that must be right because I don't think my thoughts are usually conscious (or, anyhow, consciously noticed); and, surely, my thought that it's raining is the thought that it's raining, whether or not I'm aware of having it.[53]

For myself I'm eirenic, but my terminology is adamant. It says that if occurrent non-experiential states can be truly mentally contentful, then truly mentally contentful states can be found in zombies, robots, calculators, and so on.[54] But they can't so they aren't. Fodor contraposes: they are so they can. But it's only terminology, as Cole Porter said. We don't disagree on the facts. We're sticking over a word. I'm happy to allow that any content or 'content' or 'aboutness' that can be ascribed to goings on in experienceless entities can be equally well ascribed to certain of our non-experiential neural states goings on, and vice versa. In fact I think one has to allow this to get a remotely plausible picture of how the world works. But there is nothing truly mentally contentful going on in this case (so too there is nothing truly musically contentful going on in a CD, and nothing truly breaking or broken in the panes of glass in the window in front of me), and there is no intentionality.

The alternative is to say that calculators and so on have intentionality in every sense in which we do. But I say to you again, no intentionality without mind, and no mind without, in a word, *mind*.

—What about a Freudian unconscious belief? However much you obfuscate in other cases, in this case it's absolutely clear that you are in a state that is about Great Aunt Lulu. This is fact, objective fact about the concrete world. It is a fact about you as a physical system considered now in your intrinsic physical nature. That means it's a fact about you now considered wholly independently of everything else including your past and shaping causes. There is Lulu-intentional content lodged in you, period.

---

[52] That, you say, is how the problem you had when you set out for Scotland was solved when you got there even though you hadn't given it any thought.

[53] Fodor, private correspondence (2002).

[54] In Strawson (2004) I argue that one can't stop there—one has to let in footballs, electrons, everything. The aim of the argument is a *reductio ad absurdum* of the view that there can be non-experiential intentionality.

So far as dispositions are concerned, the case of Freud-unconscious beliefs is no different from that of any other beliefs: dispositions aren't and can't be mentally contentful entities. Nor can the categorical neural grounds of mental dispositions, fully describable by physics and neurophysiology, be mentally contentful entities. But the Freudian unconscious pulls hard on people's intuitions. Surely, we think, there is a little packet of intrinsic Lulu content somewhere in the folds of my brain right now? If Wilder Penfield poked his neurosurgical probe in the right place, I would light up with a dread memory of Lulu in her satin combinations. So surely Lulu stamped Lulu-content into me in such a way that it is in me, now, intrinsically, considered simply as the physical system I now am, and so considered wholly independently of my undeniably Luluish past?

I think nearly all philosophers reject the idea of little packets of intrinsic content thus conceived. And yet the idea that there is absolutely nothing intrinsically mentally contentful and in particular Lulu-contentful inside Louis, when one of these Freud-unconscious states is actively moving him, may seem hard to defend; even though whatever is going on in him is by hypothesis non-experiential.

This is the issue just raised: can occurrent non-experiential goings on, at least, be said to be mentally contentful? How do I respond? First, I repeat that there is nothing special about the case of Freud-unconscious occurrent goings on, for the sub-experiential processes that go on in me when I find myself ready with a reply to your last remark cannot be less worthy, as candidates for mental contentfulness. Anything else? Not really. I grant that the intrinsic-content intuition is intensely natural for us given our actual unquestioned causal-environmental embeddedness, but my position remains the same. The sense in which there is something intrinsically mentally contentful here is exactly the same as the sense in which occurrent, processual radio waves travelling out into space from the studios of BBC Radio Three are, considered in their intrinsic physical nature as it is now and so wholly independently of everything else including its past and shaping causes, intrinsically Shostakovich's-15th-Quartet-contentful. There is no more intrinsically resident musical content in the occurrent radio-wave process than there is in the CD.

Some may find my terminological preferences counterintuitive to the point of offence or error, but I am sure, as already remarked, that I do not disagree with them on any matter of fact.[55]

There is much more to say, but my general terminologico-substantive position is clear. Intentionality is essentially categorical, never dispositional. More than that, it is essentially 'live', occurrent, mental, and indeed experiential. This, I propose, is the best way to talk. Fodor once disagreed when he said that a 'good theory of content might license the literal ascription of (underived) intentionality to thermometers',[56] and the proposal is obviously revisionary relative to current terminological fashion. But the claim remains: everything true that can be said in the current standard terms can be said equally clearly, and I think better, in the term I am proposing. The claim

---

[55] See further *MR* 160–2, 168–72. Obviously many intuitions are highly context-sensitive. I can pull my own in different directions by altering the surround.
[56] (1990: 130).

that mental dispositions are themselves intentional phenomena is not only metaphysically incoherent; it also puts one on a slippery slope that slides all the way down to intentional thermometers and beyond. The same slippery slope awaits the (admittedly far less bizarre) claim that occurrent non-experiential mental phenomena can be truly intentional phenomena. These points are something about which Fodor, for one, has always been very clear. But it's just a way of talking, and I want to try another way. I would be astonished if Fodor and I disagree about any relevant matter of fact.

You have to choose your implausibility. If you allow that states of a person in dreamless sleep can be genuinely intentional phenomena, your problem is to stop the slide down to intentional thermometers and beyond without invoking the seemingly arbitrary Only In An Experiential Being thesis.[57] That's Fodor's problem, but of course he doesn't think it's really a problem. If on the other hand you deny that occurrences in and states of a person in dreamless sleep can be genuinely intentional phenomena, your problem is to stop the intentional realm shrinking into the experiential realm. That's my problem, but then I don't think it's really a problem.[58]

Many who dismiss the Only In An Experiential Being thesis may want to deny that puddles and mirrors (and perhaps thermometers) have intentionality while insisting that robots, cruise missiles, and so on do. They are drawn to what one might call the *Only In A Behaviourally Purposive Being* thesis, which is, I take it, extensionally equivalent to Dennett's notion of the 'intentional stance' according to which intentional phenomena are to be found only (and also *ipso facto*) in a being to which we naturally or usefully attribute beliefs and goals when we attempt to explain or predict its behaviour.[59]

It seems to me, though, that the Only In A Behaviourally Purposive Being thesis is no less arbitrary than the Only In An Experiential Being thesis. It is, furthermore, quite unclear what should count as behavioural purposiveness. Most of those who are drawn to the Only In A Behaviourally Purposive Being thesis would not attribute intentionality to a plant that responds variously to environmental conditions (say), or to a developing embryo operating according to a fixed programme, or to a host of other such things. But it is entirely unclear what, other than a certain zoomorphic prejudice, can justify including robots that operate according to a fixed programme while excluding plants and so on.[60]

The arbitrariness of the Only In A Behaviourally Purposive Being thesis is not a problem for Dennett, of course. It is something that he is quite clear about, given his

[57] Note that it imposes a looser requirement than Searle's 'Connection principle' (Searle 1992).

[58] In Strawson 2004 I argue that the other way of talking saddles you with far too much intentionality.

[59] See Dennett 1971, 1981, 1991a. I say 'extensionally equivalent' because I think that some who endorse the Only in a Behaviourally Purposive Being thesis reject Dennett's profoundly anti-realist attitude to intentionality, consciously or not.

[60] The Only in a Behaviourally Purposive Being thesis has interesting variants, e.g. the Only in a Behaviourally Purposive Being Capable of Misrepresentation thesis, and the Only in a Behaviourally Purposive Being Capable of Learning thesis. Some think they can stop the slide down to intentional thermometers in such highly specific ways (see e.g. Dretske 1988, 1995). I'm sceptical, though, as is Fodor. For other functionalist strategies to stop the slide see e.g. Tye (1995), Lycan (1996). I reject these briefly in Strawson (2004) and also in *Intentionality!*

wholly behaviourist, anti-realist, functionalist, instrumentalist, interpretationist approach to questions of mind. It is, indeed, something he rather welcomes. There isn't, for him, any genuine metaphysical issue about the nature of intentionality. Like many, I utterly disagree, and am dismayed that the real metaphysical issue has been lost. This essay is an attempt to recover it, but it is only the beginning.[61]

REFERENCES

Ayers, M. R. (1990) *Locke* (London: Routledge).

Chalmers, D. and Clark, A. (1998) 'The Extended Mind', *Analysis* 58: 7–19.

Clark, A. (2001) *Mindware—An Introduction to the Philosophy of Cognitive Science* (Oxford: Oxford University Press).

Dennett, D. (1971) 'Intentional Systems', *Journal of Philosophy* 68: 87–106.

——(1981) 'True Believers: The Intentional Strategy and Why it Works', in *Scientific Explanation*, ed. A. F. Heath (Oxford: Oxford University Press).

——(1991a) 'Real Patterns', *Journal of Philosophy* 88: 27–51.

——(1991b) *Consciousness Explained* (Boston: Little, Brown).

——(2001) 'Are We Explaining Consciousness Yet?', *Cognition* 79: 221–37.

Dretske, F. (1985) 'Misrepresentation', in *Belief: Form, Content, Function*, ed. R. Bogdan (Oxford: Oxford University Press).

——(1988) *Explaining Behavior* (Cambridge, Mass.: MIT Press).

——(1995) *Naturalizing the Mind* (Cambridge, Mass.: MIT Press).

James, W. (1890/1950) *The Principles of Psychology*, vol. i (New York: Dover).

Fodor, Jerry A. (1990) *A Theory of Content and other Essays* (London: MIT press).

——(2000) *The Mind Doesn't Work That Way* (Cambridge, Mass.: MIT Press).

Harman, G. (1998) 'Intentionality', in *A Companion to Cognitive Science*, ed. W. Bechtel and G. Graham (Oxford: Blackwell).

Loar, B. (2003) 'Phenomenal Intentionality as the Basis of Mental Content', in *Reflections and Replies: Essays on the Philosophy of Tyler Burge*, ed. Martin Hahn and Bjorn Ramberg (Cambridge, MA: MIT Press).

Lycan, W. (1996) *Consciousness and Experience* (Cambridge, Mass.: MIT Press).

Pitt, D. (2004) 'The Phenomenology of Cognition, or What is it like to think that *p*?', *Philosophy and Phenomenological Research*.

Pyle, Andrew (2003) *Malebranche* (London: Routledge).

Russell, B. (1927a/1992a) *The Analysis of Matter* (London: Routledge).

——(1956/1995) 'Mind and Matter', in *Portraits from Memory* (Nottingham: Spokesman).

Schopenhauer, A. (1819/1969) *The World as Will and Representation*, volume I, trans. E. J. F. Payne (New York: Dover).

Searle, J. (1992) *The Rediscovery of the Mind* (Cambridge, Mass.: Bradford/MIT Press).

Siewert, C. (1998) *The Significance of Consciousness* (Princeton, NJ: Princeton University Press).

Steward, H. (1997) *The Ontology of Mind* (Oxford: Clarendon Press).

Strawson, G. (1986) *Freedom and Belief* (Oxford: Clarendon Press).

——(1994) *Mental Reality* (Cambridge, Mass.: MIT Press).

[61] This essay began as an unfinished presentation to the 2002 NEH Summer Institute on 'Consciousness and Intentionality' held at Santa Cruz in 2002. I would like to thank the participants—especially David Chalmers and John Hawthorne—for their sceptical comments.

Strawson, G. (1999) 'The Self and the SESMET', *Journal of Consciousness Studies* 6: 99–135.

—— (2003) 'Real materialism', in *Chomsky and his Critics*, ed. L. Antony and N. Hornstein (Oxford: Blackwell).

—— (2004) 'Real intentionality', in *Phenomenology and the Cognitive Sciences* 3.

—— (forthcoming) 'Why Physicalism entails Panpsychism'.

—— (in preparation) *Intentionality!*

Tye, M. (1995) *Ten Problems of Consciousness* (Cambridge, Mass.: MIT Press).

3

On the Inescapability of Phenomenology

Taylor Carman

Abstract: Dennett's intellectualist theory of consciousness trades on an equivocation between weaker and stronger claims that might be leveled against traditional psychology and epistemology. The evidence he enlists for his account of perceptual awareness, however, supports only the weaker, not the stronger, claims. Merleau-Ponty, by contrast, while also denying that sense experience consists in the passive registration of discrete sensations, or qualia, points out that intellectualism takes for granted the constancy hypothesis by denying the presence of sensory qualities in the absence of corresponding stimuli. O'Regan and Noë advance an alternative 'sensorimotor' approach to perception that takes seriously the phenomenal character of our bodily relation to the environment. Unfortunately, their account, like Dennett's, remains within the orbit of behaviorism inasmuch as it describes perceptual experience as constituted by a knowledge of causal contingencies between sensory inputs and behavioral outputs, whereas the intentionality of perception involves our inhabiting a world in virtue of the normative structure of motivational necessities. Perception is not just what we *do*, it's what we *are*. Phenomenology is inescapable, since it is what allows us to specify at the outset what any theory of perception or consciousness must be a theory *of*.

There is no such phenomenon as really seeming—over and above the phenomenon of judging in one way or another that something is the case. (Dennett 1991: 364)

To return to the things themselves is to return to that world prior to knowledge of which knowledge always *speaks*...Perception is not a science of the world, it is not even an act...it is the background from which all acts stand out, and is presupposed by them. (Merleau-Ponty 2002: pp. ix–x, xi)[1]

I. INTRODUCTION

There is sometimes a difference between the way things are and the way they seem. There is also sometimes a difference between the way things are and the way we *think* they are. But it is a different difference, for we do not always think things are as they seem,

---

[1] Here and throughout I have made minor changes to the translation of Merleau-Ponty's *Phenomenology of Perception*.

nor do things always seem the way we think they do. The first point is obvious, but the second is not, for the distinction between how things seem and how we think they seem cuts against the temptation to suppose that judgments about one's own experience are incorrigible. Just as there is no such thing as an illusory pain, some have supposed, so too there can be no false judgments, say, that the shirt looks blue, or that the water feels hot, or that I believe your sister is on the plane, or that I want dessert. But this is implausible; people often turn out to be wrong about their emotions, their beliefs, their desires, even their perceptual experiences. Indeed, there is an emerging consensus that incorrigible knowledge is simply not to be had. Where there is knowledge, Wittgenstein said, doubt and error must be possible, and where doubt is strictly speaking senseless, then so too is any assertion of knowledge.[2]

And yet one way of banishing the very idea of incorrigibility is curiously self-defeating, for it proceeds not by insisting that our judgments can be mistaken vis-à-vis facts about our experience, but more radically by denying that there are any facts about our experience independent of what we judge them to be. There are no brute subjective qualities or seemings, on this view, only judgments purporting subjective qualities and seemings of various kinds, judgments which themselves run the gamut from reflective thought to unconscious and involuntary neural processes. Far from being incorrigible, the argument goes, such judgments are either about nothing at all, hence presumably false, or else they are in reality about the physical states of the organism, hence fallible.

But this kind of eliminative assault on the notion of incorrigibility is ironically self-undermining, for what it rules out is precisely the possibility of my being wrong *about my experience*, which is to say, my experience having some definite phenomenal quality or character and yet my *judging* otherwise. Denying incorrigibility in this way is like denying papal infallibility by denying the existence of God: it rules out infallibility, but only by excluding the possibility of genuine objective error, as opposed to mere conceptual confusion or failure of reference. For the eliminativist, that is, pronouncements about one's own experience are either oblique assertions about physical states of affairs, or they are so confused as not to count as factually incorrect in any straightforward sense. The eliminativist can therefore maintain that we are fallible. But fallibility is not the same as corrigibility, which implies the possibility of correction or amendment by way of getting it right. But if there's no getting it right simply because there's no *it*, then there's a sense in which there's no getting *it* wrong, either; there's just wrongheadedness.

The phenomenological alternative to eliminativism is to insist that although we can be wrong about some of the features of our perceptual experience, we can also be reasonably certain about others. This is so because of the peculiar *intentionality* of judgments about one's own experience. Such judgments, that is, are directed or aimed at one's own experiences not simply by purporting or asserting something about them, but by *resting on* and *presupposing* them as conditions of the possibility of the judgment itself. Judgments do not just describe, but grow out of experience, in such a way that experience is never wholly alien to judgment, but inhabits and informs it from within. As all the major figures in the phenomenological tradition have maintained, though in

---

[2] See Wittgenstein (1958: §§246, 288; p. 211) and (1972: §121).

different ways, judgment presupposes other more basic forms of intentionality and understanding. Any robust notion of corrigibility thus presupposes a distinction between judgments about experience and experience itself. If that distinction collapses, as it does on traditional Cartesian and more recent cognitivist conceptions of the mind alike, though in different ways, then so too does the very idea of meaningful objective error. At the same time, judgment can never fully detach itself from the underlying stratum of experience that informs it and makes it possible. Our own perceptual experiences are therefore never altogether alien objects over against the judgments we form about them.

Daniel Dennett is a firm believer in the fallibility of judgments about consciousness, and yet the 'heterophenomenological' approach he espouses in his theory of consciousness (see *CE*, ch. 4) proceeds very much along the lines of an atheistic debunking of papal authority. Dennett's approach, that is, involves a seemingly open-minded, but at bottom incredulous, acknowledgment of first-person reports concerning the structures and qualities of conscious experience. His philosophical orientation is thus the opposite of the phenomenological approach; indeed, he denies the very possibility of phenomenology understood as a coherent descriptive enterprise distinct from the physical sciences. The reason Dennett denies the possibility of phenomenology is that he denies the existence of its object, namely phenomenal experience. Instead, on his view, experience is nothing other than the judgments we form about it, judgments he is content to describe in purely functional, physicalistic terms.

I think Dennett's view is not just false, but incoherent, and in what follows I want to contrast it with what strikes me as the much subtler and more plausible description of perceptual experience in Maurice Merleau-Ponty's *Phenomenology of Perception*. Merleau-Ponty anticipates many of Dennett's objections to Cartesianism and empiricism, but unlike Dennett he does not reject the very idea of perceptual givenness itself. Merleau-Ponty makes a convincing case that exposing rationalist and empiricist (mis)descriptions of experience as theoretically motivated errors in no way threatens our common-sense assumption that objects and situations are *given* to us in perception, prior to our *taking* them up in thought or judgment. Merleau-Ponty wants to defend that common-sense notion of perceptual givenness while at the same time dismissing, as Dennett does, the distortions and simplifications it tends to engender in both professional and folk psychology.

II. HETEROPHENOMENOLOGICAL ELIMINATIVISM

It might be objected at the outset, as he himself has objected to his critics, that Dennett is not really an eliminativist, appearances notwithstanding.[3] Surely his theory of consciousness is not, indeed no theory of consciousness could be, simply a denial of the existence of consciousness. But this reply is disingenuous; indeed, on close scrutiny, his theory amounts to just such a denial. Dennett makes a more plausible, if

---

[3] See Dennett, 'Real Consciousness', in Dennet (1998a), and Searle (1997).

still not entirely convincing, case that his theory of intentionality does not deny the reality of intentionality, but should instead be understood as a kind of 'mild realism'. His realism about intentionality is 'mild' because he does not assume, as 'industrial strength Realists' like Jerry Fodor do, that the structure of beliefs and desires is literally mirrored in the linguistic structure of sentences describing and expressing them. Nevertheless, intentional attitudes are not just fictions posited by false folk psychological theories; they are 'real patterns' truly, if only roughly, captured by intentional locutions in psychological discourse. Language can be misleading, however, if regarded as a direct and literal reflection of the cognitive realities underlying it, and we should no more expect intentional content to be carved up in discrete sentence-like chunks than we should expect landscapes to look like road maps. Rather, as Dennett puts it, 'the multidimensional complexities of the underlying processes are projected *through linguistic behavior*, which creates an appearance of definiteness and precision, thanks to the discreteness of words'. The reality of intentional content lies in 'the brute existence of pattern',[4] albeit patterns of behavior, indeed patterns we could in principle dismiss as less real than the underlying physics, provided the physical stance offered greater explanatory and predictive power than the intentional stance.[5]

Dennett likewise denies denying the existence of consciousness, but in this case the denial is less convincing. More precisely put, his theory of consciousness seems to equivocate between on the one hand a subtle and plausible challenge to a cluster of assumptions about consciousness that have dominated philosophy and psychology since Descartes, and on the other hand a boldly counterintuitive conjecture that challenges not just expert opinion but also common sense, indeed manifest appearance (assuming there is such a thing). Dennett says explicitly that he intends his theory to depart sharply from ordinary understanding: 'I will soon be mounting radical challenges to everyday thinking', he announces, for he admits that his own theory of consciousness 'is initially deeply counterintuitive' (Dennett 1991: 45, 17). And when his imagined interlocutor objects that 'there seems to be' more to phenomenology than mere *judgments* about how things are, Dennett replies, 'Exactly! *There seems to be phenomenology*. . . . But it does *not* follow from this undeniable, universally attested fact that *there really is* phenomenology' (Dennett 1991: 366). Finally, referring to the various labels philosophers have attached to the phenomenal qualities of experience— 'raw feels', 'sensa', 'qualia'—Dennett confesses, 'In the previous chapter I seemed to be denying that there are *any* such properties, and for once what seems so *is* so. I *am* denying that there are any such properties. But . . . I agree wholeheartedly that there seem to be qualia' (Dennett 1991: 372).

---

[4] Dennett, 'Real Patterns' (1998a: 114, 120).

[5] This is why I say Dennett's disavowal of eliminativism is not especially convincing even with respect to intentionality. For even if physicalistic descriptions of behavior (some day) better serve the explanatory and predictive interests of science, why should that weaken our commitment to the existence of intentionality understood as an intelligible pattern in its own right? Dennett's eliminativism is, at bottom, his scientism, that is, his insistence on equating reality with scientific utility. Hence his dogmatic stipulation that 'physical stance predictions trump design stance predictions which trump intentional stance predictions' (1998a: 119 n. 19). Perhaps the trumping goes that way for the purposes of natural scientific explanation. But those are not our only, and certainly not our most cherished, purposes.

What does it mean to deny 'that there are *any* such properties'? Dennett's denial of the reality of qualia, it seems to me, equivocates between a weaker and a stronger pair of assertions. The weaker pair are (in my words):

(1) that the qualitative aspects of experience are neither discrete objects internal to the mind nor fully determinate properties of consciousness observable and describable in terms comparable to those in which we observe and describe external objects and their properties; and

(2) that there is no sharp boundary, only a gradual difference, between the qualitative aspects of experience and the propositional contents of attitudes such as belief or judgment.

These are by no means trivial claims. But although they depart from traditional philosophical and psychological orthodoxy, they pose no threat to phenomenology. They certainly imply nothing like eliminativism with respect to phenomenal consciousness. At best, they remind us to resist the temptation to assimilate our understanding of subjective experience to our understanding of the external world and its objective features.

Now compare those two weaker claims with the following stronger claims (again, in my words):

(3) that people often suppose that conscious experience has qualitative features of its own, distinct from the qualities of the objects of our awareness—but they are mistaken, for there are no such qualities; and

(4) that people suppose that things are *given* in perception and really *seem* a certain way, as distinct from and as the basis of their judgments about them—but again they are mistaken, for perception is itself just a form of thought or judgment.

Does Dennett give us any reason to believe theses (3) and (4), over and beyond (1) and (2)? Consider the evidence he appeals to in motivating the more radical claims.

One particularly fascinating perceptual effect Dennett discusses is the phi phenomenon, or phi movement, first so called by the Gestalt psychologist Max Wertheimer. In experiments conducted by Paul Kolers, prompted by questions from Nelson Goodman, subjects were shown the single flash of a red spot, followed quickly by a displaced green spot, followed by another flash of the original red (each flash lasting about 150 milliseconds, with a gap of about 50 milliseconds in between). The subjects report seeing not two discrete spots, but one spot rapidly moving over and back again. So far, so good. But what about the change of color from red to green? Interestingly, the subjects report the spot changing color about halfway through its journey from the initial flash to the second. The effect is the same with respect to shape when the first spot is circular and the second one square: subjects report seeing it change shape gradually as it moves.[6]

---

[6] Kolers and von Grünau (1976); discussed in Dennett (1991: 114, 120 ff.); cf. Goodman (1978: 15–16, 72–3).

This is a surprising result, and in reporting it Goodman reasonably enough asks how we are able 'to fill in the spot at the intervening place-times along a path running from the first to the second flash *before that second flash occurs*' (Goodman 1978: 73). The subjects cannot be peering into the future, after all. If we want to ascertain the true phenomenal quality of their conscious visual experience, we must ask instead how the second flash manages retroactively to affect their avowed experience of seeing the moving spot change color midway between the two points. Dennett considers two hypotheses: either we concoct false memories of *having seen* the spot change color, though in fact we had no immediate sensory awareness of the change (this is what he calls the 'Orwellian' hypothesis, suggesting a kind of *ex post facto* rewriting of history); or else we really do have a genuine, albeit delayed, sensory awareness of the light moving continuously and changing color, thanks to a kind of tape delay and rapid editing process that fills in the missing data and presents the finished product directly to the mind's eye (this is the 'Stalinesque' hypothesis, reminiscent of the cooked-up evidence presented in show trials, which does in fact make a genuine appearance in court, notwithstanding its fraudulence).

Dennett's thesis is that it is impossible in principle to decide between these two hypotheses. It is not just that one is true and the other false and that we lack sufficient data to determine which, but that there is no empirical difference between the two descriptions. The intuition that one must be correct to the exclusion of the other, he thinks, is part of the crippling legacy of the idea of a 'Cartesian Theater', a single discrete place in the mind or brain where consciousness finally happens, subsequent to its physical causes and preceding its physical effects. Dennett's own 'Multiple Drafts' model of consciousness, by contrast, deliberately blurs the line between putative events of consciousness and the various cognitive attitudes we ordinarily regard as higher-order processes responding to, but distinct from, phenomenal awareness. There is no difference, he thinks, between how things *seem* to us and how we *think* they seem. He concedes that it *seems* to us as if there is a difference between what we might call *real* seemings and merely *apparent* seemings, but this seeming is itself no more a real seeming than any other, prior to and independent of our judgment; it is instead just our (admittedly rather poor) *judgment* concerning what we (wrongly) take to be the purity and plenitude of phenomenal consciousness, distinct from all our psychological and folk-psychological judgments about it. 'There seem to be qualia, because . . . it seems that what is in here can't *just* be the judgments we make when things seem colored to us' (Dennett 1991: 372).

The conclusion Dennett wants to draw, then, is that there is no *perceptual* or sensory seeming at all, distinct from the *conceptual* contents of judgments we make about how things seem to us. There is simply no distinction to be drawn, he thinks, between how things seem to us, and how we judge that they seem; seemings and judgings collapse into a single cognitive effect:

Consider how natural is the phrase 'I judged it to be so, because that's the way it seemed to me'. Here we are encouraged to think of two distinct states or events: the seeming-a-certain-way and a subsequent (and consequent) judging-that-it-is-that-way. . . . There must be 'evidence presented' somewhere, if only in a Stalinesque show trial, so that the judgment can be caused by or grounded in that evidence.

Some people presume that this intuition is supported by phenomenology. They are under the impression that they actually observe themselves judging things to be such *as a result of* those things seeming to them to be such. No one has ever observed any such thing 'in their phenomenology' because such a fact about causation would be unobservable (as Hume noted long ago). (Dennett 1991: 133)[7]

This conclusion, that perceptual content is itself constituted by acts of thought or judgment, is what Merleau-Ponty calls 'intellectualism'.[8] Indeed, it almost seems as if Merleau-Ponty has a premonition of Dennett's view when in *Phenomenology of Perception* he criticizes intellectualism for in effect obliterating the phenomenon it purports to analyze. Intellectualist accounts of perception, he argues, fail to acknowledge the embodiment and environmental situatedness of experience, reducing perceptual content to the abstract, free-floating judgments of a disembodied subject:

Perception is thus thought about perceiving. Its incarnation furnishes no positive characteristic that has to be accounted for, and its hæcceity is simply its own ignorance of itself. Reflective analysis becomes a purely regressive doctrine, according to which every perception is just confused intellection, every determination a negation. It thus does away with all problems except one: that of its own beginning. The finitude of a perception, which gives me, as Spinoza put it, 'conclusions without premises', the inherence of consciousness in a point of view, all this reduces to my ignorance of myself, to my negative power of not reflecting. But that ignorance, how is it itself possible? (Merleau-Ponty 2002: 44)

Intellectualist accounts of perception, including Dennett's, not only rely on grossly implausible phenomenologies, then, but fall into incoherence by offering a theory of something the existence of which the theory itself cannot acknowledge. But if sensory awareness is just ignorance or illusion, it is precisely the kind of ignorance or illusion that a theory of sensory awareness is obliged to recognize and describe.

Does Dennett make a convincing case for the intellectualist position? It is not hard to see how the two weaker claims, (1) and (2), gain support from what he says. There are often no good answers to questions about the precise qualities of our perceptual experience. *How much* bigger does the moon look on the horizon than at its zenith? By *how much* do the Müller-Lyer lines differ in length? At what angle do the lines in Zöllner's illusion appear to diverge? Which object do you see just inside the outer boundary of your visual field? What does the edge of your visual field look like? And of course we do sometimes draw a merely verbal distinction between how things seem

---

[7] Dennett's parenthetical appeal to Hume here is misleading. Hume insisted on the unobservability not of causal *regularity*, but of causal *necessity*. If I can reasonably say that the cue ball causes the eight ball to move, then I can with no less embarrassment say that my perception causes me to form a judgment. Indeed, Hume conceived of beliefs in precisely those causal terms, as effects of impressions. Dennett is like Hume in his tendency to blur phenomenological distinctions, such as that between perception and thought, but he has even more in common with Descartes, a fellow rationalist who sought to assimilate all mental phenomena to thinking (*cogitare*).

[8] Although the term 'intellectualism' was common in the psychological literature around the turn of the twentieth century, its meaning sometimes varied. William James, for instance, identifies intellectualism with the Kantian thesis that sensations exist but '*are combined* by activity of the Thinking Principle' (James 1950: ii. 27; cf. 218–19). Merleau-Ponty, by contrast, often restricts the term to the more radical idea, common to Descartes and Dennett, that sensation just *is* a kind of thought; that perception is cognitive 'all the way down'.

and how we judge them to be. To say that the price of something 'seems' high to us is just to say that we judge it to be high, and it would indeed be pseudoexplanatory to say that we judge it to be high *because* that's how it seems to us. It is also clear that our beliefs often trickle down and color our perceptual experience, just as our perceptual experience reaches up and shapes our beliefs. But even common sense knows this. Squeamish eaters are a reminder that the taste of food can be highly sensitive to what you think you are ingesting, just as we all know that pain is made more intense by fear and the expectation of injury. Eagerly expecting to see your sister in the airport can produce multiple false sightings, since every remotely resembling physical trait tends to leap out at you and 'catch your eye'. Finally, perhaps most strikingly, a language will look and sound very different to you depending on whether or not you understand it: foreign speech sounds like a continuous stream of noises; intelligible speech sounds like a series of discrete words.

So then, what about Dennett's more radical claims, (3) and (4)? What, specifically, does the phi movement in Kolers's experiment tell us about the reality of phenomenal consciousness and its distinctness from judgment in general? Dennett may be right that there is nothing to choose between *a priori* in the two claims in this case: on the one hand, that the subjects *literally see* the spot seeming to move and change gradually from red to green, or from circular to square, by 'filling in' the missing stages in its journey, after which the doctored evidence reaches consciousness intact (the Stalinesque show trial); and on the other hand, that they instead concoct false judgments and memories of *having seen* its continuous transition, though in fact they did not (the Orwellian rewriting of history). But can Dennett plausibly extend his skepticism beyond this special case? Two points are worth noting.

First, it is worth remembering that these experiments involve perceptions (or misperceptions) occurring on a scale of only fractions of a second. If we turn our attention to a wider temporal framework, it becomes much harder to swallow the idea that there is no difference in principle between immediate sense experiences and memories or judgments. Even if our present sensory awareness blurs gradually into a retention of the immediate past, it does not follow that there is no difference at all between perceptual experience and processes such as memory or judgment. Why should we generalize ambiguities on the micro scale to the macro perceptual world in which we readily distinguish such psychological operations? As Merleau-Ponty says, 'Ordinary experience draws a clear distinction between sense experience and judgment'. However, 'This distinction disappears in intellectualism, because judgment is everywhere pure sensation is not, which is to say everywhere. The testimony of phenomena will therefore everywhere be impugned' (Merleau-Ponty 2002: 39). Hasty generalizations from microstructures and a contempt for the phenomena are as ill advised in phenomenology as they are in physics, and we have no more reason to abandon the distinction between perception and judgment in normal cases in deference to isolated experimental effects than Sir Arthur Eddington had to infer from the vast stretches of empty space between atoms that his desk was not a perfectly solid object. Solid oak desks *are* solid physical objects, and the proportion of intervening space at the atomic level is irrelevant to that fact.

Second, conversely, if the phi phenomena in Kolers's experiment seem to undermine any sharp distinction between immediate sensory awareness and short-term memory and judgment, surely the conclusion to draw is that such common-sense psychological categories, which figure so prominently in everyday life, fail to apply in any obvious way on a very small scale and in highly artificial experimental conditions. This might sound like Dennett's own conclusion, namely, that common sense is a notoriously unreliable guide when we set out to construct a sound scientific theory of consciousness. But my point is different. It is not that the results of such experiments reveal for the first time the real facts about consciousness, rendering the categories of our ordinary understanding obsolete. Rather, they serve to point up qualitative inde-terminacies that specify lower spatiotemporal thresholds beneath which some ordin-ary concepts pertaining of perception fails to get a grip. That such concepts have only a limited range of application is hardly surprising.

If we are unable to choose between the Stalinesque and the Orwellian hypothesis in the case of perceptions of very quickly flashing spots of light, then, it is not because the two hypotheses are equally *good* when extended to the general case, as Dennett seems to suggest, but because they are equally *bad*. Indeed, neither hypothesis seems particu-larly plausible, even in the experiment as Dennett describes it. On the one hand, to say that the subjects had distinct visual sensations of a red spot appearing, moving to one side, turning green at a single discrete instant, or changing shape at a constant rate at every point on its path, reversing direction, moving back, instantaneously turning red again, or again changing shape perfectly gradually, then disappearing, would obvi-ously be to overstate their visual acuity. On the other hand, to deny that the subjects saw *any* continuity, movement, or color change at all is implausible, and it would be utterly preposterous to suggest that no one ever really sees continuity, movement, or color change in phi phenomena. To bite *that* bullet would indeed be to deny the phe-nomenon you're pretending to explain.

Phi movement occurring in an isolated stimulus within a fraction of a second is an interesting effect, then, but I think it reveals nothing especially deep about the application of our ordinary concepts of perception, memory, and judgment under nor-mal conditions; at best, it points up a kind of boundary condition for the application of those concepts. Far from showing that there is no difference in general between seeing and judging, Kolers's experiment shows only that our ordinary notions of seeing and judging break down with appearances on such a small scale. An interesting result, but hardly a reason to deny the existence of qualitative sensory experience as distinct from judgment wholesale, as Dennett does. Denying that there is any distinction at all between phenomenal seemings and cognitive judgings is a drastic conclusion to draw from the evidence. We should not infer from a few ambiguous cases in highly artificial conditions that there is *never* a difference between how things seem to me and how I judge them to be, or indeed how I judge them to *seem*, as if those distinctions were just conceptual or verbal confusions, like the distinction between pain and the feeling of pain.

What is especially striking about Dennett's proclaimed 'disqualification of qualia', however, is his admission that '*There seems to be phenomenology*'. This apparent concession sounds conciliatory at first blush: 'I wholeheartedly agree that there seem to be qualia', he says (Dennett 1991: 366, 372). But in fact it is no concession at all to our ordinary understanding of perceptual seeming, and his agreement with his phenomenological interlocutor is not as wholehearted as it sounds. For it sounds superficially as if Dennett is admitting that, when it comes to the *seeming of seeming*, in this case at least, we have a genuine *nonjudgmental* seeming on our hands, a 'real' seeming. But of course this is not what he means. He means only that we are all initially prone to *judge* that things really seem to us a certain way, independent of our judgment. What he is acknowledging is not a real seeming at all, but rather what he regards as a quasitheoretical intuition—not a Kantian kind of intuition, but an 'intuition' in the philosopher's sense of a naive judgment. What he grants the phenomenologist, in short, is not the phenomena, only reflective judgments *about* the phenomena.

But this begs the question, for whether there can be a difference between our judgments about our experience and that experience itself is precisely what is at issue between Dennett and phenomenology, and for that matter between Dennett and common sense. Dennett recognizes no difference between perceptual phenomena and what we report about them upon reflection. This is the methodological point of his heterophenomenological perspective, which regards experiential reports as just so much behavioral evidence to add to the mix of empirical evidence for any theory of consciousness. Dennett chides 'the Husserlian school(s) of Phenomenology' for the method of *epoché*, or 'bracketing', which, he says, 'excuses the investigator from all inquiry, speculative or otherwise, into the underlying mechanisms' of consciousness.[9] But considering that most of the major representatives of that movement rejected the *epoché* as a phenomenologically unmotivated dogma,[10] what Dennett is really chiding them for is the fact that they all took the perceptual phenomena seriously, as distinct from the judgments we form about them on reflection.

I believe Dennett ignores that distinction at his peril. Indeed, renouncing the dogma of incorrigibility means recognizing, as phenomenologists have, the various ways in which we can be, and often are, mistaken in our judgments concerning the structures and qualities of our own experience. Merleau-Ponty's work, for instance, is rich in the kind of thick description that resists assimilation into long-standing theoretical prejudices and ingrained reflective habits of common sense. Good phenomenology, like good observation and description of any kind, captures appearances fresh and pulls our attention away from preconceived opinions and hasty classifications that might be correct and convenient in other ways and for other purposes. Good phenomenology resists ready-made assumptions and ad hoc redefinitions in favor of getting it right about how things actually show up for us, prior to our reflecting and theorizing about them.

Precisely because he took that project of careful and sincere description seriously, Merleau-Ponty was able to anticipate much of what Dennett and others have said about the indeterminacy of sensory quality, while at the same time refusing simply to redefine terms and redraw conceptual boundaries as a way of satisfying other theoretical commitments. For example, like Dennett, Merleau-Ponty rejects any analysis of consciousness in terms of sensations, sense data, or qualia, which is to say pure qualitative raw material that has determinate objective properties of its own, independent of the intentional content of experience. What makes the notion of sensation intelligible

---

[9] Dennett, 'Hofstadter's Quest: A Tale of Cognitive Pursuit', in Dennett (1998a: 235).
[10] For more on this, see Carman (2003: ch. 2), (2005), and (1999).

is precisely the intentional setting in which we see objects and their properties. The *of* in 'sensation of red' is not the *of* in 'sensation of pain', for the first sort of sensation has an object while the second does not. We rarely, if ever, simply experience free-floating qualitative data; we see objects, people, places, events. Even a pain is not just an abstract feeling, but a pain in my leg, or my hand, or my head. As Merleau-Ponty says, 'elementary perception is . . . already charged with *meaning*', and 'a figure on a background is the simplest sense-given available to us . . . The perceptual "something" is always in the middle of something else, it always forms part of a "field".' Consequently, 'The pure impression is . . . not just undiscoverable, but imperceptible and thus inconceivable as a moment of perception' (Merleau-Ponty 2002: 4).

The theoretical concept of pure sensation, or qualia, thus finds virtually no support in our experience, however firmly planted the term may be in both ordinary and technical discourse. Why then do we so readily find ourselves talking about perception as if it were composed of discrete qualitative units? When the concept of sensation arises, Merleau-Ponty suggests, 'it is because instead of attending to the experience of perception, we overlook it in favor of the object perceived' (Merleau-Ponty 2002: 4). We are naturally focused on, or as Merleau-Ponty says 'geared into' (*en prise sur*) (Merleau-Ponty 2002: 292), perceptual objects in such a way that when we try to turn our attention to perception itself, we tend to project back onto it the qualities of the things we perceive:

we transpose these objects into consciousness. We commit what psychologists call the 'experience error', which means that what we know to be in things themselves we immediately take to be in our consciousness of them. We make perception out of things perceived. And since perceived things themselves are obviously accessible only through perception, we end by understanding neither. (Merleau-Ponty 2002: 5)

The language of sensation is conceptually parasitic on, perhaps inevitably tangled up with, the language with which we refer to the objects of perception. The very words we use to describe our experience are typically drawn from a vocabulary adapted in advance to external uses: 'When I say that I have before me a red patch, the meaning of the word "patch" is given by prior experiences that have taught me the use of the word' (Merleau-Ponty 2002: 17).

Merleau-Ponty's critique of the concept of sensation, then, is the rejection of a mistake common to both folk and professional psychology, a natural error that persists in everyday thinking and theoretical discourse alike. But what it supports is the weak claim (1), that we cannot describe experience in the same terms in which we describe the objects of experience, not the strong claim (3), that sense experience as such has no intrinsic qualities of its own, independent of our judgment. Eschewing the experience error lends no comfort to the eliminativist repudiation of the very idea of phenomenal quality.

III. SENSORIMOTOR ENACTIVISM

Inspired in part by the phenomenological tradition, and therefore much in the spirit of what I have said so far, Alva Noë and his colleagues have in recent years advanced powerful objections to Dennett's account of perceptual consciousness. I therefore want to second their response to some of the implausible conclusions he draws from both well-known and newly discovered facts about visual awareness. However, although Noë and his co-authors offer a compelling critique of Dennett up to a point, I believe they do not go far enough in challenging his underlying methodological assumptions, in particular his assimilation of lived experience to observable neuro-physiological behavior, hence his radical repudiation of phenomenology understood as an autonomous descriptive enterprise distinct from the explanatory aims of empiri-cal psychology. In spite of their advances beyond Dennett, that is, the alternative program they propose, what they call the 'sensorimotor' approach to perception (O'Regan and Noë 2001), still bears the marks of the behaviorist tradition it has in common with Dennett's heterophenomenology.[11]

Consider one of Dennett's most widely discussed examples. You walk into a room decorated with wallpaper featuring a pattern of hundreds of identical images of Marilyn Monroe. You see the regularity of the pattern without looking directly at the majority of the individual pictures. Yet, as Dennett says, what you see is precisely an array of seemingly identical Marilyns, not just one 'Marilyn-in-the-middle sur-rounded by various indistinct Marilyn-shaped blobs' (Dennett 1991: 354).

So, is your brain 'filling in' the hundreds of Marilyns in painstaking (Stalinesque) detail, or is it just telling you a neat (Orwellian) story, namely, that your experience is continuous and that you really are seeing all the Marilyns, even though you aren't? Citing the demonstrable, and indeed shocking, poverty of parafoveal vision (which is about ten times less discriminating than the two or three degrees at the center of the visual field), together with the relatively slow saccading of your eyes from one point to another (only about four or five times a second), Dennett in this case opts for the Orwellian hypothesis and insists that your brain is engaging not in detailed filling-in, but in blanket spin control: 'Having identified a single Marilyn, and having received no information to the effect that the other blobs are not Marilyns, it jumps to the con-clusion that the rest are Marilyns, and labels the whole region "more Marilyns" with-out any further rendering of Marilyn at all' (Dennett 1991: 355).

As Noë, Pessoa, and Thompson have argued, there are several problems with this line of reasoning. First, as they and others have observed, whether the *brain itself* can be said to be 'filling in' gaps in the visual field, for example the blind spot, with the kinds of neurological activity characteristic of visual processing, is an empirical ques-tion that cannot be decided on the basis of conceptual considerations of the sort Dennett offers here.[12] Dennett can only insist, reasonably enough, that we cannot assume a priori that the brain *must* be filling in, as if that were the only way to explain the inconspicuousness of objective gaps or impoverishments in the visual field.

Second, even if Dennett were right about the empirical issue of *neural* filling-in, his conclusion about conscious perception as such would not follow. Taking it for granted

---

[11] The affinity is well attested on both sides. Dennett, for example, suggests that O'Regan and Noë 'need not try so hard to differ with me. . . . we are on the same team' (Dennett 2001: 982). And they concur: 'It may be—indeed, it is likely—that our phenomenological analysis can be accom-modated by heterophenomenology' (O'Regan and Noë 2001: 1014).

[12] See Churchland and Ramachandran (1993); Pessoa, Thompson, and Noë (1998); and Thompson, Noë, and Pessoa (1999).

that sensory filling-in does not occur in cases where a mere thought or epistemic 'label' would suffice to efface some deficiency in the visual field, Dennett proceeds to infer that, although it may *seem* that you are seeing, say, a pattern of hundreds of identical Marilyns, you are not *really* seeing them, but merely *surmising* that they are there. We are, on his account, frequently and indeed profoundly mistaken about what we are really seeing. But Dennett is able to impugn common sense in this way only by tacitly embracing an assumption that he seems otherwise eager to deny, namely, that there must be some close correlation or 'isomorphism' between neurological activity and conscious experience. Dennett rejects that assumption, but only by rejecting the very idea that there is such a thing as subjective phenomenal quality, or 'how things seem'.

But notice that such a hard line against the phenomena takes for granted that *if there were* such a thing as how things seem, it could *only* be explained by the occurrence of underlying isomorphic neurological processes. Our eyes have neither the parafoveal resolution nor the muscular swiftness necessary to get discrete foveal impressions of the many Marilyns in the short time it takes you to recognize the regularity of the pattern, Dennett argues, and since the brain is presumably not in the business of filling in such sensory detail, the neurological effects necessary for distinct visual awareness must also be absent. Therefore we can have no real sensory experience of the many Marilyns, only some kind of ersatz thought or judgment to the effect *that they are there*. Eager to dismiss the crude notion that visual perception involves an inner homuncular spectator looking at a mental picture in the 'Cartesian Theater', Dennett denies that the regular pattern before one in such circumstances is perceptually *given* at all.

Noë, Pessoa, and Thompson point out, correctly, that this is a non sequitur. As it happens, Merleau-Ponty anticipated their argument sixty years ago when he criticized intellectualist theories of perception for taking for granted, no less than their empiricist counterparts, what the Gestalt psychologists called the 'constancy hypothesis',[13] the idea that discrete sensations must correspond to local sensory stimuli. Accordingly, Dennett seems to reason, since objects in my blind spot, or in the edges of my visual field, cannot be affecting my eyes in the way required for clear and distinct vision, I therefore cannot really be seeing them. As Merleau-Ponty says, 'intellectualism limits sense experience to the action of a real stimulus on my body' (Merleau-Ponty 2002: 39), and where the stimulus is lacking, consciousness can only be an artifact of judgment, just as Dennett concludes.

The contemporary version of the argument as formulated by Noë, Pessoa, and Thompson substitutes internal neurological processes for surface sensory stimuli, but the point is otherwise the same. Facts about underlying neurological mechanisms, like facts about sensory stimuli, imply nothing directly concerning the phenomenal character of experience. Noë, Pessoa, and Thompson argue plausibly that Dennett has in effect collapsed a distinction he himself draws elsewhere between *personal* and *subpersonal* levels of description, that is, between entire organisms or 'intentional systems' exhibiting behaviors in the context of an environment and functional neurological subsystems operating according to a design.

[13] Köhler, 'On Unnoticed Sensations and Errors of Judgment', in Köhler (1971).

But is Dennett's error just a mistake? Has he inadvertently drawn a bad inference from subpersonal neurological process to phenomena at the personal level of description? The suggestion would be plausible only if there were reason to believe that Dennett takes seriously the idea that there *are* any phenomena at the personal level to recognize and describe correctly. But Dennett's entire enterprise is predicated on *not* taking that idea seriously. 'What about the *actual* phenomenology?' Dennett imagines his interlocutor asking. 'There is no such thing', he replies (Dennett 1991: 365).

What Noë, Pessoa, and Thompson see as an illicit inference from the neurology to the phenomenology, then, is not just a momentary lapse of judgment on Dennett's part, but a natural consequence of his denial of the existence of the phenomena. This becomes clearer in Dennett's response to their critique of the 'grand illusion' hypothesis, which Dennett in effect anticipated in the example of the wallpaper. Recent vision research has confirmed that we are much worse than we normally suppose at recognizing detail and change in our parafoveal vision.[14] Such empirical results seem to confirm Dennett's insistence that 'Consciousness is gappy and sparse, and doesn't contain half of what people think is there!' (Dennett 1991: 366).

But does 'change blindness' really imply that we are subject to an illusion with respect to the apparent breadth, richness, and resolution of our own visual experience? Are we wrong even about how things *seem* to us visually? Noë, Pessoa, and Thompson offer what seems to me the correct response to this conundrum. Dennett's description, they observe, 'is completely unfaithful to the character of perceptual experience: the Marilyns do not seem to be present in your experience or in your mind (whatever that might mean); they seem to be present there on the wall' (Thompson, Noë, and Pessoa 1999: 187).

The main sense in which we take our visual experience to be uniform and continuous is that we take ourselves to be perceptually aware of a spatio-temporally continuous environment. And in this belief we are right. Furthermore, to say that we (ordinary perceivers) normally think we perceive all environmental detail with equal focus and clarity—as if we were looking at a fixed picture—is to misdescribe the character of perceptual experience. (Noë, Pessoa, and Thompson 2000: 102)

Elsewhere Noë writes,

It just is not the case that we, normal perceivers, believe we see a complete, dynamic picture of a stable, uniformly detailed and colourful world. Of course it *does* seem to us as if we have perceptual access to a world that is richly detailed, complete and gap-free. And we do! (Noë 2002: 6)

Noë is certainly right to suggest, as he does with tasteful understatement, that 'we need to reflect more carefully on the phenomenology' (Noë 2002: 10).

Of course, all involved in the debate reject the notion that perceptual awareness is a plenum, in spite of the fact that, as Dennett seems to suppose, 'it seems to be a plenum' (Dennett 1991: 366). But Dennett's reply to Noë's view is instructive. People really do believe 'that they have a detailed picture of the world in their heads', he insists (Dennett 2002: 16), and their regular expressions of surprise at being shown the

---

[14] O'Regan, Rensink, and Clark (1999: 34), and Blackmore, Brelstaff, Nelson, and Troscianko (1995).

effects of change blindness are themselves 'data in good standing, and in need of explanation' (Dennett 2001: 982). Happily, Noë has a good explanation: 'The surprise is explained simply by supposing that we tend to think we are better at noticing changes than we in fact are' (Noë 2002: 7). What is really surprising about change blindness, one might say, is just how surprising it is, and indeed continues to be. The labor of proofreading has for centuries made painfully obvious how difficult it can be to see what is 'right before your eyes'. And yet we continue to be astonished by our failure to notice typographical errors that seem unmistakable in retrospect. Moreover, as Noë observes, 'we are not surprised or in any way taken aback by our need to move eyes and head to get better glimpses of what is around us' (Noë 2002: 7). After all, if people naturally regarded their own visual fields as a kind of plentiful inner representation, like a framed picture, they would never move their eyes to look at anything, only their heads.

Merleau-Ponty was familiar with such phenomena, far ahead of his time. He knew, however, that perceptual consciousness is not simply 'gappy and sparse', as Dennett says; rather, 'the perceived contains gaps that are not mere "failures to perceive". I may, by sight or touch, recognize a crystal as having a "regular" shape without having, even tacitly, counted its sides' (Merleau-Ponty 2002: 13). For Dennett, by contrast, a gap in *what* I perceive can only be a *failure* to perceive, compounded by a further failure to recognize the poverty of the experience. On his account, then, we are doubly ignorant, for we fail to notice *that* we fail to notice what is not in fact present to us. We fail to see, but we also fail to judge *that* we fail to see, so we are left with what amounts to a mere *presumption* of sensory continuity and plenitude.

But my inability to see all sides of an object at once, like my inability to see that a stack of eleven books is a stack of *exactly* eleven books, is not evidence of poor vision. Rather, it tells us something about the structure of perception, in this case its perceptival situatedness and its relative conceptual inarticulation. So too, the fact that I see a figure against an inconspicuous background is not a defect, but a formal feature, of visual awareness. As Merleau-Ponty says,

To see an object is either to have it on the fringe of the visual field and be able to fix on it, or to respond to the solicitation by fixing on it. When I do fix on it, I become anchored in it . . . I continue inside one object the exploration that just now hovered over them all, and in one movement I close up the landscape and open up the object. The two operations do not just happen to coincide: it is not the contingent aspects of my bodily organization, for example the structure of my retina, that obliges me to see my surroundings vaguely if I want to see the object clearly. Even if I knew nothing of rods and cones, I would realize that it is necessary to put the surroundings in abeyance to see the object better, and lose in ground what one gains in figure, because to look at the object is to plunge into it, and because objects form a system in which one cannot show itself without concealing others.   (Merleau-Ponty 2002: 78)

Once we remind ourselves of the peculiar indeterminacy of perceptual experience, we realize that our awareness never *really did seem* to have the determinate contents and crisp boundaries that we might have thought it had, or that we might have thought it *seemed* to have. We may *think* that our experience seems to have all the determinate qualities of an object or a representation, but it does not seem to. Nor does our *thinking* that it seems to have such qualities establish that it *does* seem to. Dennett is wrong to suppose that the mere fact of your *judging* that things seem to you a certain way entails that they *do* seem that way to you. I believe the water coming out of the tap is hot, and I expect it to feel hot, so I pull away just as the water touches my hand. For a moment I judge that the water *feels* hot. But then I come to realize that it did *not* feel hot, but cold. The cold was startling, so I *judged* that it felt hot. But it didn't, it felt cold.

Why is Dennett so unmoved by these kinds of phenomenological objection to his theory? Not, I suspect, because he fails to appreciate their plausibility, but rather because his theory silences them in advance as a matter of principle. Dennett's hostility to phenomenology is no mere oversight or failure of imagination, that is, but a deliberate methodological, indeed ontological, commitment. Its consequences, as Noë and his colleagues see, are disastrous. But the disaster cannot be averted simply by pointing out the error and advocating a more attentive phenomenology. Escaping the eliminativism entailed by Dennett's heterophenomenological program calls instead for a radically different approach to the nature of perceptual consciousness.

And indeed, Noë and his colleagues set out to construct just such an alternative account. Do they succeed? Although, as I said, they have been inspired in part by Merleau-Ponty, I believe their sensorimotor account of vision differs crucially from his phenomenology of perception and embodiment, and that the contrast reveals what is lacking in their theory.

For O'Regan and Noë, 'seeing is a way of acting . . . a particular way of exploring the environment' (O'Regan and Noë 2001: 939). As such, 'Visual consciousness is not a special kind of brain state, or a special quality of informational states of the brain. It is something we do' (970). More precisely, perception is '*the activity of exploring the environment in ways mediated by knowledge of the relevant sensorimotor contingencies*' (943). Perception is not a static condition of the organism, but a kind of causal interaction between organism and environment, which moreover involves the agent's *knowledge* of the many subtle and fine-grained dependencies obtaining between itself and its surroundings. What kind of knowledge is this? O'Regan and Noë make it clear that 'Knowledge of sensorimotor contingencies is a practical, not a propositional form of knowledge' (944). More precisely,

Sensorimotor contingencies are laws describing input–output relations. . . . It is *the perceiver's exercise of mastery of the laws of sensorimotor contingency* that provides the basis for the character of experience. . . . Our relation to our environment when we perceive is bodily and grabby and . . . we implicitly understand the nature of this relation.   (O'Regan and Noë 2001: 1015)

The knowledge constitutive of perceptual experience, then, is not theoretical or propositional, but rather a kind of practical mastery of patters of causal input–output relations.

This account of the bodily nature of perception is at once empirically plausible and phenomenologically promising. There is clearly something right in the idea that perception consists not just in isolated subjective mental states, or for that matter states posited by a hypothetical theoretical observer from the intentional stance, but in an actual dynamic reciprocity between embodied agents and the environments with which they interact. And yet, it seems to me, there is one crucial aspect of perceptual experience that the sensorimotor theory tends to neglect or obscure, namely its *normative* dimension.

What are 'sensorimotor contingencies', after all, and what is it to 'know', 'grasp', or 'master' them? They are, according to O'Regan and Noë, 'the *structure of the rules* governing the sensory changes produced by various motor actions' (O'Regan and Noë 2001: 941). There is, they continue, 'a lawful relation of dependence between visual stimulation and what we do', and 'our brains have extracted such laws' (O'Regan and Noë 2001: 944). Again, O'Regan and Noë do not mean that we, or any other animals for that matter, a theoretical grasp of rules or laws explicitly articulated in the form of propositions, but that 'the animal, or its brain, must be "tuned to" these laws of sensorimotor contingencies. That is, the animal must be *actively exercising* its mastery of these laws' (O'Regan and Noë 2001: 943).

I take it that, notwithstanding their talk of rules 'governing' sensorimotor interactions, O'Regan and Noë mean by 'rule' and 'law' something more like causal *pattern* or *regularity* But this is crucial, for once we understand that the laws in question are mere regularities, and not *intelligible* forms or structures of experience with *normative* import for the agent, we see that, although the organism's 'mastery' of them may be practical and nonpropositional, as opposed to theoretical and explicit, nevertheless *what* an agent thereby grasps is just a complex web of causal relations.

In this respect, I want to argue, the account is wrong—wrong phenomenologically, and so too therefore wrong at the personal level of description. The theory might be correct as an account of the neurological and ecological conditions that make perceptual experience possible. What it cannot account for, however, is the *intentionality* of perception, including above all the intentional aspects of our proprioceptive sense of ourselves and our bodies. Indeed, O'Regan and Noë might themselves be guilty of conflating the personal and the subpersonal, or the phenomenological and the neurological. Is it, after all, 'the animal' or 'its brain' that must be 'tuned to' the laws of sensorimotor contingency? If it is the brain or nervous system, then what O'Regan and Noë call its 'grasp' of those laws looks less like a form of *understanding* than simply an additional set of emerging regularities, namely the neurological processes induced or generated by the organism's interaction with its environment. This is 'understanding' in an attenuated Humean sense, at best. If, however, it is the animal or agent as a whole that is supposed to respond to the sensorimotor contingencies, then it seems to me O'Regan and Noë have misdescribed the character of that responsiveness. More precisely, they describe it in such a way as to eliminate the normativity, hence the *intentionality* that, as I said at the outset, characterizes our grasp of the structures and contents of our own experience.

As it happens, the phenomenologist to whom O'Regan and Noë's theory is most indebted is not Merleau-Ponty, but Husserl. In the First Book of *Ideas* Husserl describes what he calls relations of 'motivation' among perceptions, to distinguish them from explicit judgments or inferences. Seeing an object from one side, for example, motivates an anticipation of seeing its back side, were I to rotate it or walk around it, without my having to *reason* that if I move thus and such, then I will see thus and such.[15] Husserl occasionally insists, however, that the concept of motivation refers above all to rational relations, being 'a *generalization* of that concept of motivation with respect to which we can say, for example, that willing the end motivates willing the means' (Husserl 1922: 89 n., my translation). In the Second Book of *Ideas*, however, he applies the concept to relations among kinaesthetic bodily sensations and sensations tied to externally perceived objects:

if the eye turns thus, *then* the 'image' changes thus; if it turns in a certain way otherwise, the image does so otherwise, accordingly. Here we constantly find this double articulation: kinaesthetic sensations on the one side (the motivating); sensations of features [of the object] on the other (the motivated).   (Husserl 1952: 58, my translation)

Here the relation sounds more causal than rational, and yet Husserl was sensitive to the objection that mere empirical psychological regularities, Humean 'associations of ideas', could never capture the *intentional* content of our awareness of our own bodies.

Merleau-Ponty's appropriation of the concept of motivation in *Phenomenology of Perception* gets much closer to the phenomena than Husserl's account. Moreover, I think it points up what is missing in O'Regan and Noë's theory. For while they avoid the rationalistic high road by denying that the agent's 'grasp' of sensorimotor contingencies amounts to a kind of theoretical knowledge, they seem to take the Humean low road instead by describing those contingencies as mere causal regularities. But the kind of motivation suited to an account of the bodily structure of perception must be neither fully rational nor merely causal, but rather something intermediary between the two.[16] Merleau-Ponty writes,

the phenomenological notion of *motivation* is one of those 'fluid' concepts that must be formed if we want to get back to the phenomena. One phenomenon releases another, not by some objective efficacy, like that which links events in nature, but by the meaning it offers—there is a *raison d'être* that orients the flux of phenomena without being explicitly posited in any one of them, a sort of operant reason.   (Merleau-Ponty 2002: 57)

Consider a concrete example. As Gareth Evans has observed, 'When we hear a sound as coming from a certain direction, we do not have to *think* or *calculate* which way to turn our heads (say) in order to look for the source of the sound' (Evans 1982: 155). Noë alludes to this passage by way of distancing himself from the behavioristic temptation he rightly senses in Evans's account, namely the temptation to *define* the content of such an experience in terms of dispositions to move one's body in certain ways. Noë does not want his theory to be behavioristic in that way:

When we see a flicker on the right, we know—in a practical, implicit way—that movements of the eyes to the right bring (or would bring) the flicker better into view. The experience of the flicker as on the visual egocentric right consists not in our disposition to move in certain ways, but in our possession of a kind of practical knowledge of how *movement* would bring the thing into view. A different rule of sensorimotor contingency applies if the flicker occurs on the left.   (Noë 2004: 89)

[15] Sean Kelly (2004) describes the differences between Husserl and Merleau-Ponty concerning background features and hidden aspects of perceptual objects.
[16] For more on the intermediate status of motivation, see Wrathall (2004).

The example is powerful, but I think neither Evans nor Noë manages to capture its true significance. Indeed, what it points up is the frequently overlooked distinction between our *normal* habituated perceptual orientation on the one hand, and deviations from or interruptions of the norm on the other. It is no accident that Evans appeals to Charles Taylor, who was in turn drawing on Merleau-Ponty. Yet Evans omits some of the most crucial remarks in the passage he quotes from Taylor, for although he emphasizes the links between perception and movement, he says nothing of the *normative* structure of the perceptual field itself. It is worth quoting Taylor's original comments more fully than Evans does:

Our perceptual field has an orientational structure . . . In those rare moments where we lose orientation, we don't know where we are; and we don't know where or what things are either; we lose the thread of the world, and our perceptual field is no longer our access to the world, but rather the confused debris into which our normal grasp on things crumbles. . . . It is not just that the field's perspective centers on where I am bodily—this by itself doesn't show that I am essentially agent. But take the up-down directionality of the field. What is it based on? Up and down are not simply related to my body; up is not just where my head is and down where my feet are. For I can be lying down, or bending over, or upside down . . . I have to maintain myself upright to act, or in some way align my posture with gravity. Without a sense of 'which way is up', I falter into confusion.   (Taylor 1978–9: 23)

Merleau-Ponty makes the same point in his account of bodily-perceptual anomalies brought about by artificial means. Normally, a landscape looks fixed and motionless even as we look out across it, moving our eyes and head. A subject whose oculomotor muscles have been paralyzed, however, sees the entire scene shift to the left when he thinks he is moving his eyes in that direction (Merleau-Ponty 2002: 55). Of course, the subject does not *infer* the movement of the landscape from his beliefs about the positions of his eyes. But neither is the static retinal image merely the *cause* of the ensuing perceptual effect. The turning of one's gaze is neither a reason nor a cause, but a motivating element in a meaningfully oriented phenomenal field:

For the illusion to be produced, the subject must have intended to look to the left and must have thought he moved his eye. The illusion regarding the body entails the appearance of movement in the object. The movements of the body are naturally invested with a certain perceptual significance and form, with the external phenomena, such a well articulated system that external perception 'takes account' of the movement of the perceptual organs, finding in them, if not the *explicit explanation*, at least the *motive* for the changes brought about in the spectacle, and can thus understand them instantly.   (Merleau-Ponty 2002: 55)

For Merleau-Ponty, as for Taylor, the motivational structure of perception is not just a complex network of causal relations between sense experience and bodily movement that the organism has mastered or grown accustomed to, but a *normative* structure of significance that we *grasp*:

the immobility of images on the retina and the paralysis of the oculomotor muscles are not objective causes that produce the illusion and carry it readymade into consciousness. Nor are the intention to move the eye and the landscape's passivity in relation to this impulse premises or reasons for the illusion. But they are the *motives*.   (Merleau-Ponty 2002: 56)

Like Evans, O'Regan and Noë neglect this normative dimension of perceptual experience. What they overlook as a result is the phenomenological difference between *normal* motivational structures and abnormal, hence evidently *contingent*, causal regularities. Indeed, their theory tends to describe the sensorimotor structures of perception as if they were *all* nonstandard, hence contingent and arbitrary.

But consider the difference between normal embodied perception, for example, turning one's head to see where a sound is coming from, and a genuinely contingent linkage or 'coupling' of a bodily movement and a sensory experience, for example pushing on one of your eyes to produce a double image, or spinning around and getting dizzy. In these latter cases, we experience the bodily movement and the ensuing perceptual effect as discrete phenomena, the former causing the latter. We sense no necessary connection between them, though we can grow accustomed to the predictable association of the one with the other. Nevertheless, even after the effect has become familiar, the two things still strike us as, precisely, two things bound together in a regular, perhaps lawful way.

The situation is utterly different phenomenologically in the case of *normal* sensorimotor integration. In this case, I do not experience the sensory effect and the bodily movement as heterogeneous elements arbitrarily linked together. Instead, they are essentially fused or intertwined in a way that strikes me as not just natural, but *necessary*. We seem to have no trouble on reflection drawing a conceptual distinction between experience and movement. In experience itself, however, they are as inextricable as coffee and cream, or better, the three primary colors that combine to produce a full-color image. When I move my body, that is, the movement does not stand out as a discrete phenomenon alongside its sensory effect. Rather, my movements are subordinated to the *demands* of the situation. My body does what it *must* do in order to get me where I *need* to be, to do what *needs* to be done. As Merleau-Ponty says, 'my body appears to me as an attitude with a view to a certain actual or possible task.... If I stand in front of my desk and lean on it with both hands, only my hands are stressed and the whole of my body trails behind them like the tail of a comet' (Merleau-Ponty 2002: 114–15).

The sensorimotor integration belonging to embodied perception is thus constituted not by causal *contingencies*, but by motivational *necessities*. When I understand myself as perceptually oriented in a world, I am not merely accustomed to the fact that *if* I turn my head, I *will* see the tree. Rather, I know that *in order to* see the tree, I *need* to turn my head. Seeing the tree *requires* that I turn to look at it. It is not just that the environment presents me with sensory input that I know as a matter of fact to be correlated in various ways with the movements of my body, even granting that I master that fact in a skillful way without calculating or thinking about it propositionally. Rather, insofar as my environment is not just a structured domain of objects and relations with which I skillfully interact, but an intelligible world that I inhabit, it always confronts me with a field of possibilities and likewise imposes demands on me. A world *qua world* affords, invites, and facilitates, just as it obtrudes, resists, thwarts, eludes, and coerces. Things present themselves to me with positive and negative valence of all kinds, primordially and inextricably fused with my own bodily needs and capacities.[17]

This fusion is what Merleau-Ponty, following Heidegger, calls our 'being in the world' (*être au monde*). It is what he would later more colorfully describe as the 'intertwining' (*entrelacs*) or 'chiasm' of body and world, which always belong to one and the same 'flesh' (*chair*) (Merleau-Ponty 1968: 130–55). The crucial point here is that our intertwinedness with the world is not just a 'coupling' of discrete things, say, sensory stimuli and bodily movements. Moreover, the difference is a phenomenological difference. That is, although the *causal* relation between our sensory systems and the environment may well involve precisely the sort of interconnections O'Regan and Noë describe, our *intentional* orientation in a meaningful world does not show up for us as a merely contingent interdependence of discrete elements. We experience our embeddedness in the world not as contingent but as necessary, indeed as definitive of us, for it constitutes not just what we *can* do and what *will* happen, but moreover what we *need*, hence what we *must* do. Perception thus consists not just in the skillful mastery of complex causal interconnections between heterogeneous bodily movements and sensory experiences, but in finding oneself with an orientation in a normatively articulated field of perceptual significance—in short, a *world*. As Merleau-Ponty tried to show, perception has not just practical but *ontological* import. It's not just what we do, it's what we *are*.

IV. CONCLUSION

Although I believe their account is phenomenologically incorrect, O'Regan and Noë do at least take the phenomena seriously. Unlike Dennett, they are careful not to blur important distinctions, for example between perception and judgment, experience and thought, and practical and theoretical knowledge. This attentiveness is crucial, for as Merleau-Ponty says, once such reductions and conflations are envisioned, 'The testimony of phenomena will . . . everywhere be impugned' (Merleau-Ponty 2002: 39). But of course impugning the evidence of phenomena is possible only up to a point, beyond which theories of consciousness and intentionality lose the very points of reference that define them as theories of consciousness and intentionality to begin with. For a theory of consciousness to obliterate the distinction between perception and cognition, for example, is for it to saw off the phenomenological branch it is sitting on. More generally, it is wrong to suppose that cognitive science and the philosophy of mind can avoid the subtle and difficult work of phenomenology and ignore our first-person understanding of our own experience, putting in its place an account of mere verbal behavior. Even those who make it a matter of principle to hold the phenomena

---

[17] Samuel Todes (2001) refers to the constitutive role of bodily 'needs' in the articulation of a meaningful perceptual world. Sean Kelly similarly stresses the normative dimension of perceptual perspective and context. The privileged context for seeing something, he writes, is 'the distance one *ought* to stand from the object, the orientation in which the object *ought* to be with respect to the viewer, the amount of surrounding illumination that *ought* to be present' (Kelly 1999: 120).

in contempt must eventually put their own phenomenological cards on the table, and not just as a gesture of candor, but by way of identifying what their theories are meant to be theories *of.* To infer the unreality of qualitative phenomenal experience from its conceptual indeterminacy and its peculiar resistance to objective description is to lose hold of the domain of discourse in which any theory of perception or consciousness is obliged to make sense.[18]

REFERENCES

Blackmore, S. J., Brelstaff, G., Nelson, K., and Troscianko, T. (1995) 'Is the Richness of our Visual World an Illusion? Transsaccadic Memory for Complex Scenes', *Perception* 24: 1075–81.

Carman, T. (1999) 'The Body in Husserl and Merleau-Ponty', *Philosophical Topics* 27: 205–26.

—— (2003) *Heidegger's Analytic: Interpretation, Discourse, and Authenticity in 'Being and Time'* (Cambridge: Cambridge University Press).

—— (forthcoming) 'The Principle of Phenomenology', in C. Guignon (ed.), *The Cambridge Companion to Heidegger*, 2nd edn. (Cambridge: Cambridge University Press).

Churchland, P. S. and Ramachandran, V. S. (1993) 'Filling In: Why Dennett Is Wrong', in B. Dahlbom (ed.), *Dennett and his Critics* (London: Blackwell).

Dennett, D. C. (1991) *Consciousness Explained* (Boston: Little, Brown & Co.).

—— (1998a) *Brainchildren: Essays on Designing Minds* (Cambridge, Mass.: MIT Press).

—— (1998b) 'No Bridge Over the Stream of Consciousness', *Behavioral and Brain Sciences* 21: 753–4.

—— (2001) 'Surprise, Surprise', *Behavioral and Brain Sciences* 24: 982.

—— (2002) 'How Could I Be Wrong? How Wrong Could I Be?' in A. Noë (ed.), *Is the Visual World a Grand Illusion?* (Charlottesville: Imprint Academic).

Evans, G. (1982) *The Varieties of Reference*, ed. J. McDowell (Oxford: Oxford University Press).

Goodman, N. (1978) *Ways of Worldmaking* (Indianapolis: Hackett).

Husserl, E. (1922) *Ideen zu einer reinen Phänomenologie und phänomenologischen Philosophie. Allgemeine Einführung in die reine Phänomenologie*, 2nd edn. (Tübingen: Niemeyer).

—— (1952) *Ideen zu einer reinen Phänomenologie und phänomenologischen Philosophie. Zweites Buch: Phänomenologische Untersuchungen zur Konstitution* (*Husserliana* IV), ed. M. Biemel (The Hague: Martinus Nijhoff).

James, W. (1950) *The Principles of Psychology*, 2 vols. (New York: Dover).

Kelly, S. (1999) 'What Do We See (When We Do)?', *Philosophical Topics* 27: 2 (Fall 1999): 107–28.

—— (2004) 'Seeing Things in Merleau-Ponty', in T. Carman and M. Hansen (eds.), *The Cambridge Companion to Merleau-Ponty* (Cambridge: Cambridge University Press).

Köhler, W. (1971) *The Selected Papers of Wolfgang Köhler*, ed. M. Henle (New York: Liveright).

Kolers, P. A. and von Grünau, M. (1976) 'Shape and Color in Apparent Motion', *Vision Research* 16: 329–35.

Merleau-Ponty, M. (1945) *Phénoménologie de la perception* (Paris: Gallimard).

—— (2002) *Phenomenology of Perception*, trans. C. Smith (London: Routledge; Routledge).

---

[18] Thanks to Bert Dreyfus, Alva Noë, and Amie Thomasson for their helpful comments on earlier drafts of this essay.

—— (1968) *The Visible and the Invisible*, trans. A. Lingis (Evanston: Northwestern University Press).

Noë, A. (2002) 'Is the Visual World a Grand Illusion?', in A. Noë (ed.), *Is the Visual World a Grand Illusion?* (Charlottesville: Imprint Academic).

—— (2004) *Action in Perception* (Cambridge: MIT Press).

Noë, Pessoa, L., and Thompson, E. (2000) 'Beyond the Grand Illusion: What Change Blindness Really Teaches Us About Vision', *Visual Cognition* 7: 102.

O'Regan, J. K. and Noë, A. (2001) 'A Sensorimotor Account of Vision and Visual Consciousness', *Behavioral and Brain Sciences* 24: 939–1031.

O'Regan, J. K., Rensink, R. A., and Clark, J. J. (1999) 'Change-Blindness as a Result of "Mudsplashes"', *Nature* 398: 34.

Pessoa, L., Thompson, E., and Noë, A. (1998) 'Finding Out About Filling-In: A Guide to Perceptual Completion for Visual Science and the Philosophy of Perception', *Behavioral and Brain Sciences* 21: 723–802.

Searle, J. (1997) *The Mystery of Consciousness* (New York: New York Review of Books).

Taylor, C. (1978–9) 'The Validity of Transcendental Arguments', *Proceedings of the Aristotelian Society* 79: 151–65; reprinted in Taylor (1995).

—— (1995) *Philosophical Arguments* (Cambridge, Mass.: Harvard University Press).

Thompson, E., Noë, A., and Pessoa, L. (1999) 'Perceptual Completion: A Case Study in Phenomenology and Cognitive Science', in J. Petitot, F. J. Varela, B. Pachoud, J.-M. Roy (eds.), *Naturalizing Phenomenology: Issues in Contemporary Phenomenology and Cognitive Science* (Stanford: Stanford University Press).

Todes, S. (2001) *Body and World* (Cambridge, Mass.: MIT Press).

Wittgenstein, L. (1958) *Philosophical Investigations*, 3rd edn., trans. G. E. M. Anscombe (New York: Macmillan).

—— (1972) *On Certainty*, ed. G. E. M. Anscombe and G. H. von Wright (New York: Harper & Row).

Wrathall, M. (2004) 'Motives, Reasons, and Causes', in T. Carman and M. Hansen (eds.), *The Cambridge Companion to Merleau-Ponty* (Cambridge: Cambridge University Press).

PART II

SELF-AWARENESS AND SELF-KNOWLEDGE

4

Consciousness with Reflexive Content

David Woodruff Smith

Abstract: A mental act is conscious, on the classical view, if it includes a certain self-consciousness, or better, if the subject is aware of its transpiring. What is the form of that inner awareness? Many philosophers have proposed that consciousness involves some form of higher-order monitoring of the mental act, a simultaneous inner observation of the mental act. This approach has well-rehearsed problems. Here a different model is considered. Inner awareness of a conscious mental state consists in a modal character of the experience, part of the way one is conscious of this or that object. On the present model, this modal character involves a certain form of reflexive content ('in this very experience I sees such-and-such'). The following essay explores the way this reflexive content works, considering how consciousness can include an awareness of itself without a higher-order activity that rides along with the basic act of consciousness. What follows is an analysis of the phenomenological structure of this reflexive inner awareness. The analysis is guided in part by considerations of the logic of indexical expressions.

INTRODUCTION

What makes a mental act or state conscious, in the view of early modern philosophy (Descartes, Locke, Leibniz, et al.), is self-consciousness, that is, the subject's awareness of the mental act's transpiring. This view was developed further in some of the classical literature of phenomenology (by Brentano, Husserl, and Sartre). Yet the proper form of inner awareness (as I prefer to call it) remained elusive. Some years ago I proposed a phenomenological analysis of inner awareness (Smith 1986, 1989). The proper form, I proposed, is that of a reflexive character bearing a special reflexive content: 'in this very experience I see or think or will such-and-such'. More recently, consciousness has come center stage in the literature of analytic philosophy of mind. Recent 'higher-order

This essay has benefited from discussions in two forums. One was a symposium with John Perry, Charles Siewert, and myself at the American Philosophical Association, Pacific Division, the Society for the Study of Husserl's Philosophy (now The Society for Phenomenology and Analytic Philosophy), meeting in Seattle on 28 March 2002. The other was my seminar on 'The First Person' at the University of California, Irvine, Spring Quarter 2002, continuing a lively discussion group meeting Winter Quarter 2002. Thanks to participants in both forums.

theories' of consciousness define our awareness of our mental states as a higher-order inner perception or thought or monitoring of our own mental states (see the essays by Armstrong, Rosenthal, and Lycan at the end of Block et al. 1997). These higher-order models share the problems I had observed in classical higher-order analyses: phenomenologically, we do not experience a second act of introspective observation of the original mental act—in which we perceive or think about or monitor the act, something we do in addition to the original act. Kindred arguments against higher-order models have been developed elsewhere (see Siewert 1998 and Thomasson 2000). These discussions place the issue of inner awareness once again at the center of consciousness theory—dare I say, center stage in the theater of consciousness. (For the state of play in contemporary philosophy of mind on these issues, see the essays in Kriegel and Williford 2005. A study of the phenomenological issues and their historical development is Smith 2004, ch. 3, 'Return to Consciousness'. A distinct but related issue is the structure and role of attention in consciousness: see Smith 2005, Ford 2005, Ford and Smith 2005.)

Here I hope to update, sharpen, and amplify my earlier analysis of inner awareness. First I shall recapitulate the analysis and expand on certain aspects (extending the presentation in Smith 1986, 1989, 2004). Then I shall turn in greater detail to the reflexive character of inner awareness. I'll focus ultimately on John Perry's recent account of 'reflexive contents' (in Perry 2000, 2001a, 2001b) and reflect on how my account differs. My point is to explore just how reflexive content (a particular type of indexical content) can be used in the analysis of inner awareness, in an analysis that avoids higher-order models altogether.

1. THE PHENOMENOLOGY OF INNER AWARENESS

Reflecting on inner awareness, in the context of contemporary phenomenology cum philosophy of mind, we should keep in mind the aim of phenomenology: to analyze (describe, interpret, analyze) our own familiar forms of conscious experience—as we experience them from our own first-person perspective within the horizon of our familiar circumstances. (See Smith 2002c, 2003.)

We are thus concerned with everyday human experience. In a paradigmatic form of conscious experience like my seeing a frog in the garden, I have a certain awareness of my visual experience as it transpires. If prompted by the question, 'What did I just see?', I can immediately recall and begin to recount my experience, to describe and interpret and analyze the experience as I just lived it. Of course, this recounting depends on my short-term recollection of my visual experience, and that recollection depends on my awareness of the experience as it transpired. The contrast, much emphasized in recent cognitive science, would be with blindsight, where I saw but had no awareness of seeing (see Siewert 1998 and Smith 2004, ch. 3). Here then is the phenomenon of inner awareness: it is not something I carry out in addition to seeing the frog; it is rather an integral part of my consciously seeing the frog. The phenomenology of inner awareness aims to analyze the form of that awareness.

That type of awareness is characteristic of everyday human consciousness as we know it. Stepping outside the experience, and aside from its phenomenological analysis,

I join the community of modern neuroscience in theorizing that this form of mental state is realized in a complex of neural activity some part of which realizes my inner awareness of my visual experience presenting this frog. The image of one part of the neural system monitoring another part leaps to mind. But phenomenological reflection leads us to reject the suggestion that there are two mental acts here. Instead, the inner awareness is already an integral part of the experience of conscious perception: all realized, we go on to theorize, in an appropriate pattern of neural activity. From both phenomenological and neural perspectives, I submit, inner awareness should be modeled as a specific part of a rather complex activity of consciousness. (In this vein LaBerge 1995, 1997, 1998 offers a model of three parts of the brain involved in attention in vision, from which one might begin to construct a neural basis for the inner awareness that is integral to ordinary perception. See Ford 2005 and Ford and Smith 2005.) From a naturalistic perspective we may go on to allow that not all forms of mental activity in lower animals, realized in different neural patterns, are characterized by inner awareness, that is, what we have recounted in our own experience. In other words, we can pull back from the strong thesis that a mental state (realized in any neural system) is conscious if and only if it includes (in the proper form) the type of inner awareness that we are concerned with here. If the lowly snail or the lofty dog does not have this type of inner awareness, it may still have consciousness. And perhaps we humans have mental states that do not involve inner awareness yet should count as conscious, such as sensory or emotional states of which we can readily become aware in a moment's recollection or reflection though they do not themselves include such awareness as they transpire—perhaps we also have some such states of which we cannot readily become aware. Or so we may allow for present purposes. (The allowance is developed in Smith 2004, ch. 3.)

In other words, the present task—a task of phenomenology—is to analyze that type of inner awareness which we characteristically find in our ordinary human experiences, as ordinary as seeing a frog (consciously). If there are lower or different types of consciousness that do not involve such inner awareness, that is beyond the scope of our present phenomenological analysis.

Siewert (1998) warns us to be wary of the 'conscious-of' trap: the tendency to say that 'whenever one has a phenomenally conscious experience, one is invariably "conscious of" it' (p. 195). Siewert's target is higher-order thought models of consciousness, encouraged perhaps by the verbal advance from 'is conscious' to 'is conscious of seeing/thinking/etc.'. However, the present analysis of inner awareness does not step into the trap. It is important to see, on phenomenological grounds, that there are different forms of awareness of one's experience. I can become aware of my own experience in recollection, especially in short-term memory (what was I just hearing or thinking?). But I can also be aware of my passing experience as a matter of course through what Husserl called a pattern of retentions and protentions (see Smith 2004, ch. 3, for a relevant version of this view). I can also be marginally or peripherally aware of my current experience, and its place in my stream of consciousness including bodily awareness, through a distribution of attention. (See Gurwitsch 1985, Smith 2004a, Ford and Smith 2005.) Indeed, these different forms of awareness are likely grounded in different patterns of neural activity involving different parts of the brain (subserving memory, temporal awareness, attention). Nonetheless, many, perhaps most, of our conscious activities characteristically involve a kind of inner awareness of the activities as they transpire, an awareness that is distinct in kind from recollection, reflection, time-consciousness, and peripheral attention. That type of inner awareness—built into an experience without any accompanying higher-order monitoring—is the focus of the present study.

2. THE FORM OF INNER AWARENESS

According to my prior analysis (in Smith 1986, 1989, 2004, ch. 3), the form of inner awareness may be articulated in the following form of phenomenological description of a simple case of visual experience:

> Phenomenally in this very experience I see this jumping frog

or, in the case of a cognate visual judgment,

> Phenomenally in this very experience I see that this frog is jumping.

Phenomenological descriptions like these, reporting on one's own experiences, are formulated in the first person: 'I see/think/imagine/will . . .'. Husserl practiced phenomenology in a similar style, 'bracketing' the question of the existence and nature of the object of one's consciousness and focusing instead on the form of one's consciousness in being directed toward such an object (Husserl 1913). (See Thomasson 2005 on the methodology of bracketing.) More recently, analytic philosophers have again stressed the importance of the first-person approach to understanding the nature of mind (Searle 1992, Chalmers 1996, Siewert 1998). The above phenomenological descriptions take a specific form (on which we comment below). Phenomenological philosophers may view this form as marking out the formal character of an experience, from which we may fan out into richer and more substantive features of such experiences (not least including the 'horizon' of meaning in the background of the experiences). Analytic philosophers should note that only the second form of description ascribes a properly propositional attitude, an intentional state whose content is a proposition (a type of intentional content expressible, ideally, by a complete declarative sentence, here 'this frog is jumping'). The first form of description ascribes a different form of perception, one whose content is a visually demonstrative sense (a type of content expressible, ideally, by the demonstrative phrase 'this jumping frog' keyed to what I see). We shall address both forms of experience along the way. But for now let us stay with the case of seeing 'this jumping frog'.

We are used to asking after the mode of presentation of an object of an intentional experience or attitude, the 'way' it is 'given' in experience. The object of my perception might be presented as a rock or as a frog, depending on how I take the brute object on which my eyes are gazing. At first, we may suppose, it simply looks like a grey rock in the garden. Then it moves, and it looks like a frog. It jumps from one rock to another, and it looks like a jumping frog. But there is an essentially demonstrative or indexical element in the mode of presentation: what I see is presented as 'this jumping frog', not as 'Calabasas' or 'jumping Calabasas', if my pet frog is named 'Calabasas', certainly not as 'the jumping from frog from Calabasas County' (there is no unique frog therefrom). No, the object of my perception is presented as actually now here before me, as 'this' particular object and moreover as 'this jumping frog'. (See the detailed phenomenological analysis in Smith 1989, ch. 1.)

But there is much more to the content of my experience. I am not simply presented 'this jumping frog' (in a pure act of 'presentation', as Brentano put it). Rather:

I *see* this jumping frog.

Generally, I am presented with such an object in a certain intentional attitude, a certain type of intentional activity: visual perception of it, not auditory perception of it (hearing 'rivet, rivet'), not daydreaming about it, not wishing for it. Part of the content of my experience is 'seeing' as opposed to 'hearing' or 'wishing' or whatever. So we must distinguish two basic parts of the content of my experience: what I called the modality of presentation, including 'see', and the mode of presentation, here 'this jumping frog'. Husserl called these elements of content the thetic character of the act and the sense of the act (Husserl 1913/1963) or the quality and matter of the act (Husserl 1900/2001). (See Smith and McIntyre 1982 for a detailed account of Husserl's distinction.) John Searle has called these elements the psychological mode and the propositional content of the intentional state (Searle 1983, but note that we do not here assume, with Searle, that every intentional experience is propositional).

There is still more, however, to the modality or thetic character of an act. I do not merely see: I see clearly or vaguely (to some degree), I see attentively or inattentively (to a degree), I see with more or less conviction ('is this a dagger I see before me?'), I see with pleasure or displeasure or with emotional feeling (say, with love or anger or disgust). With other psychological modalities, the qualifications abound further. These characters of the intentional attitude are reflected in the phenomenological structure of the experience, thus, in what we call the full 'content' of the experience.

Still a different element of content or structure is the act's character of proceeding from 'me' so that 'I' am seeing. The intentional structure of the experience consists not only in its being directed in a certain way toward an object, 'this frog', but also in its being directed from a subject, 'I'. Putting these last two items of modal or thetic character together, we say:

... *I see* this jumping frog.

(Self-awareness goes along with inner awareness of one's experience, but is not our target here. Zahavi 1999 develops an insightful phenomenological analysis of awareness of self and other. Natsoulas 1991–2 pursues self-awareness in a rich psychological context. See Ford and Smith 2005 on peripheral awareness of self.)

Having begun to factor the intentional structure of an act into different elements of content, we may specify elements that are not usually articulated well in our phenomenological analyses. What is the difference, then, between conscious and blind sight? We give a name to the difference when we say:

Phenomenally I see this jumping frog.

The character of phenomenality is what distinguishes conscious sight from blindsight: this character 'phenomenally' is present in conscious vision but absent in blindsight.

(We idealize about the clarity and semantic content of blindsight, which is less clear than conscious sight and less precise in specifying the properties of the object seen.) This character 'phenomenally', I proposed (1986 and 1989), is the 'qualitative' character that philosophers since Peirce have emphasized in seeing colors and shapes, or 'qualia', the sensed properties of color, shape, etc. And notice that the syntactic position of this character is in the modality of presentation, not the mode of presentation. If the frog is presented as greyish-green, where I see 'this greyish-green jumping frog', the presentation of color 'greyish-green' is not merely a conceptualized presentation of a certain shade of color. Rather, the color-presentation has a 'qualitative' character: it is sensuously presented, that is, 'phenomenally I see this greyish-green jumping frog'. So, on my proposal, the distinctively phenomenal presentation of color, as opposed to merely intellectual or conceptual presentation of the same color, is defined by the character 'phenomenally' in the modality of presentation.

Now, the awareness I have of my experience as it transpires is still another element of the overall content or structure of my experience. On my proposal, the specific form of inner awareness is that of the reflexive character ascribed by 'in this very experience' in the phenomenological description:

Phenomenally *in this very experience* I see this jumping frog.

Within the modality of presentation, the overall thetic character of the experience, I proposed, lies the element of content 'in this very experience'. This content indicates the mental act itself: it does so reflexively, indicating the experience itself.

The first point to emphasize is that the reflexive content 'this very experience' enters into the modality of presentation. The second point to stress is exactly how this content works. The second point will occupy us in detail below. The first point will recur later, but we should bring out its importance already at this point.

As noted, Husserl distinguished the two basic parts of intentional content we have called modality and mode of presentation, and others have marked similar distinctions. Yet there is novelty in this distinction, as familiar as it may seem today. Many philosophers today, writing in the analytic tradition, simply assume that an intentional attitude consists in a person's relation to a proposition—end of story. But we must distinguish much more by way of intentional structure or content, as the examples above show. I have tried to indicate distinct 'formal' positions in the structure of consciousness for four categorially distinct types of content in the modality of an act. These four elements of content are indicated by the successive underscored phrases in the phenomenological description:

Phenomenally in this very experience I see this jumping frog,

or, in the propositional form of perception,

Phenomenally in this very experience I see that this frog is jumping.

The modality of the act includes then: phenomenality, reflexivity, egocentricity, and of course psychological modality (vision rather than imagination or desire or whatever).

We have parsed the 'syntax' of an experience accordingly into several different formal types of intentional structure. The syntax of our phenomenological description is designed to articulate just these 'logical' or 'syntactic' features of phenomenological form. And our main concern here is with the form of inner awareness defined by the modal feature 'in this very experience'.

3. THE LANGUAGE OF PHENOMENOLOGICAL DESCRIPTION

In a study involving both phenomenology and analytic philosophy of mind cum language, we need to be clear about the connection between language and experience. We need to be clear where our concern is consciousness and where it is language about consciousness. In the above phenomenological description of my seeing a frog, I am using language to articulate a form of experience. The visual experience, with its phenomenological structure or content, is one thing; the sentence I use to articulate the structure or content of the experience is something else, a piece of language used for a specific purpose. This technique is a rather special approach to the practice of phenomenology, to phenomenological description, so let us pause to reflect on this methodology. (See Smith and McIntyre 1982 on connections between the intentionality of an experience and the semantics of 'intensional' sentences ascribing the experience.)

When I see that this frog is jumping and formulate a phenomenological description of my visual propositional attitude, I use a sentence with a logical form much studied in philosophical logic and philosophy of language. Initially, for accidents of history, when logic-minded philosophers addressed intentional attitudes, they focused (following Russell) on sentences reporting (what Russell dubbed) 'propositional attitudes'. Their concern was with issues of reference for terms in sentences reporting beliefs, sentences such as these:

Smith believes that frogs jump,
Smith believes that Calabasas jumps,
Smith believes that the winner of the frog race jumps.

The form of phenomenological description used above is partly guided by the logic of such sentences. Yet the point is to use the description to bring out features of visual experience.

Demonstrative pronouns like 'this' raise complications of context-sensitivity. Thus, if I (D. W. Smith) say,

This frog is jumping,

then my utterance of 'this' or 'this frog' is keyed to the context of my utterance as I see and typically point at a particular object, the frog now jumping around before me. If however another person, say, H.-N. Castañeda, says of me,

Smith believes that this frog is jumping,

then his utterance of 'this', in his mouth in the relevant context, is normally understood as keyed to his (Castañeda's) context of utterance: where he is near me and indicates a particular object in his and my purview. However, as Castañeda (the real-world philosopher) shrewdly observed, there is a special reading in which the demonstrative (let us add an asterisk to indicate this special use) is to be understood as keyed rather to the belief-subject's context:

Smith believes that this* frog is jumping.

Here the relevant context for the 'quasi-indicator' word 'this*' is not ascriber Castañeda's circumstance, but rather ascribee Smith's circumstance. (See the classic essay Castañeda 1966. For a recent parsing of relevant issues of phenomenology, semantics, and pragmatics for propositional attitudes and reports thereof, see Smith 2000.)

Now, in my phenomenological analysis above, I assumed (without explicitly stepping back into the semantics of such sentences) that a phenomenological description follows this logic but in the first-person form. When I say in phenomenological description,

I think that this frog is jumping,

I ascribe to myself a state of thinking and describe that state from my own first-person perspective. Given the task of phenomenology, I formulate a phenomenological description that ascribes and describes my experience of thinking 'as' I experience it. So the context of utterance as I say,

I think that this frog is jumping,

is precisely the circumstance that consists in my having an experience of thinking whose content is articulated and ascribed to myself in this form of sentence. The difference Castañeda stressed here collapses: 'this frog' has the same semantics as 'this* frog' in my phenomenological description here. The content 'this frog' in my thinking intentionally prescribes a certain object visually before me on that occasion, and accordingly the demonstrative expression 'this frog' uttered in my sentence above semantically prescribes that object perceptually before me on that occasion. (See Smith 1989, ch. 1, for details.) In short, I am using a technique of phenomenological description that is guided by the semantics of these forms of sentence.

Similarly, when I say in phenomenological description as earlier,

Phenomenally in this very experience I see this jumping frog,

or in the propositional case of visual judgment,

Phenomenally in this very experience I see that this frog is jumping,

I am ascribing to myself a visual experience with a certain phenomenological, intentional structure. Of course, while this description would specify the formal structure of my visual experience, there is a great deal more to say, as we see in the wonderful impressionistic prose of Merleau-Ponty's phenomenology of perception (Merleau-Ponty 1945/1996). By the way, contemporary analytic philosophers of mind often assume that phenomenology concerns only or primarily qualia, the subjective feel of pain or seeing a color; this assumption is quickly dispelled by reading Merleau-Ponty and Husserl, for whom our visual experience is rarely a matter of seeing only qualia and is normally rich in conceptual and associative meaning.

When Husserl introduced the phenomenological method of bracketing in *Ideas* I (1913/1963, §31), the technique was widely misunderstood. We are to 'bracket' the natural world, Husserl proposed, in order to focus on the nature of consciousness. But this does not mean we are to deny or ignore the world around us. Thomasson (2005, this volume) has argued that we should understand bracketing as akin to quotation. When I say,

'This frog is jumping,'

I am talking about a peripatetic amphibian in my physical environs. When you then quote me by saying:

Smith says, 'This frog is jumping',

you are talking about my speech activity, quoting the words I just used. And if you instead say:

Smith thinks, 'This frog is jumping',

you are talking about my cogitative activity, 'quoting' as it were the form of experience I just had. And if I say, as above,

I think, 'This frog is jumping',

I am in effect quoting the content of my own thought, though in the special attitude of phenomenological reflection (I do not normally report or need to report to myself on what I am experiencing). In fact, Husserl went on to use quotation marks explicitly as a device to 'quote' the content or sense (*Sinn*) of an experience (*Ideas* I, 1913/1963, §89). To paraphrase Husserl: when in phenomenological reflection on my 'reduced' or 'bracketed' experience of seeing the frog, I describe 'the perceived as such', the perceptual sense, as I say, 'this spotted green jumping frog', I am using the quotation marks to indicate that my concern is not the frog itself, but rather the content through which I am visually presented the object. Husserl's technique of 'semantic ascent' (to adapt Quine's term) can be amplified along the lines of the preceding paragraphs. (Smith 1970 uses a device of sense-quotation following Husserl. Smith and McIntyre 1982, ch. 4, explore the issue of the expressibility of noematic content, noting that linguistic expression abstracts away from some of the content of experience, notably the 'intuitive' or sensory aspects, including what are commonly called sensory qualia.)

4. INDEXICAL EXPERIENCES AND INDEXICAL EXPRESSIONS

All that said, let us look into two items of indexical content in this intentional structure: let us contrast the demonstrative content 'this frog' or 'this jumping frog' with the reflexive content 'this very experience', noting their respective roles in the mode and modality of presentation.

Indexical experiences, let us say, are those whose intentional content is keyed to the context in which the experience occurs; that type of content is an indexical content. When I see a frog jumping around before me in the garden, when I see (as we have been saying) 'this jumping frog', the content 'this jumping frog' in my experience pre-scribes or refers to the object appropriately before me and affecting my eyes on that occasion, in that context of experience. We use indexical expressions to express such contents and to give voice to indexical experiences, as in the first-person reports of experience drawn above as phenomenological descriptions. My point in *The Circle of Acquaintance* (1989) was precisely to develop a phenomenological analysis of indexical awareness in those forms of experience which we call direct acquaintance: percep-tual awareness of 'this object', inner awareness of one's experience as 'this very experience' and of oneself as 'I', and empathic awareness of 'you' or 's/he' (another 'I'). Inner awareness of 'this very experience' is thus a special case of indexical awareness.

The significance of indexical expressions has been richly explored by David Kaplan in his classic treatise 'Demonstratives' (1989), which was widely circulated in the 1970s and finally published nearly twenty years after its first drafting. The broad implications of this form of language are indicated by Kaplan's subtitle: 'An Essay on the Semantics, Logic, Metaphysics and Epistemology of Demonstratives and Other Indexicals'. What is missing in Kaplan's account of demonstratives and other indexical expressions, how-ever, is their connection with phenomenology. (Otherwise it is a beautiful system; and in all fairness note that 'Epistemological Remarks', 529 ff., is the very last section of philosophical discussion, before the formal system of logic is presented.) Kaplan distin-guishes two levels of meaning (if you will), which he calls 'character' and 'content'. The character of a sentence is or corresponds to its general semantic role, while the content of a sentence is a proposition (understood in Russellian fashion). Suppose (in Frege's famous example) Dr Lauben says, 'I am wounded'. For Kaplan, the character of the sentence (token) 'I am wounded' is the rule that governs its use in context, whereby the speaker refers to himself by uttering 'I', and the content of the sentence uttered in the given context is the (Russellian) singular proposition that Lauben is wounded. (Formally, the character may be represented by a function from contexts to contents, and the content by a function from possible worlds to truth-values; but the intended interpretation of the formal system is as stated.)

Consider what Kaplan then says about cognitive contents. Puzzling over Frege's remarks about the word 'I' and the Lauben case, Kaplan writes, promisingly:

What is the particular and primitive way in which Dr Lauben is presented to himself [as Frege said]? What cognitive content presents Dr Lauben to himself, but presents him to nobody else? Thoughts [or propositions] determined this way can be grasped by Dr Lauben, but no one else can grasp that thought determined in that way. The answer, I believe, is, simply, that Dr Lauben is presented to himself under the character of 'I'.   [533]

Here, it seems, the content of Lauben's thought includes the 'manner of presentation' expressed by his uttering 'I' and specified by the character of 'I'. This sounds like an astute piece of phenomenology (or 'epistemology' in Kaplan's idiom): character = cognitive significance of a thought or proposition (as he says explicitly, 530). Thus, for Kaplan, what Lauben thinks, the proposition that is the 'object' of his thinking, is composed of

Lauben himself and the property of being wounded, while the 'character' expressed is the cognitive significance of that thought or proposition for Lauben. (Notice in the above quotation that Kaplan is moving the term 'content' from the character to the singular proposition.)

Unfortunately, however, given Kaplan's ontology of 'content' and 'character', we might as well be zombies or robots. Kaplan's semantic machinery would work just as he says even if the sentence-shaped noises were produced with no consciousness, even if there were no minds involved at all, even if 'we' were all mindless automata. I don't mean to suggest that Kaplan thinks of us and our language in that way, but his account of indexicals leaves out the relevant phenomenology. The problem begins with terminology. Husserl (1900/2001) had sharply distinguished the 'content' and 'object' of an act of thinking or judging. In Lauben's case, the object of thought is the state of affairs that the individual Lauben had the property of being wounded, and that object is presented or 'intended' in one way (there are others) through the content 'I am wounded', a propositional sense, or thought or proposition, that prescribes the state of affairs indicated. It is unfortunate that Kaplan and his followers have co-opted the term 'content' and even 'proposition' for the type of entity that plays the role of object of thought, namely, a (putative or possible) state of affairs. When Kaplan turns to 'epistemological remarks' (529), his question is, 'How do character and content serve as objects of thought?' Observing Husserl's distinction, we find this terminology confused. We want to ask about the intentional content of, say, Lauben's thinking 'I am wounded'. And that content should not be identified with the state of affairs consisting in the individual Lauben having the property of being wounded. The whole point is that this state of affairs (external to Lauben's thinking) can be presented in different forms of thinking, through different contents, different 'propositions' or 'thoughts'. Phenomenology would analyze that content, whereas the corresponding state of affairs calls for medical attention.

Kaplan argued that demonstratives and indexicals refer 'directly', rather than by way of a Fregean sense containing or tied to a 'manner of presentation'. But Kaplan assumes (adapting Russell and modifying Frege) that the manner in which an object (say, Venus) is presented in thought is an entity constructed from properties (such as rising in the sky at dusk or rising at dawn). (See 494 on constituents of propositions as being either individuals or attributes or complexes of attributes, and 530 ff. on manners of presentation and cognitive significance.) But that is not right. Properties are features of individuals in the world: universals instantiated by particulars (in the traditional idiom following Aristotle). The 'way' something is 'given' in thought or experience, however, is something else again: something whose ontology concerns intentionality in thought rather than the qualification of particulars *in re*. Indeed, any property can itself be given in different ways, just as any individual can be given in different ways. (Venus can be given as 'the morning star' or as 'the evening star' or as 'that star [or planet]' or as 'Venus'. Similarly, the property of being a star can be given as 'a hot, luminous, gaseous body in space' or as 'a point of light in the night sky', etc.; even the property of being red can be given differently in different lighting conditions.) 'Ways-of-givenness' are, to the logician, 'intensional' entities, and so are properties. But ways-of-givenness are their own kind of entity: what Husserl called 'intentional contents' or 'noemata' or '(noematic) sense [Sinn]'—updating what Kant meant by 'phenomena', or things-as-they-are-presented (as opposed to 'noumena', or things-as-they-are). (See Smith 2003 on 'phenomena' in phenomenology.)

Still, in Husserlian phenomenology, the type and level of 'sense' that serves as the content of an intentional act or attitude deserves cautious appraisal when we turn to what is expressed by an indexical expression such as 'this' or 'I'. Kaplan's theory is well-crafted until we reach the role of intentional content (following Husserl's, not Kaplan's, usage of the term 'content'), where Husserl has much to say.

Husserl already (in Husserl 1900/2001) distinguished two levels of meaning (like Kaplan's) for 'essentially occasional' expressions like 'I', 'this', etc., that is, indexicals. One level, called the 'indicating meaning' of the word, reflects the 'general semantic function' of the word; the other, called the 'indicated meaning' of the word for the given occasion, is an intentional content specific to that occasion of experience. What type of sense or content the 'indicated' meaning might be is a question for phenomenological analysis. My strategy in *The Circle of Acquaintance* was to develop an explicit analysis of the intentional force of indexical contents, of how properly indexical contents (like 'this', 'I', and 'you') work in appropriate contexts of experience. This was not evident in either classical phenomenology or contemporary philosophy of mind-cum-language. And so I set out to develop an analysis of indexical contents, guided by the emerging semantics of indexicals, but looking to the phenomenology itself rather than the semantics, looking to indexical awareness rather than indexical expressions. (See the semantic distinctions drawn in Husserl 1900/2001: I, §26, VI, §5, and see Smith 1982 for a reconstruction of Husserl's semantics in relation to Kaplan's.)

Meanwhile, John Perry has worked for decades on issues of indexicality, moving closer than Kaplan to the phenomenology I seek and to an account of (what I call) the intentional force of indexical contents. In 'The Problem of the Essential Indexical' (published in 1979 and gathered with other essays in Perry 2000), Perry argued—utterly persuasively—that indexicals are unique in kind and cannot be replaced by any other type of expression. More recently, he has argued (in essays in Perry 2001b) that indexicals refer by virtue of their 'reflexive' character. Moving from language to mind, moreover, he has argued (in Perry 2001a) that 'reflexive contents' play a privileged role in consciousness. It is this latter view that I should like to explore here.

5. PERRY'S ACCOUNT OF REFLEXIVE CONTENTS

In *Knowledge, Possibility, and Consciousness* (2001a) Perry argues that there are different types and levels of 'contents' for beliefs and statements. Recent philosophy of mind has focused often on beliefs, but phenomenology is primarily concerned with occurrent mental acts (involving inner awareness), so let us focus on thoughts (events of consciously thinking) rather than beliefs (dispositions to think, and also to act). With that change, we may outline Perry's theory of contents as follows. I'll modify Perry's presentation a bit so as to line up with my phenomenological analysis, with the aim of adapting key parts of Perry's account of reflexive contents to my system.

Contemporary philosophers of mind and language, Perry charges, have wrongly assumed that contents are invariably of a certain sort: they have assumed that 'the content of a statement or a belief consists in the conditions that the truth of the statement or belief puts on the objects and properties the statement or belief is about'—'the subject matter fallacy' Perry calls it (p. 20). But that doctrine of content ignores the context-sensitive contents that Perry is interested in (as am I). To distinguish 'reflexive' contents from 'subject matter' contents, Perry offers a thought experiment (119 ff.), which I'll transform so as to feature first-person ascriptions of occurrent thoughts.

Suppose that I have read about the philosopher Fred Dretske, learning that he wrote *Knowledge and the Flow of Information*. At a party I find myself conversing with an interesting philosopher, discussing the way that knowledge depends on a causal flow of information from the environment. By association I find myself having a thought about Dretske:

(T1) I think that Fred Dretske wrote *Knowledge and the Flow of Information*.

A friend approaches and calls my conversationalist by name, 'Fred'. I suddenly realize whom I have been talking with, and I have a new thought about the man visually before me:

(T2) I think that this man is Fred Dretske.

And now I think about his remarkable book:

(T3) I think that this man wrote *Knowledge and the Flow of Information*.

In this scenario we need to distinguish two very different types of intentional contents: the nominal content 'Fred Dretske' and the demonstrative content 'this man', and so the respective propositions in which they occur.

The content of thought T1—the proposition 'Fred Dretske wrote *Knowledge and the Flow of Information*'—is what Perry calls a 'subject matter' content. This content includes 'a notion of Dretske associated with various ideas I had gotten from reading things by and about him' (120), a notion which is 'sort of like [an] internal file folder' containing ideas about Dretske (120), and which does not depend on the immediate context of experience to prescribe its object. By contrast, the content of thought T3—the proposition 'this man wrote *Knowledge and the Flow of Information*'—is an indexical content, a context-sensitive proposition. This content includes a 'perceptual buffer' (121) attached to my perception of 'this man': 'Buffers are new notions associated with the perception and used to temporarily store ideas we gain from the perceptions until we can identify the individual, or form a permanent detached notion of him, or forget about him' (121). Perry here uses a model of information storage to give a rendering of the contents representing an individual in different ways. The details are consonant with my own phenomenological analyses of different types of 'individuation in consciousness' (see Smith and McIntyre 1982, ch. 8, and Smith 1989, ch. 5). As I might put it, my seeing 'this individual [x]' introduces a 'sense of individuality [x]' which carries into my concurrently thinking that 'this man [x] wrote *Knowledge and the Flow of Information*' and into my later thinking that 'he [x] talked of academic life on The Farm' (tracking the sense of identity here, a bit artificially, with the variable 'x').

Perry will analyze the content of thought T3 as involving a 'reflexive' content, but that part of the theory comes later in our discussion. First we need to recognize that the contents of thoughts T1 and T3, these propositions, are of essentially different type. Analogously, the sentences 'Fred Dretske wrote...' and 'this man wrote...' are of essentially different type, because the indexical term 'this man' cannot be reduced to any other type of expression, such as a proper name 'Fred Dretske' or a definite description 'the philosopher who first applied Shannon-Weaver information theory to philosophy of mind'. But remember, our concern here is intentional content rather than language used to express it.

Granted that the content 'this' is essentially and irreducibly indexical in type, we may put it to use in addressing one of the peculiarities of conscious experience: the experience of 'what it is like' to see a certain color. Perry writes:

When we are attending to a subjective character [of an experience] in the subjective way and wish to communicate what we are feeling or noticing, we use our flexible demonstrative, 'this,' as in 'This feeling is the one I've been having.' Let's label this use of 'this' as an inner demonstrative: 'this$_i$.' [146]

Accordingly, when I am looking at a red ripe tomato, I may attend to what it is like to see red and then think about the qualitative look of red:

I think that this$_i$ sensory character [in my seeing this red ripe tomato] is what it is like to see red.

The inner-demonstrative content 'this$_i$' in my thought prescribes the subjective character to which I am attending in my perception. In this case I am performing both a visual perception of a tomato and an inner observation about a sensory quality, or quale, in that perception. The inner observation is a type of higher-order thought about the perceptual experience I am currently having. So I am doing two things at once. Note that this form of inner observation is not the same as inner awareness. (Compare Thomasson 2000, 2005.)

By using a theory of demonstrative content keyed to subjective character, Perry proposes (146 ff.) to solve the 'knowledge' problem about qualia (Jackson 1997): what is it that Mary the neuroscientist knows when she sees red for the first time in her life?—after a career of studying the neural processes involved in human vision while she herself lived in a colorless laboratory. The answer: Mary comes to know and think that 'this$_i$ is the quale [the subjective character] of seeing red'. In Kaplanesque terms, there is an inner demonstration of the quale, not a pointing of one's finger but a directing of one's attention to the quale, where the intentional character of 'this$_i$' specifies that it prescribes the object of that inner attention. And recall the point of Husserl's phenomenological method of bracketing: to turn one's attention from the object of experience to the experience itself, here to the sensory quale in the experience.

Beyond the issue of qualia, however, there are other forms of inner ostension in which our experience intentionally designates some aspect of our own consciousness. For instance, the paradoxical Cretan thinks as follows:

I think that this$_i$ thought is false.

In this experience the content 'this$_i$ thought' intentionally prescribes the very thought (event of thinking) in which the content itself occurs. And if the Cretan is enough of a logical realist about propositions as abstract or ideal contents, he may think as follows:

I think that this$_i$ proposition [which I am now thinking] is false.

In that experience the content 'this$_i$ proposition' intentionally prescribes the abstract or ideal proposition that is the content of the thought. So there is plenty of work for contents of inner ostension.

'Content,' Perry says, 'is a way of classifying cognitive and linguistic events by their truth conditions (and success conditions more generally)' (125). Indeed, for Husserl, the intentional content of an act of consciousness is its 'ideal species' (1900/2001: I, V), and what an act's content does is direct the act in a certain way toward an appropriate object. Thus, the content of an act of thinking-that-p is a proposition 'p' which represents the corresponding possible state of affairs that p. Today, reflecting Tarski's theory of truth (Tarski 1944/1952), we may say: the content of a person's thinking that p is true if and only if it is the case that p. In this way the intentional force of a thought's content is defined by its truth conditions. This neo-Tarskian view fits the broadly Husserlian phenomenological theory of intentionality (see Smith and McIntyre 1982 on the relation of intentionality cum content to truth conditions in possible worlds). To explicate the context-sensitivity of indexical contents, however, we need to modify the simple schema of truth conditions. Perry proposes 'the content analyzer' formula (125), rephrased here for thoughts:

> If C is a content of an act of thinking T, then:
> CA: Given [*such and such*] C is true if and only if *so-and-so*.

As I understand the new schema, *such-and-such* is the context in which the thought (or belief or statement) occurs, and *so-and-so* is the possible situation or state of affairs that would make C true in that context. The truth conditions for a content are thus relative to the context of thought: in that context the content represents that possible situation which if actual would make the content true. (The schema could be stated in terms of possible worlds, but even if we bring in possible worlds of an appropriate sort, we need to work with situations or states of affairs within those worlds.)

I would import into Perry's schema an explicit ontology of situations or states of affairs (situations as in Barwise and Perry 1983; even better, states of affairs as in Armstrong 1997). And I would assume, as noted earlier, that propositions are distinct from but intentionally represent states of affairs. If we read Perry literally, he actually goes so far as to identify contents with truth conditions of statements or thoughts (126). For our purposes I want to loosen this identification: truth conditions 'define' contents in the sense that they define important constraints on the intentionality of thoughts bearing those contents. But it is crucial to bear in mind that thoughts, their contents, and their truth conditions are distinct though logically related things. How are they related? By intentionality, I submit.

Accordingly, we should see the contextualized truth condition schema CA as a schema of intentionality. In fact, it is a corollary of the following contextualized intentionality schema relating Content to Object:

> If C is a/the content of an act of consciousness A, then:
> CO: In context K content C in act A prescribes or is satisfied by object O
>   if and only if *so-and-so*,

where K is the appropriate context in which A occurs, and *so-and-so* consists in an appropriate circumstance wherein O obtains or exists, that is, a state of affairs involving

O in an appropriate way. This is indeed the form of analysis of intentional content that I used in *The Circle of Acquaintance*. The form is more explicitly schematized here. And how do truth conditions appear in this form? Well, if the content C is propositional in form, then what it prescribes in a thought T in or given a context K is a possible state of affairs S. And then its truth conditions are stated in the form:

> If C is a content of an act of thinking T, then:
> CA*:   In context K C in T is true if and only if
>   the state of affairs S prescribed by C in T in context K is actual.

With context-sensitive truth conditions, we can explicate the difference in content between the thoughts T1 and T3 in our Perry-esque thought experiment. In the context of T1 it matters not who is in my immediate visual environment as I think that 'Fred Dretske wrote *Knowledge and the Flow of Information*': in the context of my thinking (lost in thought at the party), the content of my thought T1 is true if and only if Dretske wrote *Knowledge and the Flow of Information*. By contrast, in the context of T3 it matters who is visually before me as I see 'this man' and think that 'this man wrote *Knowledge and the Flow of Information*': in the context of my seeing 'this man' and so thinking, the content of my thought T3 is true if and only if the man visually before me wrote *Knowledge and the Flow of Information*. Thus does context constrain the intentional force of the content of thought: the content of T1 is a 'subject matter' proposition, while the content of T3 is an indexical proposition, a 'reflexive' content according to Perry. 'These [reflexive] contents,' Perry says, 'are not merely conditions on the subject matter but conditions on the utterances or thoughts themselves.' (21) (If I'm not mistaken, my account of satisfaction conditions for indexical contents in *The Circle of Acquaintance* fits well with Perry's account of context-sensitive truth conditions in the content analyzer schema CA. However, my account of intentionality, including the force of indexical contents, is not restricted to propositional attitudes, hence the wider form of CO.)

Perry intimates that he is ramifying Kaplan's conception of 'content' (see 124–31), acccording to which 'singular propositions' are in effect just possible states of affairs (with further intentional work to be done by 'character'). I think, however, that the closer Perry digs into contents, especially indexical and reflexive contents, the closer he gets to my account of content, where a 'proposition' prescribes or represents but is distinct from a corresponding state of affairs. For a subject-matter proposition as in T1 represents a state of affairs quite directly and independently of the immediate context of thought, while an indexical proposition as in T3 may represent the same state of affairs also directly but in a different and context-sensitive way. This is the point of distinguishing content and object of thought. (Again, see Smith and McIntyre 1982 for a detailed analysis of the alternative 'content' and 'object' approaches to intentionality. And the point of Smith 1989 was to analyze 'direct' awareness in perception and other forms of acquaintance but in a way that honors the phenomenological content of acquainting experiences.)

When Perry treats contents like that of T3 as 'reflexive' contents, he alludes to Hans Reichenbach's 'token-reflexive' analysis of words like 'this', 'I', 'here', etc. According to Reichenbach, 'this' refers to what its utterer is pointing at, 'I' refers to its utterer, 'here' refers to the location of the speaker uttering it, etc. On each occasion of use, that is, an indexical word refers to an entity appropriately tied to the utterance of that word. Perry adapts the token-reflexive view to contents of statements or beliefs or thoughts (124–31). Thus, the truth conditions of the content 'this man wrote *Knowledge and the Flow of Information*' in the thought T3 are, if we may put it so, reflexively tied to that very thought, that concrete token experience in the appropriate context. (I won't try to bring in Perry's picture of 'loading' information into conditions of truth (125 ff).)

There are real problems, however, with the token-reflexive analysis of the indexical contents 'this', 'I', 'now', 'here'. For instance, as I proposed (Smith 1989), the visually demonstrative content 'this' is equivalent in intentional force with 'the object actually now here before me and causing this very experience'. But the equivalence holds only in standard circumstances: not in cases where my experience is caused by a Cartesian evil genie or (as in the science fiction film *The Matrix*) by a cyber-neural AI system (whose ontology remains to be specified)—in such a case 'this' is not tied in the normal way to the experience in which it occurs. Again, the self-presenting content 'I' is normally equivalent with 'the subject who is actually now having this very experience'. But there are bizarre circumstances in which 'I' does not designate the subject of the thought in which it occurs: say, where an alien being is thinking the thought and making it seem to me as though it is my thought—and so 'I' is not reflexively tied to that token thought. (See the thought experiments laid out to this end in Smith 1989, 216 ff.; and see Natsoulas 1991–2 on this psychological possibility.) Still, I want to buy into the unique form of reflexivity that Perry is emphasizing.

On Perry's view (implicit in 126–7), every thought (or belief or statement) has a range of contents, and there is reflexive content in every thought, but only in indexical thoughts does this reflexive content impose conditions of truth involving the thought's role in the relevant context. I think this view goes with the assimilation of content to truth conditions, since the conditions of truth for a thought range widely. But this view fails to mark a crucial distinction between content and background. We must distinguish the primary content of a thought, the proposition in one's mind, from the wide range of background ideas and propositions on which it depends (see Smith 2004, ch. 5). Still, so long as we explicate content solely in terms of the truth conditions it imposes, we will miss the peculiar form of inner awareness and the role of reflexive content therein.

6. INNER AWARENESS THROUGH REFLEXIVE CONTENT

We laid out the form of inner awareness in phenomenological description as follows:

Phenomenally in this very experience I see this jumping frog.
Phenomenally in this very experience I think that this frog is jumping.

Whereas the perceptual content 'this frog' or 'this jumping frog' demonstratively prescribes an object of the act of consciousness, the content 'this very experience' reflexively prescribes the act itself, but without in any way thereby making the act its own object. To appreciate this form of awareness, we need bring out two points. First, inner awareness is achieved through a unique type of indexical content, an irreducibly reflexive content. Second, this content occurs in the modality (or thetic character) of the act, rather than in the act's mode of presentation of the object.

There are several important types of indexical content including at least 'this', 'I', 'here', and 'now', each keyed to a distinctive type of context. The demonstrative content 'this' typically occurs in perception, keyed to one's visual circumstance, as when I see 'this jumping frog' or think that 'this frog is jumping'. A different type of demonstrative content is that we called an inner-demonstrative content 'this$_i$', which is keyed not to my visual environment, but to part of my passing experience itself, as when I think that 'this$_i$ quale is the subjective character of seeing red' or when I think that 'this$_i$ thought is false'. These contents work in different ways in different types of context. To bring out the differences, we may use the content schema CA* discussed above.

If T is my experience of thinking that 'this frog is jumping', whose content C is the proposition 'this frog is jumping', then the truth conditions of C are:

> In the context K the content C in the thought T is true if and only if there is a frog visually before the subject of T in K and it is jumping,

where K is the context consisting of my being confronted by a certain frog light from which is (partly) causing my visual experience. Here the perceptually demonstrative content 'this' in the content C in my thought T is keyed to an object visually before me in the context K.

By contrast, if T is my experience of thinking that 'this$_i$ thought is false', whose content C is the proposition 'this$_i$ thought is false', then the truth conditions of C are:

> In the context K the content C in the thought T is true if and only if the very thought in which C occurs as content in K is false,

where K is the context consisting simply of my thinking that proposition. (We allow that an act of thinking is true/false just in case its content, a proposition, is true/false.) Here the inner-demonstrative content 'this$_i$'—part of the proposition C—is keyed to the very act of thinking in which 'this$_i$' occurs in context K. I leave to logicians the problem of the paradoxical character of so thinking: my job as a phenomenologist is to observe how its content works, featuring the content 'this$_i$'.

Now, clearly the inner-demonstrative content 'this$_i$ experience', or 'this very experience', is unique in type: its intentional force is to designate the very act in which it occurs as content, and that act itself is the relevant context. No other content works like that. It is, we may say, an essentially reflexive content. Remember, though, that on my account we do not reduce any other indexical contents to reflexive contents. On this point I diverge from Perry (in Reichenbach's wake).

In thinking like the Cretan as above, I am thinking about my very act of thinking, thinking about 'this$_i$ thought', or 'this very thought' (as I put it). But that higher-order thinking is not the same as inner awareness. We must distinguish two different roles of the content 'this$_i$ experience', one in mode of presentation and one in modality of presentation. Consider the full phenomenological description of my Cretanesque act:

Phenomenally in this$_i$ thought I think that this$_i$ thought is false.

—or in my earlier idiom:

Phenomenally in this very thought I think that this very thought is false.

Where 'this$_i$ thought' occurs in the proposition 'this$_i$ thought is false' in my act, it presents the object about which I am thinking—my act-of-thinking itself. But where 'this$_i$ thought' occurs in the reflexive character 'in this$_i$ very thought' in my act, its role is not to present the cogitative act itself (or to present anything at all). Its role here is to effect inner awareness of the act transpiring. It reflexively indicates the act itself, but without in any way making the act a higher-order 'intention' of itself.

And so, on my model, inner awareness consists in a modal character of an experience, and not any sort of separate higher-order 'intention' of the experience.

7. PRIVACY REVISITED

Many philosophers still believe Wittgenstein undermined the very concept of consciousness through his private-language investigation (Wittgenstein 1997/1953, §§269 ff.), and many go on to think that the practice and even coherence of phenomenology are thereby vitiated. But Hector-Neri Castañeda (1986) saw, correctly I think, that Wittgenstein's problem can be dissolved by a careful study of the way words like 'I' and 'he himself' work. Perry joins Castañeda in this view (xiii), and so do I. Moreover, the practice of phenomenology as above joins with the logic or semantics of indexical expressions to explicate the 'privacy' of consciousness as we know it. Though I cannot go into this issue in detail here, I should like to close with the basics of the vindication of privacy. (See Smith 2004, Coda, 'The Beetle in the Box'.)

As noted above, I am presented to myself in a way that I am not presented to anyone else: namely, as 'I', through the content 'I', for instance when I think that 'I wrote *The Circle of Acquaintance* on a MacPlus configured by my Ontek colleagues'. Furthermore, I am presented with qualia in my perceptual experience in a way that my qualia are not presented to anyone else: as 'this$_i$ quality of my seeing red'. (Private awareness of a sense datum, in the classical empiricist sense, was probably Wittgenstein's target in the private-language discussion.) Again, I am presented with my own cogitation in a way that it is presented to no one else: as 'this$_i$ thought', when for instance I think that 'this$_i$ thought is false'. Moreover, I have an inner awareness of my own experience, a form of awareness no one else has of my experience: namely, through the reflexive content 'this$_i$ experience', as when 'phenomenally in this$_i$ experience I think that Castañeda was on the right track'. We do not say my experience is presented to me in inner awareness; we say I am aware of my experience in that reflexive and 'inner' way.

And that way is part of the primordial form of consciousness as we know and live it: Privately. Not incommunicado. And not beyond the reach of intersubjectively practiced phenomenology.

REFERENCES

Armstrong, D. M. (1997) *A World of States of Affairs* (Cambridge and New York: Cambridge University Press).
Barwise, John, and Perry, John (1983) *Situations and Attitudes* (Cambridge, Mass.: MIT Press).
Block, Ned; Flanagan, Owen, and Güzeldere, Güven (eds.) (1997) *The Nature of Consciousness: Philosophical Debates* (Cambridge, Mass. and London: MIT Press).
Brentano, Franz (1874/1995) *Psychology from an Empirical Standpoint*. Edited by Oskar Kraus; English edition edited by Linda L. McAlister; with a new introduction by Peter Simons. Translated by Antos C. Cancurello, D. B. Terrell, and Linda L. McAlister (London and New York: Routledge). German original, 1874.
Castañeda, Hector-Neri (1966) ' "He": On the Logic of Self-Consciousness', *Ratio*: 130–57.
—— 'Self-Profile' (1986) In James E. Tomberlin, (ed.), *Hector-Neri Castañeda* (Dordrecht and Boston: D. Reidel Publishing Company, now Springer/Kluwer Academic Publishers), 3–137.
Chalmers, David J. (1996) *The Conscious Mind* (Oxford: Oxford University Press).
Dennett, Daniel C. (1991) *Consciousness Explained* (Boston: Little, Brown and Company).
Descartes, René (1988) *The Philosophical Writings of Descartes*, vol. ii, trans. John Cottingham, Robert Stoothoff, and Dugald Murdoch (Cambridge and New York: Cambridge University Press).
Ford, Jason (2005) 'The Attention Model of Consciousness' (Doctoral dissertation, University of California, Irvine).
Ford, Jason, and David Woodruff Smith (2005) 'Consciousness, Self, and Attention', in Uriah Kriegel, and Kenneth Williford (eds.), *Consciousness and Self-Reference* (Cambridge, Massachusetts: MIT Press).
Freud, Sigmund (1933/1965) *New Introductory Lectures on Psycho-Analysis* (New York: W. W. Norton & Company). [German original, 1933.]
Gurwitsch, Aron (1985) *Marginal Consciousness*, ed. Lester Embree (Athens, Oh.: Ohio University Press).
Husserl, Edmund (1900/2001) *Logical Investigations*, vol. i–ii. trans. J. N. Findlay. London and New York: Routledge. First edition of the translation, 1971. German original, first published in 1900–1. An abridged version is *The Shorter Logical Investigations*. London and New York: Routledge.
—— (1893/1991) *On the Phenomenology of the Consciousness of Internal Time (1893–1917). Lectures from 1893–1917*, trans. John Barnett Brough. Boston and Dordrecht: Kluwer Academic Publishers, 1991. From the German text edited and organized by Edith Stein, then slightly edited under his name by Martin Heidegger for the 1928 text from which the translation was prepared. This edition includes further texts gathered by Brough.
—— (1913/1963) *Ideas* I, trans. Boyce Gibson, from the German original of 1913 (New York: Collier Books, 1963). [Originally titled *Ideas pertaining to a Pure Phenomenology and to a Phenomenological Philosophy*, First Book, and known as *Ideas* I.]
Jackson, Frank (1986/1997) 'What Mary Didn't Know', *Journal of Philosophy* 83 (1986): 291–5. Reprinted in Ned Block, Owen Flanagan, and Güven Güzeldere (eds.), *The Nature of Consciousness: Philosophical Debates* (Cambridge and London: MIT Press).
Kaplan, David (1989) 'Demonstratives. An Essay on the Semantics, Logic, Metaphysics and Epistemology of Demonstratives and Other Indexicals' and 'Afterthoughts'. In Joseph Almog, John Perry, and Howard Wettstein, editors. *Themes From Kaplan* (New York and Oxford: Oxford University Press), 481–614.

Kriegel, Uriah, and Williford Kenneth (2005) *Consciousness and Self-Reference* (Cambridge, Massachusetts: MIT Press).

LaBerge, David (1995) *Attentional Processing: The Brain's Art of Mindfulness* (Cambridge, Massachusetts: Harvard University Press).

—— (1997) 'Attention, Awareness, and the Triangular Circuit', *Consciousness and Cognition* 6:149–81.

—— (1998) 'Defining Awareness by the Triangular Circuit of Attention', *Psyche* 4/7 (June 1998).

Leibniz, G. W. (1714/1998) 'Principles of Nature and Grace, Based on Reason' (1714). In G. W. Leibniz, *Philosophical Texts*, trans. and ed. R. S. Woolhouse and Richard Francks (Oxford and New York: Oxford University Press, 1998). [Texts from 1686–1714.]

Locke, John (1694/1979) *An Essay Concerning Human Understanding*, ed. Peter H. Nidditch (Oxford and New York: Oxford University Press, 1975, 1979). [Original, 1694.]

Lycan, William G. (1987) *Consciousness* (Cambridge, Massachusetts: MIT Press).

McIntyre, Ronald, and David Woodruff Smith (1989) 'Theory of Intentionality', in J. N. Mohanty and William McKenna, (eds.), *Husserl's Phenomenology: A Textbook* (Washington, D.C.: The University Press of America, Washington, D.C.; and Pittsburgh: The Center for Advanced Research in Phenomenology), 147–79.

Merleau-Ponty, Maurice (1945/1996) *Phenomenology of Perception*, trans. Colin Smith, 1962 edn.; rev. (London and New York: Routledge, 1996). [French original, 1945.]

Miller, Izchak (1984) *Husserl, Perception and Temporal Awareness* (Cambridge, Massachusetts: MIT Press).

Natsoulas, Thomas (1991–2) ' "I am Not the Subject of this Thought": Understanding a Unique Relation of Special Ownership with the Help of David Woodruff Smith: Part I' and ' "I am Not the Subject of this Thought": Understanding a Unique Relation of Special Ownership with the Help of David Woodruff Smith: Part II', In *Imagination, Cognition and Personality* 11: (1991–2): 279–302 and 331–52.

Perry, John (2000) *The Problem of the Essential Indexical and Other Essays*, expanded edn. (Stanford, California: CSLI Publications).

—— (2001a) *Knowledge, Possibility, and Consciousness* (Cambridge, Massachusetts: MIT Press).

—— (2001b) *Reference and Reflexivity* (Stanford, California: CSLI Publications).

Petitot, Jean, Varela, Francisco J., Pachoud, Bernard, and Roy, Jean-Michel (eds.) (1999) *Naturalizing Phenomenology: Issues in Contemporary Phenomenology and Cognitive Science.* (Stanford, California: Stanford University Press, in collaboration with Cambridge University Press).

Sartre, Jean-Paul (1943/1963) *Being and Nothingness*, trans. Hazel Barnes (New York: Washington Square Press, 1963). [French original, 1943].

Searle, John R. (1983) *Intentionality* (Cambridge: Cambridge University Press).

—— (1992) *The Rediscovery of the Mind* (Cambridge, Massachusetts: MIT Press).

Siewert, Charles (1998) *The Significance of Consciousness* (Princeton, New Jersey: Princeton University Press).

Smith, David Woodruff (1970) *Intentionality, Noemata, and Individuation: The Role of Individuation in Husserl's Theory of Intentionality* (Doctoral dissertation, Stanford University, Stanford, Calif.)

—— (1982) 'Husserl on Demonstrative Reference and Perception', in Hubert L. Dreyfus (ed.), *Husserl, Intentionality and Cognitive Science* (Cambridge, Massachusetts: MIT Press).

—— (1986) 'The Structure of (Self-) Consciousness', *Topoi* 5: 149–56.

—— (1989) *The Circle of Acquaintance: Perception, Consciousness, and Empathy* (Boston and Dordrecht: Kluwer Academic Publishers).

Smith, David Woodruff (1995) 'Mind and Body', in Barry Smith and David Woodruff Smith (eds.), *The Cambridge Companion to Husserl* (Cambridge and New York: Cambridge University Press).

—— (1999/2004) 'Intentionality Naturalized?', in Bernard Pachoud, Jean Petitot, Jean-Michel Roy, and Francisco Varela (eds.), *Naturalizing Phenomenology: Contemporary Phenomenology and Cognitive Science* (Stanford, Calif.: Stanford University Press). Reprinted in David Woodruff Smith, *Mind World: Essays in Phenomenology and Ontology* (Cambridge and New York: Cambridge University Press).

—— (2000) 'The Background of Propositional Attitudes and Reports Thereof', in K. M. Jaszczolt (ed.), *The Pragmatics of Propositional Attitude Reports.* Current Research in the Semantics/Pragmatics Interface, vol. 4 (Elsevier Science Ltd., Oxford, New York, 2000), 187–209.

—— (2002a) 'What is "Logical" in Husserl's Logical Investigations? The Copenhagen Interpretation', in Dan Zahavi and Frederik Stjernfelt (eds.), *100 Years of Phenomenology: Husserl's Logical Investigations Revisited* (Boston and Dordrecht: Kluwer Academic Publishers, now Springer).

—— (2002b) 'Intentionality and Picturing: Early Husserl vis-à-vis Early Wittgenstein', *Southern Journal of Philosophy* (2002).

—— (2002c) 'Phenomenology', in *Encyclopedia of Cognitive Science* (London: Nature Publishing Group Reference, Macmillan Reference Ltd). [Forthcoming in print and electronic form.]

—— (2003) 'Phenomenology', in *The Stanford Encyclopedia of Philosophy*; CSLI, on-line at http://plato.stanford.edu/.

—— (2004) *Mind World: Essays in Phenomenology and Ontology* (Cambridge and New York: Cambridge University Press).

—— (2004a) 'The Structure of Context and Context-Awareness'. In Lester Embree, editor, *Gurwitsch's Relevancy for Cognitive Science* (Dordrecht and Boston: Springer).

Smith, David Woodruff, and McIntyre, Ronald (1982) *Husserl and Intentionality: A Study of Mind, Meaning, and Language* (Boston and Dordrecht: D. Reidel Publishing Company (now Kluwer Academic Publishers, now Springer)).

Tarski, Alfred (1944/1952) 'The Semantic Conception of Truth', in Leonard Linsky (eds.), *Semantics and the Philosophy of Language.* Urbana: University of Illinois Press. Originally published in *Philosophy and Phenomenological Research* 4 (1944).

Thomasson, Amie L. (2000) 'After Brentano: A One-Level Theory of Consciousness' *The European Journal of Philosophy*, 8/2: 190–209.

—— (2005) 'First-Person Knowledge in Phenomenology' this volume: D. W. Smith and A. L. Thomasson, editors. *Phenomenology and Philosophy of Mind* (Oxford and New York: Oxford University Press).

Wittgenstein, Ludwig. 1953/1997. *Philosophical Investigations*, 2nd edn., trans. G. E. M. Anscombe (Oxford and Malden, Massachusetts: Blackwell Publishers, 1997, first published in German/English in 1953).

Zahavi, Dan (1999) *Self-Awareness and Alterity: A Phenomenological Investigation* (Evanston, Ill.: Northwestern University Press).

5

First-Person Knowledge in Phenomenology

Amie L. Thomasson

Abstract: An account of the source of first-person knowledge is essential not just for phenomenology, but for anyone who takes seriously the apparent evidence that we each have a distinctive access to knowing what we experience. One standard way to account for the source of first-person knowledge is by appeal to a kind of inner observation of the passing contents of one's own mind, and phenomenology is often thought to rely on introspection. I argue, however, that Husserl's method of phenomenological reduction was designed precisely to find a route to knowledge of the structures of consciousness that was *independent* of any appeal to observation of one's own mental states. The goals of this essay are to explicate Husserl's method of phenomenological reduction in contemporary terms that (1) show its distance from all inner-observation accounts, (2) exhibit its kinship to and historical influence on outer-observation accounts of self-knowledge popularized by Sellars, and (3) demonstrate that a contemporary 'cognitive transformation' view based on Husserl's method may provide a viable contribution to contemporary debates about the source of self-knowledge.

There must be some means of first-person access to experience if phenomenology, or any study like it, is to be possible at all.[1] For phenomenology is supposed to provide the basis for a first-person study of the mind, and thus requires some first-person way of acquiring knowledge about mental state types, their contents, and so on. If there is not, then the only possible means of acquiring knowledge of the mind will involve third-person access via external behavioral or physiological studies. Anyone who thinks that phenomenological descriptions have some role to play in philosophy of mind thus owes an account of how such distinctive first-person knowledge can be acquired.

But an account of the source and possibility of a kind of first-person knowledge about our own experiences is not just a theoretic need for those engaged in phenomenology or

Portions of this paper draw on work in my (2003) 'Introspection and Phenomenological Method', *Phenomenology and the Cognitive Sciences* 2: 239–54. Thanks to Kluwer Academic Publishers for kind permission to use this material.

[1] It does not necessarily, however, require that this first-person access yield *infallible* beliefs about our own experience. This is a separate issue, and clearly phenomenology, like so many other studies, could provide knowledge even if it is not an infallible source of knowledge. Nor does it require that we have first-person knowledge of *all* of our own mental states. There may be limits to the scope of such knowledge without it failing to provide useful information in those cases in which it is present.

other first-person approaches to the mind. For there is a great deal of apparent evidence that we have a distinctive first-person knowledge of our own conscious mental states, which any theory of mind must either be able to account for or explain away. It certainly seems that, if I am lying quietly in bed, I can know that I'm thinking about last night's movie even if no external observer would have grounds for knowing this (cf. Siewert 1998: 33–6). Similarly, it seems that we can each have knowledge about our own mental states even when others have reason to believe the *contrary*—we can knowingly lie about and mislead others about our own thoughts, feelings, or experiences (Siewert 1998: 31–2). But it has remained an enduring philosophical puzzle, subject to much recent discussion in analytic philosophy of mind, how this apparent first-person knowledge of our conscious states is possible, and what its source might be.

One standard way to account for this apparent first-person knowledge (which I will call 'introspectionist', following the literal meaning of 'introspection' as a quasi-perceptual way of being spectators of our inner states of mind) has been to posit a special faculty enabling us to observe our inner states, much as perception consists in observation of external states of the world. But such quasi-perceptual methods of introspection have been considered discredited. I will argue that at least to some extent these criticisms are apt, and that such views cannot in any case provide an adequate understanding of self-knowledge.

It is often thought that phenomenological knowledge must be based on an internal inspection of our mental states, and so phenomenology must fall with introspectionism, so conceived (Dennett 1987: 154, 157–8). But does phenomenology really rely on 'using some sort of introspection' (Dennett 1987: 154)? And is there no other way of explaining the source of our apparent first-person knowledge?

I will argue that the answer to both questions is 'no'. Far from relying on inner observation of our mental states, Husserl explicitly rejected introspectionist views of self-knowledge, and developed the method of phenomenological reduction as the route to a very different understanding of the possibility and source of knowledge of our own conscious states. Indeed Husserl's account of phenomenological method bears much more resemblance to accounts of self-knowledge developed by Wilfrid Sellars, Fred Dretske, and Sydney Shoemaker—based in the idea that knowledge of one's own experiences is in some sense based on *outer* observation of the world, rather than a direct *inner* observation of one's own experiences—than to inner observation accounts.[2]

The goals of this essay are both historical and thematic. First, I hope to explicate at least the early stages of Husserl's phenomenological method in a way that makes it clear how different his account is from inner-observation models of self-knowledge, thus showing that it would be completely misguided to dismiss phenomenology with introspectionism. Secondly, I will elucidate the thematic and historical connections between the method of acquiring first-person knowledge Husserl championed in the

---

[2] Certainly these are not the only approaches to self-knowledge. Charles Siewert (2001) develops a different sort of approach to self-knowledge based in the idea that first-person judgments about appearances aren't subject to the same kinds of error as world-oriented judgments are, since correctly classifying one's experience is a precondition for even understanding our expression of judgments about appearances.

phenomenological reduction, and the 'outer observation' accounts popularized by Wilfrid Sellars (among others) in analytic philosophy of mind—thereby setting the historical record straight, showing the relevance phenomenology not only can have but has had to analytic philosophy of mind, and (I hope) providing some insight into both views. Finally, in §4, I will develop what I call the 'Cognitive Transformation' view of self-knowledge, based on Husserl's suggestions about how the phenomenological reduction can work, enabling us to proceed from first-order, world-oriented experience to knowledge about our own intentional conscious states and their ways of presenting the world. Insofar as it is successful, this development may show that not only is Husserl's view not open to easy dismissal; it may provide the basis for a viable contribution to the contemporary debate about the source of first-person knowledge.[3] In closing I will address some challenges that remain for stories like Husserl's about how we could acquire knowledge of our own conscious states.

1. INNER OBSERVATION

One traditional method of accounting for our first-person knowledge of our own mental states is to postulate a faculty that enables us to be 'spectators' of our own inner states, in much the way that perception enables us to be spectators of an external world (Rosenthal 1997: 752 n. 59). As David Armstrong puts it, 'Introspective consciousness . . . is a perception-like awareness of current states and activities in our own mind' (1997: 724). Such inwardly directed observations are higher-order states, since they take our first-order mental states (perceptions, thoughts, desires, etc.) as their objects. The idea that our knowledge of our own mental states is based in inwardly directed observation can then explain the distinctive first-person character of knowledge of our mental states, since in each case this form of observation is possible only for one's own mental states.

Such introspectionist views of the source of self-knowledge thus go quite naturally with higher-order views of consciousness, that take consciousness to consist in those states of which we have a perception-like awareness (Armstrong 1997, Lycan 1997). If a state's being conscious entails that it is the object of a higher-order act of perception-like awareness, and that awareness is capable of providing knowledge of the state, then that would explain how all conscious states may be accessible to a distinctively first-person form of knowledge.

But such higher-order views of consciousness have recently come under attack for a variety of reasons (Thomasson 2000: 198–9), among others that if a state is conscious only if there is a higher-order state that takes it as an object, then we are left with either an infinite regress of higher-order mental states or with the odd situation in which we must postulate a huge number of unconscious mental states for which existence we have no other evidence (Chalmers 1996: 230–1) and which (although they are themselves unconscious) can make other states conscious (Smith 1986: 150). Thus others

---

[3] However, the epistemic project of determining whether or not the apparent self-knowledge so derived has the status of genuine knowledge, incorrigibility, etc., must be left for another occasion.

have attempted to formulate a one-level understanding of consciousness (Siewert 1998, Thomas 1997, Thomasson 2000). But the challenge remains for such one-level views of consciousness to account for how knowledge of our own conscious mental states is derived, if they aren't typically accompanied by higher-order experiences of them (Thomasson 2002a).

One could of course reject the idea that being the object of an introspective state was definitive of consciousness, while retaining the idea that such higher-order observations are nonetheless *frequently* present and provide the basis for our first-person knowledge of those mental states they accompany. But on closer examination, the very idea that we have a distinct higher-order perception-like awareness of (many of) our mental states is hard to make sense of. It seems simply implausible to claim that there is such a higher-order perception-like awareness since such purported pseudo-perceptual states would lack any distinctive qualia of their own (Dretske 1997: 784–5). Indeed such purported states of perception-like awareness seem to lack *any* characteristics that could distinguish them from our mere (conceptual) judgments about our first-order experiences. As Charles Siewert puts it 'The problem I have with this suggestion is that, as far as I can tell, there is no sense in which my experience "appears" some way to me, in which its appearing this way to me is a self-reflexive intentional feature distinct from my thinking or judging it to be some way' (1998: 187–216).

Even if we can make sense of this idea of a pseudo-perceptual observation of our mental states, it is far from clear that it can provide the basis for an acceptable account of self-knowledge. Sydney Shoemaker (1996: 25–49, 201–42) argues that this is an unacceptable view of self-knowledge because (among other reasons) on such a pseudo-perceptual view the link between our higher-order observations and the first-order mental states to which they are directed should be contingent. Just as it is possible that a rational individual with developed visual concepts be blind to all visible objects before her, so (on this view) it should be possible that a rational person with developed concepts of mental states fail to introspectively perceive her own mental states. Yet Shoemaker argues (1996: 30–49) that this is not possible, casting doubt on the whole picture of self-knowledge being based in higher-order perception-like observations of one's own mental states.

These problems with higher-order perception views might be thought to cause problems for phenomenology for two reasons. First, such views have long been associated with the phenomenological tradition from Brentano onwards (Güzeldere 1997: 789), so problems with them might be thought to be problems with phenomenology. Secondly, the practice of phenomenology obviously requires some means of first-person knowledge; without a higher-order introspective perception of them, it is hard to see how any access to our mental states is possible beyond that reachable through third-person behavioral or neurophysiological means.

But despite the common association of phenomenological views with this kind of view, the founders of the phenomenological tradition did not actually endorse the idea that all conscious thoughts are accompanied by a higher-order observation of them. I have argued elsewhere (2000) that, far from providing the beginning of contemporary higher-order views, Brentano actually argued against higher-order conceptions of consciousness and sought to develop a one-level view of consciousness according to which consciousness is intrinsic to those states that possess it, not imposed on them through being objects of other mental states. Brentano does, however, admittedly locate the source of our knowledge of our mental states in a kind of 'inner perception', which he distinguishes from what he calls 'inner observation', based in the fact that the former includes (as he puts it) a 'secondary' presentation built in to the original mental act itself, not a separate 'inner observation' of one act by a separate, higher-order act (1995: 29 and 128–9). Such a view would clearly be superior to higher-order views, if it could be made to work, but unfortunately it is not obvious whether (a) we have reason to think that all conscious states include such secondary presentations of themselves or (b) it is even possible for one and the same state to have both a 'primary object' and a 'secondary object'—and if not, the Brentanian view risks collapsing into a higher-order view after all (Thomasson 2000).[4]

Husserl goes further than Brentano, putting aside the theory that all consciousness is accompanied by an inner perception that takes first-order conscious states as objects, whether this inner perception is considered a separate act of observation or (as Brentano would have it) a secondary awareness built into the first-order act itself. He denies that such inner perception can be a source of infallible knowledge of our own mental states, since as long as our mental acts are taken as real psychological events that become the *objects* of consciousness (whether primary or secondary, higher-order or built-in), the object perceived will be *transcendent* in relation to the perception, with real features that forever outrun any of our experiences of it, and there will be room for inadequacy and error in that perception just as in the perception of 'external' objects. 'Exactly regarded, all psychic phenomena seen in natural or empirical-scientific attitudes are perceived transcendently' (Husserl 1913/2000, 860). Husserl not only rejects inner perception as the basis for infallible knowledge of our mental states, he even doubts that there are such inner perceptions accompanying all our conscious states. He calls Brentano's inner perception view 'a conception fraught with too many grave difficulties' (1913/2000, 543), and emphasizes that such a view remains extrinsic to phenomenology, as long as 'the need to assume the unbroken activity of inner perception cannot be phenomenologically demonstrated' (1913/2000, 543).

Nonetheless, the basic problem remains for anyone who takes seriously our apparent knowledge of our own experiences (even in situations where no outsider would have warrant for beliefs about them), and who hopes to save the possibility of a study of the mental from the first-person perspective: If not by means of a kind of inner perception, how is our apparent first-person knowledge possible at all?

2. OUTER OBSERVATION

An entirely different approach to self-knowledge has occasionally been proposed: that our apparent knowledge of our own mental states is based not in a special observation *of* our mental states, but in awareness at least apparently directed *outwards*, towards

---

[4] See Smith (1986, and 1989: ch. 2) for a neo-Brentanian account of 'inner awareness' that is explicitly distanced from all higher-order accounts.

the world (not towards our own minds).[5] Such is the basic insight of what I will call 'outer-awareness' views, views developed in some form by Wilfrid Sellars, Fred Dretske[6], and Sydney Shoemaker. I will suggest below that this insight also lies at the basis of Husserl's phenomenological method.

In the contemporary tradition, the idea was popularized by Sellars' (1956/2000) attempt to turn on its head the traditional empiricist idea that knowledge of the world is based on knowledge of our sense data, by urging that instead all sense-data talk, and indeed all talk about *appearances* is parasitic on world-talk: 'the concept of *looking green*, the ability to recognize that something *looks green* presupposes the concept of *being green*' (1956/2000: 43). On this view, we learn to employ 'looks' talk when we notice the fallibility of our 'is' talk, particularly in certain circumstances, e.g. as Sellars' mythical tie salesman John learns to shift from 'that tie is green' to 'that tie looks green' when he discovers the fallibility of his color judgments in odd interior lighting. So employing 'looks' talk is a way of withholding the commitment about the world that comes with 'is' talk, while retaining the same propositional content (1956/2000: 50).

But even if we begin from the observation that 'looks' talk arises from 'is' talk about the world, when once we decide to withhold our commitment about how the world *really* is, a critical question remains. Once we have arrived at 'looks' talk by means of this route, should our talk about how things look or appear to us be understood as:

1. Still talking about the world, but doing so non-committally, without making any claims, or:

2. Shifting to make (committing) claims about our experiences rather than the world?

Robert Brandom reads Sellars as holding the former view, that appearance sentences should not be understood as *reporting* any facts or making any claims at all (2000: 139–43). The whole point of appearance talk, on this view, is to *withhold* one's endorsement of claims about the external world, and so when John says 'that tie appears green to me', he should not be understood as making any kind of report, but rather 'evincing a disposition' to say that it *is* green (not even reporting that he has such a disposition) (2000: 139) 'in saying that something *looks* green, one is not endorsing a claim, but *withholding* endorsement from one' (2000: 142).

This sort of view is in fact not a view about the source of our apparent self-knowledge at all, since it denies that apparent claims about how things appear to one are reports that make genuine *claims* at all that could be candidates for knowledge. It is rather an explanation of the source of the *language* of looks-talk and of some of the distinctive features of that language that can be made without appeal to any sensory impressions or other 'inner episodes'. First, it explains the apparent incorrigibility of appearance

<hr />

[5] I'll speak of this as externally directed world-talk, since this is the paradigm case and makes it easy to speak of the difference (and relation) between experience of the world and knowledge about our experience. Everything that I say below, however, regarding the acquisition of experience-knowledge from world-oriented experience also goes for knowledge about our experiences that may be directed towards our own mental states or those of others.

[6] For critical discussion of Dretske's 'displaced perception' view of introspection, see Aydede (2002) and Bach (1997).

reports (and of first-person knowledge generally), since one cannot be wrong if one is not making a claim at all (though of course one cannot be *right* either, and so the claim that such appearance statements represent infallible knowledge *of* something would have to be dropped, if they are considered not to be reports at all). Second, it would also explain the impropriety of iterating looks-talk: It makes little sense to move from 'x looks red' to 'x looks like it looks red', since the commitment is already withheld in the initial move from 'x is red' to 'x looks red', as Brandom puts it 'There is no further withholding work for the second "looks" to do. There is nothing left to take back' (2000: 142).

But although I think there's something right about the idea that looks-talk derives from is-talk, and despite the above virtues of the view as Brandom describes it, several problems arise for the view that appearance talk does not make any claims, not even about one's own experience (or dispositions), but merely withholds endorsements from claims about the world. One problem Brandom mentions himself (attributing it to Joe Camp) is that certain uses of 'looks' talk, as in 'that looks blurry to me', involve terms such as 'blurry' that apply only to representations, not the world, and so can't plausibly be held to be merely describing the world non-committally (rather than describing appearances committally) (2000: 143–4 n. 11). Some other story will have to be told about how 'looks' talk functions in these cases.

A more general problem is that we can make statements about how things appear to *other* people (that chair looks green to John), and here we clearly are not merely evincing some disposition of *ours*.[7] Such statements are pretty clearly descriptions, which may be right or wrong. We may be reporting on a disposition of his, but then we end up with a strangely disjunctive analysis of appearance statements: those in the first person are not making any reports at all, those in the third person are making reports about someone else's disposition. And if we have such a disjunctive analysis, then it seems (implausibly) that, while I can make claims about how things appear to John, John cannot correct me, for his apparent counter-statement 'no, it doesn't look green to me, it looks blue to me' is making no claim at all.

Perhaps the most telling problem for the no-commitment interpretation of all appearance talk is that we can *lie* about how things appear to us. Not wanting glasses, a child can lie and say the letters appear sharp to her when they appear blurry; an *unscrupulous* tie salesman can lie and say a certain tie looks blue to him (and thus should match perfectly) when it looks green to him; a person going deaf but desiring to keep that secret can say the television sounds loud and clear to him when he can barely make it out. Of course Brandom's Sellars could say that such individuals are being insincere by 'faking' their evincing of a disposition (as one might by saying 'ouch' when nothing hurt), but mere insincerity is not enough to capture the normal idea that these are *lies*, since a lie must be an insincere *and false* claim made with the intention to deceive others. If any appearance statement could, in principle, be a lie, such statements must be making *claims* about *something*, although it is clear that such statements are not making, but rather avoiding making, claims about the world.

---

[7] This point was suggested to me by Charles Siewert.

While the 'no commitment' view of looks talk endorsed by Brandom's Sellars may have resources to respond to each of these problems individually, the very fact that it needs to offer a disjunctive analysis of talk about things looking blurry versus looking green, and of talk about appearances from the first- and third-person perspectives, combined with the need to refigure apparent data about the possibility of lying, suggest that taking looks talk as non-committal has serious costs—costs that, perhaps, only seem worth paying to those with other motivations for avoiding all talk of appearances or experiences. We may be able to offer a more uniform theory that better fits the pre-theoretic data by simply allowing that appearance statements involve a shift from talking about the world (especially or originally when our confidence about the world is undermined or put aside) to make (committing) claims about something else—our own experiences.

In fact, contrary to Brandom's interpretation, it does not seem that Sellars himself would deny that looks reports do involve commitment to certain claims, though the relevant claims, naturally, would be claims about one's own *experience*, not the world. He glosses his own view as follows: ' "x looks red to S" has the sense of "S has an experience which involves in a unique way the idea *that x is red* and involves it in such a way that if this idea were true, the experience would correctly be characterized as seeing that x is red." ' (1956/2000: 49). Similarly, while he argues vehemently against the idea of, e.g. red, triangular sense-data as the objects of 'immediate awareness' that provide the basis for knowledge of red, triangular things in the world, Sellars does not deny the existence of the relevant experiences or sensations, otherwise conceived, nor does he deny that there are legitimate forms of language that do involve making claims about them. As he says, this:

does not imply that private sensations or impressions may not be essential to the formation of these associative connections [between the word 'red' and red physical objects]. For one can certainly admit that the tie between 'red' and red physical objects—which tie makes it possible for 'red' to mean the quality red—is *causally* mediated by sensations of red without being committed to the mistaken idea that it is 'really' sensations of red, rather than red physical objects, which are the primary denotation of the word 'red'.   (1956/2000: 64)

In the end, Sellars introduces the myth of Jones (1956/2000: 102–17) as a way of showing how talk of visual sense impressions (e.g.) may be introduced as a kind of *theoretic* talk of 'unobserved' episodes. According to the 'theory' championed by Jones, these impressions are supposed to be the (normal) effect of physical objects and processes impinging on our eyes, and are supposed to explain our overt verbal behavior, as well to explain why it sometimes looks to me as if there is a red object over there. But although it is introduced as theoretic talk, it is nonetheless ontologically committal talk about states of individual perceivers; like electrons, sense impressions are unobserved, but postulated on the basis of observations that they are used to explain (1956/2000: 104).

So while Sellars holds that statements about how things appear are ultimately derived not from a kind of pseudo-perceptual inspection of our own mental states or sense-data, but rather from withholding commitment about how the world is, ultimately he seems to acknowledge that appearance statements can be committal statements providing knowledge about something else: our own mental states.

3. PHENOMENOLOGICAL REDUCTION

The fundamental and revolutionary Sellarsian idea that knowledge of one's own mental states is based in outer-awareness of the world—while withholding commitment regarding its real existence and nature—is the centerpiece of Edmund Husserl's method of phenomenological reduction, developed more than forty years earlier. Indeed Husserl regarded the phenomenological reduction as his greatest discovery (Moran 2000: 12), for it was the method that was supposed to provide the route to acquiring knowledge in his new field of phenomenology.

The resemblance between Sellars' account of self-knowledge and Husserl's phenomenological method is not likely to be pure coincidence. As Sellars writes in his 'Autobiographical Reflections', as a young teaching assistant in Buffalo he was introduced to Husserl's work by Husserl's own student, Marvin Farber. He writes of Farber, 'His combination of utter respect for the structure of Husserl's thought with the equally firm conviction that this structure could be given a naturalistic interpretation was undoubtedly a key influence on my own subsequent philosophical strategy' (1975: 283). Unlike many in the analytic tradition,[8] Sellars did not see the work of phenomenology as separate from the conceptual analysis characterizing analytic philosophy, writing 'for longer than I care to remember I have conceived of philosophical analysis (and synthesis) as akin to phenomenology' (1978: 170). Moreover, Sellars elsewhere (1978, 170 and 1963/1991, 5; cf. Huemer forthcoming) makes repeated references to the Husserlian idea of 'bracketing', or withholding the natural commitments that our experiences are veridical (see below), which is the core of Husserl's method of phenomenological reduction. For example, in *Science, Perception and Reality*, Sellars writes that in speaking of the manifest and scientific images 'I do not mean to deny to either or both of them the status of "reality". I am, to use Husserl's term, "bracketing" them, transforming them from ways of experiencing the world into objects of philosophical reflection and evaluation' (1963/1991: 5).

There are of course substantial differences in the goals and contexts in which Husserl develops the phenomenological reduction, and those in which Sellars discusses appearance talk. Husserl is primarily concerned with developing a method practitioners can follow to enable them to acquire knowledge in phenomenology—not even with offering a theoretic account of how such knowledge is possible, though obviously the acceptability of the method presupposes that some account is available of how the method proposed could provide phenomenological knowledge. Sellars, on the other hand, is concerned to offer a philosophical account of the role of appearance talk in (especially world-oriented) empirical knowledge (and whether appearances can provide a 'given' that can form the basis for empirical knowledge). So in fact neither is primarily focused on providing a philosophical account of the basis for possible first-person knowledge. Nonetheless, strikingly similar accounts can be drawn out of their work.

---

[8] With the important discussion of Ryle, who arguably arrived at the idea that conceptual analysis is or should be the core project of philosophy based at least in part on his study of the work of Brentano and Husserl. See my (2002b).

Much as it was his loss of confidence in his own color judgments that brought Sellars' John to shift from talk about ties to talk about how things *look* or *appear* to him, so it is adopted as a general method by Husserl that to enable us to shift to consider *phenomena*, our ways of consciously and intentionally representing the world, rather than simply considering the world, we must bracket the assumption that our judgments are true, our experiences veridical:

When objects are intuited, thought of, theoretically pondered on, and thereby given to us as actualities in certain ontic modalities, we must direct our theoretical interest away from such objects, not posit them as realities as they appear or hold in the intentions of our acts ... We must keep out the falsifying intrusion of all assertions based on the naïve acceptance and assessment of objects, whose existence has been posited in the acts now receiving phenomenological treatment.   (1913/2000: 255–6)

There are also, however, some important differences between Sellars' observation that 'looks' talk arises from 'is' talk (allowing that we may ultimately gain knowledge about how things seem to us by observing the world and withholding commitment) and Husserl's recommendation of the phenomenological method as a way of acquiring phenomenological knowledge. First, Sellars' John makes the move to looks talk when he has some positive reason for doubting his world-oriented judgments (such as odd lighting). But for Husserl, employing the phenomenological reduction (as he repeatedly emphasizes) does not presuppose or entail any reason for *doubting* one's world-oriented experience, and in fact subjecting experiences to the reduction should not be considered a form of *doubting* them at all. If it were a matter of something like Cartesian doubt, then the phenomenological reduction would inevitably *change* the character (or force) of the original act to be studied, e.g. by altering the experienced *conviction that* P, to an experience of *doubting that* P, and thus alter the very phenomenon we sought to describe. While we might still be able to examine the content (that P), this would make it impossible in principle for such a method to provide insight into the force (or what Husserl calls 'thetic character') of mental states, since that would be transformed by the study itself.

Instead, phenomenological reduction is based in the method of 'bracketing' (*Einklammerung*), which:

is not a transformation of the thesis into its antithesis, of positive into negative; it is also not a transformation into presumption, suggestion, indecision, doubt (in one or another sense of the word); such shifting indeed is not at our free pleasure. *Rather it is something quite unique. We do not abandon the thesis we have adopted, we make no change in our conviction*, which remains in itself what it is so long as we do not introduce new motives of judgment, which we precisely refrain from doing. And yet the thesis undergoes a modification—whilst remaining in itself what it is, *we set it as it were 'out of action,' we 'disconnect it,' 'bracket it.'* It still remains there like the bracketed in the bracket, like the disconnected outside the connexional system ...   (1913/1962: 97–8)

The use of the typographical term 'bracketing' is far from accidental, for it is rather like putting a linguistic assertion, command, question, etc. in quotation marks, to be studied as a piece of language rather than believed, followed, answered—but which leaves its force as well as its content intact to be studied, once it is placed in quotation marks. In fact, Husserl elsewhere explicitly draws out the parallels between the bracketing involved in phenomenological reduction, and the use of quotation marks in language, writing:

It is clear that all *these* descriptive statements [about the contents of perceptual acts], though very similar in sound to statements concerning reality, have undergone a *radical* modification of meaning... 'In' the reduced perception... we find, as belonging to its essence indissolubly, the perceived as such, and under such titles as 'material thing,' 'plant,' 'tree,' 'blossoming,' and so forth. The *inverted commas* are clearly significant; they express that change of signature, the corresponding radical modification of the meaning of the words.   (1913/1962: 240)[9]

By placing a sentence in quotation marks, its force is not transformed from an assertion to a question, but rather it (force and content) is placed before us as an object of linguistic study, rather than remaining part of our living interaction with the world used to make utterances, issue commands, or pose questions. So similarly, the idea of bracketing in phenomenology is to preserve both force and content of the original experience (whether it is one involving conviction, doubt, etc.), but use the brackets to disconnect it from our ordinary world-directed concern so that it can be studied as a *phenomenon*, a way of experiencing the world, rather than being put to use in our engagement with the world: 'The thesis is experience as lived (*Erlebnis*), *but we make "no use" of it*' (1913/1962: 98).

A second difference between Sellars' and Husserl's accounts is that, for Sellars' John, looks-talk arises in quite limited spheres—on those occasions where there is some room for doubting one's original experience. But Husserl employs the phenomenological bracketing or 'epoché' with a much broader scope—we are to bracket not just this or that individual thesis about the world represented in experience, but rather to bracket all at once the whole 'natural' view that there is a mind-external natural world of spatio-temporal, physical, biological, and cultural entities experienced by me:

We put out of action the general thesis which belongs to the essence of the natural standpoint, we place in brackets whatever it includes respecting the nature of Being: this entire natural world therefore which is continually 'there for us', 'present to our hand,' and will ever remain there, is a 'fact-world' of which we continue to be conscious, even though it pleases us to put it in brackets. If I do this... I do not then deny this 'world', as though I were a sophist, I do not doubt that it is there as though I were a sceptic; but I use the 'phenomenological' epoché, which completely bars me from using any judgment that concerns spatio-temporal existence.   (1913/1962: 99–100)

The fact that this bracketing is wholesale in scope is crucial, since it can thereby aim to enable us to grasp the full character of our phenomena: not just 'individual' mental states (which in fact are never entirely separate from each other), but such broader features as the field of consciousness as a whole, the unity of consciousness, the implicit background in conscious experiences, time-consciousness, etc.

The most crucial difference between Husserl and the Sellars *of Brandom's interpretation* (seemingly different from the historical Sellars), however, is that for

---

[9] For further discussion of the idea of 'quotation' of the content (noema) of an experience, see Smith (1971).

Husserl the withholding of world-regarding commitment is not the end of the story, but rather is supposed to provide the means for acquiring a whole new branch of knowledge: knowledge about experience and its ways of representing (or intending) the world.[10] The goal of the phenomenological reduction is '*the winning of a new region of Being*... the Being to be thus shown up is neither more nor less than that which we refer to on essential grounds as "pure experiences" "pure consciousness" ' (1913/1962: 101). It is consciousness, or conscious experience, that remains 'left-over' after the bracketing of phenomenological reduction, and so it is that reduction that enables us to turn from our customary interest in the world represented to gain knowledge about consciousness itself and the ways in which it represents an external world to us: '*Consciousness itself has a being of its own which in its absolute uniqueness of nature remains unaffected by the phenomenological disconnexion*. It therefore remains over as a "*phenomenological residuum*," as a region of Being which is in principle unique, and can become in fact the field of a new science—the science of Phenomenology' (1913/1962: 102).

It is important to note that it is knowledge of consciousness in this full-blooded sense as *intentional* that is the target of Husserl's phenomenological method—he seeks knowledge of how we *represent* or *constitute* the world and its features in our experience, not knowledge of mere sensory qualia (1913/1962: 226–30). In fact according to Husserl, experiences to be considered by phenomenology have both a 'material' or sensuous/qualitative component, and a 'formal' or 'noetic' component, which 'animates' and 'bestows meaning on' the sensory stratum, making the experience intentional (1913/1962: 226–7). Of these, 'the incomparably more important and fruitful analyses belong to the noetical [intentional] side' (1913/1962: 230). I will return in Section 4 below to discuss the problem of knowledge of mere sensory qualia.

Ultimately, it is not knowledge of my or anyone's *individual* conscious experiences that Husserl hopes to acquire through phenomenology, but rather of the *essences* of *types* of conscious experience and their interrelations. Thus Husserl follows the first stage of world bracketing with a second stage of phenomenological reduction: Bracketing also the question of the real existence of my (or anyone's) individual experiences *qua* individual occurrences to focus instead on the relevant *essences* involved.[11] In the remainder of this essay, however, I will focus just on the first stage of reduction, as this is most immediately relevant to answering our central question of what the source could be for our apparent first-person knowledge of our own experiences.

According to Husserl, the method of bracketing is supposed to reduce our mental acts to their *intentional content* and intentional mode or force—that is the sense in which the method involves a 'reduction'. Thus phenomenological method is based on a *shift of attitude* within our experiences: regarding them merely as *appearances*,

---

[10] As I have argued above, it seems that the historical Sellars actually allows that we may talk committally about, and acquire knowledge of, mental states themselves (thus agreeing with Husserl). Nonetheless, Sellars' idea that talk of these states is introduced as a kind of *theoretic* talk analogous to the talk of the theoretical posits of the natural sciences is apparently un-Husserlian.

[11] The account of phenomenological method given here follows that in the second edition of the *Logical Investigations* and *Ideas*. Husserl's exposition of the method varies, and other stages of the reduction are described in later Husserlian texts.

as *representing contents*, rather than simply *using* them to acquire information about the world. This method may potentially be applied to any first-order conscious state (though in fact we often do not apply them), and so potentially can provide self-knowledge of any such state by 'modifying' it in reflection (1913/1962: 106–7), to enact 'a shifting of the glance from something we are conscious of objectively to the subjective consciousness of it' (1913/1962: 201):

every variety of '*reflexion*' has the character of a *modification of consciousness*, and indeed of such a modification as every consciousness can, in principle, experience.

    We speak of modifications here just in so far as every reflexion has its essential origin in changes of standpoint, whereby a given experience or unreflective experience-datum undergoes a certain transformation—into the mode, that is, of reflective consciousness... *Every* experience can now be translated in accordance with essential laws into reflective modifications... (1913/1962: 200–1)

But what are these modifications in standpoint, these transformations, effected by bracketing, that can bring me from experience of the world to apparent knowledge of something else entirely—the intentional structures of my own conscious states? The first thing to emphasize is that they are *not* a matter of acquiring additional empirical information via further experiences; instead, they are based in *a priori* 'essential laws' regarding the *essences* of the kinds of experience involved:

We must, however, be quite clear on this point that *there is no question here of a relation between a psychological event—called experience (Erlebnis)—and some other real existent (Dasein)—called Object*—or of a *psychological connexion* obtaining between the one and the other *in objective reality*. On the contrary, we are concerned with experiences in their essential purity, with *pure essences*, and with that which is *involved in* the essence '*a priori*' in *unconditioned necessity*... In the very essence of an experience lies determined not only *that*, but also *whereof* it is a consciousness, and in what determinate or indeterminate sense it is this.   (1913/1962: 108)

So we are looking for general *a priori* laws governing these 'essences' of experiences, which enable us to shift from world-oriented experience to a reflective knowledge of our own mental states.

    These laws seem, quite generally, to be what Husserl would call 'logical' laws describing the essential connections among the concepts involved—and revealing them is closely allied to what would later be called 'conceptual analysis'. (Husserl understands logic not merely in terms of a system of formal syntactic operations, but also as encompassing relations among concepts or meaning types.) Indeed as I have argued elsewhere (2002b), the form of conceptual analysis of mental state types that Ryle popularized and practiced is a direct development of the work on the 'essences' of types of conscious state developed by Husserl and earlier by Brentano.

    Husserl says less than one might hope about exactly what these laws are and how the relevant transformations work, but his remarks and practice will provide the basis for an answer. Consider the following passage:

It is an *essential insight*... that, from the objectively given, as such, a reflective glance can be transferred to the object-giving consciousness and its subject; from the perceived, the corporeally 'there' to the perceiving act; from the remembered, as it 'hovers' before us as such, as 'having been,' to the remembering; from the statement as it comes from the given content to the stating activity, and so forth . . . It is evident that essentially . . . it is only though reflexions of this kind that such a thing as consciousness or conscious content . . . can become known.   (1913/1962: 209–10)

These remarks suggest that it is part of the very idea of experiences of these sorts that a certain cognitive transition is permitted from represented to representation, and that the shift from consideration of objects known to the representing consciousness parallels a shift one can make from the 'content' of a statement to the 'stating activity'. Indeed '*Every* experience can now be translated in accordance with essential laws into reflective modifications' (1913/1962: 201).

The 'essential laws' enabling us to transform first-order, world-oriented experiences, to knowledge of our own mental states, involve licenses to move from intending (or 'meaning') a certain object or state of affairs (e.g. the blooming pear tree) to intending (or 'meaning') the experience that enabled us to intend it (1913/1962: 240–1). In the section that follows I will attempt to draw out a story in contemporary terms to elucidate how such transformations might work. While the terms of discussion are not Husserl's own, the exposition is intended as a way of showing (perhaps more clearly than Husserl's own words can in the contemporary context) how such a method of phenomenology may provide a source for least a great deal of apparent first-person knowledge without adverting to any pseudo-perceptual observations of experience.[12] The logical transitions will be easiest to see if we separate them out into two steps (not explicitly distinguished by Husserl), and if we begin not directly with the transition from (e.g.) the perceived to the perceiving act, but rather from the case Husserl himself acknowledges as parallel: the transition from a statement to stating activity.

4. THE COGNITIVE TRANSFORMATION VIEW

Suppose someone states 'Bonnie is on the train'. Normally, in our 'lived' experience, such a claim directs our attention to the state of affairs represented, involving Bonnie and the train, and we are unconcerned with the meaning or force of the claim itself. It can, however, happen, e.g. in cases where some doubt arises about the trustworthiness of the reporter, that we shift our attention, and retreat to note only that Bob stated that Bonnie is on the train. Much the same retreat to explicitly noting the representational content and force of the original claim occurs in cases where the truth of the claim is not actually relevant or in question—e.g. when it appears in a work of literary fiction, a critic may be concerned not with Bonnie and the train (both of which are acknowledgedly fictional), but rather with the fact that *according to the story* Bonnie is on the train. Similarly, in cases of testimony in court, the retreat must be made— whether or not there is any positive reason for doubting the witness—to suspend judgment on the truth of the claim, and consider only the fact that, according to the witness, Bonnie was on the train.

---

[12] Despite its fundamental similarity to the Sellarsian account, I do not intend to imply that the Cognitive Transformation view below is an exposition of Sellars or a view he would have endorsed.

Cognitive transformations that take us from the original *use* of a *basic* sentence ('Bonnie is on the train') to a *transformed* sentence expressly *about* what is asserted, questioned, commanded, etc. ('It was stated that Bonnie is on the train'), I will call 'reductive' transformations, since they involve reducing the claims made in the original use of the sentence to claims merely about its representational content and mode. This kind of transformation is widely used in discussions of works of fiction, of the content of failed theories, of testimony, etc. in which transformations are made from the relevant pretense of asserting things about people (in the fiction case), or attempts to assert truths about the world (in the case of theory or testimony), to discuss what is true *according to* the story, theory, or witness. We can then talk about what was stated *according to* the witness while being entirely noncommittal on whether the witness was speaking the truth. In all of these cases, the retreat from the use of the statement to the description of the stating activity preserves us from certain sorts of error: 'It was asserted that (or according to the story, or witness) Bonnie was on the train' does not rely for its truth on any claims about Bonnie or the train (nor even about there being such individuals). So we move to what is at least a more secure epistemological ground, protected from certain kinds of error to which the original claim was subject.

There is an intimate logical[13] relationship between the basic and transformed sentence—namely that the appropriate *use* of the original world-oriented sentence is logically sufficient to guarantee the *truth* of the latter sentence. According to the rules of use of the concept *stated*, Bob's assertion 'Bonnie is on the train' provides logically sufficient conditions for it to be true that 'It was stated that Bonnie is on the train' (though not for 'Bonnie is on the train' to be true). Such transformations have two aspects: The content (Bonnie is on the train) is transformed into a proposition (that Bonnie is on the train), and the force (stated) is extracted from the *way* in which the proposition is presented in the basic sentence (in this case assertion). A different, say, questioning expression of the same propositional content in the basic sentence 'Bonnie is on the train?' would license transformation (ultimately) to 'it was asked whether Bonnie is on the train'.

Reductive transformations may be subjected in turn to hypostatizing transformations, so that we can move in the first instance from 'Bonnie is on the train' to 'it was stated that Bonnie is on the train' to nominalize 'stated' and get 'the statement that Bonnie is on the train was made'.[14] While the basic sentence mentioned only Bonnie and a train, at this stage we clearly have introduced a singular term for a kind of thing not mentioned in the original sentence (a statement), where that singular term is

---

[13] Again, in something like Husserl's broad use of 'logic'.

[14] The discussion here parallels in certain respects Stephen Schiffer's (1990, 1994, 1996) work on pleonastic transformations yielding terms for events, states, fictional characters, etc. But it is important to note that, although the singular term 'the statement' was derived through these hypostatizing transformations, this should not give us the slightest inclination to think that statements don't really exist, aren't to be taken ontologically seriously, or aren't *really* anything different than people and trains. In Thomasson (2001) I argue that the general move from noting that a certain term is pleonastically derivable to treating its referent as being language-created or having an ontologically reduced status is not successful.

apparently guaranteed to refer, given the original use of the basic sentence.[15] These transformations, similarly, seem to be licensed by the logical relations among the concepts involved: Part of possessing the concept of 'statement' is being able to make the hypostatizing move from 'x stated that P' to 'the statement that P was made', and to recognize that move as irreproachable when made by others.

As Husserl remarked, the shift one can make from the 'content' of a statement to the 'stating activity' parallels the cognitive shift from consideration of objects known to the representing consciousness.[16] In fact, I think that these cognitive transformations we have seen in the case of language (from statement to stating activity), also apply to experiences, and can provide a way to understand and explain the relevant cognitive transitions Husserl spoke of as forming the basis for phenomenological method, and for understanding how certain forms of self-knowledge may come about without requiring an introspective observation of our experiences.

Knowledge of our own experiences, their contents, and representational modes, it seems, is achieved by transforming our original world-oriented experience by means of both a reductive and a hypostatizing cognitive transformation. We begin with the performance or 'use' of experiences, in which they are normally simply employed in our activities of understanding and interacting with the world. The first transformative stage involves a reductive transformation from these experiences that present the world as being a certain way, to judgments about how things seem to me, i.e. from being visually presented with a red apple, to making the judgment 'it appears as if there is a red apple'. As in the linguistic case, these transformations are licensed by the logical connections between the use or performance of the original conscious act and the conditions of satisfaction for applying a term such as 'appears', which are guaranteed to be fulfilled given the original apple-oriented experience. Understanding such relations, and being able to make the move from visual presentation of a state of affairs that P to claiming 'it appears that P' is at least in part constitutive of competent possession of the concept *appears*.

But *pace* Brandom's Sellars, the derivation of 'appears' talk from 'is' talk (or *appearance* judgments from *is* judgments) does not mean that we should take such statements as merely revoking commitments about the world without making any new claims. There are implicit claims already in the reductively transformed sentences about the way things appear to us—commitments that may be made explicit by engaging in a separate hypostatizing transformation from talk (or judgment) about

---

[15] While the examples I have treated so far are linguistic, they appear to be instances of a quite general license to make a cognitive shift from a represented entity to talk about the *representation* as such. Similar transformations are also licensed, e.g., from a pictured woman in a hat in a photograph, to the judgment that there is a photographic representation as of a woman in a hat (again, one that can be made without prejudging the facts in a courtroom, and shifts the subject of discussion from the be-hatted woman to the photographic image), or from (apparent) observation of people in movies to discussion of the visual presentation in the movie, and what is the case according to it.

[16] Sellars also notes a parallel between the ability to talk about what statements of various sorts *mean* and the acquisition of mental concepts: 'For characteristic of thoughts is their *intentionality, reference*, or *aboutness*, and it is clear that semantic talk about the meaning or reference of verbal expressions has the same structure as mentalistic discourse concerning what thoughts are about' (1956/2000: 93).

how things appear to be, to talk (or judgment) explicitly about appearances.[17] As in the linguistic case, the reductive transformation can be subjected in turn to a hypostatizing transformation, so from 'it appears as if there is a red apple' we can get 'there is an appearance as-if of a red apple' or 'there is a red-apple-appearance'. By this route, we acquire a singular term for a new kind of entity—in this case an appearance—not mentioned in the original experience (which was only about an apple). And again in this case, the singular term so derived is guaranteed to refer to the newly named kind of entity (an appearance), whether or not the original experience was veridical. Part of possessing the concept of *appearance* is knowing that one may legitimately make the hypostatizing inference from 'it appears that P' to 'there is an appearance as-if P'. These later hypostatizing transformations are what enable us to speak (or think) of appearances, experiences, etc. as the subjects of our sentences, and thus to acquire knowledge about our own experiences and their contents based on what were originally thoughts, experiences, etc. directed outwards towards the world.[18] Together, these reductive and hypostatizing cognitive transformations can help explain how it was that Husserl thought the phenomenological method of bracketing could enable us to acquire knowledge of a 'new region of Being'—that of consciousness and its ways of representing the world (including appearances, thoughts, etc.)—based in first-order world-oriented experience, the practice of bracketing, and competent deployment of the relevant experience concepts.[19]

A difficulty commonly raised for outer-observation accounts of self-knowledge is that, even if they can provide a story about how we can know the *content* of our experiences, they inevitably leave out the mode or force of those experiences, so we cannot know whether we are believing, doubting, or entertaining the proposition that P, or seeing, hearing, or smelling P. This is why understanding the bracketing properly is important—as not involving a change in the original mode or force of the experience (e.g. from one of belief to doubt), but rather simply placing the force 'out of action' by setting it in typographical marks for examination *as* a way of presenting (e.g. affirming) the proposition that P rather than doubting what is presented. Just as the linguistic case involved transforming both the content of the original speech-act and its mode (whether as asserting, questioning, doubting, etc. that Bonnie is on the train),

---

[17] And just as the derivation of the term 'statement' gave us no reason to think that there aren't *really* (in an ontologically robust sense) statements, so similarly, the fact that we can arrive at experience terms through these kinds of cognitive transformation gives us no reason to think that there *really* aren't experiences, or that these are somehow ontologically 'deflated' or reducible to the entities represented.

[18] This is an idea Sellars seems to just notice, but not develop, as he writes in describing how Jones could train people to reliable non-inferentially report on their own sense impressions: 'Notice that the evidence for theoretical statements in the language of impressions will include such introspectible inner episodes *its looking to one as though there were a red and triangular physical object over there*, as well as overt behavior' (1956/2000: 115).

[19] This account bears some resemblance to Shoemaker's account of self-knowledge as supervening on first-order beliefs and desires, plus rationality and possession of the relevant concepts (1996: 34). They differ somewhat, however, e.g. in the elucidation of the cognitive transformations involved, and in the fact that the Husserlian account does not entail that there is any (even tacit) self-knowledge in cases in which the relevant transformations are not *explicitly* undertaken by people competently possessing the relevant concepts, and so does not include a self-intimation thesis for any mental states.

so transformations from experience involve transforming both the *content* of the original experience into the *represented as such*, and the *way* in which the original experience did the representing (e.g. whether as visual, auditory, or tactile experience).

Thus far I have dealt directly only with the case of how we can each know how things *appear* to us, but perceptual appearances are of course only one variety of experience, and ultimately we would like a unified account of how one can also acquire first-person knowledge of one's own beliefs, intentions, desires, etc. Although space constraints prevent a complete discussion here, it is clear how at least some of these can be handled in ways parallel to our handling of appearances above. Thus, e.g. the thought 'today is Wednesday' (apparently speaking about the day) may be transformed reductively to 'I believe today is Wednesday', from which a hypostatizing transformation can yield apparent knowledge that 'I have the belief that today is Wednesday'. The self-command 'pick up the car at four' (with content concerning the car) may be transformed reductively (in this case, bracketing whether or not the car really will be picked up at four) to 'I intend to pick up the car at four' and hypostatized to provide apparent knowledge that 'I have the intention of picking up the car at four'. Learning to make such transformations competently is arguably part of acquiring the relevant concepts of appearance, belief, intention, etc., just as learning to make the parallel linguistic transitions is part of acquiring the concepts of statement, question, command, etc.

As I have presented it, first-person knowledge is based not in a separate (pseudo)-perception of one's mental states, but rather in cognitive transitions based on 'essential laws' governing the concepts involved. In the case of reductive transformations, it is laws connecting the *performance* of a certain conscious act (or *use* of a certain expression) with the concepts of experiences or speech acts of different types. In the case of hypostatizing transformations, it is laws connecting the concepts associated with verbs like 'appears', 'states', and 'thinks', with their nominalized forms referring to appearances, statements, and thoughts. These transitions together, I have argued, are what enable us to move wholesale from world-oriented experience to discussion of the 'new region' of entities (experiences) that are the subject of phenomenology.

These are not, however, the sole source of phenomenological knowledge, for once we are working with experience-concepts, other essential relations among these may become evident. Thus, e.g. as Husserl notes, there are such 'essential connexions' between the propositions 'I remember [seeing] A' and 'I have perceived A' (1913/1962: 201)—as we might say, the first logically entails the second, since the very concept of (visual) remembering requires, as part of its conditions of satisfaction, that the state of affairs remembered by someone have been perceived by her. Similarly, as Husserl often points out, the very idea of *experiencing something as* a physical object involves experiencing it *as* in principle outrunning any experience of it.[20] The fact that these logical interrelations among mental concepts play a crucial role throughout

---

[20] Strictly speaking, Husserl tends to put the point more in terms of connections among the *essences of experiences* of certain types (corresponding to the connections among concepts of experiences of those types) than in terms of connections among *concepts* or *ideas*. I do not think, however, that such distinctions play a crucial role here.

Husserl's phenomenology lends additional credence to the idea that it is similar logical relations that are used to get us up to discussion of the phenomenological level in the first place (though the first stage must involve relations between lived experiences and concepts, not just among concepts).

Another question that might be raised for the above model is how we can acquire knowledge, not just that P is being believed, but rather that *I* believe that P: How does the *self* get into self-knowledge on this account? This, again, I think is based in unraveling the logical presuppositions behind the original world-oriented experiences.[21] The 'I', as it can be known phenomenologically, is logically presupposed by the experiences so known: 'The "being directed towards," "the being busied with," "adopting an attitude," "undergoing or suffering from," has this *of necessity* wrapped in its very essence, that it is just something "from the Ego," or in the reverse direction "to the Ego"; and this Ego is the *pure* ego' (Husserl 1913/1962: 214).

But so known, the 'I' logically presupposed by experiences is simply the 'pure' Ego, myself *qua* bearer of these experiences, not myself *qua* actual human being in the world. Whether or not one agrees that such an 'I' is logically presupposed (an issue that cannot be treated here), it is at least clear that here, as elsewhere, the 'I' is introduced not through a direct self-acquaintance nor any empirical observations, but rather through what Husserl considers 'logical' (conceptual) entailments between the very idea of experiences, and the very idea of an experiencing pure Ego.

5. ADVANTAGES AND REMAINING CHALLENGES

This account of the source of our apparent first-person knowledge can explain several apparent features of that knowledge without averting to any sort of introspective pseudo-perceptual observation of one's own experiences. It can, for example, explain our apparent first-person privilege with respect to knowledge of our own experiences, and how we can lie to others about these. While speech acts such as statements are *public* representations, so that anyone is licensed to make the relevant shift from x's stating, 'Bonnie is on the train' to speak of 'x's statement that Bonnie is on the train', the original world-oriented experiences from which self-knowledge claims are transformed are not public in this way, and so it is only the individual having the experience who is in a position to make the transformation from the original world-oriented thought or perception to draw direct conceptual conclusions about the nature of her experience.

Others can only acquire more or less probable inferential knowledge based on observations of behavior and environment, and in cases where this is insufficient to draw conclusions they may remain completely in ignorance about the mental states that the subject can know by means of these simple conceptual transformations.

---

[21] This seems to be the sense in which phenomenological knowledge of ourselves and our experiences is *transcendental* rather than empirical knowledge, on Husserl's account, as he particularly emphasizes in his later work, e.g. the *Crisis*. For a compelling contemporary account of knowledge of ourselves and the nature of our experiences as transcendental, see Mark Rowlands (2003).

This explains how lies about one's own experience are possible, and why we have the potential for fooling outside observers. For since one must begin these transformations from one's own experience, a lie is simply a case in which one willingly casts aside the normal transformation rules and makes claims about one's own experience (that the television sounds loud and clear to me) not based on transformations from the way the world is presented (the television being presented as noisy) but based, say, on a desire to hide one's hearing impairment. Others lacking the original experience cannot detect the lie by noting the falsified transformation; they can at best infer a falsehood by noting inconsistencies between the subject's verbal reports and behavior.

The apparent infallibility of statements about one's own experiences, thoughts, etc. can be explained by the fact that transformed sentences about experiences, such as 'I have an appearance as-of a red apple'—as long as they are appropriately derived from the original experiences—may be true whether or not the original world-oriented perception (presenting a red apple) was veridical, and so are protected from certain kinds of error to which the original experiences were subject.[22] A full epistemic examination of the level of certainty and means of justification of such judgments must be carried out separately, but the protection from these sorts of error can help explain at least some of the *apparent* incorrigibility that (since Descartes) has contributed to the philosophical interest of first-person experience reports. Note that this does not, however, involve claiming that all judgments about one's own experience are infallible or that all statements about appearances are guaranteed to be true. Judgments about one's own experience not derived via such transformations but by means of other routes, such as speculation, the desire to preserve good feelings about oneself, or inferences made externally by observing one's own behavior (as a blindsighter might observe that she reaches to the right and thereby judge that it must 'appear' to her that the ball is on the right) of course are not covered by this account. Nor does it entail that all mental states are known to their possessors. For the transformations we have been discussing are only available from an original *conscious* presentation of the world as being a certain way; if a blindsighter lacks conscious experience of an object in front of her, she has nothing which she can conceptually transform into the relevant description of appearances.

This model of self-knowledge can also explain the fact noted by Shoemaker that certain kinds of mistake about one's own beliefs are not possible. If self-knowledge were conceived of on the model of a pseudo-perception of one's own mental states, we would expect it to be possible to mistake one belief for another, as it is perceptually possible to mistake one person for another. But if we acquire our knowledge of our mental states by simple conceptual transformations from the world-oriented experience, the possibility of mistaking one belief for another simply doesn't arise.

But despite its virtues and despite the fact that it clearly avoids the problems supposed to plague inner-observation accounts, certain objections may arise to this account, and certain challenges certainly remain for any view of self-knowledge based

---

[22] This seems to be behind Descartes' observations (1641/1993: 23) that, in trying to acquire knowledge of an external object such as a piece of wax, I in fact acquire much more secure knowledge about my own mind.

in externally oriented experiences combined with cognitive transformations. While space constraints prevent a full discussion of any of them here, I will at least suggest what difficulties remain and some routes that might be taken to overcome them.

One worry that might arise is that treating knowledge of our experiences as derived by transformations in this way makes such knowledge as we can acquire about our own experiences trivial or obvious.[23] Indeed some sorts of knowledge *are* fairly trivial—such as knowledge of how things appear to one or what one believes—and are plausibly considered available to all competent speakers of English who grasp the relevant concepts of belief and appearance. But not all relevant phenomenological concepts are as obvious or widely shared as those of appearance and belief, just as not all linguistic concepts are as obvious or widely shared as those of statement and question. Properly understood, the cognitive transformation account does not trivialize phenomenological knowledge as a whole any more than the fact that all one needs to acquire knowledge of grammar is the basic ability to speak about the world, plus the ability to engage in the relevant cognitive shifts to speak about the ways of representing the world and the concepts and analytical tools of linguistics, suggests that grammatical knowledge is trivial or obvious. As Husserl notes, in contrast to the introspectionists, the ability to acquire knowledge of our own mental states phenomenologically is by no means guaranteed by our simple ability to experience the world (as higher-order theories would have it), but requires extensive specialized training in undertaking the cognitive shifts demanded by phenomenological reduction and acquiring and learning to apply an array of specialized concepts. This training, of course, is what Husserl sought repeatedly to supply in his various texts subtitled as 'introductions' to phenomenology. Moreover, such knowledge as can be acquired by these kinds of transformations should not be thought to exhaust phenomenological knowledge, as (once we have acquired the ability to describe the realm of experience) all manner of further essential connections may be revealed among experience types, the transcendental necessary preconditions for experiences of various sorts may be uncovered, and so on.

Finally, two sorts of powerful objection are often raised to accounts that would base self-knowledge in cognitive transformations from world-oriented thoughts and experiences. One is this: Clearly the same sort of cognitive transformation from (apparently) seeing a red apple, to 'it appears that there is a red apple', to 'there is an appearance as-if of a red apple' may be trivially made whether or not there is any sensuous appearance at all. Thus, the same sorts of cognitive transformations can move us from the judgment 'the stock market will rise' to 'it appears that the stock market will rise' to 'there is an appearance of the stock market rising', although intuitively there is nothing like a full-blooded (sensuous) *appearance* of anything here. But if the transformations to appearance-talk can be made where there seems to be no robust appearance whatsoever, this might seem to threaten the idea that, in other cases, such cognitive transformations are not merely trivial but in fact lead us to knowledge of a realm of appearances (etc.).

It is important to note, however, that for Husserl, phenomenology is not concerned with knowledge of *mere* sensuous appearances or qualia, but rather with acquiring

---

[23] Thanks to Charles Siewert for raising this issue.

knowledge of our various ways of representing (meaning, intending) the world—which need not be sensory or quasi-sensory. In that sense, there is a way in which (and mode and force with which) the stock market is presented to me as prone to rise, and that and other 'empty apprehensions or comprehensions' may be known by means of 'reflective modifications' just as the apple-appearance may be (Husserl 1913/1962: 203). In neither case should the cognitive transformations be considered trivial; in both they should be considered to provide us with knowledge of genuine representing structures of consciousness. The question remains whether the account of self-knowledge on offer can *distinguish* properly *sensuous* appearances (as Husserl would put it, those with a hyletic element) from sensuously 'empty' appearances, or enable us to acquire knowledge of the specifically *sensory* character of experience. This question would have to be solved by other routes that cannot be pursued here.[24]

The second part of the challenge for Cognitive Transformation views is that at least certain sorts of concepts applied to experience seem not to be derived—or in some cases not derivable—by transformations from world-regarding experiences. Thus, e.g. as we saw, one problem Brandom's Sellars faces is how to account for apparent descriptions of (e.g.) visual experiences as blurry, since this is not a term we ever apply to the world. Similarly, simple proprioceptive qualia such as pains, itches, and tickles, seem not to be known by means of transformations from world-oriented representations (e.g. of bodily damage); if anything, we infer that there is such bodily damage on the basis of our pains (Aydede 2002: 10–11).

Husserl says less about such cases as pains and itches than one might expect, since (again) his primary interest is not in qualia but rather in ways in which consciousness constitutes a world for us—thus focusing on full-blown intentional experiences. He treats 'sensile impressions of pleasure, pain, tickling, etc.' as 'components in concrete experiences of a more comprehensive kind which as wholes are intentional . . . so that over those sensile phases lies as it were an "animating," *meaning-bestowing* stratum . . . a stratum through whose agency, out of the *sensile element which contains in itself nothing intentional*, the concrete intentional experience takes form and shape' (1913/1962: 226–7). Even so, if these experiences are intentional (and so directed), an objector might urge that they are not *world*-directed, and so the reductive and hypostatizing transformations discussed above will not be the appropriate means of acquiring knowledge of such experiences.

Perhaps one should acknowledge that, in cases such as these, our attention *is already* turned from the world to our experience, without the need for bracketing to so turn our attention and application of concepts. In these cases, perhaps, all one needs is the direct application of the phenomenal concept to the experience, without the need for reductive and hypostatizing transformations. Certainly such an account is open to Husserl in these

[24] The relevant difference for Husserl is whether or not the experience involves hyletic data (cf. 1913/1962: 226), but it's not clear how knowledge of *whether* or *what* hyletic data an experience involves is to be acquired. An account of phenomenal concepts such as that developed by Chalmers (2002) might be of assistance. It might be that only sensory or quasi-sensory first-order experiences permit transformations to higher-order introspective beliefs involving direct phenomenal concepts, though all conscious experiences permit transformations to yield some apparent self-knowledge and may be described as 'appearances' in an explicitly broader sense.

special cases (since, unlike Brandom's Sellars, he readily acknowledges the existence of experiences and the possibility of reporting on them), and so he may acknowledge different routes for reaching these experience reports that do not require use of his phenomenological method—though such routes still require further specification.

Whatever the ultimate fate of the Cognitive Transformation view of first-person knowledge, I hope that I have at least made progress in forestalling some common misunderstandings of the methods of phenomenology, distancing it appropriately from views that consider the source of introspective knowledge to lie in a kind of pseudo-perceptual observation of one's own mental states, and suggesting how a different account of first-person knowledge may be able to be developed in a way that is harmonious with the practice of phenomenology and with a one-level theory of consciousness. Though much work remains to be done, it seems that Husserl's phenomenological reduction may not only be of historical interest, but also provide the roots for a promising way of accounting for at least much of first-person knowledge. Re-examining the classical Husserlian method of bracketing may thus not only help set the historical record straight about phenomenology and its relationship to the history of analytic philosophy of mind, but also help provide a way forward through one of the most interesting problems in contemporary philosophy of mind.[25]

REFERENCES

Armstrong, David M. (1968) *A Materialist Theory of the Mind* (London: Routledge & Kegan Paul).
—— (1981/1997) 'What is Consciousness', in Block et al. (1997).
Aydede, Murat (2002) 'Is Introspection Inferential?', in Brie Gertler (ed.), *Privileged Access: Accounts of Self-Knowledge* (Ashgate Publishing, Epistemology and Mind Series).
Ayer, A. J. (1945) 'The Terminology of Sense-Data', *Mind*, NS, 54/216: 289–312.
Bach, Kent (1997) 'Engineering the Mind', review of *Naturalizing the Mind*, by Fred Dretske. *Philosophy and Phenomenological Research* 57/2: 459–68.
Brandom, Robert (2000) 'Study Guide to *Empiricism and the Philosophy of Mind*', in Sellars (1956/2000).
Block, Ned, Flanagan, Owen, and Güzeldere, Güven (eds.) (1997) *The Nature of Consciousness: Philosophical Debates* (Cambridge, Mass.: MIT Press).
Brentano, Franz (1874/1995) *Psychology from an Empirical Standpoint*, ed. Oskar Kraus and Linda L. McAlister, trans. Antos C. Rancurello, D. B. Terrell and Linda L. McAlister (London: Routledge).
—— (1982/1995) *Descriptive Psychology*, trans. and ed. Benito Müller (London: Routledge).
Chalmers, David (1996) *The Conscious Mind* (New York: Oxford University Press).
—— (2003) 'The Content and Epistemology of Phenomenal Belief', in Q. Smith and A. Jokic (eds.), *Consciousness: New Philosophical Perspectives* (Oxford: Oxford University Press.)

[25] Earlier versions of this essay were presented at the University of Kent conference 'Consciousness in Historical Perspective' (Canterbury, England, May 2002), and at the National Endowment for the Humanities Summer Institute on Consciousness and Intentionality (Santa Cruz, California, July 2002). My thanks go out to all those who participated in the discussions for many incisive questions and comments that helped improve the essay. Special thanks for further detailed comments and/or suggestions go to David Chalmers, Willem de Vries, Wolfgang Huemer, Sean Kelly, Paul Livingston, Charles Siewert, David Smith, and Alan Thomas.

Dennett, Daniel (1987) *The Intentional Stance* (Cambridge, Mass.: MIT Press).

—— (1991) *Consciousness Explained* (New York: The Penguin Press).

Descartes, René (1641/1993) *Meditations on First Philosophy*, trans. Donald A. Cress (Indianapolis, Ind.: Hackett).

Dretske, Fred (1995) *Naturalizing the Mind* (Cambridge, Mass.: MIT Press).

—— (1997) 'Conscious Experience', in Block et al. (1997: 773–88).

Güzeldere, Güven (1995/1997) 'Is Consciousness the Perception of what Passes in one's own Mind?', in Block et al. (1997: 789–806).

Huemer, Wolfgang (forthcoming) *The Constitution of Consciousness: A Study in Analytic Phenomenology* (London: Routledge).

Husserl, Edmund (1913/2000) *Logical Investigations*, 2nd ed., 2 vol., trans. J. N. Findlay (New York: Humanity Books).

—— (1913/1962) *Ideas: General Introduction to Pure Phenomenology*, trans. W. R. Boyce Gibson (New York: Collier).

—— (1954/1970) *The Crisis of European Sciences,* trans. David Carr (Evanston, Ill.: Northwestern University Press).

Lycan, William (1990/1997) 'Consciousness as Internal Monitoring', in Block et al. (1997: 755–72).

Moran, Dermot (2000) *Introduction to Phenomenology* (London: Routledge).

Rosenthal, David M. (1997) 'A Theory of Consciousness', in Block et al. (1997: 729–54).

Rowlands, Mark (2003) 'Consciousness: The Transcendentalist Manifesto', *Phenomenology and the Cognitive Sciences*, 2/3: 205–21.

Schiffer, Stephen (1990) 'Physicalism', *Philosophical Perspectives* 4: 153–85.

—— (1994) 'A Paradox of Meaning', *Noûs* 28/3: 279–324.

—— (1996) 'Language-Created Language-Independent Entities', *Philosophical Topics* 24/1: 149–67.

Sellars, Wilfrid (1956/2000) *Empiricism and the Philosophy of Mind* (Cambridge, Mass.: Harvard University Press).

—— (1963/1991) *Science, Perception and Reality* (Atascadero, Calif.: Ridgeview).

—— (1975) 'Autobiographical Reflections', in Hector Neri Castañeda (ed.), *Action, Knowledge and Reality: Critical Studies in Honor of Wilfrid Sellars* (Indianapolis: The Bobbs-Merrill Company, Inc).

—— (1978) 'Some Reflections on Perceptual Consciousness', in Ronald Bruzina and Bruce Wilshire, eds., *Crosscurrents in Phenomenology* (The Hague: Nijhoff), 169–85.

Shoemaker, Sydney (1996) *The First-Person Perspective and Other Essays* (New York: Cambridge University Press).

Siewert, Charles (1998) *The Significance of Consciousness* (Princeton, NJ: Princeton University Press).

—— (2001) 'Self-Knowledge and Phenomenal Unity', *Noûs* 35/4: 542–68.

Smith, David Woodruff (1971) *Intentionality, Noemata, and Individuation: The Role of Individuation in Husserl's Theory of Intentionality* (Ph.D. Dissertation, Stanford University, Stanford California, 1970; Ann Arbor: UMI).

—— (1986) 'The Structure of (Self-) Consciousness', *Topoi* 5/2: 149–56.

—— (1989) *The Circle of Acquaintance* (Boston: Kluwer).

Thomas, Alan P. (1997) 'Kant, McDowell and the Theory of Consciousness', *The European Journal of Philosophy*: 283–305.

Thomasson, Amie L. (1999) *Fiction and Metaphysics* (Cambridge: Cambridge University Press).

—— (2000) 'After Brentano: A One-Level Theory of Consciousness', *European Journal of Philosophy* 8/2: 190–209.

—— (2001) 'Ontological Minimalism', *American Philosophical Quarterly* 38/4: 319–31.

—— (2002a) 'Two Puzzles for a New Theory of Consciousness', *Psyché* (e-journal) 8: http://psyche.cs.monash.edu.au/v8/psyche-8-03-thomasson.html

—— (2002b) 'Phenomenology and the Development of Analytic Philosophy', *Southern Journal of Philosophy* Volume XL, Supplement: 115–42.

6

Phenomenology and Cortical Microstimulation

John Bickle and Ralph Ellis

Abstract: We begin by surveying both historical and recent neuroscientific research that activates tiny patches of cortex in human and non-human primates to induce phenomenological experiences. Recent experiments dissociate sensory features of external stimuli and the induced cortical microstimulation, demonstrating that the neural event rather than the external stimulus determines a subject's perceptual judgment. Consensus holds that the best explanation of these carefully controlled experimental data is that cortical microstimulation induces subjective experiences with phenomenological features similar to experiences produced through normal sensory channels. This research appears to create difficulties for classical phenomenology. But the fact that intentional contents may be physiologically manipulated creates no conflict between phenomenology and physicalism. Husserl wanted to get away from our natural, everyday tendency to read empirical assumptions about physical objects into our understanding of experience. His phenomenological reduction brackets dualism as much as it brackets naive empiricism; the reduction entails no assumption about the relationship one way or the other between experiences and the causal physiological mechanisms that apparently subserve them. Moreover, Merleau-Ponty's notion of psychophysical forms as an approach to the mind–body problem requires that differing phenomenological experiences be correlated with differing physical brain processes. As our case study here reveals, combining phenomenological methods with mainstream neuroscientific investigations might prove useful for addressing 'hard problems' about conscious experience and neuronal activity.

It is no longer uncommon to read claims by neuroscientists like the following: 'The most remarkable hypothesis of modern neuroscience is that the entirety of our personal experience—from our perception of the external world to our experience of internal thoughts—results solely from patterned electrical activity among the several billion neurons that comprise the central nervous system' (Liu and Newsome 2000: R598). Many neuroscientists have grown bolder in asserting their discipline's philosophical

Bickle is the principal author of sections 1 and 3. Ellis is the principal author of section 2. However, this is a combined effort in that both authors have reviewed, edited, and revised each other's contributions. Agreement on empirical evidence, arguments, and conclusions extends considerably—further than one might normally expect between a ruthless reductionist (Bickle) and a nonreductive physicalist and phenomenologist (Ellis).

relevance. And do notice that Jing Liu and William Newsome's explicit explanatory target is '*personal experience*', not some ersatz laboratory stand-in.

Liu and Newsome continue this passage with a remark on how best to test this hypothesis: 'Ultimately, the most stringent test of this hypothesis is to create realistic experiences and mental operations artificially, by directly activating known circuits of neurons in the brain in the absence of the external inputs that normally elicit such mental operations' (2000: R598). Cognitive neuroscience is now full of claims like this one. But what makes Liu and Newsome's claim especially interesting is that it is offered by *cellular physiologists* who create these artificial experiences via *cortical microstimulation*. Remarking on the 'single-cell approach,' Newsome has also claimed recently:

> We have not yet begun to exhaust its usefulness. . . . Exciting to me . . . is the recent trend toward applying the single unit approach in behaving animals trained to perform simple cognitive tasks. More laboratories are now employing clever behavioral paradigms (frequently adapted from the experimental traditions of psychophysics and behavioral psychology) to investigate neural substrates of perception, attention, learning, memory, and motor planning, to name but a few. A wealth of new insight is emerging from these efforts, and I believe we have only scratched the surface of what can be learned.   (Gazzaniga 1997: 57–8)

For reasons that will become obvious in the next section, we'll refer to these artificially created experiences and operations as 'phenomenology induced by cortical microstimulation'. Our aim is to survey historical and recent results of this scientific research (section 1) and sketch its relevance and potentially fruitful interactions with the Husserlian phenomenological tradition (section 2). We'll close with some brief remarks about mainstream current neuroscience (i.e. cellular and molecular neuroscience), the 'hard problem' of consciousness, and a role that phenomenology might play in attempts to bridge them (section 3).

1. CORTICAL MICROSTIMULATION, PAST AND PRESENT

In the late 1930s neurosurgeon Wilder Penfield developed a procedure for performing brain surgery on awake human patients. He and his colleagues at the Montreal Neurological Institute used it as part of a surgical treatment for otherwise intractable epilepsy. Since brains lack pain receptors, patients whose scalps, skulls, and underlying connective tissue had been deadened with local anesthetics could comfortably remain conscious while surgeons ablated (removed) the site(s) of their seizure origins. In conjunction with this procedure, Penfield used mild electrical stimulation through a small ball electrode placed on the cortical surface. The technique was a clinical milestone. If electrical stimulation at a specific site evoked epileptic symptoms, this was evidence that the site is one of seizure origin. And by probing responses of a conscious patient during announced and unannounced stimulations, the surgeon could explore the functional significance of tissue he considered removing.

In one review essay, Penfield and Phanor Perot (1963) report quantitative data and case histories of patients over the previous twenty-five years (1938–63) at the Montreal

Institute who had exhibited 'experiential responses' to electrical microstimulation. During that period, Penfield and his surgical colleagues performed 1,288 surgeries on 1,132 patients. Five hundred and twenty cases involved exposing and exploring the temporal lobe; 612 involved other neural regions. Electrical stimulation produced 'experiential responses' in none of the latter 612 cases, while it did so in 40 of the former 520 cases (7.7%). Experiential responses were characterized as states 'more complex than sensory or motor phenomena' like simple whirring or buzzing sounds, color flashes, or involuntary limb movements. (These sensations were produced routinely by electrical stimulation to appropriate sensory or motor cortical regions; see Penfield and Perot 1963: 597.) Instead, true experiential responses resembled the spontaneous 'experiential hallucinations' and 'dreamy states' characteristic of temporal lobe epileptic seizures. Experiential responses induced by electrical stimulation were 'sometimes extensive and elaborate, sometimes fragmentary', and often included 'the sights and sounds and the accompanying emotions of a period of time, and the patient usually recognizes it spontaneously as coming from his past' (1963: 596). Auditory responses were most frequent, including a voice or voices, music, or other meaningful sounds. Experiences of music were surprisingly prominent. Visual responses were also frequent, often of a person or group of persons, a scene, or other recognizable objects. Auditory-experiential and visual-experiential responses sometimes occurred in combination, usually as scenes with appropriate sounds or a person or people singing or talking. In patients who commonly suffered from spontaneous experiential hallucinations during their seizures, electrically invoked experiential responses often resembled their spontaneous hallucinations. Experiential responses elicited from one site were often similar to responses elicited from nearby sites.

Transcripts from the forty case histories published in the Penfield and Perot (1963) review illustrate all these features. Here we present one for illustration.[1] After removing the anterior tip of D.F.'s right temporal lobe (Penfield and Perot 1963: Case 5, 619–20), the surgeon stimulated a site on the cut surface of the superior and medial region of the first temporal convolution. On the second stimulation D.F. reported, 'I hear some music.' When the stimulation was repeated without warning, D.F. reported, 'I hear music again. It is like the radio.' She was unable to name the tune, but claimed it was familiar. Upon a later stimulation to this same site, D.F. reported, 'I hear it.' The electrode was kept in place and D.F. was asked to describe her experience. She hummed the tune. The operating room nurse named the tune and D.F. agreed with her judgment. The nurse agreed that D.F.'s humming captured the tune's proper timing and tempo. On further inquiry D.F. claimed that the experience was not that of 'being made to think about' the tune, but that she 'actually heard it'.

Penfield and Perot (1963) offered a number of clinical and neuropsychological conclusions that speak directly to the issue of 'phenomenology induced by direct cortical electric stimulation'. For example, they write

The conclusion is inescapable that some, if not all, of these evoked responses represent activation of a neural mechanism that keeps the record of current experience. There is activation too

---

[1] Bickle (2003: ch. 4, sect. 4) contains additional examples and a more detailed discussion of the technique and Penfield and Perot's (1963) conclusions about its significance.

of the emotional tone or feeling that belonged to the original experience. The responses have that basic element of reference to the past that one associates with memory. But their vividness or wealth of detail and the sense of immediacy that goes with them serves to set them apart from the ordinary process of recollection which rarely displays such qualities.   (1963: 679)

They emphasize the connection between memory and the stream of consciousness during past experience: 'At operation it is usually quite clear that the evoked experiential response is a random reproduction of whatever composed the stream of consciousness during some interval of the patient's past waking life' (1963: 686–7). They conclude that 'there is within the adult human brain a remarkable record of the stream of each individual's awareness or consciousness. Stimulation of certain areas of cortex, lying in the temporal lobe between the auditory sensory and the visual sensory areas, causes previous experience to return to the mind of the conscious patient' (1963: 692).

That documented cases of 'experiential response' phenomenology induced by cortical microstimulation exist at all is interesting and relevant for questions about the neural basis of consciousness. But philosophical caution is appropriate here. Penfield and his associates elicited experiential responses in only a minority of temporal lobe cases, and nowhere else (though they constantly elicited simple auditory and visual sensations when stimulating the appropriate regions of sensory cortex). And these limited results were elicited in epileptics' brains, near their sites of seizure origin, where electrical activation was admittedly 'facilitated' by the organic damage. The evoked experiences were limited to only items stored in long-term memory, and also only to certain types of memory items; Penfield and Perot (1963: 689) present a list of memory experiences that were never invoked by electrical stimulation. Finally, this evidence does not even support the localization of these memory experiences to the site of stimulation. As Penfield and Perot note explicitly, during subsequent interviews days or weeks after their surgeries, patients could recall the experiential responses evoked—even when the site of stimulation had been ablated at a later stage of the surgical procedure (1963: 689). In terms of the neural basis of phenomenological memories, the most that these results show is that regions in the temporal cortices, especially ones superior to the first temporal convolution, 'play in adult life some role in the subconscious recall of past experience, making it available for present interpretation' by 'activating connections with that part of the record of the stream of consciousness in which hearing and seeing are the prominent components' (Penfield and Perot 1963: 689).

These deflationary remarks might seem like a resounding thud to philosophers of consciousness, but electrical stimulation of the primate brain did not stop with Penfield's surgical technique (which, incidentally, is still used in human neurosurgery today, with numerous refinements). Recent results from primate labs provide additional compelling evidence for phenomenology induced by cortical microstimulation.

Area MT (*M*iddle *T*emporal cortex) in primates (including humans) is the gateway to the 'dorsal' visual processing stream (Figures 6.1 and 6.2). The dorsal stream, also called the 'where' or 'how' stream, extracts information from visual neurons earlier in the processing hierarchy about objects' locations (Mishkin, Ungerleider, and Macko 1983), leading to actions guided by vision (Goodale and Milner 1992). Both lesion studies and electrophysiological recordings reveal MT's role in visual judgments about motion direction. Most MT neurons are *direction selective*, spiking at highest frequency

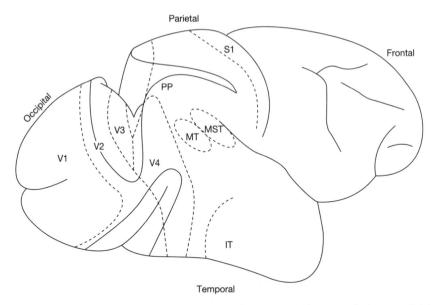

Figure 6.1 Prominent sensory regions (mostly visual) in primate (rhesus monkey) cortex. Sulci and gyri have been 'flattened' to better indicate regional locations. Abbreviations: V1, primary visual cortex; V2, V3, V4, extrastriate visual cortex; PP, posterior parietal cortex; MT, middle (or medial) temporal cortex; MST, medial superior temporal cortex; IT, inferior temporal cortex; S1, primary somatosensory cortex. (Illustration by Dave Winterhalter.)

to a visual stimulus moving in a single direction in their receptive fields, a bit less frequently to motion in related directions, and not at all (above baseline spiking rates) to motions unrelated to their preferred direction.[2] Like many cortical regions, MT has a columnar organization. Neurons in a given perpendicular MT column share similar receptive fields and motion selectivity. These features vary in neurons from column to column, and MT in its entirety realizes a 'map' that represents all motion directions at all regions of the visual field (Albright, Desimone, and Gross 1984).

William Newsome and his collaborators at Stanford University developed a method for quantifying the strength of a motion stimulus (Salzman *et al.* 1992) (Figure 6.3). A pattern of dots appears on a computer screen. The strength of a motion stimulus, expressed as a 'percentage correlation', reflects the percentage of dots that are re-plotted on subsequent screens at a fixed spatial interval and direction from their original position. All other dots are re-plotted at the same spatial and temporal intervals but in random directions from their original positions. This re-plotting and the temporal interval between the screens give the illusion of visual motion, with some percentage of the dots seeming to move in a particular direction and the rest appearing to move in random directions. For example, in a '50% correlation vertical stimulus',

---

[2] A visual neuron's receptive field is the portion of the overall visual field in which a stimulus evokes a response above baseline firing (action potential) rate.

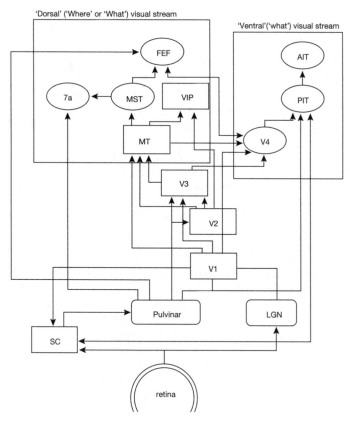

'Dorsal' ('Where' or 'What') visual stream

'Ventral'('what') visual stream

Figure 6.2 Schematic of the two visual processing streams. Abbreviations as in Figure 6.1 above, except: SC, (midbrain) superior colliculus; LGN, (thalamic) lateral geniculate nucleus; 7a, Brodmann's area 7a (of posterior parietal cortex); VIP, ventral intraparietal area; FEF, frontal eye fields; PIT, posterior inferior temporal cortex; AIT, anterior inferior temporal cortex. (Illustration by Dave Winterhalter.)

half of the dots on the original screen are re-plotted on later screens at a fixed upward interval, providing the illusion of vertical motion, while the other half are re-plotted randomly.

Newsome's lab also developed a behavioral paradigm in which rhesus monkeys express visual judgments about motion direction. Their full litany of controls is elaborate but the basic idea is straightforward. The monkey fixates on a central point on a computer screen display and maintains fixation while a visual motion stimulus of a particular strength is presented (a particular percentage correlation in some direction). Both the fixation point and the motion stimulus are extinguished and target lights (LEDs) appear at the screen's peripheries. The 'preferred' (Pref) LED is located in the direction (from the original fixation point) of the motion stimulus; the 'null' LED is located in the opposite periphery. The monkey indicates its judgment of stimulus

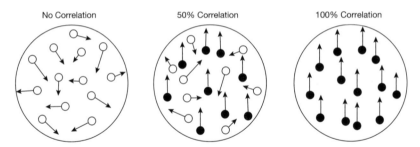

Figure 6.3 Strength of motion stimulus in Newsome and colleagues MT microstimulation studies. Percent correlation refers to the ratio of dots re-plotted on later screens to provide the appearance of visual motion in a single direction (e.g. vertical) compared to all dots. All other dots are re-plotted to give the illusion of visual motion in random directions. (Reprinted with permission from Figure 1 in Salzman *et al.* (1992: 2333), copyright 1992 by the Society for Neuroscience.)

motion direction by saccading (moving its eyes quickly) to one of the LEDs. Its saccade is its report of perceived motion direction. The monkey is only rewarded when it saccades correctly, to the Pref LED in the direction of the percentage correlation motion stimulus. Using standard single-cell electrophysiological recording procedures, Newsome's group first locates an MT neuron's receptive field and preferred motion selectivity. A percentage correlation motion stimulus is then presented only to that neuron's receptive field (as the monkey maintains fixation on the central point). They can then compare the monkey's report about stimulus motion direction across differing motion stimulus strengths (percentage correlation) when electrical stimulation is applied to that neuron through a stimulating electrode and when it is not.

Penfield and his associates induced electrical stimulation through a monopolar silver ball electrode with an area of cortical contact approximately 1.5 square mm. Their typical electrical stimulation was a square wave pulse with a 2–5 millisecond duration at a frequency of 40–100 Hz (cycles per second) and an electrical potential difference of 1 to 5 volts. The resistance was 10,000–20,000 ohms, yielding a current that varied between 50–500 milliamperes (Penfield and Perot 1963: 602). Thus vast numbers of neurons were stimulated directly by the electrical current on a single stimulation. Newsome's lab microstimulates MT neurons using tungsten microelectrodes with an exposed tip length of 20–30 *microns*. Stimulating pulses are biphasic, each with an 0.2 millisecond duration, with a frequency of either 200 Hz or 500 Hz and an amplitude of 10 *micro*amperes (μA). Citing a study by Stoney, Thompson, and Asanuma (1968) on primate motor cortex, Newsome and his colleagues report that a single cathodal 10 μA current pulse directly activates neurons within 85 microns of the electrode tip. The number of neurons stimulated directly by their electric current is thus orders of magnitudes smaller than the number directly activated by Penfield's electrodes and pulses. Current electrophysiological techniques thus allow Newsome's group to insert stimulating electrode tips into 250–500 micron clusters of sensory neurons with similar receptive fields. Technology marches forward!

The percentage correlation measure of stimulus motion strength and behavioral paradigm permit Newsome's group to plot the proportion of monkeys' reports of apparent motion in stimulated MT neurons' preferred direction as a function of stimulus motion strength. Figure 6.4 represents a monkey's performance with a choice bias slightly in this neuron cluster's preferred direction of motion stimuli. Data points and the sigmoid regression line drawn through them represent the monkey's performance in the absence of electrical microstimulation. When even a small percentage of the dots appear to be moving in this neuron cluster's preferred direction (e.g. >20% correlation), the monkey correctly judges motion in the preferred direction on nearly every trial (1.0 Proportion Preferred Direction (PD) judgment). When a moderate percentage of the dots appear to be moving opposite this cluster's preferred direction (e.g. <−50% correlation), the monkey correctly judges motion in the null direction on nearly every trial (0.0 Proportion PD). If microstimulation to this direction-selective MT neuron cluster adds signal to the neural processes underlying visual judgments of motion direction, then it will bias the monkeys' reports toward the stimulated neurons' preferred direction. When graphed, this would produce a leftward shift of the psychometric function (Figure 6.4, line A).

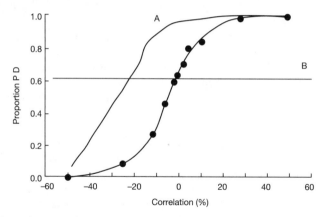

Figure 6.4 Psychometric function graphing percent correlation of visual motion stimuli against the proportion of motion judgments made by the monkey toward the 'preferred direction' (PD) of motion stimuli for the direction-selective MT neuronal cluster being microstimulated. Positive values on the x-axis represent percent correlation trials in the cluster's preferred direction; negative values represent percent correlation trials in the cluster's null direction. Data points (dots) and the sigmoid regression function drawn through them represent results on trials when no microstimulation was delivered. (A) If microstimulation adds signal to the neuronal processes underlying judgment of motion direction, the psychometric function will shift to the left. (B) If microstimulation adds noise to the neuronal processes underlying judgment of motion direction, the psychometric function will be shifted toward a line through the monkey's inherent choice bias value (y-intercept at 0° correlation), with a slight decrease at high negative percent correlations and a slight increase at high positive percent correlations. (See text for explanations.) (Reprinted with permission from figure 3 in Salzman *et al.* (1992: 2335), copyright 1992 by the Society for Neuroscience.)

Microstimulation to this cluster will make the monkey more prone to judge motion in the Pref direction, even when fewer of the dots actually appear to move in that direction. If microstimulation adds noise to the neural processes underlying motion judgment, this will exacerbate the monkey's choice bias. When graphed, this would produce nearly constant judgments around the y-intercept of the original function at 0° correlation, with only a slight increase for highly correlated preferred stimulus direction and a slight decrease for highly correlated null stimulus direction (Figure 6.4, line B).

Newsome and his colleagues continually observed the 'adds signal' result of microstimulation to direction-selective MT neuron clusters, under a variety of percentage correlations (stimulus motion strengths) and microstimulation frequencies (Salzman *et al.* 1992, especially Figures 4 and 8; Murasugi, Salzman, and Newsome 1993, especially Figures 2 and 5). At nearly every percentage correlation, microstimulation of a direction-selective MT neuron cluster biased the monkeys' saccades significantly to the Pref LED. This bias occurred even in the presence of strong motion stimuli *in the other (null) direction* (e.g. $> -50\%$ correlation). Recall that monkeys were only rewarded when they report stimulus motion direction (percentage correlation) correctly. They never received a reward for their continually incorrect choices under conditions of actual motion stimuli in the null direction and applied microstimulation. Increasing microstimulation frequency (up to 500 Hz) increased the proportion of motion reports in the neurons' preferred direction, no matter what the direction and strength of actual motion stimuli.

These results lead naturally to the question of what the monkeys *see*—what they *experience visually*—during microstimulation trials. Are the monkeys *conscious* of motion in the microstimulated neurons' preferred direction, even when the actual motion stimulus is strongly in the opposite direction? Newsome and his colleagues admit that their results cannot answer this question conclusively. But they don't shrink from speculating: 'A plausible hypothesis is that microstimulation evokes a subjective sensation of motion like that experienced during the motion aftereffect, or waterfall illusion. . . . Motion therefore appears to be a quality that can be computed independently within the brain and "assigned" to patterned objects in the environment' (Salzman *et al.* 1992: 2352). They are suggesting that *visual motion qualia* are generated in the brain and attached to other internal visual representations of external objects. Happily, in ordinary circumstances, our 'internal assignments' of features to representations tend to correlate with features and relations of the objects represented. Natural selection was crueler to creatures whose 'internal assignments' were more haphazard. But under appropriate conditions our internally generated and assigned qualia and the external features can be dissociated. Apparently that happens in Newsome's MT microstimulation-motion studies.

Neuroscientist Rodolfo Llinás and neurophilosopher Patricia Churchland have coined a term, 'endogenesis', that denotes the general idea behind this suggestion. Their idea is that 'sensory experience is not created by incoming signals from the world but by intrinsic, continuing processes of the brain' (1996: x). Incoming signals from sensory receptors keyed to external physical parameters serve only to 'trellis, shape, and otherwise sculpt the intrinsic activity to yield a survival-facilitating, me-in-the-world representational scheme' (1996: x). Natural selection—and hence adequacy for exploiting an available environmental niche, not truth—determines a given scheme's success.

Microstimulation motion effects are not specific to nonhuman primates. Newsome and his colleagues point out that 'it has recently been reported that crude motion percepts can be elicited with electrical stimulation of the human parietal-occipital cortex' (Salzman *et al.* 1992: 2352) These reports bring their results in line with Penfield's. Nor are microstimulation effects specific to visual motion. Newsome and his collaborators have also succeeded in affecting judgments of an object's stereoscopic depth compared to a fixed location by way of cortical microstimulation of MT neuron clusters that respond selectivity to binocular disparity (the relative positions of the image of the object on the two retinas) (DeAngelis, Cumming, and Newsome 1998). Nor are microstimulation effects on vision specific to one lab. Changing patterns of visual motion on the retinas as we move through space, called 'optic flow', provides a rich source of information about direction of self-movement or 'heading'. Earlier work with rhesus monkeys indicated that the medial superior temporal area (MST) (Figures 6.1 and 6.2 above) contains neurons selective for optic flow information and for stimuli that simulate the visual effects of self-motion. Ken Britten and Richard van Wezel (1998) presented rhesus monkeys with visual displays that simulated a cloud of dots at a visual depth from 1–10 m. All dots were re-plotted at a particular angle and distance to provide visual stimuli of self-motion through space at a particular angle and direction ('heading') (Figure 6.5a, b) Stimulating electrodes were inserted into the center of MST clusters with diameters of at least 250 μm in which all neurons were tuned to a similar leftward or rightward heading direction and angle. Here again,

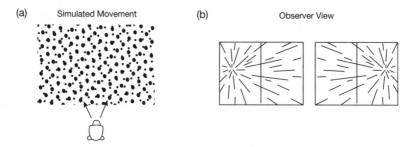

Figure 6.5 Visual 'heading direction' stimuli in Britten and van Wezel's MST microstimulation studies. (a) Dot field gives the illusion of depth from 1-10m to observing monkey. (b) Appearance of left-and right-heading stimuli, as seen from the observing monkey's perspective. The length of each line shows the illusion of speed for each re-plotted dot, which is inversely proportional to its observed depth. Vertical dashed lines correspond to a heading of 0°, or 'straight ahead'. (Reprinted with permission from Figure 1 in Britten and van Wezel (1998: 60), copyright 1998 by Nature Publishing Group.)

microstimulation adds signal to the neural processes underlying visual judgments of heading direction. Even when the dot field indicated a rightward heading of 4°, when without microstimulation the monkey indicated rightward heading on 75% of the trials, microstimulation of a leftward heading-tuned MST cluster biased the monkey to choose the *leftward* heading target dot in 90% of the trials (Britten and van Wezel 1998: Figure 2, p. 60).[3]

Nor are microstimulation effects limited to *visual* stimuli. Ranulfo Romo and his collaborators at the National Autonomous University of Mexico trained rhesus monkeys to distinguish differences in frequency between two flutter stimuli delivered to a fingertip site. Humans report sensations of 'flutter' when mechanical vibrations between 5–50 Hz are applied to the skin. Such stimuli activate neurons in primary somatosensory cortex (area 3b of S1) (Figure 6.1 above) whose tactile receptive fields include the stimulation site. 'Quickly Adapting' (QA) neurons are strongly activated by periodic flutter vibrations and fire with a probability that oscillates exactly at the input frequency. In other words, their mean firing rate correlates directly with the frequency of the mechanical vibration applied to their receptive fields (appropriate portions of the skin) (Mountcastle, Steinmetz, and Romo 1990). These neurons are also arranged in columnar clusters that share similar receptive fields. In their first study (Romo *et al.* 1998), monkeys judged whether a second 'comparison' stimulus, either mechanical or cortical microstimulation to the appropriate QA neurons, was higher or lower in frequency compared to an initial mechanical 'base' stimulus. The experimenters were seeking to discover 'whether the animals could interpret the artificial signals [microstimulation "comparison" frequencies] as flutter' (Romo *et al.* 1998: 388). So long as base and comparison stimuli consisted of two current pulses with amplitude >65 μA, monkeys achieved over 75% correct responses for both mechanical and microstimulation comparison frequencies, even when the comparison frequency differed from the base by only 8 Hz. The monkeys showed no statistically significant differences at these frequencies whether the comparison frequency was actual mechanical stimulation to the fingertip or cortical electrical microstimulation directly to the appropriate QA neurons. When the base frequency was held constant over trials at 20 Hz, monkeys made the correct judgment to comparison frequencies better than 75% of the time when they were ≤15 Hz or ≥25 Hz, with no statistically significant difference between mechanical stimuli and microstimulation (Romo *et al.* 1998: Figure 2, 388). Regarding our issue of 'induced phenomenology', Romo and his collaborators conclude:

Animals continuously switched between purely mechanical and microstimulation conditions with almost identical performance levels. Such high accuracy, based on the interaction between natural and artificially evoked activity, is consistent with the induction of a sensory percept. . . . Thus the microstimulation patterns used may elicit flutter sensations referred to the fingertips that are not unlike those felt with mechanical vibrations.   (Romo *et al.* 1998: 389–90)

---

[3] Bickle (2003: ch. 4, sect. 5) presents full details of the experimental methods and results of the microstimulation work discussed in this and the next two paragraphs.

In a subsequent study, Romo and his colleagues (Romo *et al.* 2000) reversed the base and comparison stimuli of their original study. Now on half the trials the base stimulus was mechanical vibration at the fingertip while on the other half it was cortical microstimulation. The comparison stimulus was mechanical stimulation at either a higher or lower frequency. In their original study, the monkeys had to compare the result of microstimulation with the base frequency represented and stored in working memory through normal means, beginning with actual mechanical stimulation of the fingertips. In this second study, however, if the monkeys are to succeed with microstimulation base stimuli comparable to their performance with actual mechanical base stimuli, then cortical microstimulation alone must engage the entire range of cognitive processes involved: sensation, working memory, and comparative decision-making. Besides its intrinsic scientific interest, this study is especially relevant for our question of 'induced phenomenology' because at least one prominent psychologist, Bernard Baars (1998), has urged the tight connection between working memory and consciousness. Even when base and comparison frequencies differed by as little as 4 Hz, monkeys were able to respond correctly about which frequency was lower on 75% of the trials. There were no statistical differences between performances on trials with mechanical or microstimulation base stimuli. As a final control, Romo and his collaborators tested monkeys when both base and comparison frequencies were microstimulations alone, comparing results to cases of identical base and comparison frequencies where both were actual mechanical stimuli. In the former cases, there were now no actual mechanical stimulations to induce sensory, working memory, or comparative decision-making processes in the normal fashion. Yet monkeys performed nearly identically in the two types of cases (although there was more variance within sessions with the purely artificial base and comparison stimuli).

Is there a foreseeable limit to this latest wave of cortical stimulation studies? Color perception continues to pose formidable technical difficulties (Newsome, personal correspondence). But looking beyond sensory stimuli, Liu and Newsome (2000) recently have raised the possibility of microstimulating the appropriate neurons involved in the working memory and comparative decision-making aspects of tasks like Romo's. Cells with 'working memory fields', that fire selectively following specific visual stimuli during short delay periods (up to 12 seconds), have been found in monkey prefrontal cortex (Funahashi, Chafee, and Goldman-Rakic 1993; Goldman-Rakic 1995; Romo *et al.* 1999). Might microstimulation to clusters of cells sharing working memory fields and properties induce causally efficacious 'memories' (of events that never actually occurred)? As Liu and Newsome put this question, 'might it be possible to influence or change the monkey's memory by electrically stimulating such neurons?' (2000: R600). Current physiological knowledge has not yet established that these neurons are grouped anatomically into columns or clusters with others sharing similar activation properties. However, as Liu and Newsome note, 'only a few years ago the complexity of the cerebral cortex would have led most sensory physiologists to declare Romo and colleagues' current microstimulation experiments a fantasy' (2000: R660). 'For now,' they insist, 'all bets are off until the experiments are actually tried' (2000: R660).

2. HOW DOES MICROSTIMULATION OF PERCEPTION
FIT WITH PHENOMENOLOGY?

The fascinating facts of induced phenomenology confirm the insistence of Edmund Husserl that even empirical experience must be phenomenologically reduced, so that its intentional contents are clearly distinguished from actual physical objects that may cause a perception (or apparent perception), if our understanding of the subject–object relationship is to be freed from naive-realist presuppositions. If this naive realism is what Paul Churchland (1983/1987) finds most objectionable about 'folk psychology', then phenomenology is at an opposite pole from folk psychology—contrary to Dennett's presumption from *Content and Consciousness* (1969) through *Consciousness Explained* (1991). By contrast to folk psychology, the phenomenological *epoché* brackets the objective reality-claims of particular experiences in order to lay bare the structures of the subjective acts through which we experience them. The result is a better understanding of the direct experience, as opposed to what is added by our supposed knowledge of physical reality. This is not to deny the relevant physical realities of either the physical events that may cause experiences or the physiological events that subserve them; it is meant only to bracket these assumptions in order to place the subjective experience within such a perspective that it can be examined in its own right.

The 'intentional content', the meaning of an experience as intended, must not be taken as equivalent with any physically existing 'object' in the actual world. If naive realism is part of 'common sense experience', this is because (as Einstein is said to have remarked) common sense is the repository of the prejudices of our childhood. The purpose of phenomenology is to establish a method for carefully examining our direct experience, as distinguished from everyday assumptions about their physical referents. As Thomasson puts it (this volume), the purpose is to study our modes of experiencing rather than the objects we seem to experience. To be sure, as Thomasson is quick to add, we learn about the modes of experiencing *by means of* the experience of an object; but the bracketing of the reality-claims connected with the object shifts our focus to the 'phenomenological residuum' that is left over after the reality-claims have been suspended, and this is a way to study the structures of subjective experience from a first-person point of view. In this respect, phenomenology is poles away from what most would think of as 'folk psychology'.

Induced perceptual experience through direct stimulation constitutes one of the great 'odd facts' of the neurosciences, along with Benjamin Libet's (1985) finding that action commands begin prior to the conscious decision to do the action; the strange phenomenon of 'change blindness' in which subjects fail to see a change that is clearly an obvious feature of a display (Rensink, O'Regan, and Clark 1997); and Joseph LeDoux's (2000) finding that the emotional reaction to a stimulus begins prior to its perceptual processing. Such findings tend to elicit a 'gee whiz' response; they disarm everyday ideas about the status of subjective experiences in the physical world.

Husserl was at home in the realm of odd facts. The odd facts of his day were simpler—the Gestalt findings that the longer line may appear shorter, the straight stick may look bent, and the colored background may seem gray. The original aim of phenomenology was precisely to get away from the natural, everyday tendency to read empirical assumptions about physical objects into the understanding of experience itself, as 'folk psychology' is especially (but not exclusively) prone to do, and to create a more sophisticated approach to reflecting on our own consciousness itself *through* the phenomenologically reduced experience of objects. This is why the 'phenomenological reductions' and the '*epoché*' are the centerpieces of Husserl's (1931, 1964) phenomenology. As Thomasson (this volume) puts it, the idea of the *epoché* is not to introspect into our experience quasi-perceptually, as we would inspect objects, but to shift attention from truth claims about the object we are experiencing until what is left is simply an understanding of the experience itself. From Husserl's standpoint, the 'odd facts' will seem counterintuitive only for those who assume that the content of experience is just what it initially seems, that the percept is simply caused by the object, which is physical, and that the object is as it appears with no distortions resulting from the workings of the subjective process.

However, some may still suspect that odd facts present problems for phenomenology. Empirically oriented philosophers and cognitive scientists (for example, Dennett 1969, 1991; Fodor 1983; Paul Churchland 1983/1987) are inclined to believe that phenomenology is an uneasy fit with the notion that consciousness can be produced by physical manipulations. The odd fact of cortically induced phenomenology seems to reduce phenomenal experience to the same kind of mechanism that produces non-conscious information processing, just as in a sophisticated computer or as in the image-producing mechanisms in film or recording studios. If conscious experience can be produced in the same way as the corresponding non-conscious information processing, then many believe that consciousness itself reduces to just another physical mechanism which can best be understood in physical rather than subjective terms (for example, P. M. Churchland 1983/87; Jackendoff 1996; Warren 1995; Wegner 2002). Penfield's patient D.F. subjectively experienced music when her temporal lobe was stimulated, but (so goes the argument) the objective fact is contrary to what the consciousness seems to present: in reality, the music is not actually present in D.F.'s physical environment, as she takes her experience to present it as being. This leads many contemporary empiricists (too hastily, I shall argue) to assume that subjective consciousness is a misleading guide to what is really going on in mental operations.

If consciousness can represent a mere illusion as a reality, the question naturally arises whether it may just as well misrepresent its own operations according to the familiar confusions of folk psychology. At first glance, this might seem to be the same kind of objection that led to the demise of introspectionist psychology in the nineteenth century. Subjects could not report how they had solved problems; the solution seemed to appear magically, so it finally came to be assumed that subjective consciousness does not really play a role in mental operations, but is merely an epiphenomenon of them—and a fickle and ephemeral one at that. Paul Churchland (1983/1987) goes still further to suggest that whatever can be offered by way of even a sophisticated phenomenology will be best supplanted by the more reliable results of the scientific understanding of brain functioning.

Husserl's (1931, 1964) response to this problem is highly relevant to some of the most pressing problems in current psychology and philosophy of mind. Husserl carefully distinguishes between the 'object as intended' in an experience, the subjective meaning through which the experience presents itself as 'referring' to something, as being 'about' something, and on the other hand the *physical objects* in the environment that the experience might represent, or which may or may not cause it to appear. What non-phenomenologists might casually call the 'object' of a perception is not the same as the object-as-intended in Husserl's sense, but rather a *physical* correlate of the experience, the physical object to which the experience may (to varying degrees) or may not correspond. In the case of phenomenology induced by cortical microstimulation, we have an extreme example of this distinction. D.F.'s heard music is an intentional content for D.F., but does not exist as a physical object in the world. Similarly for the 'illusory' motion and flutter percepts in Newsome's and Romo's microstimulated monkeys.

To blur this distinction between physical objects and objects-as-intended causes many problems. For example, many recent theorists of mental representation define 'representation' as a relation in which the 'object' that is represented *physically causes* an isomorphically related brain state (for example, see Fodor 1983). Such a theory sounds as if it assumes that the relation between mental act and object intended can be construed as a physical cause and effect relationship. Such theories of representation have been criticized because they allow almost any cause and effect sequence in nature to count as a representation, as long as the effect is somehow isomorphically related to the cause (Newton 2001; Thelen *et al.* 2001).

When I represent my car keys, the objects-as-intended (which I take to be on my desk in plain view) may or may not correspond to any actual car keys on my desk. Even when I see what I had taken to be my car keys on the desk, they may turn out to be only an oddly shaped piece of cardboard. The object-as-intended,[4] which in some instances may exist only in my imagination, consists of an image of my car keys, and an accurate description of it will include a characterization as to whether I intend it as merely fancied (as an act of imagination) or as actually present (as an act of perception). But even if the keys turn out to be a hallucination, an accurate description will still characterize my experience as *intending* the object as an object of perception rather than of imagination, and this characterization will be different from the characterization of intending it as a mere mental image, regardless of whether the keys are really on my desk or only a hallucination. If we then learn that the hallucination was caused by the oddly shaped piece of cardboard in conjunction with a tumor in my brain, neither of these factors is the *object-as-intended* in my experience, although they may be physical objects that are related to it in various ways. Similarly, D.F. experiences

---

[4] Some (for example, Lauer 1965; Nenon 1996) refer to what we are calling the 'object-as-intended' as the 'intentional object'; others (for example, Smith, see below) call it the content. We shall attempt to remain neutral with regard to this terminological problem (which really has to do with questions about the ontological status of the object-as-intended); the point we are making about the phenomenology of induced intentional experience by microstimulation should be equally applicable in either case. The phenomenological method, on either interpretation, is perfectly compatible with the observed facts in such experiments.

the music as actually present, not as imaginary. But there is nothing paradoxical about this phenomenon, or contrary to phenomenology as a veridical first-person exploration of the meaning of the experience, unless one overlooks the necessary distinctions to begin with.

David Woodruff Smith (this volume) sets this distinction into a fuller picture of Husserl's project by describing a fourfold relation between subject, act, content, and object. In the example of the car keys, I am the subject; my entertaining the image of the keys *as a perceptual one* is the act (regardless of whether the perception accurately depicts the keys); the idea of the keys as I take them to be (on the desk), with all I take 'keys' to mean (assuredly different from a piece of cardboard), comprises the intentional content—the *meaning* that is experienced; and the apparent specific keys (as existing-rather-than-merely-imagined) are the object, even though this appearance may be deceptive in the sense that there really are no keys, but only a piece of cardboard. The experience posits an object as existing in the actual world, even though what it posits may not actually exist, or may not be exactly as is intended.

Importantly for our purposes, the object-as-intended, the content or meaning intended, including the impression that the keys are actually seen rather than merely imagined—all of these intentional meanings are distinguishable from any *physical* objects that may or may not be similar to the object-as-intended in the experience. For example, Georgalis (2000) points out that, if I form a mental image of my grandmother, but the image looks more like, say, Saddam Hussein than my grandmother, the object of my imagination is my grandmother, not Hussein. I am representing my grandmother, but doing so very inaccurately; I am not representing Hussein while mistaking him to be my grandmother. The object-as-intended is the object that I *intend*, regardless of how veridical it is as a correspondence to something in the physical world.

Husserl also discusses the relationship between the conscious subject for whom an experience occurs, in the sense of the 'I' who has experiences, and the physiological substratum of the experience (the 'psychophysical subject' discussed in his *Phänomenologische Psychologie*, or 'Lectures on Phenomenological Psychology', published in 1962). Within the 'psychophysical subject', he further distinguishes between a *Körper* and a *Leib*—between a body in the sense of a collection of matter to be pushed around and a body that I experience myself as animating from the inside. But regardless of whether the body I take myself to be animating is as I take it to be, I am still the subject of the experiences of it, accurate or inaccurate though they may be.

So, to speak of the relationship between a state of consciousness and its intentional object as if this were simply equivalent to a causal relationship between a physical object and my body in the *Körper* sense, as a recipient of causal force from the object, is to assume many equivalences that may or may not be warranted under various circumstances. The piece of cardboard that causes my hallucination of the car keys is not what the experience is intended as an experience *of*, what it represents, or what it refers to. To ignore the Husserlian distinctions, then, can cause a great deal of confusion in theories about mental relationships and intentional representation.

A similar problem occurs in thinking about the meaning of emotions and feelings. In the realm of emotion studies, the argument is often made that, if a certain physical object in the environment *causes* us to feel a certain emotion, then this object must be the *intentional referent* of the emotion. This leads to a very oversimplified understanding of what emotions are about. When a motorist's cutting us off in traffic causes anger, we would verge on alexithymia if we did not realize that this trivial event only triggered feelings that are about much more important frustrations in our personal or professional lives, to which we may not even be paying conscious attention at the moment. Here, as in the preceding examples, phenomenological reduction shows that our feelings, no less than other conscious states, cannot be simply assumed to refer to some physical event that may have 'triggered' them. A physical explanation of what caused them does not clarify their experienced meaning.

The everyday habit of experiencing in a phenomenologically unreduced way—what Husserl calls the 'natural attitude'—includes also the habit of unreflectively applying the categories that work for objects experienced as physical to ourselves-as-subjects. For example, we ignore the distinctions between the conscious state, the psychophysical subject that appears to subserve them, the intentional meaning or content of experience, and the physical object that may correspond to it. It is an oversimplification to subsume all these concepts within a twofold distinction between a psychophysical event (hastily equated with the conscious act) and a physical object that supposedly both causes the conscious state and serves as its intentional object. It is 'natural' to think of experience in this simple way because causal concepts are drawn from the causal relations we observe empirically in the environment. But when we apply them to the causation of our experience, we end up with the problems of 'folk psychology' that both serious phenomenology *and* contemporary neuroscience are interested in avoiding. The point here is not to deny that there may be physiological correlates of consciousness, but to avoid running together intentional with causal relations.

So, given the difficulties of phenomenological reduction and description, where does this leave us with respect to Paul Churchland's (1983/1987) argument that we should eschew first-person methods in favor of simply studying the physical correlates of consciousness, which in his view can be done with more reliable methods? The psychologist Sigmund Koch (1959) has suggested that, even if we had a perfect theory of human psychology, to use this theory in understanding actual human behavior would often be like trying to use the principles of aerodynamics to explain why a particular falling leaf took the particular path it took as it drifted to earth. In principle, such an explanation is possible, but in practice it can never be done, because the facts that would be needed are so numerous, complex, and subtle that to collect them all would be a ridiculously Herculean enterprise. In the absence of such Herculean resources being devoted to the field of psychology, and also in the absence of a perfect theory, there may be many situations in which the information gleaned from rigorous phenomenological analysis of subjective experience is more useful and reliable than what can be gotten about the human body from empirical science at some particular point in its history. But the key word here is 'rigorous'. Husserl would be the last to endorse a knee-jerk 'reading off' of the supposed meanings of experiences, prior to phenomenological and eidetic reductions—in simpler terms, prior to an extensive exploration of the tacit presuppositions of the natural attitude that we are prone to bring with us to any given experience. Also, even a perfect understanding of the workings of the body still would not yield knowledge of the presumably correlated intentional meanings and their interrelations.

To think that phenomenology holds phenomenologically reduced subjective experience as proving anything about what is going on in empirical reality is to make a category mistake. It confuses the intentional object of an experience, which in principle can be a mere fantasy, hallucination, dream, or illusion (Husserl 1931), with the actual physical objects in the world—objects that may or may not correspond to our intentional objects, and to greater or lesser extents. From this perspective, what is most remarkable about induced phenomenology is that the experience may appear to the subject not merely as a mental image, as in daydreams and conjured fantasies, but as an actual percept that seems to be actually present. When D.F.'s temporal lobe was stimulated, she heard music not as if she were imagining or remembering it, but as if it were actually playing on a radio. This shows that we cannot rely on any purely subjective technique to inform us as to whether what *causes* an object to appear is a physical object in the perceptible world, or only an act of imagination. Notice that this conclusion is contrary to Sartre's discussion in *The Psychology of the Imagination* (1966), where he emphasizes that careful reflection will reveal the difference between a mental image and a percept, involving features like the greater degree of resolution and detail of the percept. But Sartre was in disagreement with Husserl on this point. For Husserl, we may notice through phenomenological reflection that we are experiencing an object as an object of perception, yet it may be merely a hallucination. And it is always possible in principle that any actual object is far from the way we constitute it in consciousness.

For Husserl, the question whether the physical body causes the subjective experience, or is identical with it, or bears some other relation to it, was to be settled *a posteriori*. This is very clear, for example, in his *Logical Investigations* (1913) and *Lectures on Phenomenological Psychology* (1962). The conceptual distinction should not prejudice the resolution of the mind–body relation, any more than the conceptual distinction between Clark Kent and Superman can settle the question whether Kent is Superman. Having begun his career as a mathematical logician, Husserl continued to recognize the possibility of a distinction without a separation, as illustrated by the factual identity of Kent and Superman, however distinguishable our eidetic concepts of them might be.

In fact, recent empirical observations about brain functions are highly consistent with many details of phenomenological reflection. In Husserl's (1913) terms, a meaning-*intention* must be in place before a meaning-*fulfillment* can occur. The meaning-intention is a category or concept, and is accompanied by vague mental imagery. The meaning-*fulfillment* presupposes this meaning-intention (i.e. this motivated, anticipatory 'looking-for'), but adds to it the actual perceptual data that facilitate a feeling that we are actually looking *at* the object, not merely *for* it. This difference between meaning-intention (looking-for) and meaning fulfillment (looking-at) is accompanied by certain phenomenologically accessed earmarks, many of which are described by Sartre in his *Psychology of the Imagination* (1966). Here again, as Thomasson (this volume) stresses, the idea that a percept presupposes a concept, just as a memory of a perception presupposes the perception, results from a purely *a priori* analysis of the phenomenologically reduced meanings of all the experiential terms, and does not require some special perception-like introspection, as if inspecting our conscious activities from the outside.

The phenomenology of this relationship between meaning intentions and meaning-fulfilling intentions is consistent with the finding of Aurell (1989) and Posner and Rothbart (1992) that, when some sensory stimulus activates the primary projection area in the brain, no *consciousness* of the object is yet present. There is consciousness of the object only when the prefrontal and parietal areas are activated, and this is the same kind of activation that would be associated with the *imagination* of the object (Richardson 1991). Activation of these areas without any corresponding sensory input corresponds to a mere imagination of the object; in this case, *efferent* activity (nervous activity directed outward toward the body's action capacities) occurs in the parietal, secondary-sensory, and frontal areas, but no matching *afferent* signals (received from the body's extremities, sense organs, or viscera) are found in the primary projection area. Relating this to the phenomenology of the experience, we can say that the efferent system has geared itself up to look *for* a certain image, but this image is not found in the pattern of input from the environment. Logan (1980), Corbetta *et al.* (1990), Pardo *et al.* (1990), Hanze and Hesse (1993), Legrenzi *et al.* (1993), Rhodes and Tremewan (1993), and other cognitive psychologists also find that, when we hold in our imagination the image of a certain object, we are more likely to see that object when flashed on a screen. By imagining the object, we gear ourselves up to look for it.

When I look at a pink wall and *imagine* it as a blue wall, I find myself 'looking-for-blue' in very much the same way as I would if I were to focus on a wall fully expecting it to be blue. This 'looking-for' phenomenon enables us to think about both the similarities and the differences between the physiological correlates of the perceptual and the imaginative consciousness of essentially the *same* cognitive content ('blue wall', for example). Every looking-at must be accompanied by a corresponding looking-for. Thus, consistently with Merleau-Ponty's (1941/62) 'We must look in order to see' (p. 232), Luria (1973) says, 'The stationary eye is virtually incapable of the stable perception of complex objects and . . . such perception is always based on the use of active, searching movements of the eyes, picking out the essential clues' (p. 100). We cannot consciously 'look-at' something without having first 'looked-for' the object. But we can 'look-for' the object with no afferent input, when the relevant efferent brain structures are active, and in this case a mere mental image of the non-present object occurs. Indeed, this appears to be what happens in Romo's (2000) most recent microstimulation studies on QA neurons in S1, when both 'base' *and* 'comparison' stimuli result from cortical microstimulation (discussed toward the end of section 1 above).

Merleau-Ponty (1941, 1942), while agreeing with the above Husserlian points, goes further than Husserl in trying to correlate phenomenology with physiology, and he picks up on this relation between meaning-intention and meaning-fulfilling intention. For Merleau-Ponty, to be perceptually conscious requires more than some brain area's receiving input from the environment that impinges on the nervous system, and then transforming the information computationally. Both the 'intellectualism' and the 'sensationalism' that Merleau-Ponty (1941) rejected made the mistake of ignoring the role of anticipatory and efferent brain activities in subserving consciousness, by trying to explain consciousness as a passive receiving of physical signals. For example, an amputee is conscious of the 'phantom limb' even though no afferent signals are received from it. The subject is conscious of the limb merely by sending efferent action commands to it—commands that are not received or acted upon, to be sure, but which facilitate consciousness of the limb nonetheless. We are conscious of our bodies not only by means of a 'body image', which is primarily afferent (based on information received from the viscera and extremities), but also by means of a 'body schema', which is based primarily on efferent signals that convey action commands to the body. Merleau-Ponty has now been confirmed in this view by the fact that when we send action commands while simultaneously inhibiting them, mental action imagery results (Jeannerod 1997).

Merleau-Ponty's account of the way consciousness correlates with the physical—an extension of Husserl's meaning-intention/meaning-fulfillment distinction combined with some physiological assumptions—leads to a prediction about perceptual experience induced by cortical stimulation. The microstimulation that induces the conscious phenomenal state, on Merleau-Ponty's view, would have to activate efferent and not just afferent processes. And this would mean that it must facilitate a widely distributed brain circuit, rather than simply activate a few local cells. This prediction is consistent with findings of Damasio (1999) and others that when we cut off the cortex from various functioning subcortical areas, we eliminate the possibility of any form of consciousness, whether through direct stimulation or not. Damasio finds that, the deeper the brain area that is impaired, the less consciousness there is, even if cortical functioning remains mostly intact. This prediction is also at least consonant with Romo *et al.*'s (2000) finding (discussed in the previous section) that cortical microstimulation of the primary somatosensory cortex can produce the full range of cognitive processes, including working memory and the comparative and decision-making processes, required to successfully perform his base-comparison stimulus matching task.

Thus one test for whether the phenomenal experiences produced by direct cortical stimulation are highly localized, or on the contrary dependent on widely distributed processes that include efferent as well as afferent aspects, would be whether a person in a persistent vegetative state could be caused to have an induced conscious state by direct stimulation. To date, there do not seem to be studies in which such conscious states have successfully been produced by cortical microstimulation in people suffering from subcortically caused persistent vegetative states but with intact cortical function. Of course, the methodological problems involved in such studies are daunting. How could phenomenal experiences be measured in such individuals?

Phenomenological considerations, while not entailing any physical commitments about objects of experience, can nonetheless contribute to interesting empirical predictions when combined with psychophysical assumptions. As Merleau-Ponty suggests, conscious processes are different from nonconscious ones not only in the subjective dimension, but also in the way they are physically realized. His may not be the only understanding consistent with the phenomenological data, but it seems to be one example. What is certainly clear is that both Husserlian phenomenology and Merleau-Ponty's attempts to mix it with psychology and neurophysiology are quite consistent with such odd findings as cortical microstimulation of conscious perceptual states.

3. 'HARD PROBLEMS', THE SOCIETY FOR NEUROSCIENCE CROWD, AND PHENOMENOLOGY AS ONE BRIDGE BETWEEN THE TWO?

There are neuroscientists who think of the brain as just another 'organ', as 'just another piece of biological tissue'. However, many pursue the discipline for reasons that historically have motivated humanists, and are not afraid to express their motives in print. A nice example is this passage from the introductory chapter of Gordon Shepherd's influential textbook: 'As we grow older, we experience the full richness of human behavior—the ability to think and feel, to remember and create—and we wonder, if we have any wonder at all, how the brain makes this possible' (1994: 3). This is not the ranting of some left-field crank, but rather from the current editor of the *Journal of Neuroscience*. Similar passages can be cited many-fold. Not all neuroscientists are philosophical philistines.

These admissions won't satisfy some philosophers, who remain jealous guardians of the 'qualitative' and 'subjective' aspects of Mind. They assume that only they—and perhaps a handful of theoretically minded psychologists—grapple seriously with 'what it is like' to be a conscious, mindful human being. They assume that these features are beyond neuroscientists' professional grasp and serious interest. But they are wrong. Consider the following passage from William Newsome, commenting on the microstimulation studies surveyed above:

I believe *the nature of internal experience matters* for our understanding of nervous system function ... Even if I could explain a monkey's behavior on our task in its entirety (in neural terms), *I would not be satisfied* unless I knew whether microstimulation in MT *actually causes the monkey to see motion*. If we close up shop before answering this question and understanding its implications, we have mined silver and left the gold lying in the tailings.   (Gazzaniga 1997: 65–6; my emphases)

Yet Newsome asks for no special discipline or methodology to address this question. He sees no shortcuts around a broadly empiricist, reductionist path, writing: 'For the time being ... I suspect we must feel our way towards these ambitious goals from the bottom up, letting the new light obtained at each level of inquiry hint at the questions to be asked at the next level' (Gazzaniga 1997: 67).[5]

Neither of us advocates replacing honest toil with theft. But the resources of phenomenology surveyed in the previous section might be a useful aid in this inquiry.

---

[5] Notice that Newsome's reductionism doesn't collapse levels, at least not methodologically, as many anti-reductionist philosophers fear. Bickle (1998) tries to make explicit the nature of this 'reductionism' implicit in mainstream neuroscience. Bickle (2003) focuses on recent scientific experiments and results to complement the philosophy of science orientation of the earlier book.

When searching for mechanisms, a useful heuristic is to know something about the phenomena we seek to explain. When that target is conscious experience, phenomenological reduction is useful for isolating its core properties—in ways we detailed in section 2 above. What must be guarded against is the tendency of phenomenologists, on the one hand, to think that they are the only ones respectful or in pursuit of the full glory of Mind; and the tendency of reductionistic neuroscientists, on the other hand, to reject potentially useful resources in their search for the cellular and molecular mechanisms of cognition and consciousness based on a caricature of what phenomenology is. As we demonstrate explicitly in this essay, the two can coexist peacefully. And the next step—which we hope to have at least initiated here—is for the two to begin assisting each other in specific transdisciplinary psycho-neural research projects.

REFERENCES

Albright, T. D., Desimone, R., and Gross, C. G. (1984) 'Columnar Organization of Directionally Selective Cells in Visual Area MT of Macaques', *Journal of Neurophysiology* 51: 16–31.

Aurell, C. G. (1989) 'Man's Tune Conscious Mind', *Perceptual and Motor Skills* 68: 747–54.

Baars, B. (1998) *In the Theater of Consciousness* (Oxford: Oxford University Press).

Bickle, J. (1998) *Psychoneural Reduction: The New Wave* (Cambridge, Mass.: MIT Press).

—— (2003) *Philosophy and Neuroscience: A Ruthlessly Reductive Account* (Dordrecht: Kluwer Academic Publishers).

Britten, K. H. and van Wezel, R. J. A. (1998) 'Electrical Microstimulation of Cortical Area MST Biases Heading Perception in Monkeys', *Nature Neuroscience* 1/1: 59–63.

Churchland, P. M. (1983/1987) *Matter and Consciousness* (Cambridge, Mass.: MIT Press).

—— (1989) *A Neurocomputational Perspective* (Cambridge, Mass.: MIT Press).

Churchland, P. S. (1986) *Neurophilosophy* (Cambridge, Mass.: MIT Press).

Corbetta, M., Meizen, F. M., Dobmeyer, S., Schulman, G. L., and Petersen, S. E. (1990). 'Selective Attention Modulates Neural Processing of Shape, Color and Velocity in Humans', *Science* 248: 1556–9.

Damasio, A. (1999) *The Feeling of What Happens* (New York: Harcourt Brace).

DeAngelis, G. C., Cumming, B. G., and Newsome, W. T. (1998) 'Cortical Area MT and the Perception of Stereoscopic Depth', *Nature* 394: 677–80.

Dennett, D. C. (1969) *Content and Consciousness* (London: Routledge & Kegan Paul).

—— (1991) *Consciousness Explained* (Boston: Little Brown).

Fodor, J. (1983) *The Modularity of Mind* (Cambridge, Mass.: MIT Press).

Funahashi, S., Chafee, M., and Goldman-Rakic, P. S. (1993) 'Prefrontal Neuronal Activity in Rhesus Monkeys Performing an Anti-saccade Task', *Nature* 365: 753–6.

Gazzaniga, M. S. (ed.) (1997) *Conversations in the Cognitive Neurosciences* (Cambridge, MA: MIT Press).

Georgalis, N. (2000) 'Mind, Brain, and Chaos', in R. Ellis and N. Newton (eds.), *The Caldron of Consciousness* (Amsterdam: John Benjamins).

Goldman-Rakic, P. S. (1995) 'Cellular Basis of Working Memory', *Neuron* 14: 477–85.

Goodale, M. A. and Milner, A. D. (1992) 'Separate Visual Pathways for Perception and Action', *Trends in Neuroscience* 15: 20–5.

Hanze M. and Hesse, F. (1993) 'Emotional Influences on Semantic Priming', *Cognition and Emotion* 7: 195–205.

Husserl, E. (1913/1970) *Logical Investigations*, trans. J. M. Findley (New York: Humanities Press).
——(1931/1969) *Ideas*, trans. W. R. Boyce Gibson from 'Ideen zu einer reinen Phänomenologie und phänomenologischen Philosophie', 1913 (London: Collier).
——(1962) *Phänomenologische Psychologie*, Lectures on Phenomenological Psychology (Den Haag: Martinus Nijhoff).
——(1964) *The Crisis of European Sciences* (Evanston, Ill: Northwestern University Press).
Jackendoff, R. (1996) 'How Language Helps Us Think', *Pragmatics & Cognition* 4: 1–34.
Jeannerod, M. (1997) *The Cognitive Neuroscience of Action* (Oxford: Blackwell).
Kim, J. (1992) 'Multiple Realizability and the Metaphysics of Reduction', *Philosophy and Phenomenological Research* 52: 1–26.
Kim, J. (1998) *Mind in a Physical World: An Essay on the Mind–Body Problem and Mental Causation* (Cambridge, Mass.: MIT Press).
Koch, S. (ed.) (1959) *Psychology: A Study of a Science*, iii (New York: McGraw-Hill).
Lauer, Q. (1965) *Phenomenology* (New York: Harper).
LeDoux, J. E. (2000) 'Emotion Circuits in the Brain', *Annual Reviews of Neuroscience* 23: 155–84.
Legrenzi P., Girotto, V., and Johnson-Laird, P. N. (1993) 'Focusing on Reasoning and Decision Making', *Cognition* 49: 37–66.
Libet. B. (1985) 'Unconscious Cerebral Initiative and the Role of Conscious Will in Voluntary Action', *Behavioral and Brain Sciences* 8: 529–66.
Liu, J. and Newsome, W. T. (2000) 'Somatosensation: Touching the Mind's Fingers', *Current Biology* 10/16: R598–600.
Llinás, R. and Churchland, P. S. (1996) *The Mind–Brain Continuum: Sensory Processes* (Cambridge, MA: MIT Press).
Logan, G. D. (1980) 'Attention and Automaticity in Stroop and Priming Tasks: Theory and Data', *Cognitive Psychology* 12: 523–53.
Luria, A. R. (1973) *The Working Brain* (New York: Basic Books).
Merleau-Ponty, M. (1941/62) *Phenomenology of Perception*, trans. Colin Smith (New York: Humanities Press).
——(1942/1967) *The Structure of Behavior*, trans. A. Fischer (Boston: Beacon Press).
Mishkin, M., Ungerleider, L. G., and Macko, K. (1983) 'Object Vision and Spatial Vision: Two Cortical Pathways', *Trends in Neuroscience* 6: 414–17.
Mountcastle, V. B., Steinmetz, M. A., and Romo, R. (1990) 'Frequency Discrimination in the Sense of Flutter: Psychophysical Measurements Correlated with Postcentral Events in Behaving Monkeys', *Journal of Neuroscience* 10: 3032–44.
Murasagi, C. M., Salzman, C. D., and Newsome, W. T. (1993) 'Microstimulation in Visual Area MT: Effects of Varying Pulse Amplitude and Frequency', *Journal of Neuroscience* 13/4: 1719–29.
Nenon, T. (1996) 'Intentionality in Husserl', in D. M. Borchert (ed.), *The Encyclopedia of Philosophy Supplement* (New York: Simon & Schuster Macmillan), 264–5.
Newton, N. (2001) 'Emergence and the Uniqueness of Consciousness', *Journal of Consciousness Studies* 8: 47–59.
Pardo, J. V., Pardo, P. J., Janer, K. W., and Raichle, M. E. (1990) 'The Anterior Cingulate Cortex Mediates Processing Selection in the Stroop Attentional Conflict Paradigm', *Proceedings of the National Academy of Sciences* (USA) 87: 256–9.
Penfield, W. and Perot, P. (1963) 'The Brain's Record of Auditory and Visual Experience', *Brain* 86/4: 595–696.

Posner M. I. and Rothbart, M. K. (1992) 'Attentional Mechanisms and Conscious Experience', in A. D. Milner and M. D. Rugg (eds.), *The Neuropsychology of Consciousness* (London: Academic Press), 187–210.

Rensink, R. A., O'Regan, J. K., and Clark, J. J. (1997) 'To See or Not to See: The Need for Attention to Perceive Changes in Scenes.' *Psychological Science* 8: 368–73.

Rhodes G. and Tremewan, T. (1993) 'The Simon and Garfunkel Effect: Semantic Priming, Sensitivity, and the Modularity of Face Recognition', *Cognitive Psychology* 25: 147–87.

Richardson, J. (1991) 'Imagery and the Brain', in C. Cornoldi and M. McDaniel (eds.), *Imagery and Cognition* (New York: Springer-Verlag), 1–46.

Romo, R., Brody, C. D., Hernandez, A., and Lemus, L. (1999) 'Neuronal Correlates of Parametric Working Memory in the Prefrontal Cortex', *Nature* 399: 470–3.

Romo, R., Hernandez, A., Zainos, A., Brody, C. D., and Lemus, L. (2000) 'Sensing without Touching: Psychophysical Performance Based on Cortical Microstimulation', *Neuron* 26: 273–8.

Romo, R., Hernandez, A., Zainos, A., and Salinas, E. (1998) 'Somatosensory Discrimination Based on Microstimulation', *Nature* 392: 387–90.

Salzman, C. D., Murasagi, C. M., Britten, K. H., and Newsome, W. T. (1992) 'Microstimulation in Visual Area MT: Effects on Direction Discrimination Performance', *Journal of Neuroscience* 12/6: 2331–55.

Sartre, J. P. (1966) *The Psychology of the Imagination* (New York: Washington Square Press).

Shepherd, G. (1994) *Neurobiology* (Oxford: Oxford University Press).

Smith, D. W. (2005) 'Phenomenology', this volume.

Stoney, S. D., Thompson, W. D., and Asanuma, H. (1968) 'Excitation of Pyramidal Tract Cells by Intracortical Microstimulation: Effective Extent of Stimulating Current', *Journal of Neurophysiology* 31: 659–69.

Thelen, E., Schoner, G., and Scheier, C. (2001) 'The Dynamics of Embodiment: A Field Theory of Infant Perseverative Reaching', *Behavioral and Brain Sciences* 24: 1–86.

Thomasson, A. (2005) 'First-person Knowledge in Phenomenology', this volume.

Warren, R. M. (1995) 'Should We Continue to Study Consciousness?', *Behavioral and Brain Sciences* 18: 270–1.

Wegner, D. (2002) *The Illusion of Conscious Choice* (Cambridge, Mass.: MIT Press).

PART III

INTENTIONALITY

7

The Immanence Theory of Intentionality

Johannes L. Brandl

Abstract: This essay starts out from the classical version of the immanence theory of intentionality, as one finds it in the writings of Franz Brentano. As will be argued in the first part of the essay, this theory is not so unreasonable as its many critics have taken it to be. If one reads Brentano's difficult texts with charity, one can see that his version of the immanence theory withstands the standard objections raised against it. Nevertheless, Brentano himself later rejected the theory because it includes the assumption of there being non-real entities existing in our minds. In the second part of the essay I argue that this commitment to an ontology of non-real entities is not an essential part of the immanence theory. A version of this theory is proposed that takes mental information bearers to be the immanent objects to which subjects are related. The merit of this proposal is that it provides a framework for explaining the subjectivity of experience within a theory of intentionality. It differs from other attempts to explain the phenomenal character of experience in intentional terms by invoking a hypothesis about the vehicle of representation that is used in subjective experiences.

1. INTRODUCTION

The immanence theory of intentionality—in its most ambitious form—aspires to be a general theory about all kinds of mental phenomena, including sensory experiences, perceptions, cognitive states like beliefs and desires, and mental acts like judgements and acts of the will. The theory says that all these phenomena involve a relation between a subject that experiences, perceives, believes, desires, judges, or wills something and a special type of non-real entities that are variously called 'immanent objects', 'intentional objects', or 'inexistent objects'. Moreover, the theory claims that only mental phenomena involve such a relation to immanent objects, and that the presence of such objects therefore provides a criterion that distinguishes mental phenomena from all other phenomena, in particular from physical phenomena.

When Franz Brentano in his *Psychology from an Empirical Standpoint* (1874) characterized mental phenomena in terms of the notion of 'intentional inexistence', he suggested a theory of that kind which he elaborated in his lectures during the following years.[1]

---

[1] Only a small number of these lectures have so far been published in Brentano 1982.

In this highly fragmentary form the immanence theory became the first theory of intentionality to inspire the phenomenological tradition. However, the theory soon lost its reputation. Brentano's students Twardowski, Meinong, and Husserl found the theory wanting for several reasons, and Brentano himself later rejected the idea that there are non-real entities contained in mental phenomena as an ontological extravagancy. The widespread assumption that henceforth guided the research in this area was the conviction that the immanence theory rests on some serious confusion and that its ontological and epistemological costs should be avoided by a more careful analysis of the concept of intentionality.[2]

Philosophical ideas tend to be long-lived, however. Some of the virtues of the immanence theory continue to attract philosophers both inside and outside the phenomenological tradition. One can see this in recent discussions of phenomenal consciousness, when the question of the ontological status of the so-called 'qualia' of experiences arises. The appealing idea of explaining the subjective nature of experience by introducing internal objects stands in conflict here with a widely shared scepticism against an ontology of mental objects. In this essay I want to propose how this conflict may be solved by reviving the immanence theory in a different form. I will thereby abstract from the more ambitious claims associated with this theory—in particular from the claim that intentionality offers us a criterion of the mental—and focus on what I take to be the core of the theory that is still defensible.

My re-evaluation of the immanence theory falls into two parts. In the first part of the essay (sections 2 and 3) I will show that some of the standard objections against the immanence theory do not withstand a closer scrutiny. An accurate interpretation of Brentano's views will make it clear that the immanence theory he adopted was not a simple-minded theory that can be easily dismissed. In the second part of the essay (sections 4 and 5) I will focus on the positive role immanent objects may play in a theory of subjective experience, and I argue that in order to play this role immanent objects need not be conceived as non-real entities. By making them part of our mental reality, the ontological resistance against taking the immanence theory seriously may be overcome.

2. BRENTANO'S EARLY THEORY OF INTENTIONALITY: AN UNTENABLE POSITION?

When Brentano stated his famous thesis that 'every mental phenomenon includes something as object within itself',[3] he thereby hoped to give a most perspicuous answer to the question of which phenomena fall under the concept 'mental'. Instead of settling this issue, however, his doctrine raised more questions than it answered and produced a real 'quagmire', as Joseph Margolis has recently put it.[4] There can be no doubt about the fundamental importance that Brentano placed on the notion of

---

[2] For further details concerning the negative reception of the immanence theory within the Brentano-School see Moran (2000: 55 ff.), and Jacquette (2004: 103 ff.).

[3] Brentano (1995: 88).   [4] See Margolis (2004: 131).

intentionality by taking it to be the most important characteristic of mental phenomena and by building his entire philosophy on this insight. But what does Brentano tell us about this special characteristic of mental phenomena?

The issue that divides interpreters of Brentano's thesis until today concerns the ontology that goes along with this doctrine. This was apparently also a great concern of Brentano himself, but unfortunately the texts he left are not very conclusive on this point. There is, however, a quite simple and straightforward reading of what he means when he speaks of there being something included as an object—or intentionally inexisting—in a mental phenomenon. On the face of it, he thereby espouses the basic idea of the immanence theory: there are mental entities that exist in the minds of subjects whose experiences and thoughts are directed at them. Robert Richardson has called this reading of Brentano's thesis its 'orthodox interpretation' and summarizes it as follows: '[M]ental phenomena *are* genuinely relational: the difference, or at least a difference, between mental and physical phenomena lies in the objects or in the mode of existence proper to those objects.'[5]

Richardson and other Brentano scholars before him have found it doubtful, however, that this is actually what Brentano meant.[6] They point out that the Scholastic terminology of 'inexistence' and 'having something as an object' also admits of an interpretation that involves no commitment to a realm of intra-mental relata of the intentional relation.[7] I will say more about these exegetical questions in the next section. First, I want to consider why one might hesitate to accept this way of understanding Brentano's thesis.

Scholars hesitate to accept the orthodox interpretation because a theory of intentionality that invokes immanent objects seems so utterly implausible to them. They find it hard to believe that a philosopher of the rank of Brentano accepted a theory that has such obvious deficits. These defects of the immanence theory are not so easy to pin down, however, as we shall see.

Let us begin with a familiar objection that we might call the 'absurdity objection'. It is the standard objection against introducing so-called 'sense-data' as the immediate objects of perceptual experiences. It says that postulating such entities has the consequence that the only entities we ever perceive are these peculiar objects existing in our own minds. The absurdity of this view becomes even greater when it is generalized to all mental phenomena. It then leads to a radical form of epistemological idealism according to which immanent objects are the only objects we can *think about*. Our thoughts would be imprisoned in our own minds, so it is said, and we would suffer from a permanent illusion that it is otherwise.

This *reductio* argument is not very impressive, however, on closer inspection. The argument only works if one construes the sense-datum theory—or the immanence

[5] Richardson (1983: 252). The main representative of this orthodox interpretation has been Roderick Chisholm; see Chisholm (1967) and (1970).

[6] See McAlister (1974), Aquila (1977), Kent (1984). See also McAlister (2004) for a recent update of her reading of Brentano.

[7] New material for such a historically guided interpretation (Richardson calls it the 'reformed interpretation' Richardson (1982: 250) has been provided in the meantime by Sorabji (1991), Caston (1998), and Perler (2002).

theory—in a highly naive way. It may certainly be doubted that Brentano subscribed to such a naive theory. Nevertheless, this view is often attributed to him. For instance, in a short introduction to phenomenology, Sajama and Kamppinen try to bring out the absurdity of the immanence theory that Brentano allegedly held by giving the following example:

> Brentano's conception of intentionality as directedness to an intra-mental object is unsatisfactory, for it implies that the object of one's perception of, say, the sun is not the heavenly body itself but some image in one's mind.
>
> However, it is easy to understand how Brentano arrived at this conception. The aim of his psychology was to describe mental phenomena such as they appear to the person who experiences them or 'lives through' them: not as they appear to an external observer. What is really present to the mind, we might now say, is the presentation (Vorstellung) or idea of the sun, not the sun itself. From this correct premise, however, he mistakenly infers that the mind is directed to this presentation or idea, i.e. to what Brentano called the content or the object of the mental act.[8]

The inference described here is fallacious for the following reason: it does not follow from the assumption that intra-mental objects are the immediate objects of perception that these are the *only* entities that we ever perceive. We must distinguish here two senses of the term 'perception'. There is the popular use of this term according to which we perceive tables and chairs that exist in the external world, and there is the technical, philosophical use of this term that takes perception to be a direct acquaintance with objects that we enjoy when we 'live through' our own mental experiences. This distinction, Sajama and Kampinnen suggest, was overlooked by Brentano and therefore his theory ended in a disaster.

Unfortunately they provide no evidence for this claim. In fact, as we shall see, Brentano was very much aware of the ambiguities involved in this kind of reasoning, and he hoped to clarify them with the help of his theory. Hence it is clearly unwarranted to suppose that his theory was so simple-minded as the absurdity objection takes it to be.

Let us, therefore, turn to a second and more interesting objection. This is a deeper worry about the explanatory power of the immanence theory. It is based on the requirement that a theory of intentionality should be able to explain how it comes that some of our thoughts are directed at objects existing in reality, while others are directed at objects that do not exist. The immanence theory is unsatisfactory, so the objection goes, because it fails to meet this requirement.

This objection is also hard to justify, however. Perhaps this is why it is often left implicit and not spelled out in detail. The most explicit treatment of it can be found in the work of Roderick Chisholm, but even there we are often left with puzzling analogies, as for instance in the following passage that contains a truncated version of this objection:

> If the doctrine of intentional inexistence is true, the very fact that Diogenes was looking for an honest man implies that he already had the immanent object; hence *it* could not be the object of his quest. Thus Brentano was later to say that 'what we think about is *the object* or *thing* and not the "object of thought"' (das vorgestellte Objekt).

---

[8] Sajama and Kamppinen (1987: 28).

The ontological use of the word 'intentional', therefore, seems to undermine its psychological use. Intentionally inexistent objects were posited in the attempt to understand intentional reference, but the attempt did not succeed—precisely because the objects so posited *were* intentionally inexistent.[9]

The first part of this passage merely repeats the absurdity objection with a different example: if the immanence theory were correct, it would be nonsense for Diogenes to look for an honest man, since the only thing he could look for would be an immanent object, and he does not have to look for that object since it is already present in his mind. It is not clear whether Chisholm actually wants to attribute this strange view to Brentano, however, since he indicates how Brentano might respond to this argument, namely by pointing out the ambiguity of the term 'intentional'. This ambiguity parallels the ambiguity of the term 'perception' mentioned above. The term 'intentional', Chisholm explains, has both an 'ontological' and a 'psychological' meaning when used in complex phrases like 'intentional relation' and 'intentional object'. It either helps to denote intentional or immanent objects that exist whenever a mental act is directed upon them—then the term is used attributively to characterize the type of object referred to. Or the term 'intentional' is used in a 'modifying' sense, as Brentano puts it. By this he means that it modifies the meaning of the terms 'object' and 'relation' in such a way that what these terms denote are *mental episodes*, not the immanent objects ('objects of thought') involved in these episodes. Chisholm therefore rightly calls this use the 'psychological' use of the term 'intentional'.

Once this ambiguity of the term 'intentional' is clarified, no confusion should arise about what Diogenes is looking for. He is in a mental state that involves an immanent object, but this immanent object merely guides his search, as we might say, and it is not what the mental episode of looking for somebody is directed at. What, then, is the objection that Chisholm raises here? Perhaps he wants to suggest that Brentano came to realize the ambiguity of the term 'intentional' only gradually. But there is no evidence he offers for this accusation. Chisholm's real objection is a quite different one and is raised only at the end of the above quote: immanent objects do not help to understand how intentional reference to mind-external objects is achieved. So how does this objection work?

Chisholm refers here to a tension between the two uses of the term 'intentional', and this is apparently what the example of Diogenes is really meant to show. If we want to understand what happens in the mind of Diogenes when he is looking for somebody, it is no help to be told that there is an intra-mental object, like an image, existing in his mind. On the contrary, postulating such intra-mental entities makes it even harder—if not impossible—to understand how a mental reference to an object in the real world is achieved.

The trouble with this objection is that it proves too much. We can see this from the fact that a similar argument would also refute theories that invoke abstract propositions as the objects of beliefs and desires. Suppose we change the example slightly and take Diogenes' desire to be a propositional attitude whose object is the abstract proposition expressed by the sentence 'I find an honest man'. How could this proposition, one

---

[9] Chisholm (1970: 139).

might ask, explain that his desire is directed at an object in the real world? The proposition is an abstract entity that exists quite independently of the external world. So we get the extra problem of explaining how such abstract objects are related to concrete things in the world.

The ontology of propositions has its well-known problems, but the present objection against invoking such entities in a theory of intentionality is simply beside the point. It overlooks that propositions are *presupposed* to fix the satisfaction conditions of propositional attitudes. When we know what proposition is the object of someone's belief or desire, we know *eo ipso* what has to be the case for this belief to be true or for the desire to be satisfied. It must therefore be *assumed* that propositions are about objects in the real world. The proposition that is the object of Diogenes' desire could not be satisfied unless he finds a real man that is honest.

The point here is this: if propositions can provide our beliefs and desires with satisfaction conditions, this must also be granted to immanent objects. Why should an intra-mental entity lack this power that abstract propositions have? There are no doubt important differences between propositions and immanent objects, but as long as it is not demonstrated how these differences affect the explanatory power of those entities, Chisholm's objection does not get off the ground.

So far, then, there is nothing an advocate of the immanence theory has to fear. His theory is neither totally implausible, nor has it been demonstrated that it suffers from a special explanatory weakness. But this is only the beginning of a possible defence of this theory. In the next section I will consider in more detail the kind of immanence theory Brentano proposed and why he eventually came to reject it.

3. BRENTANO'S LATER REJECTION OF IMMANENT OBJECTS

When Brentano published a second edition of his *Psychology* in 1911 he added some 'supplementary remarks intended to explain and defend, as well as to correct and expand upon the theory'.[10] One of these corrections he mentions specifically in the foreword to this second edition: 'One of the most important innovations is that I am no longer of the opinion that a mental relation can have something other than a thing [Reales] as its object.'[11] This is generally taken to be Brentano's official announcement of his so-called 'reistic turn'. Brentano from now on insisted that the only entities that a theory of mind should take seriously are *res*—concrete, individual things.[12]

There are two questions that arise from this change of mind. First, there is the exegetical question of how much of his earlier views about intentionality Brentano retained after restricting his ontology, and hence how far his later views on this matter differ from his earlier ones. And secondly, there is the question of how far these changes were actually necessary. Does Brentano's new ontology force him to deny that

---

[10] Brentano (1995: 271).   [11] Ibid., p. xxvii.
[12] Brentano's so-called 'turn away from non-realia' is documented in letters and manuscripts, some of which have been published posthumously in *Die Abkehr vom Nichtrealen* (1966).

mental phenomena involve a genuine relation between a subject and an intra-mental object? This latter question is the more interesting one since it asks us to consider the possibility that Brentano may have given up too much of his earlier views. Before we can address this possibility, however, we need to deal with the exegetical question first.

If one follows the orthodox interpretation described above, Brentano's reistic turn had quite dramatic consequences for his theory of intentionality.[13] Brentano could now no longer explain the intentional relation as a relation to non-real entities, and hence he needed a completely new account of this feature of mental phenomena. His new proposal was that the so-called 'intentional relation' should better be conceived as a 'quasi-relational' feature of subjects.[14] Contrary to his earlier position, mental phenomena do not require the existence of a subject *and* an object, but only the existence of a subject that is directed at an (existing or non-existing) object; hence the term 'quasi-relational'.

Critics of the orthodox interpretation deny that there is such a fundamental gulf dividing Brentano's early and later views on intentionality. According to them Brentano's later attacks on immanent objects can be mostly seen as terminological clarifications of his earlier position. Brentano had noticed that the Scholastic termino-logy he used was widely misunderstood by his contemporaries. These terms were *mistakenly* interpreted as involving a commitment to a realm of non-real entities, whereas Brentano never wanted to use them in this ontologically loaded sense. There was no need for him, therefore, to cut out these passages from the second edition, and he could still say that mental phenomena include something as an object. He only warns the reader now explicitly that this way of speaking must not be taken as introducing non-real immanent objects.[15]

How should we resolve the conflict between these two interpretations? It seems to me that something is right and wrong in both of them. There are both continuities and discontinuities in Brentano's writings, and the difficulty is to strike the right bal-ance between them. The orthodox interpretation exaggerates the discontinuities when it takes the early Brentano to have advanced a simple-minded theory of immanent objects that he *had* to give up in view of its obvious implausibility. This we have already seen in the previous section. On the other hand, it seems to me that the altern-ative interpretation goes wrong when it takes Brentano to have espoused more or less the same theory of intentionality throughout his career. Brentano did subscribe to a form of the immanence theory that he later could no longer accept, and hence we have to address the question whether he made the right moves in changing his theory.

I now want to substantiate this diagnosis by pointing out some of the textual evid-ence that needs to be taken into account. I will not offer a detailed exegetical study

---

[13] A more fine-grained account of the development of Brentano's theory of intentionality has recently been suggested in Chrudzimski (2001) and (2004). Chrudzimski distinguishes between an early, a middle, and a late period in Brentano's views on intentionality, and he takes the middle period to have been Brentano's 'Meinongian' period during which he developed a rich ontology of non-real entities including immanent objects.   [14] Brentano 1995, p. 272.

[15] So far the most elaborate attempt to bring Brentano's early views on intentionality into line with his later ontology has been made by Antonelli 2001. Further arguments for such an interpreta-tion are provided by Werner Sauer in unpublished work.

here, however; only just enough to provide the necessary background for the following considerations.

Let me begin with a quote from Brentano's so far unpublished Logic Lectures from 1884/5. Brentano elaborates here his claim that mental phenomena are directed at objects with the following caveat:

> It is good to emphasize just one thing again, namely that this relation [i.e. the intentional relation] has the peculiarity that one of its terms is real, the other not. Since one would be mistaken if one takes it to be the outer (and perhaps (often) real) object. The latter may be completely missing, the immanent one never.[16]

Brentano takes it here for granted that the intentional relation is a genuine relation between subjects and inner objects. The point he wants to emphasize is that these objects are not part of reality. Interestingly he does not take these entities to be non-real because they exist merely in the mind of a subject. Rather he argues that otherwise one would confuse these inner objects with the external objects at which mental phenomena are directed. I will come back to this point in the final section of this essay.

This passage is thus not only an explicit statement of the immanence theory, it also reveals that the introduction of immanent objects could not be a recipe for Brentano to avoid the problem of non-existing external objects. The immanent object is always there, Brentano says, but the external object may be missing. Even when it is missing, however, we talk (or think) about it as a missing entity, and hence we have to refer to it. It seems quite obvious therefore that Brentano's position involves the ontological thesis of intentionality, as Chisholm has called it, *and* the psychological thesis that mental phenomena can be directed at (existing and) non-existing objects. These two claims seem perfectly compatible with each other.

This way of understanding Brentano's theory is further supported by another aspect of it that has gone largely unnoticed so far. In several of his lectures Brentano draws a distinction between two kinds of *Vorstellungen* (presentations).[17] There are fundamental presentations, which he calls 'eigentliche Vorstellungen', and there are presentations *based* on the fundamental ones, which he calls 'uneigentliche Vorstellungen'. He does not offer a very clear account of this distinction, but a natural suggestion here seems to be this: fundamental presentations present a subject with an immanent object, whereas non-fundamental ones have the representational function of directing the mind to external objects that are *not* immanent. If this is what Brentano meant by this

---

[16] The quote is from a transcript of Brentano's logic lectures entitled 'Die elementare Logik und die in ihr nötigen Reformen', delivered in Vienna in 1884/5. The partly corrupt German passage in the transcript reads as follows: 'Nur eines wird gut sein nochmals hervorzuheben, nämlich dass diese Relation ... eigene hat, dass ihr ein ... Terminus real, der andere nicht. Denn der würde irren, der als ihn das äussere (und vielleicht (oft) reale) Object nähme. Ein solches kann ganz fehlen, das immanente nie' (Brentano Manuscript EL 72/2, p. 88, Nr. B03489). I am grateful to the Forschungsstelle und Dokumentationszentrum für Österreichische Philosophie in Graz for providing me with this transcript.

[17] Logic Lectures 1885/6, Manuscript EL 72/2, p. 232 ff. See also Brentano (1956: 64), based on a later version of these Lectures, and Brentano 1959, p. 166 f., containing material from Lectures on Practical Philosophy.

distinction, he should have given it more prominence in his writings. Much confusion about his immanence theory could thereby have been avoided.

The same can be said about Brentano's alleged confusion of the terms 'content' and 'object'. From a contemporary point of view it is indeed disturbing that Brentano uses these terms often interchangeably. It is therefore often said that Brentano was not yet aware of the fundamental importance of the content/object distinction, and that the credit goes to his pupils Höfler, Twardowski, and later to Husserl to have clarified this distinction. But this is also a mistake, I think. That Brentano did not use the terms 'content' and 'object' in the way they are used today does not show that he was confused on this point. The distinction between the 'immanent' and the 'outer' object served exactly this purpose for him. This is quite clear from the remark with which he continues the passage quoted above: 'If one says that the presented is in the one who presents something, the known is in the knower, the lover carries the loved one in his heart, we can also say: the picture is in him.'[18] This is exactly the same explanation that Höfler and Twardowksi used for introducing the content/object distinction.[19]

Together these facts make clear that the category of immanent objects was extremely important in Brentano's early theory of intentionality. It is tightly connected with his distinction between two kinds of *Vorstellungen* (presentations and representations), and it served him as a substitute for the content/object distinction. The elimination of the category of immanent objects from this theory was therefore a major step for Brentano. Why, then, did he think it necessary to rebuild his theory so extensively, and could a more modest revision have served his purposes equally well?

The reason why Brentano rejected immanent objects has already been mentioned at the beginning of this section: Brentano set out to defend a 'reistic' ontology that systematically eliminates all non-real entities, such as possible and impossible objects as well as past and future events. This quite general attack on 'fictional' entities, as he calls them, included the immanent objects as the alleged relata of an intentional relation. These objects, being mere 'fictions of language', should no longer play a role in his theory of intentionality. Brentano takes here a line quite similar to Quine's attack on intensional entities: immanent objects are superfluous entities that have been postulated without necessity.

If we look at this argument in the context of Brentano's own theory, however, we notice that it could have gone in the opposite direction as well. Brentano could have reasoned also as follows: immanent objects are certainly not superfluous entities, since they form the basis for distinguishing between presentations and representations and help to draw the content/object distinction. Yet we should not accept any non-real entities in our ontology. Hence, immanent objects have to be something *real*.

There is no hint, however, that Brentano did so much as consider this possibility. It would have required a quite different change of his view, with the advantage that in this case he could have retained the spirit of the immanence theory, namely the

---

[18] The German original is: 'Und wenn es [i.e. das äußere Objekt] vorhanden, ist es vom immanenten zu unterscheiden. Wenn man sagt, das Vorgestellte sei im Vorgestellten, das Erkannte sei im Erkennenden, der Liebende trage das Geliebte in seinem Herze, so sagen wir auch wieder: das Bild sei in ihm, . . .' (Brentano Manuscript EL 72/2, p. 88, Nr. B03489).

[19] See Twardowski 1982, p. 4.

assumption that intentionality is grounded in a real relation between subjects and immanent objects. In the second part of this essay I will now try to develop this idea from a different angle by switching to a problem in contemporary philosophy of mind.

4. THE PHENOMENAL CONTENT OF SUBJECTIVE EXPERIENCE

While Brentano's theory of immanent objects has been widely dismissed, theories that invoke other kinds of problematic entities—like Bolzano's propositions or Husserl's noemata—have been treated with greater sympathy. In what follows I want to rectify this imbalance by showing that immanent objects are designed to play a quite different role in a theory of intentionality than these alleged competitors. Their explanatory power becomes visible only when we turn to the analysis of subjective experiences. I will therefore now narrow the focus and consider the immanence theory not in the broad form in which Brentano advocated it, namely as a theory about *all* mental phenomena, but as a more specific theory about the subjective nature of experience. How far this theory can be extended to a larger domain of mental phenomena, I leave for further speculation.

It is a widely accepted assumption in philosophy of mind today that mental phenomena can be divided into two (overlapping) categories: the category of cognitive states with a propositional content, and the category of experiences with a phenomenal character. This division rests on the assumption that experiences have a specifically subjective nature that cognitive states lack. One might express this by saying that experiences are in a certain sense 'private' entities. Each of us knows what his own experiences are like, but as far as we know these experiences may be quite different from the experiences of other subjects.

Propositional attitudes are different in this respect. Subjects can share beliefs and desires with others and they can know whether or not this is the case. For instance, when two politicians claim that democracy is the best form of government, they share a vision even if their views about how this vision should be realized may be different. But when they both have a headache there need not be anything that they mentally share. Their sensations may be similar, but there need not be anything like a proposition that they both grasp and whose truth-value they can agree or disagree on. This is what constitutes the subjectivity of their sensations, in contrast to the objectivity of their cognitive or conative mental states.

One question that arises from this contrast is this: does the subjectivity of experiences rule out that experiences are intentional phenomena? This would be the case if one characterizes intentionality as the ability to grasp certain objective meaning-entities. But such a narrow understanding of intentionality is now widely rejected. Experiences may be—despite their subjectivity—intentional phenomena as well. The real question to be asked here is therefore this: can the phenomenal character of experiences be explained by—or even reduced to—their intentional content?

The recent work devoted to this question is impressive and highly sophisticated.[20] This should not make us overlook, however, the most simple question to ask at this point, namely whether experiences might be characterized as phenomena directed at immanent objects. If experiences have an intentional nature, and if their subjectivity implies that they cannot be literally shared, there seems to be no better model for accounting for these facts than the immanence theory. Immanent objects seem perfectly suited to explain whatever the difference is that exists between experiences and propositional attitudes.

It is no surprise that this question comes into view mainly in works inspired by Brentano and the phenomenological tradition. Dale Jacquette provides such an example. In a paper entitled 'Sensation and Intentionality' he proposes what he calls a 'new approach' to this topic, but as his own references make clear his proposal is very much in line with the Brentano tradition. In fact, as I shall argue, it eventually suffers from following Brentano too closely in one respect.

Jacquette starts out by introducing a distinction between what he calls 'the intentionality of perception' and 'the intentionality of sensation':

It is possible to see particular colored objects, but it is also possible to see colors themselves. The same is true of the objects of the other senses.... When experience is directed at phenomenally qualified objects, it exemplifies the intentionality of perception rather then the intentionality of sensation.... But if the subject merely sees the color blue... then the subject is directed in thought toward a shade of blue (a particular sensation or secondary quality) as the intentional object of sensation.[21]

The distinction between perception and sensation that Jacquette draws here parallels Brentano's distinction between 'authentic' and 'inauthentic' presentations mentioned earlier. And what Jacquette calls a 'phenomenally qualified object' falls into Brentano's category of immanent objects.[22] We thus get here another statement of the immanence theory: there are not just external objects that appear to us one way or other in perception, but there are also internal objects to which we are related when we have a perceptual experience, and this internal relation exists even in the case of sensations that occur without the perception of an external object.

It is true that Jacquette does not explicitly say that the phenomenally qualified objects are *intra-mental* objects that exist only as long as a subject has a certain experience. But there is nothing in what he says that speaks against such an interpretation. In particular, there is no danger that by taking these objects to be intra-mental entities his view might fall victim to the simple-mindedness of the immanence theory. Jacquette precludes this by taking sensory experiences to be basic acts on which real perceptions are founded. The danger would become even less when one adds to his proposal the

---

[20] A critical discussion of the main proposals can be found, for instance, in Carruthers (2000).

[21] Jacquette (1985: 436).

[22] A note on terminology: the term 'phenomenally qualified objects' that Jacquette uses covers one possible meaning of term 'qualia'. This latter term is also used, however, without implying that qualia are immanent objects. This non-committal way of speaking about 'qualia' is ontologically less problematic, but it leaves open the question of how the qualia of an experience can explain its subjectivity. Lycan therefore has recommended that the only proper use of the term 'qualia' is in the sense of 'phenomenally qualified object'. See Lycan (1987).

claim that sensory experiences are also directed at mind-external objects, even if—as in the case of a hallucinatory experience—such objects do not exist. Unfortunately, as we shall see, this claim is not compatible with what Jacquette proposes.

Following Brentano's goal of extending the concept of intentionality to all mental phenomena, Jacquette wants to argue that not only perceptual experiences have phenomenally qualified objects, but also bodily sensations like pain. He therefore rejects the general demand to draw a content/object distinction for each intentional phenomenon. According to him, it is a further characteristic of the intentionality of sensations—in contrast to the intentionality of perceptions—that in the case of sensations the content/object distinction collapses: 'pain as the object of sensation is also the content of the psychological experience of pain. The content and object of sensation in that case are not numerically distinct but strictly identical.'[23]

The consequences of this step are foreseeable. Following this path it must turn out that the phenomenally qualified objects to which we are related in experience cannot be anything real. They are, as one might put it, nothing else but reifications of the phenomenal content of experience. This may seem to be a great advantage since there cannot be any gap in this account between the intentional content of an experience and its phenomenal character. But from an ontological perspective we are back at the problem that Brentano faced: we have to enlarge the ontology with something non-real. There simply are no real objects that could close the gap between the phenomenal and the intentional in the way suggested by Jacquette.

A decision seems to be inevitable: either we must extend our ontology by allowing non-real entities that can play the role of qualia in a theory of experience, or the whole project of explaining the phenomenal character of experience in terms of its intentional content is in jeopardy. If these were the only two alternatives available, I would prefer the latter and follow Brentano in rejecting immanent objects. In fact, however, there is another option to be considered.

5. THE REALITY OF IMMANENT OBJECTS

Could immanent objects be real entities? From all we have seen so far this seems to be ruled out. Traditionally the role of immanent objects has always been conceived in such a way that only non-real entities can perform that role. But that tradition can be broken. Let us now see what happens when we lift this restriction on the immanence theory and develop it in a form that stays within the limits of a reistic ontology.

Taking a step back, we must consider what is actually the core of the immanence theory. When we leave out the problematic assumption that immanent objects are non-real entities, this core can be expressed by the following two claims:

(I1) Mental phenomena involve a relation between a subject and an object.

(I2) This object exists in the mind of the subject even if an external object towards which the subject appears to be directed does not exist.

[23] Jacquette 1985, p. 437.

One might think that the phrase 'exists in the mind of the subject' already implies that this intra-mental object has to be a non-real entity. But this is not so, as we can see from the fact that there are real objects satisfying the conditions in (I1) and (I2). These objects are the internal *vehicles* of representation also known as 'Mental Representations'. The capitals should indicate here that one is referring to a new type of entities, not just to mental states or episodes that have a representational function. Mental Representations are extra entities—in addition to the mental states and episodes—that are introduced for giving a more precise account of *how* mental states perform their representational function.

Mental Representations can take different forms. They may be conceived as sentence-like entities, i.e. as elements in a language-of-thought, as data-structures, as mental images, etc. But whatever they may be, they are real entities. They are as real as a picture on the wall or a sentence in a book. All such entities may describe or depict unreal things like unicorns or round squares, and they may carry a meaning that is not part of reality. But that does not make the pictures or sentences themselves unreal.[24] The same can be said about Mental Representations. They may represent non-real things and they may have a content that finds no place in reality, but the Mental Representations taken as *vehicles* of representation are definitely real.

Yet there seems to be a striking difference between pictures and sentences on the one hand, and Mental Representations on the other. In the former case we know how these things are physically realized because we can see and touch them. Mental Representations, by contrast, are not visible for us, and as laymen we know very little about how they might be physically realized in the brain. But does this really matter? Suppose we still lived in the age before the invention of writing. Then sentences would exist only as acoustic signals and we would have no clue as to how the signals we produce in speaking are physically realized. This would not make them less real, however.

By similar reasoning we can be sure that Mental Representations—if they exist— are real entities. But do they exist, and can they play the role of immanent objects? The following remarks are intended to be no more than a sketch of the path along which, I think, a positive answer to these questions can be given. As will become clear, the path differs markedly from the usual way in which the question of the existence of Mental Representations is discussed.

The common approach here is to start with a relational analysis of propositional attitudes and to argue for the existence of Mental Representations by appealing to the inferential structure and the productivity of these attitudes. This has been the way in which Jerry Fodor has defended the hypotheses of a mental language that contains Mental Representations as its elements.[25] The arguments for and against this hypo-thesis are manifold, but they need not concern us here.[26] The trouble with Fodor's strategy is that it deliberately sets aside the analysis of subjective experience.[27] It is,

[24] Even if one includes a 'mind stuff' as a possible format in which Mental Representations can exist (see Cummins 1989: 2), this stuff will be as real as a Cartesian *res cogitans*.

[25] See Fodor (1975) and (1981).   [26] See, for instance, Saporiti (1997).

[27] See Block and Fodor (1972).

however, precisely there, I want to claim, that the best arguments in favour of Mental Representations can be found.

We therefore need to take a more liberal stand on what format Mental Representations can take. It is surely implausible to assume that subjective experiences involve Mental Representations that have the format of sentences in a language-of-thought. Since the term 'Mental Representation' has become so closely associated with Fodor's hypothesis about propositional attitudes, however, I suggest we use instead the term 'mental information bearer' (or MIB, for short) as a more neutral expression for our purposes.

MIBs are the vehicle of representation used in experiences. Whether these entities can play the role of an immanent object in a theory of intentionality depends on what further features we take these MIBs to have: what kind of information they carry and how they encode this information. All we can say in advance here is what a positive answer to the above question would require. To play this role, MIBs have to be conceived as subjective entities in the following sense: each subject, we have to suppose, operates with its own set of MIBs, and each one has access only to her own MIBs. In this respect MIBs differ from all information bearers that can be used for communication. One can use a flag or a verbal utterance for communicative purposes, because different subjects have the same epistemic access to the information-bearing signal. It makes sense therefore to suppose that different subjects assign the same meaning to the same type of signal. Nothing like this can be supposed to hold in the case of MIBs. These are private entities that have only a private meaning for one subject.

It should be clear by now that defending this MIB-hypothesis will need to address quite different worries than a defence of Fodor's language-of-thought hypothesis. The main objection here seems to be Wittgenstein's argument against private entities illustrated by the 'beetle in the box'.[28] This is a powerful argument and it has convinced many to turn their backs on the immanence theory. One should notice, however, that Wittgenstein's argument is directed against invoking private entities in connection with mental states and episodes that are supposed to explain the meaningful use of a public language. It is doubtful that this argument will retain its force if the very purpose of the immanence theory is to provide an account of the subjectivity of experience in the first place.

Let me end this essay with a note of warning. One must not expect too much from a theory of intentionality that interprets immanent objects as mental information bearers. By itself this theory will not reduce the mystery inherent in the fact that we have experiences with a phenomenal character. The so-called 'hard problem of consciousness' is neither solved here, nor will it go away. In fact, it *should* not go away since real entities—as I mentioned earlier—cannot close the gap that exists between intentional and phenomenal content. Leaving this problem unresolved is therefore a welcome consequence, not a disadvantage, of taking immanent objects to be vehicles of representation.[29]

---

[28] Wittgenstein (1953: § 293).
[29] I am grateful to Glenn Stanley for helping me with the English of this text.

REFERENCES

Antonelli, Mauro (2001) *Seiendes, Bewußtsein, Intentionalität im Frühwerk von Franz Brentano* (Freiburg: Alber).

Aquila, Richard E. (1977) *Intentionality. A Study of Mental Acts* (University Park: Pennsylvania State University Press).

Block, Ned and Fodor, Jerry (1972) 'What Psychological States are Not', *The Philosophical Review* 81: 159–81.

Brentano, Franz (1956) *Die Lehre vom richtigen Urteil*, ed. Franziska Mayer-Hillebrand (Hamburg: Meiner).

—— (1959) *Grundzüge der Ästhetik*, ed. Franziska Mayer-Hillebrand (Hamburg: Meiner).

—— (1966) *Die Abkehr vom Nichtrealen*, ed. Franziska Mayer-Hillebrand (Hamburg: Meiner).

—— (1973) *Psychologie vom empirischen Standpunkt*. Hamburg: Meiner (reprint of the edition 1924 edited by Oskar Kraus; originally published in 1874 and 1911).

—— (1982) *Deskriptive Psychologie*, ed. Roderick M. Chisholm and Wilhelm Baumgartner (Hamburg: Meiner).

—— (1995) *Psychology from an Empirical Standpoint*, trans. D. B. Terrell and Linda L. McAlister (London: Routledge & Kegan Paul).

—— (unpublished), *Die elementare Logik und die in ihr nötigen Reformen* (1884/1885). Manuscript EL 72/2.

Carruthers, Peter (2000) *Phenomenal Consciousness: A Naturalistic Theory* (Cambridge: Cambridge University Press).

Caston, Victor (1998) 'Aristotle and the Problem of Intentionality', *Philosophy and Phenomenological Research* 58: 249–98.

Chisholm, Roderick M. (1967) 'Intentionality', in Paul Edwards (ed.), *The Encyclopedia of Philosophy*, vol. 4 (New York: Macmillan), 201–4.

—— (1970) 'Brentano on Descriptive Psychology and the Intentional', in H. Morick (ed.), *Introduction to the Philosophy of Mind* (Glennview, Ill.: Scott, Foresman and Company), 130–49.

Chrudzimski, Arek (2001) *Intentionalitätstheorie beim frühen Brentano* (Dordrecht: Kluwer).

—— (2004) *Die Ontologie Franz Brentanos* (Dordrecht: Kluwer).

Cummins, Robert (1989) *Meaning and Mental Representation* (Cambridge, Mass.: MIT Press).

Fodor, Jerry (1975) *The Language of Thought* (New York: Thomas Y. Crowell).

—— (1981) *RePresentations. Philosophical Essays on the Foundations of Cognitive Science* (Cambridge, Mass.: MIT Press).

Jacquette, Dale (1985) 'Sensation and Intentionality', *Philosophical Studies* 47: 429–40.

—— (2004) 'Brentano's Concept of Intentionality', in D. Jacquette (ed.), *The Cambridge Companion to Brentano* (Cambridge: Cambridge University Press), 98–130.

—— ed. (2004) *The Cambridge Companion to Brentano* (Cambridge: Cambridge University Press).

Kent, Otis T. (1984) 'Brentano and the Relational View of Consciousness', *Man and World* 17: 19–51.

Lycan, William G. (1987) 'Phenomenal Objects: A Backhanded Defense', *Philosophical Perspectives* 1: 513–26.

McAlister, Linda (1974) 'Chisholm and Brentano on Intentionality', *The Review of Metaphysics* 28: 328–38.

—— (2004) 'Brentano's Epistemology', in D. Jacquette (ed.), *The Cambridge Companion to Brentano* (Cambridge: Cambridge University Press), 149–67.

Margolis, Joseph (2004) 'Reflections on Intentionality', in D. Jacquette (ed.), *The Cambridge Companion to Brentano* (Cambridge: Cambridge University Press), 131–48.

Moran, Dermot (2000) *Introduction to Phenomenology* (London: Routledge).

Perler, Dominik (2002) *Theorien der Intentionalität im Mittelalter* (Frankfurt: Klostermann).

Richardson, Robert (1983) 'Brentano on Intentional Inexistence and the Distinction Between Mental and Physical Phenomena', *Archiv für Geschichte der Philosophie* 64: 250–82.

Sajama, Seppo and Kamppinen, Matti (1987) *A Historical Introduction to Phenomenology* (London: Croom Helm).

Saporiti, Katja (1997) *Die Sprache des Geistes* (Berlin and New York: De Gruyter).

Sauer, Werner (unpublished), 'Das Wesen der psychischen Phänomene: die Intentionalität'.

Sorabji, Richard (1991) 'From Aristotle to Brentano: The Development of the Concept of Intentionality', in Julia Annas (ed.), *Oxford Studies in Ancient Philosophy* (Oxford: Clarendon Press).

Twardowski, Kasimir (1982) *Zur Lehre vom Inhalt und Gegenstand der Vorstellungen. Eine psychologische Untersuchung* (Munich: Philosophia Verlag). [Originally published in 1894.]

Wittgenstein, Ludwig (1953) *Philosophische Untersuchungen*, in *Werkausgabe*, i (Frankfurt: Suhrkamp 1984).

8

Consciousness of Abstract Objects

Richard Tieszen

Abstract: Gödel, Penrose, and others have argued that human beings are able to know about abstract objects or truths. A similar view, but worked out in much more detail, can be found in the writings of Edmund Husserl. Husserl is one of only a few major philosophers in the last one hundred years or so who holds that it is possible to develop a philosophy of mind in which one can account for the consciousness of abstract or ideal objects. In this essay I discuss Husserl's ideas in connection with the views of Gödel and Penrose. In the later part of the essay in particular I present my own version of an argument that leads from Gödel's incompleteness theorems to recognition of the awareness of abstract or ideal objects. Husserl's view, based on his ideas about intentionality and the phenomenological reduction, shows us how to open up a space for a phenomenology of the consciousness of abstract objects.

In the recent literature in the philosophy of mind there is virtually no consideration of whether or how the mind might be able to grasp abstract or ideal objects. Most of the views of mind that have emerged in the past few decades (e.g. behaviorist, computational, connectionist, neuroscientific) are not in a position to address this issue at all since, in one way or another, they are developed as 'naturalistic' accounts and it is believed that naturalism has no place for abstract objects. Abstract objects, after all, do not have spatial extension, are not in the causal nexus like physical objects, are either timeless or omnitemporal, and so on. The phenomenological account of mind due to Husserl stands in stark contrast to this trend. In Husserl's work one finds an effort to account for the consciousness of abstract or ideal objects. An account of this kind is needed because, according to Husserl, logic and mathematics are both about such objects. Phenomenology itself is committed to abstract objects like essences, ideal meanings, and noemata.

There are, of course, many objections to efforts to account for the consciousness of abstract objects. All of the old fears about substance dualism, mysticism, and other forms of mystery-mongering quickly surface. Would it be possible, however, to develop an account of our consciousness of abstract objects that avoids these old worries and in fact situates such a view of mind in a broadly 'scientific' setting? The scientific setting here could presumably not consist only of natural science but would have

I would like to thank Amie Thomasson and the two OUP referees for comments on this essay.

to include logic, pure mathematics, and some other productions of reason where we do not suppose from the outset that these later scientific undertakings are to be understood in terms of a strict empiricist interpretation of natural science. Instead of interpreting reason and its productions in terms of empiricist principles and methods we can interpret empiricist principles and methods in terms of reason and its productions. It would be foolish to deny that natural science requires sense perception (or technological extensions of it) but it can still be claimed that there is much in natural science that cannot be accounted for on the basis of empiricist principles alone. Since logic, pure mathematics, and some other operations of reason are surely subsumed under the category 'science' we can bar the non-scientific ideas that are at the base of the worries.

One could argue that scientific theory in fact depends on the consciousness of abstract or ideal objects. It seems to me that something like this is true and while I cannot consider all of the details in this essay I will provide a few indications below about the manner in which I think it is true. Scientific thinking is not just sense perception but is instead built up from sense perception on the basis of cognitive activities of abstraction, idealization, reflection, formalization, and other 'higher-order' activities of reason that involve conscious directedness toward abstract objects. These cognitive activities are indispensable to science but they cannot be construed as being directed toward the objects of everyday sensory experience. What I have in mind here is a kind of indispensability argument.

Any progress that could be made in providing an account of the consciousness of abstract objects would be especially helpful to views like those of Kurt Gödel and Roger Penrose, for Gödel and Penrose are two of the most prominent figures in recent times who have claimed that we have a grasp of such objects. The arguments of both men are based on Gödel's incompleteness theorems (see, e.g., Gödel 1972: 271–2; Penrose 1994: 418). In what follows below (especially §§ 5–6) I will present my own version of an argument that leads from the incompleteness theorems to recognition of the awareness of abstract or ideal objects (see also Tieszen 1994, 1998a). The argument, it will be seen, is connected with a number of themes in Husserlian phenomenology. As I proceed I will also comment on some other aspects of the views of Gödel and Penrose.

Husserl thought that by adopting the proper perspective we could see how the mind operates with data that are abstract or ideal. This perspective is opened up by phenomenology itself, especially through its views on intentionality, evidence, and the phenomenological reduction. One can point to the abstract data in our experience in more or less sophisticated ways. In recent times, using the incompleteness theorems is certainly one of the more sophisticated ways of doing it. Husserl himself was not in a position to use the incompleteness theorems in this manner but Gödel (after 1959) did appeal to Husserl's views in attempting to understand how the mind could operate with abstract data (see Gödel 1961; Wang 1974, 1987, 1996; Tieszen 1992). There are also other ways of pointing to the abstract data in our experience and I shall indicate a few of these as we proceed (§§ 3–4). Some of the key ideas in my discussion derive from the notion of intentionality and I will start by discussing some important features of intentionality.

1. INTENTIONALITY AND PHYSICAL STATES

Brentano is famous for arguing that if there is a distinctive mark of the mental then it is that mental phenomena exhibit intentionality while physical phenomena do not. This means that mental phenomena—various states of consciousness—display 'aboutness' or 'directedness'. They are directed toward objects. A belief, for example, is always a belief about some object or state of affairs. Purely physical states, however, are not 'about' anything. They do not have this characteristic of referring to something or other. Brentano's thesis need not be construed as committing us to substance dualism. It would presumably be compatible with anomalous monism in the style of Davidson or with any of a range of views concerning the ontology of mind. David Smith's (Smith 1995) 'many-aspect monism' might be an especially good fit. Someone like Searle, to take another example, might hold that consciousness (which exhibits intentionality) is to the brain as digestion is to the stomach. I would like simply to set aside questions about the ontology of mind for a while, perhaps for even a very long while. I want to focus on the fact that it seems very difficult to deny that consciousness, at least in the forms most relevant to scientific thinking, exhibits intentionality. If we can speak about beliefs at all, for example, then what would it be like for a belief not to be about something or other? Imagine that you have a belief but that it is not about anything. This seems absurd.

Suppose we fasten firmly onto this idea of directedness. Once we take it seriously then we see that there are indeed many forms of conscious directedness. A number of these forms will be relevant to science and in this essay I will focus on the types of conscious activities involved in scientific thinking. In particular, sensory perception is only one form of conscious directedness and it is not the only form involved in scientific thinking. It is a condition for the possibility of some forms of scientific thinking but not necessarily for all. There is also conscious directedness involving abstraction, idealization, reflection, formalization, and other 'higher-order' cognitive activities. Our awareness is directed in different ways in imagination, memory, mathematical thinking, and so on. Following the style of phenomenology, let us say that in mathematical thinking I'm directed toward mathematical objects and states of affairs, in sensory perception I'm directed toward sensory objects and states of affairs, in imagination I'm directed toward imaginary objects and states of affairs, and so on. At the outset it will not be a good idea to run automatically the different types of object-directedness into one another. We ought not to suppose from the outset, for example, that mathematical thinking just is a species of imagination. Rather, the various connections between the two would need to be investigated and clarified.

In making these remarks I want to hold that object-directedness does not require that there be an object. Nothing about saying that imagination is object-directed requires us to say that imaginary objects exist. The same is true for states of belief. Having a belief about something does not entail that there is a corresponding object of belief. A couple of years ago I believed that I saw a house on a street in the Hollywood hills but it turned out, to my surprise, to be merely two walls of a house on a movie set. It is not like there had to be a house in order for my belief to be about what it was about. Here one can follow Husserl in holding that it is the 'content' or 'noema' of my belief that made the object-directedness possible even if there was no house. The 'noema' of my belief can, in a certain sense, be thought of as the meaning by virtue of which I am directed toward the object or state of affairs (see, e.g., Husserl 1982 or 2001: Investigation I). In order for the perceptual judgment that there was a house to be justified it would be necessary to have evidence and in Husserl's phenomenology there is a detailed theory of evidence. It is possible to investigate different forms of directedness due to the noemata of our cognitive acts, however, without considering whether we actually have evidence or not for the existence of the objects toward which we are directed by the noemata. I will consider some questions about the evidence for some particular kinds of abstract objects in section 7 below.

For the moment, we can say that there are different types of consciousness and that with these different types of conscious states there will be associated different contents or noemata that are responsible for our being directed in just the way that we are. While there is always some noema or other associated with a conscious state there may or may not be an object or state of affairs corresponding to the noema. It is important to note that in speaking only of object-directedness we have a great deal of freedom that we would not have if we thought we had first to decide all of the details about evidence for the existence of objects. Instead, we will be speaking about what types of object-directedness there are and we will come back to some questions about evidence later.

The kind of language I have been using in this section is mind language. Mind language in this style is very different from brain language. Brain states, viewed as purely physical phenomena, do not have aboutness. It is not part of the very nature or essence of a particular neurochemical activity that it somehow refer outside of itself to some other thing. In describing this neurochemical activity in the language of natural science we should not find that in addition to neurons and neurochemical interactions that there are 'contents', noemata, meanings, and so on. This is simply the wrong level of description. It is widely agreed that the sentences of neuroscience itself should be shorn of the intentional idiom. One aims for a thoroughgoing extensionalism.

I want to emphasize this point in connection with my central concern in this essay because I think we will not get very far with the question of the consciousness of abstract objects if from the outset we suppose that mind talk just is brain talk or even that the mind is in some crude way just the brain. To put it starkly: how could a brain be in epistemic contact with an abstract object? If this is the question then we can probably close up the shop and go home now. Given what a brain is and given the kinds of physical interactions in which it can be involved, and given that an abstract object is typically understood to be a non-physical object of some kind, it would seem to be a category mistake to suppose that brains could have access to abstract objects. As I say, there are many philosophers who at this point would simply say 'so much the worse for abstract objects'. If, however, it is in some sense undeniable that conscious states exhibit directedness in the manner indicated above and if mind talk involves a different level of description from brain talk then we needn't give up just yet. There is still some territory to be mapped out concerning our various forms of consciousness and it is possible that there are coherent descriptions and analyses of this territory that do justice to our experience in different domains. It is not clear to me that this possibility should be closed off in advance on account of some preconceived metaphysical or epistemological views.

It might be thought, for example, that evolutionary biology is inconsistent with the idea of conscious directedness toward abstract objects, for evolutionary biology is purely naturalistic while abstract objects are precisely not natural entities. It is important to note, however, that while abstract objects are not natural entities it is still possible that *conscious directedness* toward abstract objects has some kind of naturalistic explanation. It is conscious directedness that I want to explore. We can then distinguish forms of directedness that are scientific and evidential from forms of directedness that are not scientific and not evidential. It would be stronger to claim that the existence of abstract objects is consistent with evolutionary biology. Many philosophers would hold that this seems implausible. But even here one can point out that the matter has not yet been decided once and for all. It is a large problem to determine whether or how evolutionary biology is compatible with 'ideals' of all sorts (e.g. in ethics, in mathematics). Perhaps the existence of abstract or ideal objects could be consistent with some expanded and stratified scientific view of the cosmos that includes evolutionary biology as a part. Even a philosopher like Quine, who is very friendly to scientific thinking and to evolutionary biology in particular, recognizes the existence of abstract objects (i.e. sets). (One way in which Quine's view differs from mine, however, is that he is not friendly toward the concept of intentionality. On Quine's view we are committed to the existence of abstract objects as long as statements that quantify over them are indispensable to natural science. There is evidently no need to account for our awareness of such objects, however, unless writings like *The Roots of Reference* are supposed to address such a need.)

2. GÖDEL, PENROSE, PLATONISM, AND BRAIN PROCESSES

Kurt Gödel and Roger Penrose are two of the most prominent thinkers in recent times who have claimed that we have an awareness of abstract objects. One of my worries about Penrose's view in *Shadows of the Mind* is that he seems to think that Gödel's incompleteness theorems imply some kind of platonism but he then focuses almost exclusively on *brain processes* and on how these must be non-computational. He uses the incompleteness theorems to argue that there are non-computational procedures for *knowing* mathematical truths, but this is immediately equated with the view that there must be non-computational brain processes (Penrose 1994). It is fair to ask Penrose the question that immediately gets us into a corner: how could the brain be stimulated by abstract objects or, rephrasing it somewhat, what could the relationship between the brain (which for Penrose is not a computer) and abstract objects be? Penrose overlooks the fact that knowing is a conscious state that exhibits intentionality. One might expect him to address issues about non-computational *mental processes*, where these are not immediately equated with brain processes, but there is no phenomenology of consciousness in Penrose's work. In particular, there is no phenomenology of the consciousness of abstract objects.

It is interesting to compare Penrose's view with some of Gödel's remarks on minds and brains. Gödel has suggested, for example, that Turing's argument that mental procedures are mechanical procedures is valid if one assumes that (1) there is no mind separate from matter and (2) the brain functions basically like a digital computer (see Wang 1974: 326). Gödel evidently thought that 2 was very likely but that 1 was a prejudice of our time that might actually be disproved. Penrose, by way of contrast, denies 2 and seems to hold that the missing science of consciousness is to be a form of neuroscience that recognizes non-computational brain processes. Gödel's remarks, on the other hand, suggest that brain processes are computational but mental processes are not. In Gödel's own writing there is very little philosophical discussion of how this would be possible but it at least shows that he does not feel compelled to say immediately that brain processes are non-computational if the incompleteness theorems suggest that mental processes are non-computational. Of course there are also problems with Gödel's view. One of the worries, especially given the paucity of his remarks on the subject and some of his religious views, is that in questioning 1 he may be holding a kind of substance dualism. I have already indicated that I think we should steer clear of substance dualism. In relation to 1, let us not venture beyond the following separation: consciousness exhibits intentionality and brain states do not exhibit intentionality.

It is perhaps worth mentioning that Gödel seems to think that the non-computational character of mental processes is connected directly with the ability of the mind to grasp abstract objects. Penrose, whose argument is more like that of J. R. Lucas (Lucas 1961), has not made this connection (see also Tieszen 1996). Although I do not wish to discuss the issue whether minds are machines in this essay it seems to me that Gödel is on the right track here (see Tieszen 1994, 1996, 1998a, 1998b).

3. THE INTENTIONAL DIFFERENCE

If there are different forms of consciousness then what kind of territory can be mapped out regarding these different forms? There is a fundamental principle that we need to take seriously if we are to answer this question. I will call it the *intentional difference principle* (IDP). In order to understand the IDP it will be helpful to say a little more about intentionality and noemata. Suppose I believe that something or other is the case: I believe that S. Here we have a certain subject ('I'), a type of consciousness (belief), and what I will call the 'content' of the belief, expressed by 'S'. The type of consciousness (e.g. believing, imagining, remembering, perceiving) is called the 'thetic character' by Husserl in his book *Ideas I*. What is expressed by S is called the 'noematic Sinn'. Husserl also has some other names for it but let us just use 'content' or 'noematic Sinn' interchangeably in this essay. There can also be so-called direct-object constructions, as when I say 'I perceive the tree', 'I perceive the green tree', or 'I imagine the purple tree'. If the form here is 'I perceive x' then we still have a subject and a thetic character and a kind of noematic Sinn, but in this case the noematic Sinn is expressed by a singular term. Husserl sometimes refers to the thetic character and the noematic Sinn together as the 'full noema'. The same noematic Sinn might be combined with different thetic characters, or the same thetic character might be combined with different noematic Sinne. I will simply use the term noema for the full noema.

Let us now formulate the IDP as follows: *Every noema yields, prima facie, a different kind of directedness. We are to take the directedness of consciousness just as it presents itself and not as something else.* Noemata can differ from one another on account of either their thetic character or their noematic Sinn. If, for example, I express the noematic Sinn of one act as ' x is a triangle' and the noematic Sinn of another act as 'x is a natural number' then clearly these two Sinne yield different kinds of directedness although there may be relations between the Sinne. The claim that two noematic Sinne Φ and Ψ do not yield a different kind of directedness is something that must be shown. In fields like mathematics and logic it should in fact be proved if possible. In some cases it will be obvious to everyone that two contents do not yield a different kind of directedness but, on the whole, this will be the exception rather than the rule.

It also follows from our remarks above that a shift in thetic character makes for a shift in the type of conscious directedness. Remembering is different from perceiving, and both are different from imagining. Perceiving is different from judging. In this essay I will use the term 'perception' to refer only to sensory perception. In the discussion below we will see that consciousness of abstract or ideal objects involves certain shifts in thetic character. Given what we just said, the thetic character involved in the consciousness of abstract objects cannot be perception. Indeed, if we substitute an expression with mathematical content (e.g. $5 + 7 = 12$) for 'S' in our scheme above then it would be a kind of category mistake to combine this content with the thetic character for sensory perception.

It is important to note that the fact that *a cognitive act is directed in a particular way means that it is not directed in other ways.* If my thinking is directed by 'x is a triangle' then there are a host of ways in which it cannot be directed. Some contents will be compatible with a given content but others will not. Noematic Sinne can be consistent with one another, imply one another, and so on. There will also be categories or regions of noematic Sinne appropriate to particular kinds of object-directedness and other categories of noematic Sinne appropriate to other kinds of object-directedness. Noematic Sinne are to be understood as intensional entities and as such their identity is not to be determined extensionally.

Noematic Sinne, we might also note, always present us with a perspective on an object or situation. Consciousness is perspectival and we are finite beings and cannot take all possible perspectives on an object, state of affairs, or domain. We do not experience everything all at once. Our knowledge is thus typically incomplete in certain ways, although we might see how we could continue to perfect it.

Now it is clear that sensory perception is one type of conscious directedness. We are not, however, directed exclusively to sensory objects. To take the IDP seriously is to hold that in sensory experience we are directed toward sensory objects, in mathematical experience we are directed toward mathematical objects, in imaginative experience we are directed toward imaginary objects, and so on. This should be our starting position. It might turn out that some of these types of object-directedness can be reduced to others but in each case that will remain something to be shown. The starting position is non-reductionistic. In thinking of how to solve a problem in a number theory textbook, for example, my thinking does not seem to be directed toward sensory objects or states of affairs although there may be some sensory experience in the background. If in our experience we were directed exclusively toward sensory objects it is not clear how sciences like mathematics and logic would be possible at all.

Sensory perception itself deserves to be looked at more carefully from this phenomenological perspective. It is of concrete objects but it appears that a kind of *abstraction* is involved even at the lowest levels of the sensory perception of objects. There is a constantly changing flow of sensory input but in ordinary sensory perception we are not directed toward this sensory material. We are directed instead toward a particular object that is experienced as identical through this constantly changing flow of sensory input. There is *one* object that is 'formed' or 'synthesized' out of the multiplicity of data reaching our senses. Here we can already speak of a kind of abstraction that takes place passively or automatically in our experience. The notion of abstraction here can still be kept fairly simple: 'abstraction' simply means 'not attending to' something. Thus, not to attend to the complex flow of sensory material itself in sensory experience is to abstract from it. We are not directed toward it even though it is part of the concrete whole of the experience. To perceive a concrete sensory object, we might say, is already to abstract from a difference (or some differences). This might be what Gödel had in mind when he wrote about how even in the case of physical experience we form our ideas of objects on the basis of something that is immediately given. One of his remarks about forming our ideas of objects (Gödel 1964: 268) is that this is the function of a kind of synthesis, of generating unities out of manifolds (e.g. *one* object out of its various aspects).

Sense perception is not the same thing as scientific thinking. Rather, we should say that scientific thinking is 'founded' on sense perception. It consists of theory that, in the case of natural science, is built up on the basis of sense perception. It utilizes various forms of abstraction, generalization, reflection, idealization, formalization, and so on. In his *Logical Investigations* (*LI*) Husserl gives some examples of how abstraction (and generalization) extends further in our experience and he begins to distinguish the different types of abstraction (generalization) that are involved in different types of conscious directedness. He characterizes, for example, the difference between ordinary 'straightforward' sensory perception and what he calls 'categorial intuition' (see Husserl 2001: Investigation VI, §§ 40–52). Categorial intuition includes intuition of objects like natural numbers, sets, and states of affairs. A related distinction is drawn between sensory and categorial abstraction. There can also be forms of abstraction in which sensory and categorial elements are mixed.

In the *LI* Husserl makes the following kinds of observations to distinguish straightforward sensory perception from the consciousness of abstract objects. In sensory perception the external object appears at once, as soon as our glance falls upon it. The unity of perception in this case does not arise through our own active bringing together of the parts that we perceive but is rather an immediate fusion of part-intentions without the addition of any kind of thetic character other than perception. In ongoing straightforward perception the sense perception is merely extended. The unification of percepts is not the performance of some new act through which there is consciousness of a new object. The same object is meant in the extended act that was meant in the part-percepts taken singly. There is as it were a passive unity of identification through these acts but this is not the same thing as a separate *act* of identification. In ordinary perception we are directed toward the 'real' perceptual object, not toward an ideal identity. The *perception* is not like the case, for example, where we *judge* that a = a or a = b. Different thetic characters are involved here. Husserl says that the latter situation involves a new relational act that is not involved in straightforward perception. The perceptual series can be used to *found* such a new relational act when we articulate our individual percepts and relate their objects to one another. In this latter case the unity of continuity holding among the individual percepts provides a basis for a consciousness of identity itself but the latter type of consciousness is different from straightforward perception.

In clarifying what a straightforward percept is we are also clarifying what a sensible or 'real' (as opposed to 'ideal') object is. A real object is just the possible object of a straightforward perception. Sensible objects are, in general, the possible objects of sensible intuition and sensible imagination. We can then also define real part, real piece, real moment, and real form. Each part of a real object is a real part. In straightforward perception the whole object is explicitly given while each of its parts is implicitly given. Every concrete sensory object and every piece of such an object can be perceived in explicit fashion. Husserl distinguishes 'pieces' of objects (independent parts) from 'moments' (non-independent parts) of objects (Husserl 2001: Investigation III). A moment is just a part of an object the existence or perception of which depends upon the existence or perception of the whole of which it is a part. Moments of objects, unlike pieces, are incapable of separate being. Husserl thus holds that moments are 'abstract' in the sense that we may be able to consider them by themselves in thinking and in language even though they cannot be taken to exist by themselves. The apprehension of a moment, and of a part generally, *as* part of a whole already points to a founded (and, hence, no longer straightforward sensory) act since part-whole awareness already involves a relational kind of act. Husserl says that in these cases the sphere of 'sensibility' has been left behind and the sphere of 'understanding' entered. 'Understanding', as opposed to sensibility, can be defined as the capacity for categorial acts, i.e. acts directed toward categorial objects. It is in understanding (in this sense) that we rise up to scientific thinking.

When a sensory object is apprehended in a straightforward manner it simply stands before us. The parts that constitute it are in it but are not made our explicit objects. We can also, however, grasp the same object in an explicating fashion in articulating acts in which we put certain parts into relief. Relational acts can then bring the parts into relation to one another or to the whole. This is a new kind of active 'synthesis' that we bring to the situation since relational acts are not themselves straightforward acts of perception. Only through such new modes of interpretation will the connected and related members assume the character of 'parts' or of 'wholes'. Now the articulating acts and the act we call 'straightforward' are experienced together in such a way that new objects, the relationships of the parts, are constituted. What we have here, therefore, are categorial objects given to us in categorial acts. All such relationships of wholes to parts or parts to parts are of a categorial, 'ideal' nature. Next, suppose we *formalize* the basic relation 'x is a part of y' as '$x \leq y$'. To perceive or judge that $x \leq y$ is no longer part of straightforward sensory perception. In a similar manner, external relations like 'a is to the right of b' or 'a is larger than b', are given as states of affairs in founded acts. In these sections of the Sixth Investigation of the *LI* Husserl gives two additional examples of the consciousness of 'higher-order' objects: collectiva and disjunctiva (§ 51).

What we have in these cases is a shift in directedness (noema) from concrete sensory perception to the awareness of something else, an abstract object or state of affairs. To be conscious of the fact that 'the pen is to the left of the computer' is no longer to be engaged or immersed in straightforward perception itself. An abstraction has taken place in which some features have been lifted out of the concrete sensory experience. In such an abstraction we stand in a different relation to our sensory environment. We are, so to speak, more distant from it. In being at an even further remove from the sensory environment the gap between the human subject and the object or state of affairs becomes even more apparent. As Heidegger emphasized, this gap does not seem to be present at all when we are immersed in the most basic kinds of everyday skilled activities and practices. It is precisely because there is such a strong emphasis on skilled activities and practices in Heidegger's work, however, that one finds little help there with problems about conscious directedness toward abstract objects and related problems concerning scientific reason.

In the examples at hand there is already a form of directedness toward an abstract state of affairs, albeit one that is not very far removed from concrete sensory experience. We are simply adhering to the IDP here. We are to take the object-directedness just as it presents itself and not as something else. As a consequence we must now allow that there is directedness toward an object or state of affairs that is 'abstract'. It is useful, however, to distinguish *pure* abstract objects or states of affairs from those that are mixed with sensory components. Husserl discusses such a distinction at some length.

4. THE IDP AT HIGHER LEVELS OF ABSTRACTION AND IDEALIZATION

In the examples of categorial awareness mentioned thus far the synthetic acts are so founded on straightforward percepts that our awareness is subsidiarily directed to the objects of the founding percepts insofar as it brings them into a relational unity. There are, however, other kinds of categorial acts in which the objects of the founding acts are not intended by the noema of the founded act. In this case there is also a kind of 'abstraction' but it is not an abstraction that amounts, for example, to setting some real moment of a sensory object into relief. Instead, there can be consciousness of a genuine universal, of an 'ideal' object. It seems, for example, that we can be directed toward the redness of a particular rose or toward the redness of a particular wagon. This would be different, however, from being directed toward the ideal universal or essence 'redness' itself. To *mean* something universal is different from meaning some sensory particular. This is just the IDP at work again. We might become aware of the identity of a universal on the basis of different individual intuitions, as in the case just mentioned. Thus, we would again have an abstraction from a difference, but now at an even higher level. The essence would be given as the ideal unity through this multi-plicity. Even if this kind of abstraction, which Husserl sometimes calls 'ideational' or material 'eidetic' abstraction, rests on what is individual it does not for that reason *mean* what is individual. The awareness of the essence as an essence is not awareness of a sensory individual.

In mapping out the territory of conscious directedness we are thus led to distin-guish between different types of abstraction. There can be abstraction of essences per-taining to sensory objects (e.g. redness). Husserl holds that such essences are inexact or vague. In *Ideas I* (Husserl 1982: § 74) he says these are 'morphological' essences. Unlike such morphological essences, however, mathematical essences are exact or pre-cise. They involve certain kinds of idealizations. There can be mixed acts of under-standing in which sensory elements are combined with categorial forms. For example, we can consider the relational act of taking an object x to be an element of a collection y (in the sense of a set), which we represent formally as $x \in y$. There could then be direct-edness toward a set (collection) of chairs. Chairs are concrete sensory objects but sets themselves, as mathematical objects, are not. There could also be directedness toward a set of natural numbers. In the latter case, no sensory elements are involved at all. We have, as it were, pure categorial abstraction. Pure logic, pure arithmetic, pure geo-metry, and so on, contain no sensory concepts in their theoretical fabric. In being directed by 'x is a triangle' or 'x is a natural number', for example, we are not directed toward sensory objects. Husserl begins to develop in this manner, and on the basis of the IDP, an account of directedness toward the pure abstract objects of pure mathe-matics and pure logic (for further discussion see Tieszen 2004).

In his analyses of abstraction Husserl also employs a form/matter distinction, where 'matter' does not refer to sensory or physical matter but, roughly put, just to any judg-ment or proposition with content. For example, the following pair of propositions contain references to exact but 'material' Euclidean essences: 'all triangles are three-sided' and 'all rectangles are four-sided'. If we say that these two propositions have the *same logical form*, say $(\forall x)(\Phi x \rightarrow \Psi x)$, then once again we are abstracting from a dif-ference. In this case, however, we are dealing with yet another kind of abstraction, a formal abstraction (see, e.g. Husserl 1982, 1969). We are moving from 'material' propositions to the logical form of those propositions. Formal abstraction is thus dif-ferent from the kind of abstraction involved in obtaining (exact or inexact) 'material' essences. The relation of form to 'matter' is not the same, for example, as the relation of genus to species or of species to instance. If an object is red then it is colored, and if something is colored then it is in some sense extended. There is an abstraction going on here as we move from the more to the less specific but it is different from a formal abstraction. Now if we consider each of the three cases—'all triangles are three-sided', 'all rectangles are four-sided', and $(\forall x)(\Phi x \rightarrow \Psi x)$—we see that the mind is directed differently in each case. In the case where I think that $(\forall x)(\Phi x \rightarrow \Psi x)$ the directed-ness, as purely formal, is quite indeterminate although it is not completely lacking in determinateness. It is, for example, different from the directedness involved in think-ing that $(\exists x)(\Phi x \wedge \Psi x)$.

Similarly, when we say that the propositions 'all primes are odd' and 'all composites are even' have the same logical form we are abstracting from a difference. The natural numbers themselves would be abstract objects and so would the concepts or essences 'being prime', 'being odd', etc. Where we say that 'the pen, the pencil, and the eraser are *three*' and that 'the cup, the cigarette, and the match are *three*' we are abstracting from some differences. According to Husserl, each natural number is itself an ideal or eidetic particular.

Formalization amounts to lifting the form off of material propositions. We could then focus on the forms of propositions in a theory, obtaining an entire theory-form. This theory-form can be intended or meant as 'ideal', not as 'real'. Thus, we are not speaking of a formal system here as a concrete object that is determined by various sensory qualities associated with sign tokens (e.g. specific marks on paper with specific colors, etc). Once we have a theory-form it can be rematerialized in many possible ways. Think of all the ways in which the simple form $(\forall x)(\Phi x \to \Psi x)$ can be filled in with different content. There can obviously be many different categories or regions of such material fillings. One very broad distinction among these, as we indicated, is that some will involve exact essences and some will involve inexact essences. Formal abstraction is to be distinguished from material eidetic abstraction, and the latter may yield exact or inexact essences depending on whether idealization is involved or not. Sensory essences are vague or inexact ('morphological'), while the concepts of logic and mathematics are exact. A kind of perfection or ideality is involved in mathematical concepts that is not involved in concepts of 'real' sensory objects. Correlatively, the laws of mathematics and logic are exact, while those of the empirical sciences do not all have the same kind of exactness and precision. Instead, they involve probabilistic elements and are more or less vague generalizations from or typifications of sense experience. Indeed, as a good rationalist, Husserl thinks that the exact sciences establish norms toward which the natural sciences strive in trying to become more exact, more precise, more clear, distinct and certain, or more perfect. The sciences of the 'real' approximate the sciences of the 'ideal' more or less closely.

Husserl's own theory of the conscious directedness toward abstract or ideal objects is thus developed at some length and it could obviously be investigated in much more detail. Instead of following out the many details of Husserl's ideas, however, I would now like to consider a general program in the foundations of mathematics that might allow us to eliminate all references to pure abstract objects in mathematics. If this program were successful then we could presumably eliminate appeals to categorial or mathematical (eidetic) intuition. Before taking this up I briefly mention one more example that might be taken to show how conscious directedness toward abstract data is quite common in our experience.

It seems that for a wide range of cases we are more adept at identifying and responding to abstract data than we are to identifying and responding to the immediate, individual concrete phenomena in which they are expressed or exemplified. In written and spoken communication it is typically not the written or sounded physical word tokens toward which we are directed. We are not directed, e.g. toward the font sizes, colors of the tokens, etc. We are also not directed toward the word *types* (which are already minimally abstract). Of course we could be so directed but then it would be for a different set of interests or purposes. What typically happens in ordinary communication is that these things recede into the background and are often not noticed at all.

We might find ourselves directed toward one of these features of the sign tokens if, for example, it somehow blocks our grasp of a person's meaning. What we are directed toward and attempt to grasp, unless there is some kind of breakdown, are the meanings of the expressions. If it is the sign tokens that are concrete then it appears that the meanings toward which we are directed could not count as concrete. They are not given to straightforward sensory perception. Now consider all of the things we do not notice about the physical, concrete sign tokens or sounds in ordinary communication. There is an abstraction at work here. To grasp the meaning is again to abstract from many underlying differences in the immediate, individual concrete phenomena through which the meaning is expressed. We are again to think of this in terms of shifts in directedness. To try to interpret away such abstract data in our experience is to lose track of some basic facts about our conscious life.

5. DIRECTEDNESS TOWARD CONCRETE, FINITE SIGN CONFIGURATIONS IN MATHEMATICS

Mathematics and logic seem to many to be the last bastions of pure abstract objects. Consider the following attempt to eliminate the purported reference to pure abstract objects in mathematics. We try to view all of mathematics in terms of concrete, 'real' formal systems, as Hilbert tried at one time to do. That is, one axiomatizes mathematical theories (e.g. Zermelo-Fraenkel set theory) and then completely formalizes them. The formalization should be very precise. We specify an alphabet of signs from which the expressions of the formal system are to be composed, we present an inductive definition of the expressions of the system, and we lay down a finite set of rules of inference from which theorems are to be derived from axioms. The entire formal system is then supposed to be seen as a system of concrete, finite sign configurations and manipulations on sign configurations according to the rules of inference, which are simply rules for generating new bits of syntax from existing bits. Now the sign configurations and the rules for manipulating them are all given, at least as tokens, in what we have been calling straightforward sensory perception. If we focus on only such a concrete, 'real' formal system in place of the original (informal) mathematics that led to it we are doing what David Hilbert called 'metamathematics'. Metamathematics will be concerned only with syntax and syntactical properties. The conscious directedness would in this case be toward something given (at least in principle) in straightforward sensory perception. A 'proof', for example, is just a finite sequence of finite sign configurations called 'sentences'.

Hilbert proposed to put mathematics on a firm foundation through an approach of this sort. The idea would be to show that formalized mathematical systems were consistent using *only* a special theory, let us call it C (for 'concrete mathematics'). C could not be just any theory. What would make C special is the fact that it would possess the kinds of properties that would supposedly insure reliability or security. It should be finitary and not infinitary, for infinitely long sign configurations would extend beyond straightforward sensory perception and would already involve us in idealizations. It should be possible to understand C as a theory involving only concrete and not abstract entities. The concrete entities in this case are finite sign configurations. C should thus be concerned with what is 'real' and not with what is 'ideal'. Its sentences and proofs should be surveyable in immediate, straightforward intuition (perception). C should not be a creature of pure thought or pure reason. In Hilbert's view, C represents the part of our mathematical thinking that is contentual and meaningful. The contrast is with parts of mathematical thinking that we may regard as purely formal and 'meaningless' in the sense that we need not consider their purported references to abstract or infinitary objects or concepts.

6. AN ARGUMENT FROM THE INCOMPLETENESS THEOREMS

For formal systems T that contain enough mathematics to make Gödel numbering possible, Gödel's first incompleteness theorem says that if T is consistent then there is a sentence G, the Gödel sentence for T, such that $\nvdash_T$ G and $\nvdash_T \neg$ G. The second theorem says that if T is consistent then $\nvdash_T$ CON(T), where 'CON(T)' is the formalized statement that asserts the consistency of T. Theorem 1 tells us that G cannot be decided by T but that it is true if T is consistent. The theorem does not tell us that G is absolutely undecidable. Indeed, Gödel frequently emphasizes how sentences that are undecidable in some theories are in fact decided in certain natural extensions of those theories (e.g. by ascending to higher types or other theories more powerful than the original theory). T can be, for example, primitive recursive arithmetic (PRA), Peano arithmetic (PA), Zermelo-Fraenkel set theory (ZF), and so on. The theorems tell us that such formal theories T cannot be finitely axiomatizable, consistent, and complete. Theorem 2 suggests, generally speaking, that if there is a consistency proof for a theory T then it will be necessary to look for $\vdash_{T'}$ CON(T), where T is a proper subsystem of T'.

A very likely candidate for C is PRA. PA is arguably less suitable, given the distinctions described a moment ago. In whatever manner we construe C, however, it follows from theorem 1 that if C is consistent then the Gödel sentence for C cannot be decided by C even though it is true. It follows from theorem 2 that if C is consistent then C cannot prove CON(C). Given the way we characterized C above, it follows that deciding the Gödel sentence for C or proving CON(C) must require objects or states of affairs that *cannot* be completely represented in space-time as finitary, concrete, real, and straightforwardly intuitable. In other words, deciding the Gödel sentence for C or proving that CON(C) must require appeal to the meanings of sign configurations, to objects or states of affairs that are in some sense infinitary, ideal or abstract and not straightforwardly intuitable.

Either there are such 'abstract' entities or not. Suppose that there are no such entities or that there is no consciousness of such entities. Then it would follow, since we must remain within the perspective of C, that we must stop or 'become static' with respect to deciding the Gödel sentence for C or obtaining a proof of CON(C). That is, we could not decide some clearly posed mathematical problem. (I mean we could not decide it unless the decision were to be made arbitrarily or on non-mathematical grounds.)

However, for some T (e.g. PA) we in fact do have proofs of CON(T) and decisions of related problems. Contradiction. Therefore, there are such entities and we must have some consciousness of them.

It is worth noting that we can obtain a reasonably good understanding of the sense in which the objects or states of affairs used in the decisions or consistency proofs must be abstract, infinitary, and not completely captured in straightforward intuition. In the case of PA, for example, the consistency proof requires the use of transfinite induction on ordinals $< \varepsilon_0$, or it requires primitive recursive functionals of finite type. The level of abstraction involved here is not very substantial compared to some parts of mathematics. It would certainly be more substantial, for example, in the case of consistency proofs for real analysis or in proofs of the consistency of ZF + the continuum hypothesis (CH) or of ZF + ¬CH. In these later cases we would ascend to even greater heights of abstraction, idealization, and reflection in order to extend the science of mathematics with new concepts, methods, and results.

It needs to be emphasized again that C cannot be just any formal theory. We cannot keep extending C with new axioms that allow us to decide sentences that were previously undecidable and still expect to have concrete mathematics, for then we might as well have started with something like ZF in the first place. As a purely formal theory ZF is of course concrete in the same sense as PRA but the difference is that ZF certainly could not codify concrete, finitary mathematics. To hold that it could is to subvert completely the philosophical basis of Hilbertian proof theory.

What does an argument like this show? One thing that it seems to indicate is that the conscious directedness toward abstract objects that is part of mathematics as it is given and practiced cannot be reduced to directedness toward concrete sign configurations and purely combinatorial operations on such objects. Mathematical intuitions (or, if you like, categorial intuitions) of the type described in sections 3–4 cannot be eliminated. Put in terms of the IDP, we cannot simply substitute noemata pertaining to concrete syntax and the properties of concrete syntax for noemata of the sort that are found in standard mathematical (as distinct from metamathematical) practice. There is a sense in which we could do this, however, if our formalized theories were shown on finitist grounds to be consistent and complete, for then we could in a finitistically acceptable way identify formal provability with mathematical truth. Many people have the sense that meaningful mathematics extends beyond C. From my point of view this simply means that many mathematical statements express noemata that are not captured in purely syntactical terms. There are, as it were, intended abstract *meanings* and objects of mathematical theories that are to be taken as data in their own right. Note, by the way, that it does not follow that strict formalization is not important or not useful. All we are saying is that it does not give us the whole picture. It is part of a larger whole.

We can say that the incompleteness theorems can be used to show that mathematical (e.g. arithmetical) truth cannot be understood completely in terms of a purely formal 'real' notion of proof. Purely formal proofs in this sense are concrete and are given in straightforward perception. Moreover, they are always relative to a particular formal system. It is possible that there is some kind of absolute concept of provability or of truth but it has to be distinct from the purely formal notion of proof since the latter is always relative to a particular, specified formal system. Directedness toward concrete formal proofs, in any case, is different from directedness toward mathematical truths.

7. SCIENCE AND EVIDENCE

I have been discussing at some length the idea that there is conscious directedness toward abstract or ideal objects. I would now like to say a few more words about the evidence for the existence of such objects. It is clear, I think, that we do not have evidence for everything toward which we may be directed. Science, however, depends on evidence. There are theories of evidence that will help us to rule out many dubious non-concrete objects without eliminating all non-concrete objects. I prefer a view of science according to which science reflects the activities of critical reason in a wide sense. Science in this sense should put up barriers against superstition. I would like to rule out any alleged objects that do not do any work for us in science, either in logic and mathematics or in natural science: alleged objects like gods, angels, ghosts, round-squares, unicorns, and so on. In some cases we could rule out evidence for objects on a priori grounds (e.g. the noematic Sinn is formally or materially contradictory). In other cases we need not rule out the objects on purely a priori grounds. We can hold that there is just nothing at this time that counts as evidence for the objects and continue critically to examine the matter of whether there could possibly be anything that could count as evidence for them. When we have evidence, in the primary case, our empty intentions or noemata must be filled in by intuition to various degrees (see Husserl 2001: Investigation VI, §§ 1–29). There must be at least partial fulfillment of our intentions.

Many of the abstract objects or states of affairs toward which we appear to be directed in mathematics and logic seem to be admissible on these grounds. Indeed, logic and mathematics are our most rigorous sciences and are among the finest products of human reason. Here the evidence frequently comes in the form of proofs and some of these proofs are of existence statements. The proofs I have in mind here are the kinds of proofs one finds in mathematical practice, where this practice is not always manifested in axiom systems. Proofs, as we have said, need not be understood as purely formal proofs. We can say that Gödel's theorems show us that the purely formal concept of proof ought not to be identified with the concept of proof according to which a proof is what provides evidence. Indeed, proofs have been present in mathematics from very early times and have been considered to provide evidence since these times even though they were not cast as purely formal proofs. One could also point to many other distinctive features of mathematics as science. In addition to proofs, we might be able to trace certain mathematical concepts back to their origins in the life-world. We should consider not only the movement of thought from the particular to the universal or from the 'material' to the formal, but also the reverse direction in which we see many important and fruitful applications of mathematical concepts and forms. These remarkable applications both within and outside of mathematics distinguish the science of mathematics from other conceptual frameworks that might be thought to involve non-concrete objects. In mathematics there is also broad intersubjective confirmation of results, patterns of strict valid reasoning not found in other forms of discourse (e.g. in fiction), as well as other efforts to adhere to justificatory procedures.

In particular, some of the abstract objects that emerge in the effort to overcome the incompleteness results seem perfectly acceptable. In the case of the consistency proof for PA, for example, we can use transfinite induction on ordinals $<\varepsilon_0$. Even intuitionists countenance the existence of such ordinals. Thus, it appears that we can hold that there is a grasp of the arithmetical truths yielded by Gödel's procedure.

As I said at the outset, I would like to develop an account of our consciousness of abstract objects that is situated in a scientific setting. The setting, however, should not be so narrow as to include only neuroscience. Penrose seems to assume uncritically that the missing science of consciousness will just be neuroscience, for his reflections on the incompleteness theorems are followed immediately by some rather remarkable flights of neuroscientific speculation (Penrose 1994). He conjectures that synaptic connections between neurons are controlled at a level where there is physical activity at the quantum-classical borderline. In order to get brain processes to be non-computational Penrose suggests that in consciousness some kind of global quantum state must take place across large areas of the brain, and it is within the microtubules in the cytoskeletons of neurons that these collective quantum effects are most likely to reside. Whether such speculation proves to have any validity or not, I think our view of consciousness will need more breadth. It should include a rich phenomenology and the idea that mathematics and logic are autonomous sciences (an idea in which the IDP will again have a role to play). One would then provide careful descriptions and analyses of the types of conscious directedness involved in logic, mathematics, and the natural sciences, where these descriptions and analyses should be subjected to rational, critical analysis and development. Science in this sense depends on a broad conception of reason and critical analysis that includes many scientific specializations (many perspectives on Being) but that cannot be corralled into any one of them in particular. Thus, my view of the scientific endeavor is evidently broader than Penrose's. It is not so broad, however, as to include some of Gödel's alleged and very speculative views on religion, angels, immortality of the soul, and the like. There are at least reports of some of Gödel's ideas that make him out to be rather superstitious and I prefer to avoid such associations.

8. CONCLUSION

Does the philosophy of mind have a place for the consciousness of abstract objects? As a matter of fact, there has not been much discussion of this question in the recent literature. If there is something to what I have been saying in these pages then it should have a place for the consciousness of abstract objects. There are different forms of conscious directedness and among these we find what appears to be directedness toward abstract objects or states of affairs. Phenomenology would have us take these different forms of consciousness seriously and, unlike many other approaches to consciousness, it offers us some tools for exploring them.

REFERENCES

Feferman, S. *et al.* (eds.), (1986–95) *Kurt Gödel: Collected Works*, i–iii (Oxford: Oxford University Press).

Gödel, K. (1934) 'On Undecidable Propositions of Formal Mathematical Systems', in Feferman et al. (1986: 346–71).

——(1961) 'The Modern Development of the Foundations of Mathematics in the Light of Philosophy', in Feferman et al. (1995: 374–87).

——(1964) 'What is Cantor's Continuum Problem?', in Feferman et al. (1990: 254–70).

——(1972) 'On an Extension of Finitary Mathematics Which Has Not Yet Been Used', in Feferman, et al. (1990: 271–80).

Husserl, E. (1969) *Formal and Transcendental Logic*, trans. D. Cairns (Nijhoff: The Hague).

——(1982) *Ideas Pertaining to a Pure Phenomenology and to a Phenomenological Philosophy, Book I*, trans. F. Kersten (Nijhoff: The Hague).

——(2001) *Logical Investigations*, trans. J. N. Findlay (London: Routledge).

Lucas, J. R. (1961) 'Minds, Machines and Gödel', *Philosophy* 36: 112–27.

Penrose, R. (1989) *The Emperor's New Mind* (Oxford: Oxford University Press).

——(1994) *Shadows of the Mind: A Search for the Missing Science of Consciousness* (Oxford: Oxford University Press).

Smith, D. (1995) 'Mind and Body', in B. Smith and D. Smith (eds.), *The Cambridge Companion to Husserl* (Cambridge: Cambridge University Press), 323–93.

Tieszen, R. (1992) 'Kurt Gödel and Phenomenology', *Philosophy of Science* 59/2: 176–94.

——(1994) 'Mathematical Realism and Gödel's Incompleteness Theorems', *Philosophia Mathematica* 3/2: 177–201.

——(1996) 'Review of *Shadows of the Mind: A Search for the Missing Science of Consciousness*, by Roger Penrose', *Philosophia Mathematica* 4/3: 281–90.

——(1998a) 'Gödel's Path from the Incompleteness Theorems (1931) to Phenomenology (1961)', *Bulletin of Symbolic Logic* 4/2: 181–203.

——(1998b) 'Gödel's Philosophical Remarks on Logic and Mathematics: Critical Notice of *Kurt Gödel: Collected Works*, Vols. I, II, III', *Mind* 107: 219–32.

——(2004) 'Husserl's Logic', in the D. Gabbay and J. Woods (eds.), *Handbook of the History of Logic, Vol. III. The Rise of Modern Logic: From Leibniz to Frege* (Amsterdam: Elsevier), 207–321.

Wang, H. (1974) *From Mathematics to Philosophy* (New York: Humanities Press).

——(1987) *Reflections on Kurt Gödel* (Cambridge, Mass.: MIT Press).

——(1996) *A Logical Journey: From Gödel to Philosophy* (Cambridge, Mass.: MIT Press).

PART IV
UNITIES OF CONSCIOUSNESS

9

Husserl and the Logic of Consciousness

Wayne M. Martin

Abstract: In this essay I explore one of the most problematic and provocative theoretical commitments of Edmund Husserl's phenomenological projects: the idea of a logic of consciousness or phenomeno-logic. I show why Husserl is committed to this idea and why, at the same time, it is so problematic and out of step with contemporary approaches in the philosophy of mind. I then try to render the idea intelligible along two paths. First, to take the idea of a logic of consciousness seriously we must identify and challenge our entrenched atomistic assumptions about conscious states. If we think of conscious states as 'qualia', whose identity-conditions are fixed by their specific feel, then the relations among conscious states must always be contingent and external, and there can accordingly be no sense to the idea that consciousness has its logic. The Husserlian alternative, I argue, is to recognize the identity-conferring relations that hold among conscious states. Second, to recognize the sense in which a science of consciousness might be logical, we must come to terms with Husserl's conception of an ideal science. For on a Husserlian conception, I argue, apophantic logic and phenomenology must be seen as two varieties of ideal science: systematic articulations of the content and structure of an ideal that is constitutive for conscious experience of a world.

1. HUSSERL'S COMMITMENT TO THE IDEA OF A LOGIC OF CONSCIOUSNESS

One speaks at considerable peril in saying what is *not* contained in Husserl's voluminous corpus. To the best of my knowledge, however, Husserl nowhere uses the expression 'the logic of consciousness'. But if his commitment to this idea is not fully explicit, it nonetheless lies at the core of his understanding of consciousness and his vision for a phenomenological science. I begin with a brief defense of this interpretative claim, sketching three ways in which the logic of consciousness is called upon to play its role in connection with Husserl's more celebrated projects. Obviously these preliminary remarks cannot provide a detailed interpretation of Husserl's texts; my aim is provide a preliminary setting for an unfamiliar idea by situating the logic of consciousness in the broader framework of Husserl's phenomenological approach to the issues of mind and meaning.

Consider first the problematic of intentionality. As is well known, Husserl held the intentional character of experience to be one of the central concerns of phenomeno-logical inquiry. In a memorable passage from his 1911 manifesto for phenomenology, he offers a list of five 'riddles' which it falls to phenomenology to answer. ('All these questions become riddles as soon as reflection upon them becomes serious.'[1]) First among the riddles is that of intentionality: 'How does consciousness give or encounter an object?' How, that is, can we make sense of the fact that conscious states not only acquaint us with our own subjective psychic situation but somehow present us with features of an objective world? The riddle of intentionality has by now become a famil-iar point of reference in our thinking about mind and meaning. What is less familiar, however, is the riddle that immediately follows on Husserl's list: 'How can conscious experiences be mutually *legitimated* or *corrected* by means of each other and not merely *replace* each other or *intensify* each other subjectively?' This second riddle reflects Husserl's assumption that conscious states do indeed 'legitimate' and 'correct' each other—that conscious states exhibit evidentiary relations and that consciousness as a whole can be understood as an evidentiary structure. These assumptions pose a riddle because they call for us to say what conscious states are such that they are party not only to the 'natural relations' of succession, causation, functional interconnection, and so on, but also to the evidentiary relations of confirmation, refutation, legitimation, and the like.

The proximity of these two riddles is significant. As we shall see in further detail below, the evidentiary character of consciousness proves to be deeply interconnected with its intentionality. To hazard a first rough formulation: consciousness relates to an object only insofar as it is answerable to a call for consistency. For a conscious state to be about a state of affairs is not for it to be caused by the state of affairs, or for it to be the product of a mechanism that evolved in a context where representing that state of affairs was selectively advantageous. Its relation to an object derives rather from its place in a network of states governed by a logical demand. We shall return to consider this Husserlian idea below, but at this stage the point to emphasize is that a solution to Husserl's second riddle (and hence ultimately to the first riddle as well) requires that we somehow come to terms with the idea of a logic of consciousness. For if there are to be evidentiary relations among conscious states then there must be some governing logical framework in virtue of which we can say that some conscious states *validate* others.[2]

A second manifestation of Husserl's commitment to a logic of consciousness can be found in connection with his principled pluralism about the sciences of conscious-ness. Once again we can use the 1911 manifesto as our point of departure. In a charac-teristic crescendo Husserl there announces the advent of 'a science of whose extraordinary extent our contemporaries have as yet no concept; a science, it is true, of consciousness that is nonetheless not psychology; a phenomenology of consciousness as opposed to a natural science about consciousness'.[3] Husserl is, as we would now put

---

[1] Husserl (1911: 87–8).
[2] I discuss the evidentiary character of consciousness in connection with Dummett's critique of Husserl in Martin (1999).
[3] Husserl (1911: 91).

the point, staunchly anti-reductionist about the mind. But his resistance to any naturalistic reduction does not stem from a metaphysical dualism of mind and body; his is rather a dualism of theoretical frameworks—a dualism of sciences. On this view, the various natural sciences of the mind (psychology, neurophysiology, evolutionary biology, etc.) cannot exhaust what there is to be known about consciousness. They must be supplemented by what we might well call an *unnatural* science of the mind.

It is important to recognize, however, that Husserl's demand for an 'unnatural' science of consciousness is not driven by the idea that there is some subjective feel or quality that is known only privately and first-personally and hence eludes the third-personal stance of the natural scientific framework. Husserl is indeed concerned with the peculiarities of the first person perspective, but his resistance to naturalism does not rest on the conviction that natural science cannot tell us 'what Mary didn't know' or 'what it is like to be a bat'.[4] Rather, the principle behind Husserl's pluralism derives from his reflections on logic. Logic provides the paradigmatic case of an unnatural science—a science, as Husserl famously argues in his diatribe against psychologism, that is not based on induction, that is presupposed by (and hence cannot be justified by) empirical investigation, and whose principles are normatively constitutive for reasoning rather than descriptive of it.[5] The case of logic provides the exemplar for phenomenology, since both are concerned with the meaning-content of certain kinds of activity. An act of judgment or inference is both a particular event in the life of an organism and the bearer of a certain content. Accordingly it can be investigated with radically different theoretical orientations—either as a natural event with a particular natural history and governed by natural laws or as a meaning whose inferential significance is determined by the laws of logic. In order to secure his pluralism, Husserl relies on an analogous claim about consciousness: the natural sciences of its natural functioning must be supplemented by a phenomenological logic which governs its meaning-content.

We find yet a third niche for the logic of consciousness in connection with Husserl's remarkable late work on the fate of rational ideals in the so-called 'European Sciences'. This is not the place to recount Husserl's attempt to trace the beginnings of western science to the workshop of an imagined carpenter, idly entertaining the thought of an ideally smoothed plank or a perfectly straightened edge. Nor can we here assess his provocative and controversial interpretation of the Galilean contribution to the ancient project of discovering rational order in being itself.[6] For our purposes what is important in this sweeping genealogy is Husserl's claim that the outcome of this development has been a crisis—the Crisis, as we might put it, of the Merely Subjective.

It is striking to consider how closely the word 'subjective' has come to be linked with words like 'merely' or 'nothing but': 'That's *nothing but* his subjective opinion; we shouldn't be swayed by *merely* subjective considerations.' In such contexts, 'subjective' serves as a privation-term: to be subjective in this sense is to be less than fully objective. Furthermore, the category of the subjective is here firmly situated beyond the reach of reason. A merely subjective preference is something about which there can be

---

[4] Nagel (1974), Jackson (1986).   [5] Husserl (1900–1: esp. pp. 98–108, 225 ff.).
[6] Husserl (1938a): see in particular §9 and Appendices I and VI.

no rational dispute. A merely subjective response is one that lacks evidentiary significance—the sort of thing that a fair juror is called to put out of consideration in reaching a judgment. For Husserl this equation of the subjective and the merely subjective amounts to a crisis. It is a crisis for science insofar as science must ultimately draw its evidentiary basis from what Husserl famously calls the lifeworld—a domain which is saturated with 'merely subjective' features. But it is also, Husserl argues, a crisis for humanity. For as the category of the subjective comes to be downgraded to that of the merely subjective, we subjects find ourselves either systematically excluded from the rational order or included in ways that abstract from our subjectivity, rationalizing and deploying us as particularly complex bits of objective nature. At the crux of Husserl's diagnosis of the European situation *c*.1938 we find the claim that in this exclusion of the subjective from the rational order we find the looming crisis of European civilization.

Even more astonishing than this provocative cultural diagnosis is Husserl's further claim about the role to be played by transcendental phenomenology in meeting the crisis. And it is here, once again, that we find the implicit commitment to the logic of consciousness. According to Husserl, the crisis of the merely subjective was born of the Galilean contrast between an objective mathematizable order discoverable by science and the 'merely subjective' features of the world as we ordinarily experience it. 'Galilean' science (which is to say: modern science) calls upon us to abstract from the distorting effects of the latter in order to disclose the nomological order of the former. Husserl certainly does not propose that we give up on this Galilean strategy; on the contrary, he celebrates it as our greatest advance in the ancient rationalist project. But if the pursuit of that project is not to leave the subjective as an extra-rational remainder, he insists, then the methods of the natural sciences must be supplemented by an approach that discloses the rational structures of subjectivity. Phenomenology is thus tasked with showing that the subjective is *not* beyond the reach of reason, that it is *not* lacking in evidentiary force, that it *is* governed by logical principle.

But if all this is evidence of Husserl's commitment to the logic of consciousness, we might well also take it to be evidence that his projects are doomed and his strategies misguided. For there seems to be every good reason to suppose that the idea of a logic of consciousness is itself hopelessly incoherent. I turn next to consider some of the difficulties.

2. A CHORUS OF CRITICS

To broach the idea of a logic of consciousness is to find oneself confronted more or less immediately by a chorus of skeptical critics. Before considering how Husserl might make sense of the idea, it will be useful to distinguish a few of the more prominent voices that are united in a pre-emptive dismissal.

A first voice in the chorus is a voice of warning—calling us to guard against the popular misuse of the notion of logic. In *popular discourse*, the first voice observes, we are ever hearing of the logic of this or that. If we read the newspapers or tune to the political chat shows we will hear of the logic of the market, the logic of the air-war, the logic of corporate takeovers, and so on. Stephanopolous on CNN discusses the latest spate of negative political advertising: 'Campaigns go negative in the late stages of a close contest, particularly in contests between similar candidates; that's just the logic of the campaign.' We should not succumb to this loose talk, so the first voice warns, marking thereby a subtle intellectual class distinction. For the most part these journalistic invocations have nothing to do with *logic proper*, which concerns itself only with the forms and principles of valid inference and tells us nothing about 'going negative' in the sense Stephanopolous has in mind.

But there is more than simply sloppy usage here, we will be reminded; there are certain dangers as well. What are described as logical principles in these contexts are usually nothing more than loose generalizations about reigning local practices. To call them logical principles is to misrepresent the contingent and local as somehow inevitable, driven by the inexorable authority of logic itself. One danger is thus that sloppy usage masks false consciousness. A second danger is that we risk losing sight of what is special, and specially puzzling, about logic. After all, to lump these contingent generalizations in with logic is also to lump logic in with them—to treat logic, as in one memorable dismissal, as 'the canonization of entrenched patterns of thinking'. But this is to lose sight of one of the most remarkable and puzzling features of 'logic proper'—that one logic seems to be enough. We don't need a special logic for campaigns and another for takeovers; we don't need one for here and another for there. Logic itself somehow applies equally everywhere and to everything. Given all this, the first voice offers a counsel of suspicion. When we hear talk of a logic of this or that we should look closely. Likely we will find something that is not in fact logic at all.

If there is one sense in which logic applies to everything, there is another sense in which it only applies to one thing. Logic concerns judgment. Such is the theme of the second voice in the chorus of critics. The laws of logic articulate the inferential relations that hold among propositions; they map out the further judgments I am entitled to (and committed to) if I start out with some set of premises. But premises and conclusions must be judgments or propositions, and it is here that the possibility of a distinctive logic of *consciousness* seems to be ruled out. My conscious awareness of, say, the taste of green tea is simply the wrong sort of thing to figure as an element in an inference, since it lacks conceptual content and propositional form. But if it can't figure as either a premise or a conclusion, there can be no logic of it. The situation is not improved if we concede that the taste of green tea cannot *itself* figure as a premise or conclusion, but insist that judgments *about* that taste can. To make this move is indeed to return to the domain of logic and inference, but it is not to reach the domain of some special logic of consciousness. It is simply to return to the familiar terrain of what Husserl calls apophantic logic.[7] It is the logic of propositions, not some supposed logic of consciousness, that governs inferences involving judgments about the taste of green tea. As a general matter, then, this second voice urges dismissal of the notion of a logic of consciousness. Either consciousness is governed by ordinary propositional logic or it fails to exhibit the propositional complexity required for logical relations.[8]

---

[7] Husserl (1938b: 11–13).

[8] A canonical version of this argument is found in Sellars 1956. For a particularly insistent deployment see McDowell 1994.

The remaining voices in the chorus of critics build upon these first two, emphasizing the manifold particular ways in which consciousness is constitutionally ill suited to governance by logical principles. We can hear voices insisting on the *objectivity* of logic and contrasting it with the subjectivity of consciousness. Logic, after all, is meant to articulate inferential relations that hold quite independently of what I happen to think of them. Logical truths are in this sense objective truths—truths that I may come to recognize but which in no way depend upon that recognition. Consciousness, by contrast, is taken to be the limiting case of the 'merely subjective'— that whose very reality is dependent on how it seems to me. A closely related point concerns the *scope* of logical principles. Logic, we are told, is universal: it applies not only to any possible *object* of judgment but to every possible *judge*. No matter what our species or physiological makeup—whether human, alien, or even divine—to engage in judgment is to be bound by logic's constraints. Consciousness, by contrast, would seem to be a highly parochial matter. Inference may be the same no matter who does the inferring; but we should surely expect consciousness to vary dramatically from one physiology to another. Accordingly it seems wildly unlikely that we would find any logical principles in this domain—principles that govern consciousness per se.

Finally, and perhaps most importantly, there is the sheer contingency of consciousness. Whenever genuinely logical principles are in play we expect to find necessity: a conclusion follows necessarily from its premises; a contradiction is necessarily false. This expectation of necessity is indeed satisfied when we consider the relations among judgments: some, taken together, *entail* others. But the relations among conscious states seem to be contingent through and through. No matter how often the *taste* of green tea follows the *scent* of green tea, there is nothing about the one that necessitates the other. There will be no contradiction if the next occurrence of that scent is followed by the taste of fennel—or by perhaps the taste of hemlock, and thence by nothing at all. This last voice, then, is our Humean conscience, reminding us that the occurrence of a conscious state is ultimately a matter of fact, and that there are thus no necessary relations—and accordingly no logical relations—to be found in consciousness.

Such then are the main voices—or at least some of the main voices—making out the pre-emptive negative case. A stern voice of warning denounces the misuse and dilution of the notion of logic; a Sellarsian voice insists that logical relations presuppose propositional structure; a Fregean voice contrasts the objectivity and universality of logic with the subjectivity and parochiality of consciousness; and a Humean voice reminds us that we will find no necessity in the workings of our conscious lives. Ultimately, it seems to me, Husserl can only hope to meet this pre-emptive case indirectly—by first getting us to rethink our assumptions about the basic character and structure of consciousness. But it is certainly tempting to try a more direct reply. We have been told of the impossibility of a logic of consciousness; perhaps our reply should simply demonstrate its actuality. Perhaps we should plunge forward and try to state some axioms or possible theorems of this purported logic.

There is something admirable about this sort of foolhardiness, though in the end it is rarely effective. Let's follow out the exchange for a few steps. Suppose, for instance, that we start by directly confronting the charge that consciousness is a domain of contingency. We could meet that charge if we could name a necessary principle governing the relations among conscious states. Accordingly we may be tempted to dust off the trusty red/green principle: nothing can be experienced as both red and green all over at the same time. Here, we may be tempted to say, we have a principle that expresses a necessity, not merely a contingency, about our conscious experience: if I experience something as green all over, I *cannot* at the same time experience it as red all over. Furthermore, the universality here seems to be strict rather than merely inductive. I need not worry that I might travel to Australia and happen upon red-green swans. And strict universality is said to be a sign of necessity.

If this much be granted, then perhaps we will go on to point out that the necessity here does not derive from the principles of our ordinary apophantic logic. There is certainly no formal contradiction in the proposition '$\exists x(Gx \,\&\, Rx)$'; we shall never establish its negation as a theorem of the predicate calculus. Neither does it seem that we can account for this necessity as a mere artifact of our language—as if the very definition of the term 'green' somehow includes the clause 'not red'. (Imagine what Webster's would look like: 'Green: adj.; of the color of growing foliage; a color that is not red, not yellow, not blue, not magenta, not puce, not chartreuse...'.) Further, even if we set aside this first problem, and grant that our color language precludes assigning both red and green at the same time to the same object, surely we would want to say that this feature of our language *reflects* a fact about our experience. If our color language is structured that way then surely it is because our experience is structured that way.

We may think, then, that we have uncovered a special kind of necessity at work in our conscious experience. Consciousness is not, it seems, a domain of thoroughgoing contingency; we find certain kinds of necessary principles at work there too. Have we hit upon a theorem of the logic of consciousness (or something that ought to be provable as a theorem if only we could set out the right axioms)? Have we uncovered a logical principle governing the relation between consciousness of red and consciousness of green? If we think we have our foot in the door then perhaps we will be emboldened to try for something more ambitious. From the red/green theorem we move on to Husserl's principle of adumbration, and thence perhaps, as our confidence builds, to the principle of ontological difference.

But this whole strategy is doomed. We can expect two kinds of reply. First there will be skirmishes over counterexamples: a certain kind of satiny fabric seems both red and green. We will have to squabble over whether this is really a third color, or perhaps an alternation of colors or in fact a genuine counterexample. But the really serious trouble will come from the first voice in our chorus of critics: we will be accused of mistaking the local for the logical. If there is any necessity here, we will be told, it is physical or physiological necessity. What prevents us from experiencing double color saturation is a logically contingent fact about wavelengths on the visible spectrum, or about our rods and cones, or about the neural architecture of V1, or whatever. There is no logical fact here and no fact about consciousness per se; there is simply a fact about our particular biophysical situation. And at this point, no doubt, we can expect one of those sad stories from the neuro-wards; some poor soul has lesions which are reported to leave him reporting things as red and green all over.

The same sort of exchange will play out, I expect, with whatever possible principles we propose as candidates for a logic of consciousness. Consider briefly the central Husserlian principle of perspective—that nothing appears save as partially obscured, that perceptual consciousness is always partial and piecemeal, adumbrating further possible perspectives in horizons of further perceiving. Even here we will have to worry that we are mistaking the logical for the local and physiological. Imagine some kind of conscious intelligence that is embodied in a kind of fog. We humans perceive an object from a single perspective, but the fogging consciousness simply fogs all around it, taking in all sides at once. Many animals manage to integrate sensory input from two sides of their body; why shouldn't the fogging being integrate views of an object from every side?

It seems clear to me that there is nothing but stalemate along this path—or at best stalemate, and certainly little by way of illumination. So let's abandon the frontal assault and attempt a more roundabout approach.

3. ATOMISM, INTERNAL RELATIONS, AND THE INTENTIONALITY OF CONSCIOUSNESS

As is often the case with Husserl, we find that taking his proposals seriously requires that we first wean ourselves off some entrenched preconceptions about the character of our conscious lives. We have lots of entrenched preconceptions and accordingly our approach here can work along several discrete lines. As a first step, I focus on one obstacle that keeps us from recognizing even the possibility of a logic of consciousness: our atomistic conception of conscious states.

The opposition between atomism and holism has become a familiar and contested feature of the philosophical landscape, particularly in epistemology and philosophy of language. In confirmation theory, for instance, the holist emphasizes that hypotheses can be tested only as a corporate body. The confirmation holist denies, that is, that there can be atomistic confirmation—confirmation that proceeds one hypothesis at a time. For in any confirmation setting I am always making countlessly many background assumptions—assumptions that can in principle be called into question in the face of apparently confirming or disconfirming evidence. In the philosophy of language, analogously, the holist insists that the meaning of a single utterance depends on its place in a network of actual and possible utterances and inferences. This inferential nexus underwrites and structures the meanings ascribable at any particular node. For the meaning holist, we can always *talk* about the meaning of a single expression, but to do so is to abstract from the larger whole in which it finds its determinate sense.

How does this opposition between atomism and holism bear on our understanding of consciousness? First an observation: it is a striking feature of our contemporary philosophical situation that we have learned to take holism seriously as a thesis about confirmation, about linguistic meaning, about belief, etc., but that we often retain a naive atomism about consciousness. We tend to think of consciousness as a kind of dynamic mosaic, with the identity of each tile fixed by its own specific quality, quite independently of the role it plays in the mosaic as a whole. If we are to make room for the notion of a logic of consciousness we must start by learning to be suspicious of this atomistic construal. One step in this direction comes by way of an appreciation of the context-dependence of even the simplest conscious phenomena. The apparent shade of a color-sample, for instance, varies substantially with variation of the background against which it is viewed.[9] But to follow Husserl we must recognize a deeper source for the holism of consciousness: its intentionality.

It will be useful to approach this idea by way of some familiar observations about constraints on belief-ascription. These constraints—familiar from Davidson in one tradition and from Schleiermacher, Dilthey, and Gadamer in another—make it impossible to ascribe interpretations to a text or beliefs to a speaker one by one. In attributing a single belief to someone—say the belief that Clinton was the last US president of the twentieth century—I always implicitly attribute many other beliefs as well: that Clinton is a person; that the United States has a president; that Clinton held public office, etc. And of course each of these ascriptions involves indefinitely many more, and so on. Interpretation is not like collecting pebbles at the beach; it is systemic and holistic from the outset.

For our purposes, a particularly important point to recognize is the role played by the ideal of consistency here. Suppose we tune to AM talk radio and hear an angry caller saying that Clinton was the last president of the twentieth century but that the twentieth century did not end during his presidency. We will be puzzled and wonder what the speaker could possibly mean; we will feel the need to attribute some further belief that will somehow displace the appearance of contradiction. Is he going to explain some idiosyncratic view about the hidden meaning of the Twenty-fifth Amendment? Does he allege a conspiracy to cover up a mysterious vacuum of power during the millennial frenzy? Perhaps he believes that legitimate government in the United States ended with some particularly grievous Clintonian misdeed. Absent some such explanation we will shake our heads and tune back to the baseball broadcast. 'He isn't making any sense', we will say, meaning not simply that he is saying something silly but that we can't figure out what he believes. If he is someone whom we can't simply ignore (suppose he is our student, or our patient, or a major presidential candidate) then we will have to adopt radically different interpretative strategies. We will look for two distinct *sets* of beliefs, each largely consistent, that are here colliding with one another; or we will try to figure out what sort of speech act is being performed—some kind of joke, perhaps, or an attempt to frustrate the audience in order to divert attention from important issues. Or perhaps we will conclude that what seemed to be inconsistency was in fact misunderstanding: 'He must not be using the term "century" the way the rest of us do.'

The point here is *not* that we must adhere to a principle of charity in interpretation, if that is taken to mean that we must find a way of attributing mostly *true* beliefs. (Such a principle will not serve us at all well on the AM dial!) The point is rather that we must suppose that the one to whom we are attributing beliefs at least recognizes the authority of the ideal of consistency. Naturally we all fall short of this

---

[9] Albers (1963).

ideal in particular cases, but where inconsistency is sufficiently wanton the task of interpretation takes a very different turn. We can still find meaning in the speaker's utterances, of course, if we treat them simply as grammatical sentences of a language we recognize and understand. But if the speaker is perfectly content to utter a sentence that means *p* followed by a sentence that means not-*p* (and likewise for *q*, *r*, *s* and their negations), and if he resists or rebuffs any attempt to clarify or illuminate his unusual utterances, then we soon reach a point where we no longer take those utterances seriously *as expressions of belief*. He raves, as Kant said in another context, but he does not think.

The important question to pose here concerns the basis of these constraints on interpretation. *Why* must the attribution of belief be holistic and apply the ideal of consistency? Have we here simply given voice to the local rules of etiquette for belief-attribution? The answer is surely no. To set aside holism and the demand for consistency would in effect be to give up attributing beliefs altogether. The reason for this, I submit, lies in a fundamental connection between the ideal of consistency and what I shall call the *intentional determinacy* of a belief. To say that a belief is intentionally determinate is simply to say that it is about something in particular. My belief about Socrates is about Socrates; my belief that the Pythagorean Theorem is true is about right triangles. Intentionality can survive error and even, as Brentano famously emphasized, the non-existence of its object. But it cannot survive a loss of determinacy. A belief that is not about anything determinate is not properly a belief at all.

There is one straightforward way in which the ideal of consistency is linked to the intentional determinacy of beliefs: the demand for consistency can be used to assess a set of beliefs only insofar as those beliefs are about some common determinate object. If I say both that Alph is alive and that Alph is dead, I am guilty of inconsistency only insofar as I am talking about one and the same Alph. More generally: the ascription of contradictory properties only amounts to a contradiction where they are ascribed to one and the same entity. What is somewhat harder to see is that the same principle runs in the opposite direction: the ideal of consistency applies only where there is intentional determinacy; but intentional determinacy obtains only where representation is disciplined by the ideal of consistency.

In attributing a belief to someone I am attributing an intentional state: I am positing the believer as cognitively directed toward some determinate object or state of affairs which is in turn treated as the standard of truth for the belief itself. To attribute a determinate belief to someone is thus to situate them in a two-way relation to an objective state of affairs: their belief is *about* the object; the state of the object determines the *truth* of the belief. To demand that a set of beliefs be consistent is in effect to demand that they fit together in such a way as to specify something determinate—something that can then serve as the standard whereby the truth or falsity of those beliefs is assessed. Without the discipline of the ideal, a set of psychological states is no longer about anything determinate and hence is no longer properly treated as a set of beliefs at all. To apply the point to our example: the talkshow conspiracy-theorist who ignores not only the recognized authorities and the obvious facts but the demand for consistency as well is no longer expressing a theory at all; he is giving noisy but indeterminate expression to his discontent.

It will be useful to express this result by importing a version of Bradley's distinction between internal and external relations. An internal relation is one that at least partly determines the identity of one of its relata. The number two, for instance, is internally related to the number one, since nothing could be the number two unless it stands in the relation 'greater than' to the number one. An external relation is one that is not internal, not identity-conferring; causal relations are paradigmatically external. Brentano introduced us to the idea that the relation between an intentional state and its object is internal in this sense. This should not be taken to mean that the intentional object is itself somehow an internal part of the intentional state (though Brentano himself sometimes succumbs to that view). The point is rather that the intentional relation is identity-conferring: my belief's being about Clinton is part of its identity; substitute Gore or Bush or Kerry and I have a different belief. The Husserlian claim goes further: we find internal relations not only between an intentional state and its object, but also among intentional states themselves. Husserl's investigation of what he calls 'noematic content' is ultimately carried out through an investigation of these internal relations. For my conscious state to amount to an experience of an enduring object, or a temporally extended melody or a mannequin on display, it must be internally related to other intentional states: the expectation of a view from another side; the protention of a structure of melodic completion; the sudden surprise if it sneezes. These internal relations determine the intentional character and content of my experience.

The pattern we have found in the case of belief holds, I believe, for intentional experience generally. Wherever we find intentional determinacy we should expect to find identity-conferring systematicity and a demand for coherence as well. The form of the demand and accordingly the structure of the system will vary with the form of intentionality. The intentionality of desire or fear, for instance, is not subject to the same demand for logical consistency that the intentionality of belief requires. Reason proscribes assent to a thought content and its negation; but there is no irrationality or contradiction in both desiring and not desiring the same state of affairs. (Some things, after all, are both desirable and undesirable.) But there can nonetheless be a breakdown of rational coherence, even in these cases often celebrated for falling outside the realm of rational governance. Once again a demand for formal coherence serves to sustain the intentional content of the state. If I am afraid, for example, then the requirements of intentional coherence license us to ask what feature of my situation I believe to threaten harm. If I desire some state of affairs, then we will want to know what feature of that state of affairs I believe to be of value. In posing such questions we are situating particular desires and fears in a systematic framework of intentional states on which their identity depends. The legitimacy of the questions reflects the structural conditions of these intentional forms.

There will be cases, of course, where we find ourselves hard-pressed to answer the demand for structural coherence: 'I don't know what I am afraid of here; something just doesn't feel right.' In other cases we find that the demand is flatly violated: 'I know there is no real danger of falling here, but I can't control my fear.' This is just what we should expect: the demand for intentional coherence governs normatively rather than mechanically; ideals hold even in the breach. But as with the case of belief, a lapse in the authority of the ideal threatens to undermine the intentionality of a fear or desire. In the limiting case I find myself left in a stew of affect and agitation but without any determinate intentional content—a condition familiar to frustrated infants. It is significant that in such circumstances we adults sometimes manage to recover intentional determinacy by more or less explicit appeal to the constraints of coherence: 'What am I really upset about here? Is it really Alph, whom I have just been berating? But I like Alph, and Alph didn't do anything wrong. I guess I feel somehow threatened by Alph, but Alph is not really the threat here. . . .' In such questioning we are groping our way out of intentional confusion by holding fast to the formal structures governing intentional content. By situating our experience in its intentional context we come to a critical understanding of its identity. This is important for two reasons. First, as we shall see in the following section, this normative deployment of formal structuring principles is one of the hallmarks of the logical, according to Husserl. Second, we find in such a critical deployment important leverage for challenging the hegemony of the 'merely subjective'. When we appeal to such principles in making sense of our intentional situation we are in effect bringing consciousness back within the reach of rational assessment.

It is worth emphasizing, however, that the points we have been making take a conditional form: *if* consciousness exhibits intentionality then we should expect it to exhibit holistic systematicity and a demand for coherence. Astonishingly, the antecedent is controversial. Indeed in some circles it is now treated as obviously false. This is, I think, one of the weird artifacts of the debate about reductionism which has played such a large role in the philosophy of mind. It has been assumed that the last holdout against theoretical reduction of the mind to the body will be the so-called 'raw feels' of sensory states. Accordingly, these raw feels have often taken the front seat in philosophical discussions of the problematics of consciousness. In the aftermath of this history we have reached the strange result that the problem of intentionality is largely divorced from the problem of consciousness. Consciousness is treated as a collection of raw feels which are not of themselves intentional; discussions of intentionality systematically eschew any discussion of conscious experience for fear of falling into some form of subjective idealism. Husserl would surely have considered this outcome to be a manifestation of the crisis of the merely subjective: the paradigm of consciousness is insulated from any objective dimension in order that we can puzzle over the 'mere subjectivity' of qualia. The proper response to this situation is to wake ourselves up—as if from a very confusing dream. This is perhaps the most basic demand that Husserl makes of his students: return to the facts; let's at least hang on to the idea that consciousness is a way of being open to the world.

If we are to make sense of this worldliness of consciousness, however, we will need to overcome our atomistic prejudices. Consciousness cannot be a mosaic of self-sufficient atoms; its medium is an ordered framework of identity-conferring relations governed by an ideal of formal coherence—an ideal that can be put to work in critical self-examination. In the next section I consider how this conception of consciousness squares against Husserl's characterization of the status of logic.

4. HUSSERL'S THIRD WAY AND THE IDEALITY OF LOGIC

Thus far we have been approaching the idea of a logic of consciousness by thinking about consciousness. But it will be worth our while to consider the question from the side of logic as well. Husserl's most famous statement of his views about logic comes in the Prolegomena to his *Logical Investigations*. As is well known, Husserl there undertakes an extended critique of psychologism in logic. What is not usually remembered, however, is that in undertaking this critique, Husserl sought to situate himself on a middle path between the psychologizers and their critics: 'In the dispute over a psychological or objective foundation for logic, I, accordingly, occupy an intermediate position.'[10] It will be useful to consider one aspect of Husserl's third way, since once again we will find ourselves forced to question one of our entrenched habits of thought: the distinction between descriptions and prescriptions, and accordingly between descriptive and normative principles or inquiries.

The nineteenth-century debate over psychologism was in fact quite wide-ranging and at times diffuse.[11] And it was often characterized by that distinctive intensity and bitterness that one finds only in academic turf battles.[12] But at the center of the disputes was the question whether logic, epistemology, and even mathematics are properly understood as having their theoretical roots in empirical psychology. Thumbnail histories of twentieth-century philosophy sometimes read as if late nineteenth-century logic was characterized by a broad psychologistic consensus—an orthodoxy that was then undermined by Frege and toppled by Husserl. But in fact the battle between psychologizers and their critics was already well underway before either Frege or Husserl entered the fray, and the opposed camps were well established.[13] The program of psychologism in logic and epistemology (whether in its nineteenth- or twentieth-century forms) has often been met with a quick reply; we might call it 'the ten-second refutation'. The ten-second refutation appeals to the distinction between descriptive and normative sciences. Logic, it is said, *cannot* be part of empirical psychology, or indeed of any empirical science, because of its ineliminable normativity. Empirical psychology may describe how we *in fact* think and reason, but this is not the concern of logic or epistemology, which are concerned with how we *ought* to think and reason, with *correct* or *valid* reasoning. And these concerns are in no wise empirical matters.

The ten-second refutation of psychologism is one of the familiar and venerable (which is to say: shopworn) moves in philosophy. It was probably already old when Kant used it, and it was a standard move among the broadly Kantian nineteenth-century critics of the psychologistic agenda.[14] Husserl's dissatisfaction with the argument is

---

[10] Husserl (1900–1: 175).   [11] See Willard (1984: ch. 4).

[12] For a sense of the tone of the debate, see the second edition preface to Sigwart's *Logik*, which open with the insistence that logic be grounded 'not upon an effete tradition, but on a new investigation of thought as it actually is in its psychological foundations' (Sigwart 1873 vol. i, p. x).

[13] Sluga (1980), Kusch (1997).

[14] For Kant's formulation see Kant 1800: 16; for an example of the nineteenth-century deployment see Herbart (1850: ii. 173).

easy to miss, largely because of his considerable sympathy both for its conclusion and for one of its premises. 'The laws of logic', he writes, 'have an intrinsic prerogative in the regulation of our thought'; they are 'predestined for normativity'.[15] Despite this sympathy, however, Husserl insists that the standard anti-psychologistic argument does as much to obscure as to illuminate the distinctive character of logic.

We must first put an end to a distorted notion which both parties share, by pointing out that logical laws, taken in and for themselves, are not normative propositions at all in the sense of prescriptions, i.e. propositions which tell us, as part of their *content*, how one *ought* to judge.[16]

Husserl's initial point is in one sense quite simple. Consider, for instance, the principle of contraposition: 'If every S is P, then nothing not-P is S.' The content of this proposition, to use Husserl's words again, 'exhibits not the faintest trace of normativity'.[17] It is not imperatival; it says nothing about what one ought or ought not do; it is no more or less normative that a theorem of algebra. It simply states a relation that holds between two propositional forms.

We must be careful not to misunderstand Husserl's position here. He does not deny the normative significance of logic. On the contrary, as we have seen, he insists on it. Neither does he deny that a syllogistic principle like the one above might be *transformed* into an explicitly normative judgment: 'If you judge that every S is P then you ought also to judge that nothing not-P is S.' Indeed in the soundness of this transformation we can begin to see the crucial point. Notice first that such a transformation yields a *new* judgment: 'Everyone sees . . . that this proposition is not the original proposition of logic, but one that has been derived from it by bringing in the thought of normativity.'[18] Second, notice that this normative transformation brings with it the context 'judge that'. The new judgment makes a claim on the activity of cognitive agents: if *you* (someone, anyone) judge that all S is P then *you ought also to judge*. . . . Along with a host of celebrated logical peculiarities, the introduction of this operator brings with it two crucial elements. First, it introduces an activity that is in one sense subjective: an act of judgment is always the act of some cognitive *subject*, some cognitive agent. This form of subjectivity, however, is anything but 'merely subjective'. For with the introduction of the activity of judgment we also introduce an ideal-governed domain—a domain of activity that is partly constituted by its recognition of the authority of an ideal of consistency and theoretical unity. Husserl's normative transformation of a logical law implicitly relies on this ideal as its warrant. But further, his account of the status of logic relies on the attendant notion of an ideal law. 'The opposite of a law of nature', he concludes, 'is not a normative law . . . but an ideal law.'[19]

Here it may be useful to consider a rough analogy in the area of moral theory. Moral theory is, of course, the clearest case (perhaps the paradigm case?) of normative inquiry. Moral laws are meant to tell us something about how we ought to act, about what living well consists in. Already in this way of putting it, however, we can see a difference between two ways in which a moral theory might fulfill its normative

---

[15] Husserl (1900–1: 170, 171).   [16] Ibid. 168.   [17] Ibid. 169.   [18] Ibid.
[19] Ibid. 175.

function. On the one hand, we might expect an ethical theory to encode a set of principles with explicitly normative content. The Ten Commandments and the principle of utility express their normativity in something like this way. In Husserl's terminology, they include normativity as part of their thought-content. But an ethical theory might also carry out its normative function without explicitly yielding any pre-scriptions or imperatives. Aristotle's ethics—to take the most prominent example—contains few explicit prescriptions. But of course the *Ethics* nonetheless serve a normative function. A set of judgments here *serve as norms* not in virtue of prescriptive content but because they articulate and specify a more general, overarching ideal—the ideal of living well or living honorably. The principles that generosity is the mean between extravagance and stinginess and that justice is fairness in distribution might in this sense be deemed ideal principles. They are part of a body of descriptive judg-ments which spell out the ideal of living well—an ideal which governs the domain of human activity in the polis.

Aristotle's principles would only amount to laws in the sense relevant to Husserl if the ideals in question are domain-constitutive. Ideals are domain-constitutive where an activity of some sort is only possible for a subject who recognizes their authority.[20] This would not seem to be the case with Aristotle's ideals, since one can certainly live in the polis without recognizing their authority—most obviously as a slave or crim-inal, but perhaps as a sophist or philosopher as well. In the case of logic, however, the ideals are domain-constitutive. If I do not recognize the ethical ideals with which Aristotle is concerned then I will not live *well* in the polis. But if I do not recognize the logician's ideal then not only will I not judge *well*; I will not judge at all.

This brings us back to Husserl's account of logic. What would it mean to think of modus ponens or the rules of syllogistic reasoning as ideal laws? Here is one of Husserl's formulations:

The peculiar science of logic [is] absolutely independent of all other scientific disciplines. [It] delimits the concepts constitutive of the idea (*Idee*) of system or of theoretical unity, and goes on to investigate the theoretical connections whose roots lie solely in these concepts.[21]

For Husserl, the fundamental notion of logic is the idea of theory—or as he says here: the idea of systematic theoretical unity. A theory, in Husserl's sense, is a complex whole comprised of judgments or propositions. But not just any motley collection of judg-ments amounts to a theory. In order to count as a theory, a set of judgments must exhibit characteristic forms of order. In traditional logic there is a close analogy between the complexity of judgments and the complexity of theories: just as a collec-tion of *concepts* must be combined in accordance with a set of formal rules in order to amount to a *judgment*, so a collection of judgments must be combined in accordance with a set of formal rules in order to amount to a theory. In calling the laws of logic

---

[20] A standard example of a domain-constitutive ideal is that of check-mate for chess. The novice player who suggests that we 'play on' after check-mate has been reached is no longer playing chess but some other game with chess-pieces. Deliberative assemblies provide a more complex and interesting example of ideal-constituted domains. Where the assembly no longer recognizes the ideal of hearing minority points of views it is not properly described as a *deliberative* assembly; it becomes an elaborate formality for endorsing majority opinion. [21] Ibid. 172.

ideal laws, then, Husserl's claim is that these laws articulate the content and structure of the idea of systematic theoretical unity.

How does this land Husserl on the disputed question of the descriptive or normative character of logic? The answer is that we should resist the pressure to submit to this disjunction, which is neither exclusive nor exhaustive. The opponents of psychologism are certainly right to insist on the normative significance of logic: the principles articulated by the logician provide a general standard by which judgments can be assessed. But in an important sense this is an *application* of logic rather than its fundamental character—much as navigation is a use we make of maps, which likewise sustain normative application without normative content.[22] If we are invested in the descriptive-normative distinction, then we may insist that logic must itself be descriptive, but that it is *put to normative use* in the way that physics, for instance, is put to use in the evaluation of bridge design. But this too would be misleading. Logic is descriptive, on Husserl's account, but what it describes is an *ideal*. Its normative function is thus internal to its basic enterprise in a way that does not hold when a practical application is found for an empirical natural science.

The important result for our purposes, however, is to be found in the notion of an ideal law and an ideal science. An ideal law is a principle which articulates an ideal, the recognition of which is partly constitutive of a domain of activity. Note the elements here. An *Ideal*: an ideal science deals with principles that give normative structure to some domain. *Articulation*: an ideal science lays out the content of that ideal, by expressing its structure in a set of principles. *Recognition*: the ideal must be recognized in its domain in the sense in which an authority is recognized. That is, it is recognized as providing reasons and sustaining critical assessment. *Constitution*: the recognition is constitutive in the sense that a form of subjective activity depends for its very possibility on the domain structured by recognition of the ideal.

5. PHENOMENO-LOGIC AND THE COGNITIVE SCIENCE OF CONSCIOUSNESS

For much of the twentieth century, the problems and puzzles of consciousness were treated as philosophical in the pejorative sense: the sort of thing someone might quarrel about in coffee houses but not the stuff with which serious research programs might be concerned. It seemed worthwhile to investigate the structure of intelligence, the compositionality of language, the interpretation of texts, the social construction of meaning, and so on. But part of the attraction of these programs lay in the fact that they could approach questions about meaning without appeal to the facts or problems of consciousness. Cognitive scientists and computer programmers set about the construction of intelligent machines, but it was simply idle to ask whether such machines

---

[22] It is also worth noticing that on Husserl's construal logic is concerned only derivatively with inference, argument, and proof. I can indeed use logic to 'get around' in inferential space, but this use of logic depends on the more fundamental undertaking of articulating the structure of that space. See Husserl (1929: 98 ff.).

would or could be conscious. In philosophy, the turn toward structures of meaning in language was explicitly undertaken as a way of bypassing any theoretical concern with consciousness. Even in phenomenology, talk of consciousness was held to be suspect—implicated in a conception of subjectivity that needs to be superseded.

Recent years have seen an astonishing reversal of this trend, with consciousness suddenly a central topic not only in philosophy but in biology as well. What had seemed to be a phenomenon too subjective to be taken seriously in science has now re-emerged as the latest physiological grail, while in philosophy the debate over the possibility of zombies attained an unexpected centrality. The danger is that all this new interest and new work remains trapped in a very traditional disjunction: the study of consciousness is undertaken either as a strictly neurophysiological investigation which hopes to identify the neural mechanisms involved in consciousness, or else as a philo-sophical enterprise seeking to clarify the ontological status of consciousness through the construction of thought experiments and abstract tinker-toy models. A few brave souls combine both approaches.

What is missing in these alternatives is an approach which attempts to understand consciousness specifically as a cognitive phenomenon. Here it is worth reminding ourselves that the very word 'consciousness' (like the corresponding term *Bewußtsein* in German) bears the notion of knowledge on its face: con-sciousness; *con-scio*; with-I-know. The 'know' in 'consciousness' can be read in many different senses. Originally it seems largely to have concerned moral knowledge, as betrayed by its modern etymological cousin: 'conscience'. Too often in the modern philosophical tradition, the knowledge in question was taken to be the privileged and supposedly pristine know-ledge one is meant to have of items in one's own private sphere of subjectivity. Alternatively, one might think of 'conscious' as demarking a range of biological functions that are carried out with the knowledge of the individual: digestion is without-I-know; perception is con-scio. For Husserl, however, the most fundamental cognitive moment of consciousness is its intentionality: consciousness presents us with a world.

It is just here, I have been trying to show, that we have something to learn from Husserl. To consider consciousness as a cognitive phenomenon in Husserl's sense is to see it as an evidentiary domain—as a cognitive activity structured by ideals of consistency and intentional coherence. It is only in virtue of such ideals that con-sciousness presents me with a world; and it is only because of the capacity for criticism by appeal to those ideals that consciousness amounts to a kind of knowledge. It can be hard to see (and easy to dismiss) this construal of consciousness, in part because the relevant notion of 'activity' seems ill-suited to this domain. Consciousness seems to be something that simply happens to me rather than an activity that I under-take and that I might accordingly scrutinize and criticize by appeal to an ideal. We do of course assess and criticize the perceptual capacities of individuals—he has poor eyesight; she has a keen sense of smell. But such assessment is carried out with reference to something like a statistical normal, rather than with respect to an ideal.

Perhaps we have here found the marker for the deepest shift which Husserl proposes in our thinking about consciousness: we are to think of consciousness as a kind of act.

As usual, Husserl's most important ideas are marked by paradox: 'In talking of acts,' he writes at one point, 'all thought of activity must be rigidly excluded.'[23] But this is a riddle for another occasion. What I have tried to do here is to cultivate and articulate a Husserlian conception of a logic of consciousness, along with the conception of consciousness that is its correlate. By seeing consciousness as a domain of identity-conferring relations governed by a demand for consistency, and by seeing logic as the articulation of a domain-constitutive ideal, we can perhaps see our way toward an investigation which takes consciousness seriously as cognition.[24]

REFERENCES

Note on citations: in citing from works in German, I refer when possible to the pagination of standard English translations (as indicated below), but have sometimes modified these translations in the interest of consistency and accuracy.

Albers, Joseph (1963) *Interaction of Color* (New Haven: Yale University Press).

Herbart, Johann Friedrich (1850) *Psychologie als Wissenschaft* (modern reprint: Amsterdam, Bonset, 1968).

Husserl, Edmund (1900–1) *Logische Untersuchungen*. Citations refer to translation by J. N. Findlay, *Logical Investigations* (London: Routledge & Kegan Paul, 1970).

Husserl, Edmund (1911) 'Philosophie als strenge Wissenschaft'. Citations refer to translation by Q. Lauer, 'Philosophy as Rigorous Science', in *Phenomenology and the Crisis of Philosophy* (New York: Harper, 1965), 71–147.

Husserl, Edmund (1929) *Formale und Transzendentale Logik*. Citations refer to translation by Cairns, *Formal and Transcendental Logic* (The Hague: Martinus Nijhoff).

Husserl, Edmund (1938a) *Die Krisis der europäischen Wissenschaften und die transzendentale Phänomenologie*. Citations refer to translation by D. Carr, *The Crisis of European Sciences and Transcendental Phenomenology* (Evanston, Ill.: Northwestern University Press, 1970).

Husserl, Edmund (1938b) *Erfahrung und Urteil: Untersuchungen zur Genealogie der Logik*. Citations refer to translation by Churchill and Ameriks, *Experience and Judgment: Investigations in a Genealogy of Logic* (Evanston, Ill.: Northwestern University Press, 1973).

Jackson, Frank (1986) 'What Mary Didn't Know', *The Journal of Philosophy* 83: 291–5.

Kant, Immanuel (1800) *Logik* (Königsberg: Nicolovius); translation by Hartman and Schwarz as *Logic* (New York: Dover, 1974).

Kusch, Martin (1995) *Psychologism: A Case Study in the Sociology of Philosophical Knowledge* (London: Routledge & Kegan Paul).

Martin, Wayne (1999) 'Husserl's Relapse? (Concerning a Fregean Challenge to Phenomenology)', *Inquiry* 42: 343–70.

McDowell, John (1994) *Mind and World* (Cambridge, Mass.: Harvard University Press).

Nagel, Thomas (1974) 'What is it like to be a Bat?', *The Philosophical Review* 83: 435–50.

23 Husserl (1900–1: 563).

24 Parts or versions of this essay were read to audiences at Cambridge University, the Philadelphia Philosophy Consortium, and the Pacific Meetings of the American Philosophical Association. Thanks to those audiences, to the editors of this volume, and to the members of the UCSD Phenomenology Reading Group for their help. Paul Livingston and Bill Bristow offered a number of helpful comments on an earlier draft.

Sellars, Wilfred (1956) 'Empiricism and the Philosophy of Mind', in Feigl and Scriven (eds.), *Minnesota Studies in the Philosophy of Science*, i (Minneapolis, Minn.: University of Minnesota Press), 253–329.

Sigwart, Christoph (1873) *Logik*. Citation refers to translation by Helen Dendy, *Logic* (New York: Macmillan, 1895).

Sluga, Hans (1980) *Gottlob Frege* (London: Routledge & Kegan Paul).

Willard, Dallas (1984) *Logic and the Objectivity of Knowledge: A Study in Husserl's Early Philosophy* (Athens, Oh.: Ohio University Press).

10

Temporal Awareness

Sean Dorrance Kelly

Abstract: The problem of temporal awareness manifests itself in many ways: in our experience of the passage of time, in our experience of the movement of objects across space, in our experience of temporally separated objects as belonging together (as in the case of the notes in a melody), and so on. Each of these cases makes it clear that our experience, in some sense, extends beyond what's happening now. But what model of experience accounts for this phenomenon? I argue that two classical models, the specious present theory and the retention theory, are both unsatisfactory. I conclude by suggesting some of the richer phenomenological features that ought to play a central role in any more satisfactory account.

1. THE PROBLEM OF PACE PERCEIVED

In Sonnet 104, Shakespeare writes about a gracefully aging friend. Although three years have passed since they last met, her appearance has changed so slowly that she seems hardly to have aged at all. To highlight this fact, Shakespeare compares the imperceptible change in her appearance with the movement of an hour hand across the face of a clock:

> Ah! yet doth beauty, like a dial-hand,
> Steal from his figure and no pace perceived;
> So your sweet hue, which methinks still doth stand,
> Hath motion and mine eye may be deceived:

The image in these couplets illustrates the idea that some movements or changes—like the measured movement of the hour hand or the ever-so-gradual decline in a friend's appearance—occur too slowly for us to experience them as such. Although we can notice that a change *has occurred*, the change itself goes forever unseen. This idea is a fairly common one. Locke writes in the *Essay*, for instance, that when the motion of a body is too slow, the sense or experience of its motion is lost. In such a case, Locke observes: 'the Body, though it really moves, . . . [nevertheless] seems to stand still, as is evident in the Hands of Clocks, and Shadows of Sun-dials, and other constant, but slow Motions, where though after certain Intervals, we perceive by the change of distance, that it hath moved, yet the Motion it self we perceive not'.[1]

In addition to motions that are too slow to perceive, Locke observes that some are too swift to perceive as well. In these kinds of cases, although there is a real succession of events in the world, we experience these events as taking place all at the same instant. So for example, Locke writes:

Let a Cannon-Bullet pass through a Room, and in its way take with it any Limb, or fleshy Parts of a Man; 'tis as clear as any Demonstration can be, that it must strike successively the two sides of the Room: 'Tis also evident, that it must touch one part of the Flesh first, and another after; and so in Succession: And yet I believe, no Body, who ever felt the pain of such a shot, or heard the blow against the two distant Walls, could perceive any Succession, either in the pain, or sound of so swift a stroke.[2]

Locke concludes from these examples that our capacity to experience events as taking place in succession has both an upper and a lower bound. When events proceed too slowly, as in the case of the movement of the hour hand, we can only perceive that motion *has occurred*, without being able to perceive it *as occurring*. By contrast, when events proceed too swiftly, as in the case of the movement of the cannon-bullet, we experience events that actually take place in succession *as occurring all at once*. Thus, Locke writes, 'There seem to be *certain Bounds to the quickness and slowness of the Succession of* those *Ideas* one to another in our Minds, beyond which they can neither delay nor hasten'.[3]

Between these boundaries, however, when objects are moving at a pace that is neither too fast nor too slow, something apparently extraordinary occurs: we perceive them *to be moving*. As Locke writes, we perceive 'the Motion it Self'. The simplest and most often-cited example of this nowadays was not available to Shakespeare or Locke. It is the example of the second hand sweeping round the face of a clock.[4] By contrast to the bullet, we see the second hand as occupying successive positions on the dial. By contrast to the hour hand, however, which we can only see *to have moved* across the face of the clock, we experience the second hand at every moment as *now moving*. Emphasizing this latter distinction, C. D. Broad writes in his 1923 book *Scientific Thought*:

[I]t is a notorious fact that we do not merely notice that something *has* moved or otherwise changed; we also often see something *moving* or *changing*. This happens if we look at the second-hand of a watch or look at a flickering flame. These are experiences of a quite unique kind; we could no more describe what we sense in them to a man who had never had such experiences than we could describe a red colour to a man born blind. It is also clear that to see a second-hand *moving* is a quite different thing from 'seeing' that an hour-hand *has* moved.[5]

---

[1] Locke (1975: bk. II, ch. XIV, §11, p. 185). [Locke 1975 is hereafter referred to as *Essay* followed by book, chapter, section, and page number.] [2] *Essay* II.XIV.10, pp. 184–5.

[3] *Essay* II.XIV.9, p. 184.

[4] Russell, at least, claims that there were no second hands on the clocks of Shakespeare's day, and Locke never seems to discuss such an example either. See Russell (1948: 210).

[5] Broad (1993: 351). In normal cases, the perception of something as moving is caused by the physically continuous motion of an object in the environment. Modern technology has provided us, however, with a number of ways to generate motion perception experiences by the rapid presentation

The experience of something *as moving*, therefore, seems to be a basic and distinct kind of experience. I said before, however, that it is an apparently extraordinary one. The reason for this is that we seem to experience objects as moving *now*, at the moment we are having our experience of them. But all movement takes at least some time to occur, given the laws of physics, and all experienced movement takes some considerable time, as we have seen already from the case of Locke's cannon-bullet. If movements take place across time, therefore, it is difficult to imagine how we could experience them as occurring at a moment. This is what I will call the philosophical problem of motion perception. To borrow the phrase from Shakespeare, it is the problem of 'pace perceived'. In the next section I will discuss two traditional attempts to deal with this problem.

2. TWO APPROACHES TO THE PROBLEM OF PACE PERCEIVED

Each of the approaches I will discuss has a storied history. The idea that they should be considered as distinct approaches in dialogue with one another, however, has, to my knowledge, no precedent.[6] This is largely, I believe, a function of the narrow professionalism that has increasingly characterized the study of philosophy. For distinct sub-specialties have formed around the advocates of each approach: historical and/or continental, on the one hand, contemporary, analytic, and scientifically motivated, on the other. Nevertheless, a genuine dialogue between these views seems not only possible but also desirable. The reason for this is not just that those who are ignorant of history are doomed to repeat its mistakes; it is also because the gems of history are often hidden by contemporary concerns.

Of the two approaches I will discuss, the first, which I will call the method of Retention, finds its inspiration in Locke and Hume, and its fulfillment in Kant and Husserl. It is the starting point, too, for Heidegger's analysis of temporality, and

---

of static images (as in the case of film or television). This general phenomenon is called 'apparent motion'; the different kinds of apparent motion provide an important clue to the workings of the human motion detection system. Of the several kinds of apparent motion, 'beta motion' is the name of the smooth, continuous kind that is indistinguishable from normal cases of motion perception. Beta motion is caused by the presentation of static images at a rate of around 10 per second (100 milliseconds per presentation). See Palmer (1999: 471–81).

[6] I have found one possible exception to this claim in a relatively obscure 1929 paper by the famous Kant scholar, H. J. Paton. (See his 'Self-Identity', first published in *Mind* and then reprinted in Paton (1951).) Even this paper, however, seems to be an accident of history: Paton is discussing from a Kantian perspective the recent views of his colleague C. D. Broad. (Well, his almost-colleague: I believe that Paton was at Oxford while Broad was at Cambridge.) An anonymous referee points out that there is, of course, plenty of discussion attempting to relate the 'analytic' tradition of James, Broad and others with the 'continental' tradition centered around the work of Husserl and Heidegger. But the distinction I am making between the 'specious present' approach to the problem of temporal awareness and the 'retention theory' approach is orthogonal to the analytic/continental divide. Even so, the referee recommends several pieces that are certainly worth looking at. Among those in English are: Gallagher (1998); Gurwitsch (1966); and Brough (1970). In addition, Brough's introduction to Husserl's lectures on time consciousness is interesting.

thereby the conditions on the possibility of truth. The second approach, the doc-trine of the Specious Present, first found its popular voice in the late nineteenth-century work of William James, was made precise in the 1920s and 1930s by C. D. Broad, and has been rehabilitated in a recent book by the English philosopher Barry Dainton. I will argue that Husserl's method of Retention enjoys certain benefits over even the most sophisticated and recent versions of the doctrine of the Specious Present. This is especially interesting since Husserl's view, when it is discussed by ana-lytic philosophers at all, is often assimilated to a kind of Specious Present approach itself.[7]

Locke and Hume understood the philosophical problem of motion perception as a special case of a more general concern. This more general concern focuses on the origin of our ideas of time, and especially our ideas of succession and duration. The empiricists took it as a datum of their research that we never have a direct impression or experience as of one event succeeding another, nor do we ever perceive directly any duration of time that elapses between the occurrence of two events or over the course of a single event. Thus, Locke writes definitively that we have no perception of Duration,[8] and Hume expands upon this idea in the following passage from the *Treatise*:

The idea of time is not deriv'd from a particular impression mix'd up with others, and plainly distinguishable from them; but arises altogether from the manner, in which impressions appear to the mind, without making one of the number. Five notes play'd on a flute give us the impres-sion and idea of time; tho' time be not a sixth impression, which presents itself to the hearing or any other of the senses.[9]

One of the central issues between Retention theorists and defenders of the Specious Present turns on this point. Locke and Hume think it is obvious that we have no intu-itive faculty by means of which to experience the passage of time. By contrast, defend-ers of the Specious Present claim that we do have a direct perception of duration, that we experience the world, in other words, in temporally extended units that are taken in as a whole. As William James writes, in a famous passage from the *Principles of Psychology*:

[T]he practically cognized present is no knife-edge, but a saddle-back, with a certain breadth of its own on which we sit perched, and from which we look in two directions into time. The unit of composition of our perception of time is a *duration*, with a bow and a stern, as it were—a rearward- and a forward-looking end... We do not first feel one end and then feel the other after it, and from the perception of the succession infer an interval of time between, but we seem to feel the interval of time as a whole, with its two ends embedded in it.[10]

---

[7] Richard Gale, for instance, groups Husserl and Heidegger together with James and Broad as advocates of the Specious Present. See Gale (1968: 293–4). For a more careful treatment of Husserl see Miller (1984), and also Dainton (2000: ch. 6). For an especially readable account of Husserl's rela-tion to Kant, see Blattner (1999: 190–208). Blattner argues that the thesis of the Specious Present is, on Husserl's account, 'misleading but partially correct' (p. 199).   [8] *Essay* II.XIV.4, p. 182.

[9] Hume (1978: bk. I, pt. II, sect. III, pp. 34–5). [Hume 1978 is hereafter referred to as *Treatise* followed by book, part, section, and page number.]   [10] James (1950: 609–10).

Later in the same chapter James defines the Specious Present clearly as 'the short duration of which we are immediately and incessantly sensible',[11] and he insists that within this short duration we can discern earlier and later parts.[12]

Barry Dainton, in his recent book *Stream of Consciousness*, defines the Specious Present in a similar manner. According to Dainton, 'Whatever falls within [a subject's] specious present is sensed all at once as a whole, but a temporally extended whole'.[13] As with James, then, Dainton here denies Locke and Hume's claim that we have no perception of duration as such. According to the defenders of the Specious Present theory, what we experience at a given moment is always a temporally extended duration, and could not be otherwise.[14]

Locke and Hume do not deny, of course, that we have ideas of succession and duration; they merely deny that these ideas have their origin in a direct perceptual impression of the passage of time. Rather, according to the empiricists, we get our ideas of succession and duration by reflecting upon the succession of ideas that constantly runs across our mind. As Locke writes in the *Essay*:

To understand *Time* and *Eternity* aright, we ought with attention to consider what *Idea* it is we have of *Duration*, and how we came by it. 'Tis evident to any one who will but observe what

---

[11] James (1950: 631).

[12] James is clear, however, that we are not always correct about the temporal order of the parts of a Specious Present: '[W]hen many impressions follow in excessively rapid succession in time, although we may be distinctly aware that they occupy some duration, and are not simultaneous, we may be quite at a loss to tell which comes first and which last; or we may even invert their real order in our judgment.' (1950: 610).   [13] Dainton (2000: 137–8).

[14] Although James's definition of the Specious Present is the starting point for all modern discussion of the topic, the contemporary literature has not accepted James's notion unequivocally. Indeed, Robin Le Poidevin, in a recent review article, defines a version of the Specious Present that seems to bear no relation to James's at all. (See Le Poidevin (2004).) Further, he claims that his definition of the Specious Present characterizes the typical use of the term in contemporary literature (although this claim seems dubious to me).

On Le Poidevin's account, the Specious Present is characterized merely as the interval of time within which events are experienced as simultaneous. But all parties—both defenders and deniers of the Specious Present as it is traditionally conceived—agree that it is possible for us to experience as simultaneous two events that actually occur in succession. Locke's cannon-bullet was an example of this. Although the bullet first hits one wall and then the other, it is traveling so swiftly that we do not hear these events as succeeding one another in time; rather we hear them as simultaneous. Since all parties agree that our experience of simultaneity is relatively coarse-grained in this way, it cannot be that any useful notion of the Specious Present follows from this kind of account.

This is not to say that the notion of experienced simultaneity holds no philosophical interest. One important problem in this area concerns the transitivity of an equivalence relation like simultaneity. If A and B are experienced as simultaneous and B and C are experienced as simultaneous, then A and C, by transitivity, should be experienced as simultaneous too. Naturally, however, if the string of events is long enough there will be some event F that should be experienced as simultaneous with A (given the argument from transitivity) but as a matter of fact is not. This gives rise to a nice problem about how to define the equivalence class of events that are experienced as simultaneous with one another. The problem is formally equivalent to a problem Goodman discusses, in *The Structure of Appearance*, about the transitivity of apparent color. Russell, who discusses the problem of experienced simultaneity in chapter 6 of his 1913 manuscript *Theory of Knowledge*, happens upon exactly the same solution that Goodman recommends half a century later: the group of events that are simultaneous in experience, according to Russell, is defined such that any two are experienced together, and nothing outside the group is experienced together with all of them. On such a view, the way the experience seems to the subject at the moment does not reveal entirely the way it is.

passes in his own Mind, that there is a train of *Ideas*, which constantly succeed one another in his Understanding, as long as he is awake. *Reflection* on these appearances of several *Ideas* one after another in our Minds, is that which furnishes us with the *Idea* of *Succession*: And the distance between any parts of that Succession, or between the appearance of any two *Ideas* in our Minds, is that we call *Duration*.[15]

Likewise, Hume endorses the same idea in the *Treatise* when he says, somewhat more economically, 'from the succession of ideas and impressions we form the idea of time'.[16]

At this point, however, a notable problem arises. For how are we to make the transition from the succession of ideas that runs across our mind to the idea of one thing's following another? After all, as James points out, 'A succession of feelings, in and of itself, is not a feeling of succession.'[17]

Locke and Hume agree that the mere existence of a train of ideas is not sufficient to give rise to the idea of succession. But they seem to think that we need merely to reflect upon the succession of ideas, to watch them as they pass before our mind, and the idea of succession will occur immediately.[18] Surely, however, more is required than this. Beyond merely noticing that there is now an idea before my mind, and now an idea, and now an idea, it seems that we must keep track of the previous ideas in order to think of the current one as having followed them. For imagine a creature who at every moment experiences only what is before him *at the time*, always forgetting that which has come before. Although there may be a succession of ideas in the mind of such a creature, no amount of reflection upon them will give him the idea of one following the other. James quotes the nineteenth-century German psychologist Volkmann in order to make this point: '[I]f A and B are to be represented *as occurring in succession* they must be *simultaneously represented*; if we are to think *of* them as one after the other, we must *think* them both at once.'[19]

Defenders of the specious present, like James, seem to have found a way out of this difficulty: according to them, the earlier and later events that form the parts of a Specious Present are given to experience *all at once as a whole*. It is part of our experience immediately, on such a view, that one event succeeds another.

But this is not the only, and as we shall see in the next section not even the best, way to account for the experience of succession. Kant formulates a version of the alternative when he discusses the threefold synthesis in the A-deduction of the First Critique.[20] The key aspect of his account for our purposes is the second synthesis, the

---

[15] *Essay*, II.XIV.3, pp. 181–2.   [16] *Treatise*, I.II.3, p. 35.   [17] James (1950: i. 628).

[18] Hume, of course, recognizes a general problem in this area when he writes, in the Appendix to the *Treatise*, 'But all my hopes vanish, when I come to explain the principles, that unite our successive perceptions in our thought or consciousness. I cannot discover any theory, which gives me satisfaction on this head' (pp. 635–6). Hume is here discussing, of course, the problem as it applies to personal identity. Without any principle of connection there seems to be no way of binding together one's experiences into a simple whole that constitutes the self. But lacking this principle, it is also hard to see how Hume will derive the idea of succession from a mere succession of otherwise unconnected ideas. Perhaps he will argue that in reflection we *feel* the ideas succeeding one another, though they don't in fact belong together at all. But Hume does not pursue the point in this context.

[19] Quoted in James (1950: 629).

[20] See Kant (1965: A98–A110). Hereafter referred to solely by the standard pagination.

so-called synthesis of reproduction in imagination.[21] The motivating thought behind this synthesis is that it is always a part of our experience at a moment that we take it in the context of the experiences that have come before. The earlier experiences are 'reproduced in imagination', as Kant says, and are thereby presented simultaneously with the experience I am having now. So, for instance, Kant writes:

> When I seek to draw a line in thought, or to think of the time from one noon to another, or even to represent to myself some particular number, obviously the various manifold representations that are involved must be apprehended by me in thought one after the other. But if I were always to drop out of thought the preceding representations (the first parts of the line, the antecedent parts of the time period, or the units in the order represented), and did not reproduce them while advancing to those that follow, a complete representation would never be obtained.[22]

On Kant's view, therefore, or at least on one relatively standard interpretation of it, the experience I am having now is always accompanied by a reproduction of the experiences that immediately preceded it. To return to Hume's example, Kant accounts for my experience of the five notes as occurring in succession by filling my current experience not only with a presentation of, say, the fifth note, but also with a reproduction of the earlier presentations of the initial four. Only because my current experience is taken in the context of the earlier ones do I hear the notes as occurring in succession instead of independently.

Kant's view has the same advantage over Locke and Hume that the doctrine of the Specious Present does. In both cases the current note resides in experience along with the earlier ones. This is what makes it possible to hear them in relation to one another. The difference between the views lies in the presentation of the earlier notes. On Kant's view my earlier experience of the notes is reproduced now in imagination. According to the defenders of the Specious Present, however, I am now in direct perceptual contact with the earlier notes themselves—notice, the notes themselves, not even a representation of them—even though those notes now no longer exist. It is not at all clear that this latter notion makes sense, and I will discuss some difficulties with it in the following section. Before I move on, however, I would like to raise a problem for Kant's position as I have formulated it here.

The problem concerns the nature of the reproductive act. Kant's text itself seems to allow for several interpretations of reproduction. One standard interpretation in the secondary literature, however, understands reproduction as a kind of memory. So, for instance, Robert Paul Wolff writes:

> What I must do . . . as I proceed from one moment to the next, is to reproduce the representation which has just been apprehended, carrying it along in memory while I apprehend the next. In looking at a forest, I must say to myself, 'There is a birch; and there is an elm, plus the birch which I remember, etc.'[23]

---

[21] Much ink has been spilled by Kant commentators over the question what the relation between the three syntheses is. One popular view, emphasized by Paton, is that the three syntheses are all aspects of a single synthesis; that no one of them can be understood independently of the others. I do not mean to be taking a stand on this issue here, even though, because of space constraints, I will emphasize the second of the syntheses. [22] A102.

[23] Wolff (1963: 128).

The problem with this interpretation becomes clear when we think about how memory works. One kind of memory occurs when one is reminded of something.[24] As I am going out the door it all of a sudden occurs to me that I have left my keys behind. The experience of leaving the house, as we say, jogs my memory. But think of this kind of experience in the context of Hume's example from a moment ago. When I hear the fifth note in the melody I am not all of a sudden reminded of the earlier notes, as if I had forgotten them momentarily and now they are back in mind. Hearing the notes as a melody is not a matter of being reminded of the earlier notes at all. As Husserl says, 'A present tone can indeed "remind" one of a past tone, exemplify it, pictorialize it; but . . . the intuition of the past cannot itself be a pictorialization.'[25] This kind of memory, therefore is a bad candidate for reproduction.

Another kind of memory occurs when one entertains the memory of an event or thing. I can think fondly, for instance, of the moment in my wedding ceremony when I took the hand of my bride-to-be. I can focus on the look that ran across her face, examine the feel of her hand in mine, and luxuriate in the emotion of the moment. If I have a particularly vivid imagination, I can almost experience it as if it is actually happening now. But even if my imaginative faculties fall short of this extreme, when I genuinely entertain the memory, I have *it, the memory*, before me at the moment. Even if I am not fooled into thinking that I am now at the altar, the memory of my having been there is fully before my mind.

This kind of memory, too, seems inadequate to account for the experience of the notes. It would be as if, while hearing the fifth note, I entertain the memory of the one before. Perhaps I even hear it again in my mind. But now the two notes are presented simultaneously as a kind of chord—albeit one is a note I am hearing and the other a note I am entertaining in memory. But the experience of a chord—even a chord with these mixed components—is not like the experience of a melody. So reproduction cannot be entertaining a memory either.

For these kinds of reasons, Husserl prefers to talk of *retaining* elements of the recent past rather than of *reproducing* them. Retention, according to Husserl, is a unique kind of intentionality that is unlike any kind of reproduction or memory.[26] To retain the earlier notes in the melody is to be directed toward them as just-having-been. To bring the story back to pace perceived, I can experience the second hand as moving round the face of the clock because I perceive it as now pointing at the twelve and as just-having-been pointing at the spot before. As Husserl says,

During the time that a motion is being perceived, a grasping-as-now takes place moment by moment; and in this grasping, the actually present phase of the motion itself becomes constituted. But this now-apprehension is, as it were, the head attached to the comet's tail of retentions relating to the earlier now-points of the motion.[27]

---

[24] Blattner (1999: 206–7) discusses a category of memory like this. Wolff's example reads as if this is the kind of memory he has in mind: there is an elm, oh yes, and I must not forget the birch that I have just seen.
[25] Husserl (1991: §12, p. 33/31–2). [Husserl 1991 is hereafter referred to as *Internal Time*, followed by the section number and then the page number in this English translation and the page number in the standard German pagination.]   [26] See *Internal Time*, §12, pp. 33–4/31–3.
[27] Ibid., §11, p. 32/30.

Now, there is a genuine question whether we can make sense of this kind of intentionality. I understand what it is to think of George W. Bush *as* the President of the United States. This is the kind of intentionality—the kind of being directed toward something under an aspect—that we are all familiar with. But what could it be to experience a note *as just-having-been*? Husserl is little help here, since he defines retention principally by contrast with what it is not. What one would like is a standard set of examples that give us the feel for what it is to experience something as just-having-been. I have some sketchy ideas myself about how such a project might proceed, but I will leave those for the conclusion. Before I get to that, however, I want to present a brief criticism of the Specious Present.

3. WHAT IS WRONG WITH THE SPECIOUS PRESENT[28]

The doctrine of the Specious Present, as we have seen, proposes that we are at every moment in direct perceptual contact not only with what is now occurring but also with what has recently occurred and indeed with what is about to occur as well. As James says, the experienced present is 'a saddle-back...from which we look in two directions into time'.[29] It is very difficult to understand what this could mean. I will outline briefly three concerns.

In the first place, it is hard to understand how I could now be perceptually aware of something that is no longer taking place. One way to make sense of this possibility is to emphasize the time lag that always exists between when an event occurs and when the light from that event reaches my retina and is processed by my brain. Because of this time lag the supernova that I see in the night sky, for instance, is really an event that took place some time ago. Since there is always some lag between the occurrence of the event and my experience of it, there is a sense in which I am always perceptually aware of events that are no longer taking place. But this cannot be relevant to the Specious Present. For if it is in this sense that I am aware of the past then I cannot in this sense also be aware of the present, never mind aware of the future. If the time lag between events and experiences is the relevant fact, then I am only ever aware of what is past. But this is inconsistent with the view. Another possible option is to say that we are not aware *of* past events, but only aware of them *as past*. But this is to turn the doctrine of the Specious Present into a Husserlian kind of intentionalist theory. It is, in other words, to give up on the claim that the Specious Present is sensed immediately and as a whole. But this is the defining feature of the Specious Present, so to give up on it is to give up on the doctrine altogether.

Second, it is hard to understand how we could experience duration directly at all. Again, there is an obvious way to make sense of this possibility, but it is irrelevant to the Specious Present. The obvious trick is to say that we always experience what is in

---

[28] An anonymous referee points out that some of the following criticisms of the Specious Present theory have appeared in the literature before. See, for example, Mabbott (1951) and Mundle (1954).

[29] James (1950: 609).

fact a short duration, but we experience it as a moment in time. We saw Locke defend a version of this claim when he talked about the case of the cannon-bullet. In that case two successive events—the bullet hitting first one wall and then another—were experienced as occurring simultaneously. But the Specious Present is not about simultaneity; it is about temporal extent. The doctrine is committed not to the claim that we experience temporally distinct events as simultaneous, but rather to the claim that we experience temporal extension itself. What could count as evidence for such a claim continues to be deeply unclear to me.

Finally, it is perhaps most difficult to understand how I could now be perceptually aware of something that has not yet occurred. Not all proponents of the Specious Present include the near future as part of the short duration that we immediately perceive. On C. D. Broad's account, for instance, the Specious Present extends only backwards in time. But James, for one, is clearly committed to the idea that the future is part of what we immediately perceive. Again, this might make sense if it were the claim that we experience events *as about to occur*. Husserl, indeed, holds a view like this: the comet's tail of retentions to which the present is attached is supplemented with a leading thread of protentions as well. But these are just the kind of intentional items to which the doctrine of immediate sensory presence contrasts. So these are not available to the defender of the Specious Present. And any other account of one's awareness of the future seems to smack of parapsychology.

I hope this short list will give some sense of the difficulties in understanding the Specious Present. Even if we could make sense of the doctrine, however, it is clear that it cannot explain the possibility of pace perceived. For let us grant that we are immediately aware of the short duration during which the second hand travels from the twelve to the one; the duration, in other words, of a Specious Present.[30] Still, it is not a part of my experience that all motion comes in short, interrupted bursts. The doctrine of the Specious Present, if it works at all, can only explain my capacity to perceive an object's motion over the short period of time that the Specious Present spans. In order to account for perceived motion that lasts longer than the duration of a single Specious Present, the view would have to allow for the possibility of stringing Specious Presents together. But in this case the Retention Theory reappears. For I will need to retain the prior Specious Present in order for the current one to be experienced as part of a larger whole. The doctrine of the Specious Present, in other words, seems not even to be able to explain the very case that motivated it.

I conclude from this that Husserl's method of Retention enjoys certain benefits over the doctrine of the Specious Present. It is, in other words, a better account of the temporal structure of experience. But it is still not a very good account. That is because, as I have said already, Husserl defines retention only negatively—by contrast with what it is not. What we would like is a positive set of examples that give us the feel for what it is *now* to experience something as *just-having-been*. I turn, in conclusion, to some brief thoughts about what these examples might be like.

---

[30] There is no agreement, by the way, over how long the Specious Present lasts. Dainton, however, clocks it in the three-second range. See Dainton (2000: 170).

4. CONCLUSION: THE EXPERIENCE, NOW, OF SOMETHING'S ABOUT TO BE AND OF SOMETHING'S JUST HAVING BEEN[31]

The idea of a perceptual experience *now* representing something *as just having been* or *as about to be* may sound strange. It certainly will sound strange if we think of perceptions like pictures. For pictures seem to freeze a moment in time and present everything that was happening *at that moment*, but not at the moments before or after.[32] But perceptions are not like pictures. They have a dynamic component to them that is essential, and after all this should be no surprise. For how often does the animal in its natural environment need a representation of the present moment and nothing else? Rather, the most basic kinds of perceptual experiences are those that put us in a dynamic relation with an object and its environment. Let us consider some of these.

The most basic kind of determinate experience is the experience of a figure against a ground. I say this is the most basic kind of determinate experience, though, because much of the time experiences are indeterminate in a very particular sense: they have not yet parsed the perceived world into its figure and ground components. When this kind of indeterminacy persists it can be extremely disconcerting. Perhaps you have had the experience of driving along a dark road at night, turning round a bend, and losing your sense of what counts as the road and what counts as the forest that runs alongside it. Maurice Merleau-Ponty, the French phenomenologist, gives a good description of an indeterminate experience like this:

> If I walk along a shore towards a ship which has run aground, and the funnel or masts merge into the forest bordering on the sand dune, there will be a moment when these details suddenly become part of the ship, and indissolubly fused with it. As I approached I did not perceive resemblances or proximities which finally came together to form a continuous picture of the upper part of the ship. I merely felt that the look of the object was on the point of altering, that something was imminent in this tension, as a storm is imminent in storm clouds. Suddenly the sight before me was recast in a manner satisfying to my vague expectation.[33]

In this example Merleau-Ponty is describing the experience of not yet having parsed the scene into a ship (the figure) that stands out against a forest (the ground). How exactly to describe this kind of indeterminate experience is a delicate matter. It is wrong, for instance, to say that I saw the funnel, the masts, and the trees, but I had not yet figured out which goes with what. For I did not see funnel, masts, or trees at all, at

---

[31] In preparing this section I have benefited from discussions with Bert Dreyfus, and also from a paper by Ade Artis.

[32] I say that pictures seem to present a frozen moment in time, rather than that they do present a frozen moment in time, since I think this is even a bad account of pictures. Often when we look at a photograph we experience it as presenting someone in the midst of activity, an activity against the background of which this particular moment is understood. Michael Fried, the art historian, has brought this point out nicely in his *Absorption and Theatricality* (1980). I have tried to speak more extensively to this issue myself in an unpublished paper called 'Representing the Real: a Merleau-Pontean account of art and experience from the Renaissance to New Media'.

[33] Merleau-Ponty (1962: 17).

least not characterized as such. What I experienced was a certain kind of confusion, though one that sets up vague expectations of resolution nevertheless.

Picking up on the idea of confusion, some people will say that what is characteristic of this kind of indeterminate experience is that you haven't yet got the object in focus. But we must be careful; the metaphor of focus may make us think of a microscope with its focusing knobs turned to one extreme, and indeterminate experiences are not like this either. It's not as if you are looking attentively and carefully at an object that is presented out of focus, since there's no sense that anything counts as an object yet at all, and so there's no capacity to attend to it carefully or otherwise.

One aspect of the indeterminate experience that is important, however, is the vague sense that something is on the verge of becoming clear. As Merleau-Ponty says, there is a tension in the experience that feels as though it is about to resolve itself. And the resolution is not arbitrary either—there are certain expectations, even if they are not explicit or in any sense articulable, that are part of the imminent resolution of the scene. It is an essential part of the experience, in other words, that I am about to gain a perceptual grip on the scene presented to me. This, it seems to me, is a pretty good candidate for now experiencing something as about to happen. It is the experience of something as the thing on which I'm now gaining a perceptual grip.

By contrast, there are indeterminate experiences as of things on which I'm now losing my perceptual grip. As the person on the sidewalk approaches and walks by I go from gaining to losing my perceptual grip on her.[34] Even once she is behind my back I experience her as there, though no longer perceptually available. What it is to experience something as past, perhaps, is to experience it as the thing on which you're now losing your perceptual grip.

Gaining and losing a perceptual grip on an object are things I can now experience myself to be doing. Indeed, as we navigate through the world and our attention is caught now by this object and now by that, gaining and losing perceptual grip is something we are almost always doing. But at every moment it is a dynamic process, one that distinguishes sharply between what is imminent and what is receding. These kinds of experiences, it seems to me, bear further exploration if we are to grapple in any interesting way with the phenomena of temporal awareness.[35]

---

[34] See Todes (2001: 119–22).

[35] An anonymous referee complains that what I have given here is merely the 'intuitive/phenomenological sense of what retention and protention actually feel like' and that these descriptions have no 'explanatory power'. There is a sense in which this is right. What I mean to be doing in this conclusion is merely to describe retention and protention in terms of Merleau-Ponty's notion of perceptual grip, not to give a full-fledged analytical account of the phenomena. In a more complete positive treatment of the issue I do believe that one should go on to analyze or to systematize these phenomena—something that the 'descriptive phenomenologists' did not do. But I don't pretend to have made that step myself here. The referee goes on to say that Husserl's own account explains these very phenomena. I think this is wrong in two different ways. First, Husserl's phenomenology, like Heidegger's and Merleau-Ponty's, was not meant to explain but only to describe. As Heidegger said, phenomenology is essentially descriptive, so much so that the phrase 'descriptive phenomenology' is at bottom tautological. But second, and more importantly, these are not the phenomena that Husserl has in mind when he talks about retention and protention. The idea of perceptual grip belongs to Merleau-Ponty and was completely alien to Husserl so far as I know. Husserl did not, it seems to me, understand Merleau-Ponty's deep notion of perceptual indeterminacy, even if he used very similar terminology. See Kelly (2003) for further discussion of perceptual indeterminacy.

REFERENCES

Blattner, William D. (1999) *Heidegger's Temporal Idealism* (Cambridge: Cambridge University Press).

Broad, C. D. (1993) *Scientific Thought* (Bristol: Thoemmes Press). [This edition is a reprint of the 1923 edition.]

Brough, John (1970) 'A Study of the Logic and Evolution of Edmund Husserl's Theory of the Constitution of Time-Consciousness' (Dissertation: Georgetown University).

Dainton, Barry (2000) *Stream of Consciousness: Unity and Continuity in Conscious Experience* (New York: Routledge).

Gale, Richard (1968) *The Philosophy of Time* (London: Macmillan).

Gallagher, Shaun (1998) *The Inordinance of Time* (Evanston: Northwestern University Press).

Gurwitsch, Aron (1966) 'William James's Theory of the "Transitive Parts" of the Stream of Consciousness', reprinted in *Studies in Phenomenology and Psychology* (Evanston: Northwestern University Press), 301–31.

Hume, David (1978) *A Treatise of Human Nature*, ed. P. H. Nidditch (Oxford: Oxford University Press, 1978).

Husserl, Edmund (1991) *On the Phenomenology of the Consciousness of Internal Time (1893–1917)*, trans. John Barrett Brough (Dordrecht: Kluwer Academic Publishers).

Fried, Michael (1980) *Absorption and Theatricality: Painting and Beholder in the Age of Diderot* (Berkeley: University of California Press).

Le Poidevin, Robin (2004) 'The Experience and Perception of Time', in the *Stanford Online Encyclopedia of Philosophy*, http://plato.stanford.edu/entries/time-experience, pp. 3–4.

James, William (1950) *The Principles of Psychology*, i (New York: Dover Publications, Inc.).

Kant, Immanuel (1965) *Critique of Pure Reason*, trans. Norman Kemp Smith (New York: St Martin's Press).

Kelly, Sean Dorrance (2003) 'Husserl and Phenomenology', in Robert C. Solomon (ed.), *Blackwell Companion to Continental Philosophy* (Oxford: Blackwell), 112–42.

Locke, John (1975) *An Essay Concerning Human Understanding*, ed. Peter H. Nidditch (Oxford: Oxford University Press).

Mabbott, J. D. (1951) 'Our Direct Experience of Time', *Mind* 60: 153–67.

Merleau-Ponty, Maurice (1962) *Phenomenology of Perception*, trans. Colin Smith (New York: Routledge & Kegan Paul).

Miller, Itzchak (1984) *Husserl: Perception and Temporal Awareness* (Cambridge, Mass.: MIT Press).

Mundle, W. K. (1954) 'How Specious is the "Specious Present"?', *Mind* 63: 26–48.

Paton, H. J. (1951) *In Defense of Reason* (London: Hutchinson's University Library).

Palmer, Stephen E. (1999) *Vision: From Photons to Phenomenology* (Cambridge, Mass.: MIT Press).

Russell, Bertrand (1948) *Human Knowledge: Its Scope and Limits* (New York: Simon & Schuster).

Todes, Sam (2001) *Body and World* (Cambridge, Mass.: MIT Press).

Wolff, Robert Paul (1963) *Kant's Theory of Mental Activity: A Commentary on the Transcendental Analytic of the* Critique of Pure Reason (Cambridge, Mass.: Harvard University Press).

11

Collective Consciousness

Kay Mathiesen

Abstract: In this essay, I explore this idea of a collective consciousness. I propose that individuals can share in a collective consciousness by forming a *collective subject*. I begin the essay by considering and rejecting three possible pictures of collective subjectivity: the group mind, the emergent mind, and the socially embedded mind. I argue that each of these accounts fails to provide one of the following requirements for collective subjectivity: (1) plurality, (2) awareness, and (3) collectivity. I then look to Edmund Husserl's idea of 'social subjectivities' for a possible account, but I agree with Alfred Schutz that Husserl fails to explain how such subjectivities are constituted by the conscious acts of individuals. In an effort to provide such an explanation, I turn to a discussion of our basic capacities for social intentionality: empathy, intersubjectivity, and co-subjectivity. In the final section of the essay, I argue that individuals can form a collective subject by taking a first-person plural perspective and 'simulating' the consciousness of the collective that they form. This account has the required features of plurality, awareness, and collectivity.

INTRODUCTION

We tend to think of consciousness as the most private and individual of features and that, consequently, the idea of a 'collective consciousness' is an obvious non-starter. So, it is surprising that the word 'consciousness' has its roots in the idea of a *shared* awareness. 'The word "conscious" derives from the Latin words "cum" ("together with") and "scire" ("knowing"). In the original sense, two people who know something together are said to be conscious of it "to one another"' (Lomond 1998). In this essay, I explore this idea of a *collective* consciousness. I will not argue that it exists and we experience it—I think this needs no argument. Collective consciousness, as I will define it, is a familiar and ubiquitous part of our world. It is as common as families, clubs, tribes, churches, states, and ethnic groups. Those who would reject this idea seem to be to be motivated by an ontological fear of collectivity, rather than observation of human experience. My account of collectivity will show that this fear is unwarranted.

Ultimately, I propose that individuals can share in a collective consciousness by forming a *collective subject* and that they do this by modeling within themselves the states of consciousness of the collective. Since, as I will argue, forming a collective subject with others is partly dependent on how persons experience themselves in relation to others, any account of collectivity will have to begin with an account of the phenomenology of social experience. So, in this essay I will be focusing on the phenomenology of collective subjectivity as the persons who constitute a collective subject experience it.

I begin the essay by considering and rejecting three possible pictures of collective subjectivity. Along the way I identify three features of collective subjectivity that any account will need to capture: collective subjectivity requires plurality (i.e. that there be multiple conscious subjects), awareness (i.e. that there is *genuine* intentionality), and collectivity (i.e. that the collective subject forms a social group). I then explore the possibility that we can find an account of collective consciousness in Edmund Husserl's discussion of social subjectivity. But I find that Husserl's intriguing mentions of social subjectivities are insufficiently worked out and, as Alfred Schutz notes, do not explain how the conscious acts of individuals can form the foundation for such entities. In an effort to provide such an explanation, I turn to a discussion of our basic capacities for social intentionality. I explore how we can understand the thoughts of others and combine our thoughts with theirs, through empathy, intersubjectivity, and what I call 'co-subjectivity'.[1] In the final section of the essay, with the account of social intentionality as a basis, I provide an account of collective subjectivity. I describe how individuals form a collective subject through taking a first-person plural perspective and 'simulating' the consciousness of the collective that they form. This account has the requisite features of plurality, awareness, and collectivity.

1. THREE VIEWS OF COLLECTIVE CONSCIOUSNESS

As I noted above, the idea of a collective consciousness immediately implies the existence of some collective subject of this consciousness. Indeed, this is why philosophers often reject such a notion out of hand; it seems to imply the existence of some sort of (spooky) 'group mind'. We will not be frightened away so easily, however. We are going to look carefully and see if there is anything sensible that can be made of the idea of a collective subject of consciousness.

The question before us is how can individuals form such a collective subject. In this section, I consider three suggestions for what this collective subject is, viz., (1) the Borg, (2) the emergent mind, and (3) the socially embedded mind. Each of these is connected to a view about what a collective consciousness might be: (a) Collective consciousness is a stream of consciousness that is literally shared by more than one conscious subject. (b) Collective consciousness is a kind of emergent consciousness dependent on a number of interacting individuals. (c) Collective consciousness describes the fact that all individual consciousness is dependent on a social context. I will argue that none of these views captures what we want from an account of collective subjectivity.

---

[1] Indeed, co-subjectivity seems to capture the original meaning of consciousness—the idea of knowing (or seeing, believing, wanting, intending, etc.) together with another person or persons.

A. Group Mind—the Borg

Many philosophers assume that a collective consciousness would require the existence of a collective mind. We can agree that no such thing currently exists, but the creators of 'Star Trek: The Next Generation' imagined something like it—'the Borg'. The Borg is supposed to be a genuinely collective subject with a single unified collective consciousness. Individual conscious agents are 'assimilated' into the Borg with cybernetic implants whereby their minds are connected to all of the other minds and whereby they experience a single flow of consciousness. The idea is that each 'individual' person who is a member of this entity shares in the mental experience of all of the other persons. There is no individual thought—the thoughts of each are the thoughts of all. If we stop to think about it, however, we will notice that the Borg is not really a *collective* subject at all. A *collective* consciousness implies that there is more than one consciousness, but the Borg is simply a single consciousness distributed across a number of brains.[2] As Husserl and other phenomenologists have noted, in order for there to be more than one mind, there must be something inaccessible about the minds of the others.[3] Husserl points out that 'if what belongs to the other's own essence were directly accessible, it would merely be a moment of my own essence, and ultimately he himself and I myself would be the same person' (1960: 109). In other words, if I experience your flow of consciousness directly, then we form one consciousness. The fact that there is more than one brain doing the processing does not make a difference. In fact, it could be argued that human beings already have 'two brains', because there is a large amount of duplication between the two hemispheres,[4] but it does not follow that we each have a collective consciousness. So, a *collective* subject must be composed of a number of separate centers of consciousness, which are not directly accessible to each other. Thus, collective consciousness, far from requiring the existence of a group mind, requires that there are separate minds. I will call this the 'plurality' condition.

B. Emergent Mind

A less bizarre suggestion is that a collective consciousness is a second-order consciousness that emerges from the interaction of conscious agents. On this view, the higher-level states of consciousness are dependent on the interaction of a number of conscious individuals, but the contents of these states are not something of which any individual necessarily has awareness. It is the society or group as a whole that is the subject of these states of consciousness, not the individual members of the society or group.

---

[2] The creators of *Star Trek* seem unaware of this point. In the episode 'I-Borg' a member of the Borg says 'we' when referring to himself as a subject. 'We' means the speaker and other conscious subjects, but if all share in the same flow of consciousness, then there is only one flow of consciousness and, thus, only one self. If there is only one self, then there is only one 'I'.

[3] See e.g. Husserl (1960) and Stein (1964). For a more detailed discussion of this point see Zahavi (2001).

[4] Philosophers working on personal identity make much of this fact. They ask us to consider what would happen if each hemisphere were transplanted into two different bodies.

The sociologist Emile Durkheim is perhaps the most famous proponent of the view that there is a collective consciousness in this sense.[5] On his view, collective consciousness is a state of the entire collective (e.g., a society, church, tribe, etc.). The collective state of a group at any time is what Durkheim called a 'social fact'. The content of the collective consciousness is ontologically distinct from that of the individual members; it is this distinctness that makes the state of the collective consciousness a *social*, as opposed to a *psychological*, fact. Social facts are dependent on and are expressed through (though not necessarily reflected in) the beliefs, attitudes, and actions of individuals, but they are inherently collective—they are, to quote Durkheim, states '*sui generis* of the collective mind' (1951: 142). So, for example, in his groundbreaking work on suicide, Durkheim attempts to show that the behavior of individuals in taking their lives, expresses certain social facts, which are states of the society as a whole. Durkheim emphasizes that these states are true of the collective 'as a whole'—they are not true of each person taken separately. What this last statement means, however, may be unclear.

It might help us to get clearer on Durkheim's notion of collective consciousness by contrasting it to a more recent account that is often treated as comparable, viz. Margaret Gilbert's 'plural subject theory'. According to Gilbert, individuals can form plural subjects that intend, believe, etc. 'as a body'. Gilbert's key claim is that the collective intentions of the group are not derived from the individual intentions of its members. By this she means that the individuals are not *separately and individually* committed to the intention; their intentions, beliefs, etc. are *interdependent*. But, this interdependence is based on a joint commitment to the intention. This joint commitment, on Gilbert's view, requires that each person represents the proposed intention to herself and accepts it (albeit with an other 'as a body'). In other words, each member is aware of the intention that they share.

The emergence view, on the other hand, does not require that the members of the collective have any awareness of the contents of the collective beliefs, intentions, etc.[6] One way to see this is to look at Durkheim's methodological prescriptions for how we are to determine what these states of collective consciousness are. According to Durkheim, we discover social facts by looking at the statistics that capture the collective state of large groups of people. Durkheim states that, 'The average . . . expresses a certain state of the group mind' (1994: 436). This average state may not be a state that any individual in the collective is in. Compare the average income; it is possible that no individual member of the group actually makes that income.

While I do not want to deny here that there may be various emergent properties and 'social facts' of the type that Durkheim described, they are not forms of collective consciousness. To be conscious is to have awareness, to be a subject of mental states, but Durkheim's point is that there are states of the group mind where no one is aware

---

[5] Before I go on, it is important to note that Durkheim says a number of things about the collective consciousness. It is not clear that they are all consistent with each other. Here I am picking up on one strong vein in his comments.

[6] This distinction is often not emphasized clearly enough either by those commenting on Gilbert, or by Gilbert herself.

of the contents of the collective consciousness (either singly or collectively).[7] It is important to note that I do not mean to imply here that there would need to be a second-order awareness of the conscious states of the collective in order for the collective to be in a conscious state.[8] Rather, what is required is that there be a state of 'consciousness', that there be awareness of the appropriate sort. But Durkheim's method is an unreliable supplier of this sort of awareness—just as the average income is not an income, so the average thought is not a thought.

Another emergence view of collective consciousness focuses specifically on how collectives may produce a kind of emergent intentionality. On Durkheim's view the state of the collective is the average, while on the 'intentional system' view the state of the collective arises from the functional system that the individuals can form and which can then be interpreted through the language of intentionality. Todd Jones, for example, argues that, 'it is perfectly possible for a group to have a goal or representation that none of the people in the group has' (2001: 229). Jones bases his account on an intentional system theory where 'goals' and 'representations' need not be mental states. He uses a cell analogy—cells do not consciously coordinate their activity, but we can explain what they produce as an intentional system. According to Jones, 'Intentional biological organisms are cooperating clusters of cells which, over time, develop capacities to survive and flourish by becoming increasingly well tuned to getting their goals in their particular environments. There is no reason to believe that cooperating clusters of people can't come to be organized in a similar manner' (246).[9] So, on Jones's view, just as our neurons constitute a system with mental properties (which no individual neuron has), so too can persons constitute a system with mental properties (which no individual person has).[10]

But under what conditions does a system, whether of cells or persons, constitute an *intentional* system? According to Jones any system that becomes tuned to its environment can be understood as 'representing' the environment and acting so as to achieve its 'goals'. Since social systems composed of thinking subjects can have this characteristic, they too can be seen as intentional systems. However, there are (at least) three problems with this kind of account of collective consciousness.

First, there is an epistemological problem of how to determine what the intentions of the system are; there are notorious problems with functionalist explanations in social science.[11] The mere fact that we can tell a story about how some action x

---

[7] At least not until the social scientist does her statistical studies, but that does not make the scientist the subject of the collective consciousness any more than my knowledge of your state makes me the subject of it.

[8] In other words, I am not appealing to a second-order thought conception of consciousness.

[9] It is worth noting the verbal sleight of hand here; Jones uses anthropomorphic language to describe the clusters of cells, e.g., 'cooperation', 'their goals', which makes the comparison to human intentional agents appear more plausible.

[10] I focus here on Jones account, but there are a number of other authors who have suggested similar accounts. See e.g. Tollefsen (2002), Brooks (1986), Scruton (1989), and Wilson (2001). Ned Block (1978) famously described a thought experiment where the population of China performed the functional roles of neurons. Block, however, used this thought experiment for other purposes and was not proposing an account of group mind.

[11] See e.g. the articles in Part V, 'Functional Explanation' in Martin and McIntyre (1994).

produces some (desirable) effect y, does not show that the function of x is to produce y. Furthermore, even if you could show that the function of x is to produce y, you will still need to pick out precisely what the representation and goal are in this situation. Of course, from the difficulty of getting such intentionalistic explanations right, it doesn't follow that they are *all* incorrect or fail to capture some ontologically important phenomenon, but the next two problems are more ontologically serious.

Second, Jones's intentional system account fails to make any distinction between systems composed of such parts as cells with no intentionality of their own, on the one hand, and those composed of agents with consciousness and intentionality, on the other. One way to acknowledge the fact that human beings have their own intentionality would be to show how the intentionality of the group is a reflection of or derived from the intentionality of the members.[12] But, if that is the case, then the functional explanation approach breaks down, because we will need to pay attention to the intentionality of the parts.

Finally (and most importantly), the kind of consciousness that Jones ascribes to collectives is the result of using the language of intentionality in a metaphorical or analogous way. We may use intentionalistic language to describe the behavior of systems that appear to behave in a goal-like manner. A stream acts 'as-if' it intended to flow downhill; genes act 'as-if' they were trying to achieve the goal of surviving and replicating themselves. But to use the language of intentionality, contra Dennett, does not commit us to attributing intentional states to these entities. So, while we can look at the overall pattern of behavior among a number of persons and see that they act 'as-if' they participated in a collective mind with some particular intention, it does not follow that they do.

If one wants to give up the view that consciousness is a phenomenon that crucially includes such features as awareness, and call all self-organizing entities conscious, then there are multiple collective consciousnesses in a very trivial sense. To designate any system that responds to its environment as an intentional system, however, is to deprive the concept of intentionality of its special link to conscious awareness. Thus, as long as we insist that consciousness is a mental phenomenon—in particular, that it has something to do with experience and awareness, not simply with the ability to adapt to the environment, the intentional systems account does not give us genuine collective consciousness.[13] To sum up the main moral from this section: a group of persons whom we want to say form a 'collective consciousness' must be 'collectively conscious', that is, they must have collective awareness and genuine intentionality. I will call this the 'awareness' condition.

C. Socially Embedded Mind

Some would argue that I am framing the issue the wrong way. We should not be asking how individuals can form a collective subject, but how individuals are formed by the collectivities in which they inhere. Such 'social embeddedness' views hold that

---

[12] Indeed, this is precisely what Jones does in his examples, but then the analogy with cells breaks down. The intentionality of the system of the cells is supposed to be merely a function of the overall functioning of the system.

[13] Of course, the intentional system defender may claim that they were hoping to get rid of talk of consciousness altogether.

collectivity is the necessary precondition for individual consciousness—thus, we could say that each individual's consciousness is inherently collective. On this view each of us is a 'collective subject' in some sense, because our consciousnesses are inextricably tied up with and dependent on the social collectives in which we are born and live. All of our thoughts, beliefs, attitudes, etc. are the expression of an inherently shared collective consciousness.[14]

Two main lines of argument are made for this view. The first argument finds its historical precedent in Hegel's discussion of the master–slave dialectic, whereby individuals only become aware of themselves as conscious beings through interaction with other conscious beings. Recent arguments along these lines appeal to work in cognitive science that seems to confirm the hypothesis that interaction with others is part of the process of developing a sense of self. Citing this literature, Evan Thompson claims that, 'Individual consciousness is formed in the dynamic interrelation of self and other, and therefore is inherently inter-subjective' (2001: 1). Thus, on this view self-consciousness only arises in a collective context.

The second argument finds its historical precedent in Wittgenstein's private language argument. According to this view, without a public language and its social practices of interpretation, as embodied in a shared way of life, one could not 'think'.[15] As Philip Pettit describes this view, there is 'no act of thinking, at least as things stand with human beings, without an interactive context of thinking subjects' (1993: 172). On this view an individual conscious subject requires a social context for its thoughts to mean anything.

While these social embeddedness views make an important point about the social nature of consciousness, there is a notion of collective consciousness—the idea of a collective subject—that they fail to capture. The point of these social context views is that every act of consciousness, even the most seemingly individual and private, is dependent on a background of a social world that we share with others. This draws no distinction, however, between the hermit and an engaged and active member of a community. But the hermit does lack something that the member of the community has; the hermit cannot form a collective subject with other conscious beings like himself. In order for collective consciousness to be genuinely collective, it must be something that persons share and that ties them together into a social group.

From the above discussion we can say that, minimally, an account of a collective subject of consciousness should capture the following features. (1) *Plurality*, i.e., the collective is constituted by a number of separate conscious subjects. (2) *Awareness*, i.e., the individual members of the collective are aware of the contents of their *genuine* intentional states. (3) *Collectivity*, i.e., collective subjectivity is distinguishable from individual subjectivity—it binds people together in a social group. In the rest of the essay, I take these three features as providing criteria for an adequate account of collect-ive subjectivity. In the next section I explore whether the history of phenomenology can provide us with an account of such collective subjectivity. For this, I look to Edmund Husserl's discussion of social subjectivities in *Ideas Pertaining to a Pure*

---

[14] This thesis need not have the rather mysterious metaphysical form of Jung's collective unconscious.   [15] See e.g. Baier (1997) and Stoutland (1997).

Phenomenology and to a Phenomenological Philosophy. Second Book: Studies in the Phenomenology of Constitution (hereafter referred to as *Ideas II*).

2. HUSSERL AND SCHUTZ ON 'SOCIAL SUBJECTIVITIES'

It might be suggested that Edmund Husserl, in his discussion of 'social subjectivities' and 'personal unities of a higher order' in *Ideas II*, has provided an account of collective subjectivity that satisfies these conditions. Husserl seems to be talking about something close to what we are looking for when he says that individual conscious subjects can 'coalesce into a *social subjectivity* inwardly organized to a greater or lesser degree which has its common opposite pole in a surrounding world or an external world, i.e., in a world which is for it' [emphasis added] (1989: 206). This seems very promising, but two of his more extended descriptions of social subjectivities (what Husserl also calls 'personal unities of a higher order') raise more questions than they answer.

As Husserl describes them, personal unities,

have their own lives, preserve themselves by lasting through time, . . . have their qualities as communities, . . . their modes of functioning in collaboration with other communities and with individual persons, . . . their regulated changes and their own way of developing or maintaining themselves invariant over time . . . The members of the community, of marriage and of the family, of social class, of the union, of the borough, of the state, the church, etc., 'know' themselves as their members, consciously realize that they are dependent on them, and perhaps consciously react back on them. (1989: 191–2)

Husserl seems right on target here with his description of the features of such collectives as tribes, clubs, families, churches, etc., and their capacity to persist through time. But, overall in this passage Husserl describes the collective from the outside; he does not describe how the intentional states of the members can give rise to these properties. However, while in the first part of this passage the discussion of the qualities of personal unities sounds rather like the emergence view, the last sentence seems to hint at something more like a collective subject. Here he says that members of these personal unities 'know' themselves as members. Thus, he seems to be suggesting something like the awareness criterion.

In another passage, Husserl provides an analogy between persons and 'personal unities' which suggests that personal unities may have a kind of consciousness similar to that of individuals.

In the case of a state, a people, a union, etc., there is a plurality of bodies, standing in physical relationships something required for intercommerce, either direct of indirect . . . Each Body has its spirit, but they all are bound together by the overarching *communal spirit* which is not something beside them, but is an encompassing 'sense' or 'spirit.' This is a subjectivity of a higher level. (1989: 255)

According to Husserl, the body of the social subjectivity is composed of the bodies of the individual members who interact with each other, thus forming a physical system that is the basis of the social subjectivity. While each person also has his or her own 'spirit' or consciousness, there is also a communal spirit or consciousness which binds them together. But, again, it is not clear exactly what the relationship is between the subjectivity of the members and the subjectivity of the social subjectivity. While Husserl does say that these social subjectivities arise out of the 'intercommerce' between individuals, he does not describe exactly how the attitudes and activities of individuals mesh to form such personal unities. How do the separate individual subjectivities coalesce to produce a shared social subjectivity?

The above concerns echo some criticisms of Husserl's conception of social subject-ivities made by the phenomenologist and social theorist Alfred Schutz. Schutz wrote that those looking for insights relating to the foundation of the social sciences should look 'in other parts [of *Ideas II*] than those [quoted above] dedicated to the analysis of communication and social groups' (1966: 39). Schutz criticized Husserl's concept of personal unities as unclear and based on metaphorical language—talking of groups as 'persons' may be an appropriate metaphor at times, Schutz argues, but one should not take it too literally. Schutz compares Husserl's discussion of these personal unities to the ideas of Durkheim and other theorists who treat groups as subjects without explaining how the properties of the collective are a result of the intentionality of the members of these collectivities (1966: 38–9). According to Schutz ,'[A] project that reduces social collectivities to the social interaction of individuals is closer to the spirit of phenomenology' (1962: 80–1).[16] He notes that from the outside such collectivities may seem to form collective persons with intentions all their own. The danger is that one will then start to attribute intentions directly to the group with no explanation of how the intentions of the individual members constitute these collective intentions.

Schutz himself, however, seems to go too far in the direction of reduction. His focus on individuals and their interactions with each other lead him, for the most part, to discuss only the ways in which individual subjects interact with other individual subjects[17] (he is quite good on this, however, and I refer to some of his work on intersubjectivity below). As a result, his work never really provides the hoped-for understanding of how one-on-one interactions can give rise to the kind of personal unities described by Husserl. Below, I try to fill in the gap between Husserl and Schutz. In the end, my account may not result in something completely compatible with Husserl's account of 'personal unities', but it is inspired by the possibility of a phenomenological account of such collectivities.

3. INTERSUBJECTIVITY, EMPATHY, AND PLURAL SUBJECTIVITY

The job of the phenomenologist, Schutz claimed, is to explain how collective subjects are created by the social interaction of individuals. In the rest of this section I explore how individuals form social subjectivities that include themselves and others. I start by discussing the basic capacity necessary for any social interaction with others: the capacity to empathize with the mental states of others. This capacity for empathy is

---

[16] Schutz makes the same point in his review of *Ideas II* (1966: 38–9).
[17] See e.g. Schutz (1932).

essential for intersubjectivity, and it provides us with a passageway into plural subject-ivity and ultimately into collective subjectivity.

A key to our capacity for forming a collective subject is our capacity to see things from another person's point of view. Without this, we would be stuck in a solipsistic world where we could never take a joint attitude toward anything. Before I can take a shared perspective with another person, I must first see the other as another subject like myself and understand that she has her own unique point of view. In addition, I must also be able to somehow 'imagine' or represent to myself what that experience is like. Merely knowing that she has her own experience does not allow me understand it—think of Nagel's (1974) discussion of the difference between knowing that a bat has its own experience and point of view and knowing 'what it is like' to be a bat. Some creature's points of view may be too different from our own for us to understand 'what it is like' to see things from their perspective. Recent work by cognitive science and philosophers of mind on 'simulation theory' and the traditional phenomenolog-ical study of empathy both analyze how we conceive of others as fellow subjects of experience.[18]

According to simulation theory, we understand others by 'simulating' within ourselves what we would experience and how we would respond if we were in the other's shoes.[19] One advocate of simulation theory describes how we may simulate the experience of a climber in trouble as follows: 'I re-enact a fragment of his mental life, and so come to occupy psychological states very close to his' (Ravenscroft 1998: 178).[20] Simulation theorists often describe this as modeling while 'off-line'; in other words, we experience the fear as if we were the other person, but we do not act as if we were the other person. (Although the fear may lead us to do things *for* the other person.)

Those working in the phenomenological tradition have described the phenomeno-logy of 'empathy' in a surprisingly similar way.[21] According to Edith Stein, a student of Husserl's who wrote her doctoral dissertation on empathy, in empathy I 'am at the subject of the content in the original subject's place' (1964: 10). In other words, I do not simply 'believe' that the other is, for example, singing a song. I experience the other's singing of the song as if from her point of view—as if I am '*at* the subject' or in the subject's position. It is important to note that this is distinct from experienc-ing it as if I *am* 'the subject'—I do not experience this as 'my singing': neither in the sense that I think that she is doing my singing, nor in the sense that I am doing her singing.

---

[18] There is some debate about how empathy is possible and how it functions. See Zahavi (2001) for an excellent discussion of these issues.

[19] The rival theory to simulation theory is the 'theory-theory'. According to the theory-theory, we develop an implicit theory about how minds work and use certain inputs, such as the other's beliefs, attitudes, etc. to infer what others will do. See Carruthers (1996) for a discussion.

[20] This should not be taken to imply that I ask myself, 'What would I feel if I were in his situ-ation?' Essentially, I must have an experience as if from the *other's* point of view. See the discussion below of Adam Smith's account.

[21] It is important to note here that by 'empathy' I am not implying any kind of positive emotional or moral attitude toward the subject of my 'empathetic act'. Empathy simply refers to the capacity that we have for seeing or feeling something from another's point of view.

Some might argue that there are important differences between empathy as described by Stein and 'mind reading' as described by the simulation theorists. Indeed, it is worth noting that Stein, in contrasting her view with Adam Smith's, distinguishes empathy from something that sounds like some versions of simulation theory. On Smith's view, according to Stein, 'We put ourselves in the place of the foreign "I." If we then . . . ascribe this experience to him, we gain knowledge of his experience' (1964: 14). She claims that this is a 'surrogate' for empathy, but is not, like empathy, an *experience*. What Stein may have in mind here is that Smith's 'simulation' is an intellectual procedure, which is not connected to any 'direct' experience of the other person as a living, sensing, thinking being. Contemporary simulation theorists, however, also emphasize the importance of bodily and emotional aspects of our experience. Robert Gordon (1995), for example, focuses on 'hot' mechanisms which essentially involve emotion and Alvin Goldman (1995) discusses 'mirror neurons', 'a vehicle by which an observer *mimics, resonates with*, or *re-creates* the mental life' of others based on our direct observation of their bodily movements.[22] Another objection that might be offered to Smith's account is that it only provides us with a sense of how 'I' would feel if I were in the other's situation, not of how the other person feels in his situation. But this does not distinguish empathy from simulation either; simulation theorist Robert Gordon (1995) has made the same criticism of Smith's account.

It is true, however, that there are a number of differences in emphasis between empathy theory as elaborated by Stein and contemporary work on simulation theory. Stein's account focuses on empathy with emotional states, while the simulation theorist's account focuses on beliefs and desires. Stein is concerned with the phenomenological analysis of the lived experience of empathy, while the simulation theorists are concerned with the psychological processes whereby we perform acts of empathy or simulation.[23] Stein emphasizes the embodied nature of human beings as psychophysical units, while simulation theorists tend to focus more on human beings as rational agents. Finally, Stein is concerned with how others' experience is 'given' to us—that is, how we can see other people as subjects like ourselves, while simulation theorists are concerned primarily with our capacity to predict what others will do.

While these are interesting differences worth further discussion, the areas of agreement are more fundamental and more important for our purposes here. For example, Stein agrees with simulation theorists in distinguishing empathy from simple emotional contagion (Gordon 1995: 728–9 and Stein 1964: 22–3).[24] Both Stein and simulation theorists agree in seeing empathy as having an important epistemic function that allows us to know something about other people. Both Stein and the simulation theorist Robert Gordon compare empathy to fantasy—wherein I can live through an experience that is not happening to me at that moment. Most importantly, both Stein and the simulation theorist reject accounts that try to explain our

[22] It has been observed in some primates that when one observes another engaged in some activity, the neurons of the observer fire in a way that 'mirrors' those in the observed. See Gallese and Goldman (1998) for a discussion.

[23] Stein says: 'I would like to know, not how I arrive at this awareness, but what it itself is' (7).

[24] In this paragraph I use the term 'empathy' to refer to our capacity to understand the thoughts and feelings of others, not as a particular theory of this capacity.

understanding of the thoughts of others through some sort of analogy or comparison with our own mental processes. According to the rival to simulation theory, 'theory-theory', for example, we develop a folk psychological theory of beliefs and desires in our own case first and then learn to apply it to others. We interpret others' behavior by means of this theory. The simulation theorist and Stein agree in rejecting this sort of model and arguing that we are able directly to model the other's experience within ourselves. We can experience thoughts and experience as if from the other's point of view. If our experience appropriately matches that of the person with whom we are empathizing, then we have gained important knowledge about her.

It is not sufficient for social subjectivity, however, that I merely model the other's experience within myself—that merely provides a one-way empathetic experience. Intersubjectivity requires a reciprocal relationship between persons. For this, the other must simultaneously empathize with me. This modeling of each other will include the fact that each of us is modeling the other, etc.—giving rise to what Ingvar Johansson calls 'intentional mirror infinity' (1989: 271).²⁵ The typical example of such intersubjectivity is a conversation, but one may also find it in non-verbal interactions (washing dishes together, making love, etc.). These interactions provide a 'we-experience' where we are not just perceiving things from our own perspective, but are also aware of the other's perspective and experiences at the same time. We respond to the other and modulate our actions based on the actions of the other. Schutz describes this 'we-experience' as follows: 'Within the unity of this experience I can be aware simultaneously of what is going on in mine and yours, living through the two series of experiences in one series' (1967: 170). This is crucially different from a case where I am simply using a tool or a computer program. Husserl calls this the 'personalistic attitude': 'the attitude we are always in when we live with one another, talk to one another, shake hands with one another in greeting, or are related to one another in love and aversion, in disposition and action, in discourse and discussion' (1989: 192).

Every act of intersubjectivity simultaneously implies co-subjectivity. As Husserl describes it, 'In these relations of mutual understanding, there is produced a conscious mutual relation of persons and at the same time a unitary relation of them to a common surrounding world' (*Ideas II*, 203). Two persons engaged in an intense disagreement are intensely intersubjective, yet it may seem that what they precisely lack is a shared perspective on the world. But, even engaging in an argument implies that we understand each other, and that we have a common awareness of the world around us. If we shared no common perspective, then we would not even be able to disagree.

There is some shift that takes place, however, when we move from the 'you' and 'I' to the 'we'. Stein describes such co-subjectivity in a case where a number of others and I all feel joy at some event: 'I intuitively have before me what they feel. It comes to life in my feeling and from the "I" and "you" arises the "we" as a subject of a higher level' (1964: 17). That is, each thinks of her experience as something that 'we' are having. And yet I want to argue that there is an even more radical notion of collective consciousness—a consciousness that is not simply something that you and I share, but a consciousness that is experienced as the attribute of the collective of which we are *members*. Below I discuss how such a collective subject is formed.

²⁵ See David Lewis (1969) on common knowledge for a similar idea.

4. COLLECTIVE SUBJECTIVITY

So, what does it mean to experience yourself, not just as sharing a perspective on the world with another person, but as a member of a collective which has its own consciousness? My proposal is that when we take the collective (as opposed to merely plural) perspective, and thus form a properly *collective* subject, we take the perspective of the collective of which we are members. How is this possible? I want to suggest the following answer. As I noted above, according to simulation theory and the theory of empathy, I am able to understand and predict what another person is thinking and how they may act by 'simulating' that person's mental states within myself. I propose that we are similarly able to 'simulate' the states of a collective subject of which we are members.[26] We can think 'as' the collective—taking the first-person plural point of view; that is, we can model within ourselves the beliefs, values, etc. of the collective. The beliefs that I form through this process I then experience as those of the collective of which I am a part. However, I simultaneously conceive of these thoughts, attitudes, beliefs, etc. as being shared by my fellow members, who are similarly simulating the collective. In addition, we will communicate with each other so that we can come to a shared sense of what the collective awareness is. Thus, not only will I see my thinking as that of one thinking 'as a member of the collective', but I conceive of my experience as one that all other members do or would (if they thought about it) share.[27]

To illustrate this, take one of Husserl's examples of a personal unity, a church; in this case let us take just my local congregation. I know the principles of the church, as do my fellow members. We know that these principles express the ideals, values, and goals of our church. Some of these may actually be written down in our mission statement or some other such document. Other of these ideals, values, and goals are embedded in our practices, habits, and even the architecture of the building we use. We all talk about 'the church', its future, what it should be doing, etc., and when we do so, we have a shared conception of what we are talking about. However, we do not see it as something separate from ourselves. We all know that we collectively constitute the church. We often say such things as 'We should do such and such', 'That is not how we do things', etc. Each of us is able to think, talk, and act in the first-person plural with a clear idea of 'who' we are thinking, talking, and acting for.[28]

Prima facie it may seem that there is a bootstrapping problem here. If, in order for there to be a collective subject, we must form it by taking the perspective of the collective, then we seem to be caught in a vicious circle. In response, it should be noted that,

[26] I use the term 'simulation' rather than empathy here, because, given Stein's focus on the embodied nature of empathizing, we might think that we cannot 'empathize' with a collective given that it lacks a single sensing body. More work is needed here to get clear on exactly what the role is of emotion and our bodily natures in empathy. In this regard it is worth noting that Stein claims that empathy is also how we can understand God (and God us) (1964: 11–12). Stein does not seem to be assuming that God must have a physical body in order for us to empathize with Him and Him with us.

[27] Of course, this is in an ideal situation. Often members may disagree on some key features of the collective, how to weigh differing collective values, etc.

[28] It is worth noting that I am describing a 'congregational' church where there is little or no church hierarchy. Those in more structured and hierarchical denominations or religions may have a different experience of who 'we' are and their role in determining the identity of the church.

first, social objects generally have a sort of (non-vicious) circularity; for example, in order for something to be money, people must believe that it is; in order for some behavior to be polite, people must believe that it is, etc. There is a similar sort of circularity here—in order to form a collective, we must believe that we do. Furthermore, we can provide a developmental account of how collectivity grows out of co-subjectivity, thus avoiding the bootstrapping problem. For example, think of Marx and Engel's call to the workers of the world to unite. One way to understand the charge to the workers is as a call for them to form a collective, by recognizing their shared perspective on the world that has developed through their interdependence as workers and their common membership in an oppressed group and using this recognition as the basis for adopting the first-person plural perspective.

While I am focusing here on the phenomenology of collective subjectivity, it is interesting to note some features of the ontology of this picture. Simulating the beliefs of a collective is importantly different from simulating the beliefs of another person. In one sense the collective and the collective's beliefs, values, attitudes, etc. do not exist independently of my and my fellow members beliefs about them. There is no collective existing separately from my (our) thoughts, emotions, beliefs, and actions—the thoughts of the collective simply are the thoughts of the members qua members of the collective. So, in this sense, simulating the thought processes of a collective is like simulating the thought processes of a fictional character. A collective is like a fictional entity that is simultaneously imagined by a number of persons—it is a collective creation. It is not exactly the same as a fictional character, however, because, although we may 'identify' with a fictional character, our thinking does not constitute the thinking of the character. A fictional character may depend (partly) on our thoughts about her,[29] in a way similar to the way that a collective is dependent on our thoughts, but she is not something that we constitute. On the other hand, the collective's thoughts, beliefs, in short its *consciousness*, are simply our consciousness as we simulate the collective in our own minds.[30] This does not mean that we can never get it wrong, however. There are facts about what we did in the past, whether our current belief is consistent with our past or other current beliefs, etc.

If I am right, then individuals who form a collective subject can be said to share a form of 'collective consciousness', which is plural, aware, and collective. It is genuinely plural in the sense that it is composed of a number of persons—it is not simply an individual consciousness. The individual members of the collective are aware of the contents of their collective consciousness and the intentionality of the collective is derived from that of its members. It is collective in the sense that the individual members are united through their shared conception of the collective, which is formed and perpetuated by the relations of intersubjectivity between the members.

---

[29] For an account of how fictional characters are dependent on the conscious acts of readers, see Thomasson (1999).

[30] Here again empathy might not be an appropriate description of what we are doing, because empathy implies that there is a distinct consciousness that I am empathizing with. Perhaps it would be better to say that our capacity to think in this collective mode is similar to or made possible by the same mechanisms that allow us to empathize with others.

CONCLUSION

The above account provides just the beginning of a complete understanding of the nature of collective subjectivity and the phenomena of collective entities and the relation to their members. However, I hope it provides some impetus for phenomenologists and philosophers of mind to concern themselves with the social and collective aspects of consciousness. Hopefully, this work will draw on both analytic philosophy of mind and phenomenology. The fact that recent work on simulation theory sounds so similar to the work of Husserl and his students on empathy should provide just one indication of the important connections between these two fields.

REFERENCES

Baier, Annette (1997) 'Doing Things With Others: The Mental Commons', in Lilli Heinämaa, Sara Wallgren, and Thomas Alanen (eds.), *Commonality and Particularity in Ethics* (New York: St Martins Press), 15–44.

Block, Ned (1978) 'Troubles with Functionalism', in C. Wade Savage (ed.), *Minnesota Studies in the Philosophy of Science*, ix (Minneapolis: University of Minnesota Press), 261–325.

Brooks, D. H. M. (1986) 'Group Minds', *Australasian Journal of Philosophy* 64/4: 456–70.

Carruthers, Peter (1996) 'Simulational Self-knowledge: A Defense of Theory-Theory', in Peter, Carruthers and Peter K., Smith (eds.), *Theories of Theories of Mind* (Cambridge: Cambridge University Press).

Durkheim, Emile (1994) 'Social Facts' in Martin Michael and Lee C. McIntyre (eds.), *Readings in the Philosophy of Social Science*. (Cambridge, Mass.: The MIT Press), 433–40.

——— (1951) *Suicide* (New York: The Free Press).

Gilbert, Margaret (1989) *Social Facts* (Princeton: Princeton University Press).

Gallese, V., and Goldman, A. (1998) 'Mirror Neurons and the Simulation Theory of Mind-Reading', *Trends in Cognitive Science* 2: 493–501.

Goldman, Alvin I. (2001) 'Desire, Intention, and Simulation Theory', Bertram F. Malle, Louis J. Moses, and Dare A. Baldwin (eds.), *Intentions and Intentionality: Foundations of Social Cognition* (Cambridge, Mass.: MIT Press), 207–24.

——— 'Simulation and Interpersonal Utility', *Ethics* 105/4: 709–26.

Gordon, Robert M. (1995) 'Sympathy, Simulation, and the Impartial Spectator', *Ethics* 105/4: 727–42.

Husserl, Edmund (1960) *Cartesian Meditations: An Introduction to Phenomenology*, trans. Dorion Cairns (Boston: Martinus Nihjoff).

——— (1989) *Ideas Pertaining to a Pure Phenomenology and to a Phenomenological Philosophy. Second Book: Studies in the Phenomenology of Constitution*, trans. R. Rojcewicz and A. Schuwer (Dordrecht: Kluwer).

Johansson, Ingvar (1989) *Ontological Investigations: An Inquiry into the Categories of Nature, Man and Society* (New York: Routledge).

Jones, Todd (2001) *The Philosophical Forum* 32/3: 221–51.

Lewis, David (1969) *Convention: A Philosophical Study* (Cambridge, Mass.: Harvard University Press).

Lomond, Eric (1998) 'Conciousness', in E. Craig (ed.), Routledge *Encyclopedia of Philosophy* (London: Routledge), http://www.rep.routledge.com/article/wo11.

Martin, Michael and McIntyre, Lee C. (eds.) (1994) *Readings in the Philosophy of Social Science* (Cambridge, MA: MIT Press).

Nagel, Thomas (1974) 'What is it like to be a Bat?', *Philosophical Review* (Oct.) 83: 435–50.

Pettit, Philip (1993) *The Common Mind: An Essay on Psychology, Society, and Politics* (New York: Oxford University Press).

Ravenscroft, Ian (1998) 'What is it like to be someone else? Simultaneous and Empathy', *Ratio* 11: 170–85.

Schutz, Alfred (1962) *Collected Papers: Volume 2*, ed. A. Broderson (Boston: Kluwer).

—— (1932) *The Phenomenology of the Social World*, trans. George Walsh and Frederick Lehnert (Evanston, Ill.: Northwestern University Press, 1967).

—— (1966) *Collected Papers*, iii: *Studies in Phenomenological Philosophy*, ed. Ilse Schutz (The Hague: Martinus Nijhoff).

Scruton, Roger (1989) 'Corporate Persons', *The Aristotelian Society*, Supplementary Volume 63: 239–66.

Searle, John R. (1990) 'Collective Intentions and Actions', in Philip R. Cohen, Jerry Morgan, and Martha E. Pollack (eds.), *Intentions in Communication* (Cambridge, MA: MIT Press), 401–15.

—— (1995) *The Construction of Social Reality* (New York: The Free Press).

Stein, Edith (1964) *On the Problem of Empathy*, trans. Waltraut Stein (The Hague: Martinus Nijhoff).

Stoutland, Frederick (1997) 'Why Are Philosophers of Social Action So Anti-Social?', in Lilli Heinämaa, Sara Wallgren, and Thomas Alanen (eds.), *Commonality and Particularity in Ethics* (New York: St. Martin's Press), 45–74.

Thomasson, Amie L. (1999) *Fiction and Metaphysics*. New York: Cambridge University Press.

Thompson, Evan (2001) 'Empathy and Consciousness', *Journal of Consciousness Studies* 8/5–7: 1–32.

Tollefsen, Deborah (2002) 'Organizations as True Believers', *Journal of Social Philosophy* 33: 395–410.

Tuomela, Raimo (1995) *The Importance of Us: A Philosophical Study of Basic Social Notions* (Stanford: Stanford University Press).

Tuomela, Raimo, and Miller, Kaarlo (1988) 'We-Intentions', *Philosophical Studies* 53: 367–89.

Wilson, Robert (2001) 'Group-Level Cognition', *Philosophy of Science* 68. Proceedings: S262–S273.

Zahavi, Dan (2001) 'Beyond Empathy: Phenomenological Approaches to Intersubjectivity', *Journal of Consciousness Studies* 8/5–7: 151–67.

PART V

PERCEPTION, SENSATION,
AND ACTION

12

Perceptual Saliences

Clotilde Calabi

Abstract: Philosophers generally acknowledge that our beliefs about the world and our actions call for reasons. Against the mainstream view, which identifies reasons either with experiences or with beliefs, I argue that the perceived situation provides such reasons. More precisely, I argue that the world's being in a certain way warrants a certain perception of the world and that a warranted perception provides reasons for acting appropriately. I identify such reasons with perceptual saliences, and I offer an account of their objectivity and normativity. While they are objective properties, they are not to be read as naïve realism reads them. While they are normative, they are not to be read as antirealism reads them. My suggestion is that the best account of these reasons is in terms of cognitive irrealism.

1. PREMISE

Suppose that you are in your office: you perceive the environment around you, although you do not acknowledge (hence judge) that, for example, the table is on your right and the window is on your left. You make judgements of this kind only in unusual circumstances, for example, if you ask yourself whether you are dreaming, or whether the furniture has been moved around. Following Austin, I label those unusual circumstances 'circumstances of aberration', meaning that they are circumstances that may ground what one believes, what one does and what one feels, in a sense that I will specify.[1] By this I mean that our beliefs about the world's being in a certain way and our actions in the world do call for warrants, and one possibility that I find plausible is that the *perceived* situation provides such warrants. Or so I will argue.

I proceed in the following way. First, I present an account of the relation between perceptual beliefs and the perceptions they are based on, according to which perceptual

I would like to thank for comments on previous drafts of this article and discussion of related issues Elvio Baccarini, Carla Bagnoli, Paolo Casalegno, Luca Ferrero, Snjiezana Prjic-Samarzjia, Marco Santambrogio, Robert Schwartz, Paolo Spinicci, Gabriele Usberti and two anonymous referees. I am particularly indebted to Amie Thomasson for her comments.

[1] Many phenomenologists would agree with the idea that perceptual judgement is an aberration presupposing a background of normality. Among them, there are Husserl, Merleau-Ponty, Heidegger, and Searle.

experience discloses grounds for perceptual beliefs as well as for action; then, after distinguishing between grounds and reasons as two different types of warrants, I focus on the relation between actions and their reasons, and present three theories of such reasons, namely a content theory, an act theory, and an object theory. It is while assessing the object theory that I argue that the reason-providing object is a perceptual salience. My argument is based on a comparison between the relation between actions and their reason-providing objects on the one hand, and the relation between an appropriate emotion and its reason-providing object on the other hand. My account of perceptual saliences is an alternative to the main accounts provided by phenomenologists and philosophers of mind,[2] in that it recognizes a crucial role to the faculty of attention and contains an analysis of reasons involving a kind of irrealist cognitivism.[3]

2. PERCEPTIONS AND COMMITMENTS

According to standard phenomenological theories of perception, perceptual experiences have a representational content, by virtue of which they are directed towards objects or states of affairs.[4] The content of a perceptual experience is the way in which it represents a portion of the world. One can be either a conceptualist or an anti-conceptualist with respect to this content. Conceptualists such as Strawson, Searle, and McDowell hold that perceptual experiences require possession and usage of concepts, and hence perceptual content is conceptual. Since it is conceptual, it is also propositional. Anti-conceptualists hold the opposite view. Notwithstanding their divergences, both parties acknowledge that the content of a perceptual experience prescribes the conditions of correctness of that experience. The experience is correct if the world (a portion of it) is as the experience represents it via its content, otherwise it is incorrect. The conceptualist identifies correctness with truth, the non-conceptualist does not, confining himself to consider correctness as a relation of fit between contents and objects, the main difference being that truth is propositional, whereas fitness is not.

Consider first the conceptualist position. It amounts to the idea that in order to perceive the world as being in a certain way, one needs to possess the concept of that way. Thus, perceptual experiences are phenomenal states permeated by concepts.[5] Conceptualists provide two arguments in support of their thesis. The first argument has to do with the idea that perception is committed to truth. For a state to be

---

[2] In my analysis, the class of phenomenologists is broadly conceived. It includes not only psychologists such as Gibson and Koehler, but also philosophers such as Heidegger and Searle.

[3] Irrealist cognitivism has been introduced into the philosophical debate on normativity by John Skorupski. It amounts to the idea that the propositions about reasons are truth-apt propositions, but do not have truth-makers, that is, there are no mere facts making them true. See Skorupski (1999), (2002).

[4] Standard phenomenological theories of perception are to be found in Hussel's *Sixth logical Investigation* in Husserl (1900–1), Husserl (1952), Searle (1983), Smith (1989). A survey of post-Husserlian theories is in Crane (1992a).

[5] See Strawson (1992: 62): 'The character of our perceptual experience itself, of our sense experience itself, is thoroughly conditioned by the judgements about the objective world which we are disposed to make when we have this experience; it is, so to speak, thoroughly permeated—saturated, one might say—with the concepts employed in such judgements'. See also McDowell (1994), (1998).

truth-committed is for it to have contents that are ready to be used inferentially. Take the case of belief. Its being truth-committed means that the believer aims at having true representations of the world and, at the same time, is capable to draw inferences that are truth-preserving from those representations. This does not require possession of the concepts of entailment, logical validity, and so on, although it entails possession and usage of *some* concepts. The same is for perception: for the conceptualist, perception's goal is attaining truth and, although to perceive is not to engage in committal inferences, nevertheless it is to entertain contents that are ready to be used as contents of belief and thus ready to be used in committal inferences that are truth-preserving. McDowell's position well features the conceptualist's way of thinking, for he claims that 'the content of a perceptual experience is already conceptual. A judgement of experience does not introduce a new kind of content, but simply endorses the conceptual content, or some of it that is already possessed by the experience on which it is grounded' (1994: 48–9). Notice that the passage from perceptual experience to judgement is rendered through the verb 'to endorse'. For McDowell perception is committal (in his terminology, its content is claim-containing) in that the content, though passively received, is ready to be used inferentially in the sense I specified above. Somewhat obscurely he remarks that judging or believing requires a more active type of commitment towards the content: it involves an actual inferential use. Endorsement amounts to that actual usage of content.[6]

The second argument emphasizes the normative relation between perception and perceptual belief. This relation is identified with a relation of justification. Since the justification relation holds only between proposition-like entities, and since propositions are constituted by concepts, the content of perception is conceptual. It is worth stressing that the two arguments in McDowell are connected. Only if perception is truth-committed can it provide a justification basis to judgement: the justification basis must be propositional and propositionality is granted by the fact that perception is truth-committed. Thus, McDowell and other conceptualists defend what we may call the *reason & commitment view*: there are no reasons unless there are underlying commitments, and there are no commitments unless there are endorsable reasons. In this view, perceptual experiences provide *reasons* for perceptual beliefs, reasons being conceptual and propositional.

Three features of the *reason & commitment view* are worth stressing. First, reasons for judgements are not necessarily inferential reasons: perceptual judgements are such that the perceptions they are based on provide evidential reasons for them, and the relation between the perception and the corresponding judgement is not inferential.[7]

---

[6] Elaborating on Sellars, McDowell says that visual experiences are 'conceptual occurrences, actualizations of conceptual capacities with a suitable logical "togetherness". In that respect, they are like judgements. But they are unlike judgements in the way in which they "contain" their claims. Judgements are free exercises of conceptual capacities with a suitable togetherness. But in an ostensible seeing whose contents includes that of a given judgement, the same conceptual capacities are actualized, with the same togetherness, in a way that is ostensibly necessitated by the objective reality' McDowell (1998: 471).

[7] See Brewer (1999), Brandom (2000), both arguing that the relation between perceptual judgements and the reasons justifying them is non-inferential. See also Husserl's *Sixth Logical Investigation* in Husserl (1900–1); Mulligan (1995).

Second, the reasons for judgements, be they inferential or not,[8] are reasons that the believer *is disposed to acknowledge*: in the 'reason & commitment view', contents count as reasons through their endorsement by believers.[9] Third, changes occur when perception develops into perceptual belief.

Let me focus on the third point. Which changes are more precisely involved? To address the conceptualist–anti-conceptualist debate by focusing on this problem can help to identify the real issue. As we have seen, the conceptualist says that there is only a change in committal import, that is, the endorsement of an already propositionally structured content. Let me thus consider the anti-conceptualist view. According to it, there is both a change in function and a change in committal import and the two go together. Perceptual activity is a matter of getting things right (size, colour, distance, etc.), unlike propositional activity, which aims at providing true descriptions of the world. Thus, for the anti-conceptualist, perception is not committed to truth, but only to veridicality.[10] What exactly does the commitment to veridicality amount to? For the anti-conceptualist perception is committal in the sense that the perceiver takes his own perceptual experience at face value, that is, he takes experiences as presentations of how things are or, equivalently, as what allows him to make contact with the world. Focusing on the subpersonal level of description of the phenomena, the committal nature of perception amounts to the idea that perceptual systems aim at representational correctness: their primary function is to provide a veridical or correct representation of the environment. Another way to put this is to say that perception discloses *grounds* for perceptual beliefs, but not reasons.

I am not interested in reviewing the anti-conceptualist's arguments against conceptual content and I try to remain neutral on this controversy as much as possible. However, two remarks are in order. The first is that often the conceptualist has an excessively intellectual view of concepts and a too demanding account of commitments, according to which to possess a concept is to possess the criteria for its application, to be capable of engaging in the activity of making explicit judgements, and to be reflectively conscious of one's commitments. Some anti-conceptualists are opposed to that view.[11] The second is that also for the anti-conceptualist talk of function involves reference to norms or standards. Thus, in the anti-conceptualist's view the committal nature of perception involves the existence of standards or norms that govern the production of correct representations by the perceptual system in normal circumstances.

---

[8] Consider the case of inferential reasons. If I judge (and hence believe) that this chair is purple, I commit myself to the truth of the content of my judgement. To commit myself to the truth of that content is (a) to be disposed to consider its assertion as justifiable, *and* (b) to be disposed to consider the content of the assertion (or, equivalently, of the judgement) as the premise of an inference. Once again, no commitments, no reasons. In the case of (b) if I am disposed to consider the content of my judgement that this chair is purple as the premise of an inference, I also commit myself to assert something else, for example, that it is coloured and that it is extended.   [9] Peacocke (1999: 216).

[10] For the distinction between truth commitments and veridicality commitments see Burge (2003).

[11] McDowell is a conceptualist of this variety. See Noe (2000) for a criticism of the 'too much exalted conception of our own conceptual skills', formulated within a defence of the conceptual content of perception. See Crane (1992b) and Peacocke (1998) for an anti-conceptualist account of perceptual content.

These norms govern the well-functioning of the system for achieving veridicality and failure to meet them brings about incorrectness. If we move to the personal level, we notice that the well-functioning of the system is directly relevant not only to making contact with the world, but also to the formation of true beliefs on the part of the perceiver. As Noe puts it, although at that level perception may be belief-independent, it is not belief-indifferent.[12] This means that for both conceptualists and anti-conceptualists perceptual belief depends upon perceptual states for both its contents *and* its warrants.[13] Thus, for both conceptualists and anti-conceptualists the norms concerning the functioning of the perceptual system are relevant not only to the formation of true beliefs, but also to the norms governing these latter[14] and the transition from perception to belief is not only a causal transition, but also a normative transition. For the anti-conceptualist, to acknowledge this is precisely to acknowledge that when perception develops into a belief, it discloses grounds for that belief, that is, provides non-propositional warrants for it. In this sense, the transition is not only a causal transition.

3. PERCEPTIONS-BASED ACTIONS AND THEIR REASONS

Perception is not only connected to belief and judgement, but also to action. In this latter case, perception is neither action-independent nor action-indifferent: perception and action are mutually interdependent. For those who favour the subpersonal description of the phenomena, there are not two systems, the perceptual system and the action system, proceeding in a causally linear way; rather there exists one complex perception-action system in which causation flows in both ways.[15] Switching to the personal level of description, as Noe puts it, 'perceptual experience raises questions not only about how things are, but [also] about how we stand in relation to how things are. In keeping track of how what we do affects what we experience, we are keeping track of what our experience tells us about the world.'[16] This is because to be a perceiver one must be capable of keeping track of the ways in which one's perceptual experience depends on what one does: the ability to perceive depends on the ability to keep track of the interdependence of perception and action.

Thus, if we focus on the way perception interacts with action, we notice that there is no linear causal transition from the one to the other. Yet the existence of a double feedback is no threat to the idea that the linear model of transition is adequate for the

---

[12] Noe (1999).

[13] Obviously, the conceptualist considers perceptual content as conceptual and thus perception as reason-providing, while the anti-conceptualist considers perceptual content as non-conceptual and thus grounds-providing.

[14] As Burge remarks, 'perceptual belief and perceptual knowledge depend for their content and warrant on perceptual states. Norms governing well-functioning by perceptual systems for achieving veridicality and for serving the formation of true beliefs are directly relevant to norms governing attaining truth in perceptual belief', see Burge (2003: 521–2). [15] See Hurley (1998).

[16] Noe (2000).

rational explanation of actions.[17] Under the appropriate circumstances, the individual explains his action in terms of what he perceives. Once again, as for the case in which perception develops into perceptual belief, also in this case, when the believer becomes an agent, a normative transition affects him, and not merely a causal one. If perception becomes integrated into propositional activity and thus develops into perceptual belief, this latter may disclose reasons for the agent that make his action appropriate. My main question is what kind of reasons are these.

Consider the following case. Suppose that I am reading in my office and suddenly the light goes off. Having realized this (and thus believing now that the light is off), I may have a reason for switching it on, or for being uncomfortable. We may account for reasons in three ways. First, we may consider the entertained content (that the light is off) as what provides the reason. Yet this view is inadequate because an entertained content cannot provide a reason for action (nor for belief or for feeling) unless it is endorsed by the believer. If the entertained content per se were a reason for acting or for feeling, we could not account for, say, the difference between imagining that a huge dog is going to attack me and believing that a huge dog is going to attack me. In the former case a mere content is entertained, in the latter that content is believed to be true. Only if I also believe that that content is true may it be appropriate for me to run away. In other words, other things being equal (that is, given sameness of content), one acts if certain psychological conditions arise (namely if certain beliefs and desires occur). This is to say that content theories cannot satisfy holistic constraints. Thus, content alone has no motivational force and content theories of normativity should be rejected.

Second, we may consider the act of judging or state of believing that the light is off as reason-providing. One example of the act-theory of reasons is Davidson's. For him what counts as a reason for an action or an emotion is some mental state provided with content and occurring in a network of other mental states. Thus, there are no objective properties whose instantiation counts as a reason for doing something or for feeling something and only some general principles of rationality act as constraints establishing that one ought to do so and so, or that it is permissible/required to feel so and so. This account of normativity, unlike the content-account, satisfies the holistic requirement. Yet, it falls short of the facts. It does not capture the common sense truth that there are facts that count as reasons for doing something or for being in some affective state. Doesn't the fact that something is a shelter count, in an endangering situation, as a reason for seeking protection in it, and doesn't the fact that someone is aggressive count as a reason for defending oneself (given some *ceteris paribus* conditions)? Yes, of course, one could respond. Nevertheless, the problem is what kind of facts these are. Let me turn then to the object-account of reasons, a third option that seems to me more promising than the other two and thus deserving a more detailed discussion.

[17] Thus, I do not follow Hurley's idea that rationality should be conceived as 'a higher order property of complex patterns of response, which emerge from layers of direct dynamic couplings between organisms and their structured environments', Hurley (2001: 10). See also Hurley (1998: ch. 10). I suspect that Hurley's emergentist account of rationality entails reductionism, which I reject at the end of the essay.

4. GIBSON'S AFFORDANCES AS REASONS FOR ACTION

Gibson's theory of affordances is an interesting example of the object theory of reasons. Two aspects of it are worth stressing. The first is the idea that the senses are not channels for sensations, rather they are perceptual systems whose function is to pick up environmental information. The activity exercised by these systems is exploratory and investigative, as opposed to a performatory and executive activity, which would be exercised by sense organs, if there were any.[18] The perceptual systems explore the information available in sound, mechanical contact, chemical contact, and light and the organism immediately uses the available information for action purposes.[19] The second aspect is the idea that the activities exercised by the perceptual systems and by the basic orienting system are those of one general disposition, which Gibson identifies with attention.[20] Dispositionally defined, attention is *sensitivity to information*. The attention's goal is the recognition of affordances, which are the invariant properties of objects, which the perceptual systems recognize, despite changing sensations (of light, pressure, etc.):

The eyes, ears, nose, mouth and skin can orient, explore, investigate. When thus active, they are neither passive senses nor channels of sensory quality, but ways of paying attention to whatever is constant in the changing stimulation. In exploratory looking, tasting and touching the sense impressions are incidental symptoms of the exploration, and what gets isolated is information about the object looked at, tasted or touched. The movements of the eyes, the mouth, and the hands, in fact seem to keep changing the input at the receptive level, the input of sensation, just so as to isolate over time the invariants of the input at the level of the perceptual system.[21]

There is an intimate relation between perception and action, in that the perception of an object immediately causes the perceiver's behavioural reaction: an animal perceiving a predator runs away. Thus, an organism directly perceives the world in terms of its affordances for action, that is, in relation to the opportunities it presents for action. In this view, attention qua sensitivity to information[22] is the capacity to detect affordances in their motivational function. The actions causally sustained by affordances are primitive normative responses to what in specific contexts it is best to do:

When the constant properties of constant objects are perceived (the shape, size, color, texture, composition, motion, animation, and position relative to other objects), the observer can go on to detect their affordances. I have coined this word as a substitute for values, a term which

---

[18] Gibson (1966: 32).   [19] Gibson (1966: 58).
[20] Gibson (1966: 49–51, 58). 'Each perceptual system has its own peculiar mode of attention' (p. 251). 'What I had in mind by a psychophysics of perception was simply the emphasis on perception as direct instead of indirect. I wanted to exclude an extra process of inference or construction. I meant (or should have meant) that animals and people sense the environment, not in the meaning of having sensations, but in the meaning of detecting information. . . . I should not have implied that a percept was an automatic response to a stimulus, as a sense impression is supposed to be [in classical psychophysics]. For even then I realized that perceiving is an act, not a response, *an act of attention*, not a triggered impression, an achievement, not a reflex' (emphasis mine).
[21] Gibson (1966: 4).   [22] Gibson (1966: 58).

carries an old burden of philosophical meaning. I mean simply what things furnish, for good or ill. What they afford the observer, after all, depends on their properties.[23] For example, a path affords pedestrian locomotion from one place to another, between the terrain features that prevent locomotion. The preventers of locomotion consist of obstacles, barriers, water margins and brinks (the edges of cliffs) ...

An obstacle can be defined as an animal-sized object that affords collision and possible injury.[24]

Thus, 'Certain saliences may be reasons for types of actions, and not for others. For example, a cloud may prevent looking through, but not going through.'[25] It should also be emphasized that the recognition of saliences is obtained without the intervention of an intellectual process: perception does not necessarily depend on conception and belief.[26]

In Gibson's view, the relation 'being a reason for' that holds between a salience and an action is a causal relation, which can be more or less successfully oriented towards the achievement of a certain task. There are no differences in principle between the boring and burrowing behavior of a tick detecting butyric acid on the skin of a mammal, and the action-oriented perception of a human being.[27] As Mace puts it, 'in Gibsonian perceivings there are no right or wrong answers but degrees of clarity and sufficiency for the task at hand'.[28] In other words, given that the *motivational* relations are nothing else but causal relations, it follows that any object could be a reason or motive for performing such and such an action, and hence justify that action, under the condition of occurring in a selectively relevant niche. Yet it could be objected that not any selectively relevant cause of doing x counts as a consideration in favour of doing x, especially for beings capable of second-order thoughts and desires.

The objection I have raised is a reformulation of the so-called trivialization problem that Fodor and Pylyshyn find in Gibson.[29] Take Gibson's definition of perception as the direct pickup of invariant properties, where 'direct' means unmediated, neither by memory nor by inference. Fodor and Pylyshyn argue that this account of perception is empty, unless the notions of direct pickup and invariant properties are suitably constrained. 'For, patently, if any property can count as an invariant and if any psychological process can count as the pickup of an invariant, then the identification

---

[23] Gibson (1966: 285). Objects may have several affordances. For example, a tomato may be eaten, thrown, painted, to name only a few. It may lack other affordances, for example it cannot be used as a brick. See Reed (1988: 231).   [24] Gibson (1986: 36).

[25] Gibson (1986: 36).

[26] Gibson (1966: 2). Hence, according to Gibson, the recognition of saliences does not require inferential capacities (for him to possess and apply a concept is to exercise inferential capacities).

[27] The tick is sensitive to the butyric acid found on mammalian skin. Butyric acid, when detected, induces the tick to loosen its hold on a branch of a tree and to fall on the mammal. Tactile contact extinguishes the olfactory response and starts a procedure of running about until heat is detected. The detection of heat in turn initiates boring and burrowing. The tick relies on simple cues that are specific to its need and does not bother to represent details of other types. The case is discussed by Clark (1997). He makes the hypothesis that, like the tick's world, the humanly perceived world is equally biased and constrained. He claims that also for human beings biological cognition is highly selective and 'it can sensitize an organism to whatever parameters reliably specify states of affairs that matter to that specific form of life' (p. 25).   [28] Mace (2002: 111).

[29] Fodor and Pylyshyn (1981).

of perception with the pickup of invariants excludes nothing' (p. 177). Here is their argument:

Suppose that under certain circumstances people can correctly perceive that some of the things in their environment are of the type P. Since you cannot correctly perceive that something is P unless the thing is P, it will always be trivially true that the things that can be perceived to be P share an invariant property, namely being P. And since, according to Gibson, what people do in perceiving is directly pick up an appropriate invariant, the following pseudo-explanation of any perceptual achievement is always available: to perceive that something is P is to pick up the (invariant) property P which things of that kind have. So, for example, we can give the following disarmingly simple answer to the question: how do people perceive that something is a shoe? There is a certain (invariant) property that all and only shoes have—namely, the property of being a shoe. Perceiving that something is a shoe consists in the pickup of this property.

Fodor and Pylyshyn think that they have their way out of the trivialization problem.[30] Yet what is most interesting here is that the same problem arises with respect to affordances as reasons for action. Some constraints are needed if we want to rule out another disarmingly simple answer to the obvious question: what makes something a reason for doing F? Of course, there is a certain (invariant) property that all and only reasons for doing F have—namely, the property of affording F, and that is a causal property. Holding something as a reason for doing F would consist in the pickup of this property.[31] This leaves unanswered the main question: what makes something a reason for doing F? We cannot respond to this question simply by saying that the reason motivates. Are we forced then to reject the idea that facts count as considerations in favour of doing something? Once we have argued that Davidson's view falls short of the facts, we can now see that what appeared on a first glance as a relevant alternative to it, namely Gibson's view, falls short of rationality, by making its claims vacuous. It does so, because it flies on the face of one of the main tenets of rationality, namely holism. Gibson, while attempting to see perception as integrated with action, does not see it as integrated with thought. The first type of integration (integration with action) is blind with respect to rationality issues, unless there is also the second type of integration (integration with thought).

5. ATTENTION AS SENSITIVITY TO REASONS: THE CASE OF EMOTIONS

There is a more promising venue I want to explore. In the Gibsonian view, perceptual saliences are natural properties of objects. Alternatively, I argue that saliences are normative properties. Correspondingly, I propose a revision of the *reason &*

---

[30] They think that Gibson should abandon the thesis of unmediated perception. But this is not something he is disposed to do. I criticize their solution in Calabi (2004).

[31] Notice that the same objection can be raised if we focus on attention as the disposition to detect saliences, rather than on saliences themselves. Attention is conceived as a purely mechanical disposition that is triggered whenever the environment affords it. Now, if saliences qua objects of perceptual judgements provide reasons for action, as Gibson says, an account of them cannot ignore the sense of why it may be right to consider certain saliences as reasons for certain types of action and not for others. If attention is a disposition to detect saliences, it must be possible to set the norms for its correct application. Yet, this is not something a Gibsonian account of attention allows us to do.

commitment view and argue that this revision involves an account of attention as something quite unlike a mechanical disposition. In defending my account, I compare the normative relation that subsists between the appropriate responses and the relevant perceptual saliences on the one hand, and the normative relation occurring between an appropriate emotion and its object on the other hand. Theorists often argue that emotions are significantly similar to perceptions, and that an understanding of perception helps us to understand how emotions work. I go the opposite way by making reference to emotions in order to understand the normative relation between perception and action. I argue that both purposive action and evaluative experience involve the exercise of a faculty of attention, which I identify with sensitivity to reasons. In my opinion this account of attention accommodates both demands in that it does not fall short of the facts, nor does it fall short of rationality.

Emotions are modes of our sensitivity to certain saliences and, as such, they are modes of attention. As De Sousa rightly stresses, these modes set the agenda for beliefs and desires.[32] Consider saliences, as they are detected by emotional experiences. They are (real or illusory) properties of a real object to which the emotion relates and that motivates it: they are aspects of an object that constitute reasons for some specific emotional reaction and we may call them motivating aspects. For example, the dog's being large and barking is a motivating aspect of fear. Motivating aspects fulfil a justification function, and in order to do so, they must be rationally related to the emotion caused by their perception. This means that they must incorporate a success condition for the emotion, which varies according to the kind of emotion. An emotion is appropriate or justified if its motivating aspect instantiates the success condition for that kind of emotion. For example, being dangerous is the success condition for fear: in the above example, fear is appropriate if the dog's being large and barking makes it dangerous. Now, the relevant question in this context is what kinds of property are being dangerous and the like, which represent the success condition for different kinds of emotion.

They belong to the class of evaluative properties. An interesting analysis of these properties is McDowell's, who considers them as analogous to secondary qualities. We cannot adequately understand secondary qualities unless we view them as objective dispositions, apt to elicit some particular subjective state in individuals provided with the appropriate kind of sensitivity. Pursuing that analogy, McDowell claims that we learn to see the world on the basis of evaluative classifications, because we are endowed with dispositions that allow us to care in appropriate ways about the objects we learn to see as collected together by the same classifications. McDowell does not deny the objectivity of evaluative properties, since explanations of fear that manifest our capacity to understand ourselves when experiencing it, clash with the claim that reality contains nothing in the way of fearfulness. Any such claim would undermine the intelligibility that the explanations confer on our responses.[33] In particular, the intelligibility of fear requires that we be ready to attribute some properties

---

[32] See on this De Sousa (1987: 196): 'we might say that they [the emotions] ask the questions that judgement answers with beliefs and evaluate the prospects to which desire may or may not respond'.

[33] McDowell (1985: 176). See also Wiggins (1987) and Wiggins (1976).

to an object that would validate our fear response or invalidate it, that is, justify it or show that it is unjustified. These properties are such that they impinge on our perception and our sentiment simultaneously: unless objects were provided with such validating/invalidating properties, and unless we are provided with the appropriate sensitivity, there could be no account of the appropriateness/inappropriateness of our emotional responses, let alone of their intelligibility.[34] Thus, there is an intelligibility requirement concerning the properties' objectivity and dependence upon a perceiver's existence and the special kind of sensitivity of the perceiver.

McDowell's account surely is a worthy attempt to overcome the distinction between the subjective and the objective: evaluative properties are objective properties whose existence depends upon the existence of a perceiver who can perceive them in virtue of his sensitivity. The sensitivity, correctly educated, is required to see in specific contexts the relevant evaluative properties. Moreover, sensitivity makes it possible to see the appropriate motivational function in these properties.[35] Yet, theorists often object to McDowell that he does not really explain that motivational function, because he overlooks the fact that evaluative properties, unlike secondary qualities, are such that they *merit* (and sometimes *require*) a certain type of reaction. Ultimately he reduces the objectivity of values to an agreement on criteria for appropriateness.[36] This is not to say that one should abandon the relational account. McDowell's lesson is that the objectivity of reasons does not exclude mind-dependency and it is precisely this idea that is worth pursuing.

Constructivists take the idea seriously in a fruitful and provocative way. Although there are various kinds of constructivists, their fundamental idea is that the contents of reasons and their normative force are determined by a rational choice involving deliberation. Deliberation concerns the relations between facts and values, that is, it concerns which facts should matter as a consideration in favour of doing or not doing something, for blaming, for praising, or for laughing, ultimately, which facts should matter as reasons. As it has been stressed, for constructivists too, the problem 'is not to have some standard of salience, rather the question is how to get salience right'.[37] Yet, to get saliences right is not to recognize them when they occur by exercising some sort of insight, but rather *to constitute them*: moral saliences as normative reasons, so the constructivist says, are constructed through the activity of deliberation. The constructivist interpretation of the idea that reasons are mind-dependent forcefully stresses the process by which a reason can be extrapolated, starting from the recognition of a fact.

Let me return back to perception vis-à-vis action and attempt to apply this basic constructivist idea to the perception-action context. In what sense can we assert that perceptual saliences count as a consideration in favour of doing something, without running into the trivialization objection raised above?

---

[34] Wiggins (1987: 194).

[35] Notice that a sensitive subject is someone who is disposed to revise his/her own evaluations, and hence disposed to modify his/her own judgements.

[36] Bagnoli (2002). De Sousa's account, which relies on the notion of paradigmatic scenario, is vulnerable to the same objection.   [37] Bagnoli (2002: 130).

6. CONSTRAINTS FOR PERCEPTUAL SALIENCES

To assert that perceptual saliences count as reasons for doing or not doing something is not to say that our desires and interests cannot be ranged among the considerations that matter. It means that we find reasons for action not only in ourselves (as Davidson tries to argue) but also in the world as we see it. The normative role of saliences can be accounted for if we acknowledge that it is essentially through perceptual experiences that we have access to the way the world is. These experiences provide empirical contents for beliefs and the contents they provide have a demonstrative component that ensures the reference to mind-independent objects. To grasp these contents is a prima facie reason for endorsing them in belief. In this sense, perceptual experiences are the exercise of a capacity to make cognitive contact with the world. However, this is not the end of the story. The agent needs to recognize the authority of the beliefs he has acquired through perceptual experiences, if they should constitute a guide to action. It is not only a matter of knowing that the mechanism of perceptual belief formation is generally reliable. Reasons are not apprehended through a reliable mechanism nor through blind hunches. To understand why it is so, take the case of the blindsighter making guesses about things around him. His guesses are the result of a reliable, non-conscious mechanism for detecting objects. Yet, having no conscious experiences, he has no reasons for action. He cannot acknowledge that *experiencing that this is thus* is due to the fact that it is just so.

Thus, in my view, those reasons consisting of perceptual beliefs that the world is so and so depend on the world's being perceptually available to a perceiver *as so and so*. My idea is that, for this class of reasons, it is the world that wears the trousers, although the world is a world that the agent has in view.[38] Yet, to pursue the analogy with evaluative properties, mention of some kind of appropriate sensitivity is required. In fact, I have also said that those aspects of the world that count as considerations in favour of doing or not doing something are objects for a perceiver equipped with a certain type of sensitivity, and we should spell it out in terms of the possession of some specific capacities: recognition of perceptual saliences as reasons depends upon possession of these capacities. The capacities corresponding to the required sensitivity are the capacity for demonstrative reference, that is, the capacity to individuate objects that are in egocentric spatial relations to oneself and see them as having those egocentric relations, and the capacity for discrimination.[39]

Let me address first the capacity for demonstrative reference. The perceiver views things that are displayed in a certain way around him, that is, that are given as being in certain spatial relations with him. An appreciation of the perceived egocentric relations between the subject and the things displayed to him involves some awareness of the consequences of obtaining these relations for the action of the perceiver upon the things perceived and for the perception that he has of them. For example, to see

---

[38] See McDowell (1998).

[39] Some kind of conceptual competence is also required, to view perceived objects as motivating actions. Conceptual competence is not a secondary aspect, and it is worth stressing that stressing it constitutes a further significant departure from the Gibsonian account of reasons.

something moving behind an obstacle is not merely to see the occlusion of one surface by another, but to see the object moving out of sight, in such and such a way that the hidden object may become unhidden by a change in the point of observation brought about by specific movements (of the object, or the obstacle or the perceiver).[40] In this view, the objects enjoying some salient property, that is, motivating the agent, are displayed *as* around the perceiver, and they are perceived by means of a perceptual demonstrative content. That is, perceptual experiences, by means of which we gain access to saliences as reasons for action, have a content of the form 'That is so and so', in which the demonstrative refers to a thing having an egocentric spatial relation to the perceiver and the predicate identifies the way in which such a thing is experientially presented as being.[41]

The capacity for discrimination captures what Alvin Goldman, among others, has called 'a fundamental facet of animate life, both human and infrahuman', namely 'telling things apart, distinguishing predator from prey, for example, or a protective habitat from a threatening one'. Goldman observes that 'the concept of knowledge has its roots in this kind of cognitive activity'.[42] I think that the concept of action too, has its roots in this kind of cognitive activity, that is, has its roots in the exercising of a capacity for discrimination. However, I elaborate on Goldman's claim in a way that allows us to reply to the trivialization objection raised above. Consider Davidson's example of the man who is walking in the park and finds the branch of a tree on the trail. He thinks that someone may step on it and fall, and throws the branch behind a nearby bush. Then, he takes the bus home. At a certain moment, he realizes that the branch may be even more dangerous in that position, gets off the bus, returns to the park, and puts the branch where it was before. Does the fact that the branch is behind the bush constitute an appropriate reason for returning to the park? Obviously it does not. This person is unable to discriminate between real and unreal dangers, in those particular circumstances. In other words, given the circumstances, he is unable to determine an appropriate context of evaluation. The context should suggest what counts as a real danger and what does not, that is, the context should indicate which considerations may be relevant if one is looking for danger. Now, the identification of the proper context, that is, ultimately, the identification of the criteria of relevance for danger, is subject to deliberation. This means that a capacity for deliberation is required in order to individuate what counts as a relevant or appropriate criterion for considering something as dangerous and acting appropriately. Discrimination is discrimination with justification in view.

7. ATTENTION AS SENSITIVITY TO REASONS

The faculty of attention mentioned at the beginning of this essay, corresponds to the capacities for demonstrative reference and for discrimination, that is, the capacity to individuate the proper context of justification. By defining attention as 'sensitivity to

---

[40] Gibson stresses this point in several places, e.g. in Gibson (1972).
[41] See Brewer (1999) as an example of this kind of analysis of perceptual demonstrative content.
[42] Goldman (1988).

reasons', I consider its application as the joint exercise of both. Interestingly enough, for common sense to pay attention to something is to direct one's gaze, or focus one's mind on it, as well as to take it instead of taking something else into proper account.[43] The two aspects are obviously related. The capacity for demonstrative reference should capture the first aspect of attending; telling things apart should capture its other aspect. It should be noticed that in my account attention as sensitivity to reasons is a highly sophisticated capacity for telling things apart: as I said, it is discrimination with justification in view. In conclusion, to resume the thesis that I have attempted to articulate, we can say the following. Our perceptual systems (particularly the visual system) are such that they give us the capacity to recognize colours and shapes and provide us with experiences that are broadly speaking correct. In the case of agency, the information provided by the perceptual systems can be used by the person properly for action purposes, that is, with its correct motivational function, only if he is provided with a specific kind of sensitivity, articulated in the capacity for demonstrative reference and for discrimination. Under these latter conditions, the perceiver can individuate, given certain specific situations and his interests, what is salient in those situations, that is, what counts as a reason for doing something. The normative transition between perception and agency is constrained by the correct exercise of the proper sensitivity.

Reductionists often identify the space of reasons (that is, the appropriate context of discrimination) with a space of adaptive responses.[44] Accordingly, they consider sensitivity to information as a matter of selective adaptation. Constructivists argue that moral phenomenology requires evaluative properties as *objectively normative*, as its intelligibility condition. I have argued that a parallel requirement concerns also the phenomenology of perception: in some critical situations the perceiver should be considered as an *evaluator*, that is, an individual who discriminates, in the information that he gathers, what counts as a reason for believing, a reason for acting, and a reason for feeling, from what does not. If one adopts a reductionist perspective, then salient perceptions turn out to be only those that fit our niche well. Yet, this does not transform them, *ipso facto*, into (good or bad, right or wrong) reasons for acting, feeling, and believing. A slope may be a reason to believe one has taken the wrong path, a reason to feel fear, a reason to stop walking, or all these reasons together. But this requires capacity for discrimination and capacity for discrimination involves deliberation. Also, the perception of butyric acid may be described as a reason for the tick to behave in a certain manner. Yet, we can use this description, only if we are also ready to describe the tick as an individual that is able to individuate the proper context of

---

[43] As Ryle has stressed, there are various heed concepts, some of which are captured by the verbs 'to inspect' and 'to scrutinize'. Interestingly enough, the semantic field of those verbs, as reported by *Roget's Thesaurus*, includes the connotations of attention as sensitivity to reasons, as I have characterized it: 'to inspect' is 'to fix, to fasten to, to focus one's mind on, to review, to pass under review, to concentrate on, to bend the mind to, to give one's mind to, to direct one's thought to, to keep track of, to not lose sight of, to be mindful, to bear in mind, to have in mind, to be thinking of, to consider, to weigh, to take account of, to glance at, to look into, to dip into, to be all eyes, to be all ears, to look after, to keep in view, to keep in sight, to have an eye to, to study closely'. See Ryle (1949), (1964).

[44] A. Clark typically represents such reductionism. See Clark (1997: 50). Adaptive responses in my view include not only possible actions, but also emotional reactions, moral attitudes, and beliefs.

evaluation, and hence can divide possible reasons into good and bad. If not, the tick could be a well-fitted mechanism, but would not be an evaluator. I have attempted to indicate in what conditions perceivers could be conceived as evaluators. I have argued that the capacity for discrimination that is required is significantly similar to the capacity for discrimination involved in evaluative experiences. In both cases, one selects saliences, that is, those reasons one can endorse or can feel committed to. In both cases, the recognition of saliences is unintelligible except as a modification of some kind of sensitivity.[45]

The account of salience I have sketched should apply to organisms that are both capable of detecting aberrances in the background of normal perception, and capable of evaluating reasons as reasons for acting, feeling, and believing, that is, that are capable of deliberation. In doing so, these organisms exercise their attention. In describing the constraints that guide our perception of saliences as reasons for action, I have attempted to argue explicitly for two related theses and implicitly assumed the validity of a third one. The first is that attention is not, as Peacocke, among others, suggests, merely a resource which may be drawn upon whatever the subject's purposes.[46] Rather, attention qua sensitivity to reasons helps to shape one's purposes, that is, to individuate reasons for agency, for emotions, and for beliefs. The second claim is that, in attempting to respond to the trivialization problem, I have argued in favour of a kind of irrealist cognitivism with respect to saliences, that is, I have tried to undercut the naïve belief in the idea that reasons for action belong to a world of objects and events and for the simple-minded conviction that our senses give knowledge of these reasons.[47] The third claim consists in an implicit defence of the linear account of the normative transition between perception and action, as opposed to a multilayered-double feedback account, such as the one endorsed by Hurley.

One objection to my view can come from the following development of the blind-sighter case. Suppose that thanks to the dedicated and enduring help of nurses and caretakers the blindsighter comes to recognize that his guesses are reliable and to trust them as a normal perceiver would trust his perceptions.[48] Although he is still missing conscious experiences, he has a reliable unconscious mechanism for detecting objects

---

[45] In an analogous vein, W. Koehler considers saliences as intentional correlates of an interest attitude: 'These qualities are objective looking correlates of definite interest-attitude'. See Koehler (1939: 81).

[46] Peacocke (1999: 213). The whole passage reads as follows: 'perceptual attention serves a function of selection. It selects particular objects, events, or particular properties and relations of objects and events in such a way as to improve the perceiver's informational state concerning the selected item. The details of the nature of the improvement are a matter for empirical investigation. The improvement might be a matter of more detailed, and new, kinds of informational content; or it might be a matter of the speed with which states of given informational content are attained. Whether this capacity for improved informational states for selected items is used effectively or wisely is another matter. Attention is a resource which may be drawn upon whatever the subject's purposes' (pp. 212–13).

[47] I am paraphrasing Gibson, who claims that his account of the senses as perceptual systems rather than channels of sensation provides support 'for the naïve belief in a world of objects and events, and for the simple-minded conviction that our senses give knowledge of it'. See Gibson (1967: 168). [48] The case is discussed by Kelly (2004).

in the environment and he *knows* that the mechanism is reliable. Does he now have reasons for action? It is tempting to answer affirmatively. I think that this is a correct answer, but the new blindsighter is no counterexample to my case. In fact, he does exercise his attention and discriminates with deliberation in view. Yet, his attention is caught by what the caretakers and the nurses have taught him he can rely on. He is not exercising perceptual consciousness, although he is carefully attentive to what these people have told him and they speak, so to say, in place of what would be his own experiences, if he were normally functioning. In this case some kind of sensitivity is still necessary for deliberation, but it is no longer a perceptual sensitivity. Rather, it is a sensitivity to the teaching and the testimony of others. Thus, attention qua sensitivity to reasons, that is, qua capacity to consider aspects of the world as motivating agency, is not identical with perceptual consciousness. To deny their identity is not to deny that attention is the capacity for demonstrative reference and for discrimination. Rather, it entails that the capacity for demonstrative reference and the capacity for discrimination themselves are not identical to, or dependent upon, perceptual consciousness. I have defined above attention as sensitivity to reasons, and considered it as the joint exercise of the capacity for demonstrative reference and the capacity to individuate the proper context of justification. I have not identified attention with consciousness: the new blindsighter's case shows that both the capacity for demonstrative reference and the capacity to individuate the proper context of justification can be exercised also in the absence of perceptual consciousness. Neither condition depends upon an identification of attention with consciousness. One should finally notice that although the blindsighter has no perceptual experience of saliences as grounds for action, yet perceptual saliences exercise their normative role for him also. Although he is not conscious of them, he still refers to them as reasons for agency, and exercises the appropriate sensitivity in so referring.

REFERENCES

Bagnoli (2002) 'Moral Constructivism: A Phenomenological Argument', *Topoi* 1: 125–38.

Brandom (2000) *Articulating Reasons* (Cambridge, Mass.: Harvard University Press).

Brewer, B. (1999) *Perception and Reason* (Oxford: Oxford University Press).

Burge, T. (2003) 'Perceptual Entitlement'.

Calabi, C. (2004) 'Avoidance of Trivialization and the Given-Supplemented Divide', unpublished manuscript.

Clark, A. (1997) *Being There: Putting Brain, Body and World together Again* (Cambridge, Mass.: MIT Press).

Crane, T. (ed.) (1992a) *The Contents of Experience: Essays on Perception* (Cambridge: Cambridge University Press).

Crane T. (1992b) 'The Non-Conceptual Content of Experience', in Crane (eds.), *The Contents of Experience* (Cambridge: Cambridge University Press): 136–57.

De Sousa, R. (1987) *The Rationality of Emotions* (Cambridge, Mass.: MIT Press).

Fodor, J. A. and Pylyshyn, Z. (1981) 'How Direct is Visual Perception? Some Reflections on Gibson's "Ecological Approach" ', *Cognition* 9: 139–66.

Gibson, J. (1966) *The Senses considered as Perceptual Systems* (Boston: Houghton Mifflin).

—— (1967) 'New Reasons for Realism', *Synthese* 17: 162–72.

—— (1972) 'A Theory of Direct Visual Perception', in J. Royce and W. Rozeboom (eds.), *The Psychology of Knowing* (New York and London: Gordon and Breach), 215–27.

—— (1986) *The Ecological Approach to Visual Perception* (Hillsdale, NJ: Lawrence Erlbaum Associates).

Goldman, A. I. (1988) 'Discrimination and Perceptual Knowledge', in J. Dancy (ed.), *Perceptual Knowledge* (Oxford: Oxford University Press), 43–65.

—— (1998) *Consciousness in Action* (Cambridge, Mass.: Harvard University Press).

Hurley, S. (2001) 'Perception and Action: Alternative Views', *Synthese* 129: 3–40.

Husserl, E. (1900–1) *Logische Untersuchungen*, 1st edn. (Halle: Niemeyer); 2nd edn. *Husserliana* XVIII, XIX/1, XIX/2 (1913–21). Translation: *Logical Investigation*, trans. J. Findlay (London: Routledge & Kegan Paul, 1970).

—— (1952) Ideen zu einer reinen Phänomenologie und phänomenologischen Philosophie, ii, Husserliana IV (The Hague: Nijhoff). Translation: *Ideas Pertaining to a Pure Phenomenology and a Phenomenological Philosophy, Second Book* (Dordrecht and Boston: Kluwer).

Kelly, S. D. (2004) 'Reference and Attention: A Difficult Connection', *Philosophical Studies* 120: 277–86.

Koehler, W. (1939) *The Place of Values in a World of Facts* (London: Kegan Paul).

Mace, W. M. (2002) 'The Primacy of Ecological Realism', *Behavioural and Brain Sciences* 25: 111.

McDowell, J. (1985) 'Values and Secondary Qualities', in G. Sayre-McCord (ed.), *Essays on Moral Realism* (Cornell: Cornell University Press), 166–80.

—— (1994) *Mind and World* (Cambridge, Mass.: Harvard University Press).

—— (1998) 'Having the World in View: Sellars, Kant and Intentionality', *The Journal of Philosophy* 95/9: 431–90.

Mulligan, K. (1995) 'Perception', in D. W. Smith and B. Smith (eds.), *The Cambridge Companion to Husserl* (Cambridge: Cambridge University Press), 168–238.

Noe, A. (2000) 'Perception, Action and Nonconceptual Content', in *A Field Guide to Philosophy of Mind*, E-Symposium on Hurley's *Consciousness in Action*, http://host. unizoma3.it/Mogetti/Kant/Field/Hurleysymp_noe.htm.

Peacocke, C. (1998), 'Nonconceptual Content Defended', *Philosophy and Phenomenological Research* 58: 381–8.

—— (1999) *Being Known* (Oxford: Oxford University Press).

Reed, E. (1988) *James Gibson and the Psychology of Perception* (New Haven: Yale University Press).

Ryle, G. (1949) *The Concept of Mind* (London: Hutchinson's University Library).

—— (1964), 'Pleasure', in D. F. Gustafson (ed.), *Essays in Philosophical Psychology* (London: Macmillan): 195–205.

Searle, J. (1983) *Intentionality* (Cambridge: Cambridge University Press).

Skorupski, J. (1999) 'Irrealist Cognitivism', *Ratio* 12: 439–59.

—— (2002) 'The Ontology of Reasons', *Topoi* 21: 113–24.

Smith, D. W. (1989) *The Circle of Acquaintance* (Dordrecht: Kluwer).

Strawson (1992) *Analysis and Metaphysics* (Oxford: Oxford University Press).

Wiggins, D. (1976) 'Truth, Invention and the Meaning of Life', revised version, in G. Sayre-McCord (ed.), *Essays on Moral Realism* (Cornell: Cornell University Press), 127–65.

—— (1987) 'A Sensible Subjectivism?', in *Needs, Values and Truth* (Oxford: Basil Blackwell), 185–211.

13

Attention and Sensorimotor Intentionality

Charles Siewert

Abstract: In his *Phenomenology of Perception*, Merleau-Ponty holds that our sensory consciousness of place exhibits a kind of indeterminacy that shows it is not, properly speaking, the *representation* of space. Rather, it has what he calls 'motor intentionality', a kind of intentionality inextricable from bodily know-how. According to the interpretation and defense of this view offered here, directing visual attention involves changes to the phenomenal character of experience that cannot be specified by attributing verbal or imagistic content to it—changes that are inconceivable apart from the exercise of sensorimotor skills. And, since experience is assessable as correct or illusory in virtue of having such character, we may thus say it has *sensorimotor intentionality*. The nature of sense-experience, and what distinguishes it from verbally articulable judgment, can then be construed in terms of a distinctive form of intentionality rooted in bodily skills.

1

When contrasting *judgment* and *sensation*, or *sapience* and *sentience*, philosophers often take the first of the pair to furnish the intellect without which our senses cannot—accurately or inaccurately—show us the world. On such a view, sensation (visual, aural, tactile, etc.) has no reference or directedness to the world, no *intentionality*, but only provides material for interpretation, or triggers our beliefs. One alternative would be to hold that, while sensory experience is distinguishable from judgment or belief, it also has intentionality—albeit of its own distinctive sort.

Some recent attempts to develop the latter idea oppose the 'conceptual' intentionality of belief to the 'nonconceptual' intentionality or content of sense-experience.[1] This contrast will gain substance only by adding an account of what concepts are, and of what sensory intentionality or content is, if not conceptual. To help meet this challenge, it is tempting to assimilate sensory intentionality somehow to imagistic forms of representation: to see is to construct 'internal pictures' that represent (however faithfully or unfaithfully) an external reality.[2]

---

[1] For discussion of this by many key figures in the debate, see the articles collected in Gunther (2002). [2] See, for example, Tye (1995, 2002).

Here I want to consider a different way to affirm the distinctiveness of sensory intentionality—one that neither appeals to some conceptual/non-conceptual contrast, nor accepts anything like 'picture in the head' theories of what is special about it. On this proposal, sense-experience is not a kind of internal description, map, or picture our brains use to steer our bodies around the world. For our awareness of place is not separable, in the way this suggests, from our capacities for movement. Its appearing to us as it does is not merely contingently related to our capacity for exploratory motor activity—e.g., the sorts of head, eye, hand, and whole body movements involved in 'getting a better look' at something, and, more generally, perceiving it better or more fully. To sense where things are is to use these motor skills.

The notion that what marks sensory intentionality is its tight connection with sensorimotor know-how—what we might call the idea of *sensorimotor intentionality*—seems to have first arisen, in various forms, in the last century, and is alive and well in current philosophy of mind.[3] But I think it's fair to say we have only begun to explore proposals of this nature. Here I want to launch one expedition into this territory, taking as a point of departure some suggestions and problems in a central work of this nascent theoretical tradition—Maurice Merleau-Ponty's *Phenomenology of Perception*. While I think part of what I say does plausibly reconstruct some of his key views, that is not the main business of this essay. My primary aim is to clarify the idea of sensorimotor intentionality (or one variant of it), while illustrating how phenomenology—considered both as a historical movement, and as a style of inquiry—is relevant to contemporary philosophy of mind. My case will ultimately hinge on what phenomenological reflection reveals about visual attention and visual illusion.[4]

---

[3] My formulation of the idea of sensorimotor intentionality is indebted to reading the manuscript for Alva Noë (2004). And generally I am much indebted to many conversations over the years with Hubert Dreyfus about Merleau-Ponty's *Phenomenology of Perception* (1945/2002). Dreyfus (1992, 2001, 2002a, 2002b) has long employed Heidegger- and Merleau-Ponty-inspired considerations to argue that classically 'cognitivist' approaches to artificial intelligence are flawed by their assumption that embodiment is incidental to intelligence. Noë is one of the recent 'enactionist' theorists of perception, among whom one could also count, for example, Andy Clark, Susan Hurley, Evan Thompson, and Kevin O'Regan. (See Clark (1997); Hurley (1998); Hurley and Noë (2003); Noë, Pessoa, and Thompson (1999), O'Regan and Noë (2001).) Gibson's (1979) 'ecological' school of perceptual psychology also belongs to this current of thought. Recently, Sean Kelly (2004) has offered his own interpretation of Merleau-Pontyan 'motor intentionality', with reference to contemporary neuropsychological research, such as that of Milner and Goodale (1995). It should be noted that Merleau-Ponty's approach to sensorimotor intentionality grew out of his understanding of Husserl and Gurwitsch, and his study (and critique) of clinical and experimental research, especially that in Gestalt psychology.

[4] 'Phenomenological reflection' for me paradigmatically includes (even if it is not confined to) thought about the phenomenal character of experience, which thought enjoys that type of warrant distinctive to first-person judgments about experience. (See n. 18.) It is a central aspect of the *phenomenological tradition in philosophy*, rooted in Brentano and Husserl—as I understand it—to make use of examples, both real and hypothetical, of phenomenal experience, characterized in ways for which one can have this distinctive first-person warrant, to support general claims about what kinds of experience there are and how these interrelate—claims relevant to philosophical questions regarding, for example, consciousness, intentionality, perception, and attention. I see the argument of the present essay as belonging to the phenomenological tradition, understood in that sense. However, by these remarks, I intend to offer neither a comprehensive definition of 'phenomenological philosophy' nor a description that would apply to all that Brentano, Husserl, and those influenced by them have done under its rubric.

2

Merleau-Ponty's general notion of intentionality is expressed in a way familiar from Brentano and Husserl—intentionality is 'directedness': 'It [a sensation] is ... intentional, which means that it does not rest in itself as a thing, but that it is directed and has significance beyond itself.'[5] But, largely through considering pathological inabilities to perceive and move, Merleau-Ponty is led to distinguish a species within this genus, a kind of intentionality—which he labels 'motor intentionality', or 'motor significance'.[6] His discussion of psychopathology is intricate and elusive, but the following will, I hope, portray it accurately enough to frame the issues I want to examine.

Merleau-Ponty is fascinated by the way in which brain damage sometimes results in an inability to perform movements to order, and to engage in non-routine, self-prompted patterns of action. His star case is the patient Schneider, studied by the psychologists Gelb and Goldstein in the 1920s. While Schneider had no trouble engaging in routines with which he was already familiar—blowing his nose, lighting a match, making wallets—as the occasion for them arose, his war injury apparently left him with a variety of motor deficits. He was, for example, unable to position his arm in certain ways when asked to do so, and to pantomime acts, such as combing his hair,[7] though he sometimes tried to compensate for such deficits by clearly abnormal means: when asked to move his arm he first 'moves his whole body, and after a time his movements are confined to his arm, which [he] eventually "finds" '.[8]

Merleau-Ponty maintains that the difference between normal and abnormal cases (like Schneider's) does not entirely lie in which bodily movements can be coordinated with sense-perception. For sometimes, as in the pantomime case, there is not much to distinguish—qua mere bodily movement—what the subjects can do from what they cannot do. And the problem is not that pathological subjects fail to perceive the regions of space relevant to their motor performance. Further, we should not think that Schneider-like 'substitutions' are only slower, more labored, and inefficient versions of normal activity.[9]

To understand what's had and what's lost in such pathological cases, Merleau-Ponty thinks we need to acknowledge that there are different ways of being conscious of space. A patient can reach a certain spot in order to swat a mosquito, while unable to direct the same hand to the same spot when asked to point to it, because the former ability (the ability to grasp, reach, take hold) involves a consciousness of space different in kind from that at work in the latter (pointing) capacity.[10] And both differ from the way of being conscious of space at work in pathological substitutions. According to Merleau-Ponty, to distinguish these forms of spatial consciousness adequately, conceptual innovation is required. Fundamental to this, we need to recognize that there is a *non-representational* consciousness of place.

---

[5] Merleau-Ponty (p. 248) [All page references to Merleau-Ponty pertain to the 2002 edition of *Phenomenology of Perception*.]   [6] Merleau-Ponty (p. 127).

[7] Merleau-Ponty (pp. 118–20).   [8] Merleau-Ponty (p. 126).

[9] Merleau-Ponty (p. 124).   [10] Merleau-Ponty (pp. 118–19).

Traditional psychology has no concept to cover these varieties of consciousness of place because consciousness of place is always, for such psychology, a positional consciousness, a representation, *Vor-stellung*, because as such it gives us the place as a determination of the objective world and because a representation either is or is not, but if it is, yields the object quite unambiguously.[11]

To assess his view fully, we would need to ask whether the conclusions Merleau-Ponty draws are really warranted by the psychological evidence on which he draws, whether he adequately describes this in the first place, and how other research since his time affects his case. This would be quite a job. But the passage just quoted may lead one to wonder: how are we even to get started? There seems to be an initial problem about even understanding the thesis, prior to figuring out how one gets to it by thinking about brain damage. This idea of intentionality without representation appears odd in the context of contemporary philosophy of mind, no less than in the 'traditional psychology' of Merleau-Ponty's time. To talk about consciousness *of* a place is to speak of intentionality. But to say this is the mental *representation* of a place may seem no more than a change in terminology. And just what does this intentionality without representation have especially to do with motor abilities?

Let's try to get clearer about the challenge here, and the materials Merleau-Ponty might offer us to deal with it. He says that when one is engaged in successful sensorimotor coordination, one is conscious of 'bodily space as the matrix of [one's] habitual action, not as an objective setting'. And 'bodily space is not space thought of or represented'.[12] Again, the phrase 'motor intentionality' is coined for this type of spatial consciousness. Now, although Merleau-Ponty claims it is brought to light by consideration of abnormal cases (such as Schneider's), he clearly thinks it is found in normal movements made to order, and in spontaneous action of the sort for which Schneider has deficits. Motor intentionality is ubiquitous. It is just that its distinctiveness supposedly becomes more evident by contrast with pathological cases, which 'throw into relief' aspects of normal perception, whose very familiarity can make them difficult to distinguish.[13]

But what is it that is allegedly thrown into relief? What makes motor intentionality differ from other 'objective' kinds? It's clear that we are supposed to think of it as '*non-positional* consciousness'. While motor intentional consciousness is directed toward something or 'refers' to it, it does not '*posit*' or '*represent*' it *as an object*. Merleau-Ponty writes: 'In the action of the hand which is raised towards an object is contained a reference to the object, not as an object represented, but as that highly specific thing towards which we project ourselves, near which we are, in anticipation'.[14] That the *action of the hand* 'contains' the reference to an object hints at what is *motor* about motor intentionality. But all this leaves us with the questions: just what is the difference between object-positing and non-positional consciousness? And how can we consider the latter *intentional* without thinking of it as *representational*? The point about anticipation is important (we will return to this later). But straight off it is unclear how to construe such anticipation if not as a kind of mental representation.

---

[11] Merleau-Ponty (p. 119).   [12] Merleau-Ponty (pp. 119, 159).
[13] See Merleau-Ponty (pp. 125–6, 151).   [14] Merleau-Ponty (p. 159).

We might think the anticipation is simply a belief that something will (or is likely to) occur—and that would surely count as representational.

Merleau-Ponty does speak of motor intentionality as a non-explicit kind of consciousness.[15] So one may try appealing to the contrast between what is *explicit* and what is *implicit*, and say that one does not represent or posit something as an object, as long as one is only tacitly or implicitly (not explicitly) conscious of it. But on a common interpretation, the explicit/implicit contrast is drawn between what is *conscious* and what is not. And some will say that being explicit, and being conscious, involves accessibility to one's verbal report, or to reflection. However, this evidently won't help us make sense of Merleau-Ponty's proposal, if it gives us only a distinction between conscious and non-conscious representation. For it won't tell us how to conceive of a consciousness *of* place without regarding it as spatial representation.

Nevertheless, maybe we've found an important clue. It is central to Merleau-Ponty's philosophy to maintain that the implicit background—the 'horizon' of what we do—can never be made fully explicit, can never be fully 'thematized'.[16] Perhaps implicit consciousness is non-representational insofar as something about it inherently resists being made fully explicit—that is, fully articulated in verbalized reflection. However, here we risk ascending too soon to the grander themes of Merleau-Ponty's philosophy, and of existential phenomenology in general: the idea that our way of being-in-the-world defies any attempt to articulate it in a detached, theoretical conception. But we're unlikely to make headway by directly taking on this thesis about being-in-the-world, and attempting to clarify and reconstruct in an entirely general way these related notions (of 'horizon' and 'thematizing'), which Merleau-Ponty draws from Husserl and Gurwitsch.[17] We will, I believe, eventually be more likely to understand the grand claim, if we first get a grip on how it may emerge from the humble sensory case.

Although I will now turn the focus away from reconstruction of Merleau-Ponty's view, I will not set it completely aside, for I will suggest a view of sensorimotor intentionality which I believe is consonant with and supports Merleau-Ponty's, guided by ideas and examples drawn from his work. And I will make use of two clues gathered thus far: first, the suggestion that, in some sense, the 'horizon' of one's sensory experience of a thing cannot be made fully explicit; and second, the notion that in our sensorimotor activity we 'anticipate' something without *representing* what we anticipate. My route to sensorimotor intentionality will differ from Merleau-Ponty's, since I will appeal to aspects of vision we can appreciate without recourse to philosophical psychopathology. I do not by any means dismiss that approach, but it may not be the best way to start, and involves complications we can avoid if we work from normal, shared experience more straightforwardly accessible to phenomenological reflection.

15 See, for example, the note on representation and consciousness in Merleau-Ponty, p. 160.
16 See, e.g., p. 70: '[T]he phenomenal field as we have revealed it . . . places a fundamental difficulty in the way of any attempt to make experience directly and totally explicit.'
17 See Gurwitsch (1964). For a helpful treatment of Husserl's notion of 'horizon', see Smith and MacIntyre (1982).

3

So: we are looking for a way to think of an aspect of sensory experience as in some sense *intentional*, without regarding it as representational, and to think of its intentionality as essentially bound up with motor skills. Let's start with the Merleau-Pontyan idea that, in sense-experience, there is a consciousness of place that resists being rendered fully explicit. Now at least one way—paradigmatically—to make your sensory experience explicit is to *say what you experience*. To do that, we might think, is to attribute to the experience the content expressed by your utterance of a sentence. For example, I say, 'It looks to me as if the circle on the left is larger than the circle on the right', and thereby attribute to my experience the content I express by uttering the sentence 'The circle on the left is larger than the circle on the right'. Now if you could (in principle) say *everything* you experience, then you could make your perception fully explicit. On the other hand, suppose there are differences in your experience, differences (let us now say) in its *phenomenal* or *experiential* character,[18] which cannot be distinguished, in thought, by attributing different linguistically expressible contents to them. Then you cannot, in that way at least, make fully explicit what you perceptually experience.

There may be other ways of making the differences in what one experiences explicit. Instead of attributing to experience a verbally expressible content, one might attribute to it the contents of some imagistic representation, map, picture, or diagram. One might do this by constructing or pointing at some such representation and saying: 'This is how it looked to me'. Or one might say: 'The way it looked to me is

---

[18] What do I mean by 'phenomenal or experiential character'? I mean: that respect in which phenomenally conscious experiences (and *only* these) may differ from one another, which is distinguishable in first-person judgments enjoying the kind of warrant that is peculiar to them. Hence differences in phenomenal character are 'subjectively discernible', and accessible to 'first-person reflection'. I do not take this to entail that first-person judgments about phenomenal character are infallible. Differences in phenomenal character are, in a sense, differences in how it appears or seems to one. We might otherwise describe them as differences in the way it seems to have various experiences, or differences in *what it's like* to have an experience, *for* one who has it. For example: a difference between the way it feels to you to be in pain, and the way it feels to you to have an itch, or a difference between the way red and green look to you. But in my view differences in phenomenal character extend to much more than this. They include differences in the way a drawing looks in a 'gestalt switch' and the way it seems to us to think non-imagistic verbally expressible thoughts. (See Siewert 1998: chs. 6–8.)

Although I reject the notion that differences in phenomenal character are purely qualitative non-intentional aspects of mental life, I do recognize that not all differences reportable as differences in the way it *looks* to someone need be differences in the phenomenal character of visual experience. (For example, Bobby may look to you about twelve, though he looks older to me—but this doesn't entail that our visual experiences differ in phenomenal character.) For the purposes of this essay, context will have to help make clear when I am claiming that a difference in how it looks to someone constitutes a difference in the phenomenal character of experience.

My notion of 'phenomenal character' is also, obviously, dependent on my interpretation of 'phenomenal consciousness'. Phenomenal consciousness, as I understand it, is both: (1) a feature shared (at a minimum) by experiences of its looking, feeling, sounding, tasting, and smelling some way to someone, and by corresponding modalities of imagery; and (2) a feature whose occurrence one would deny who maintained that certain kinds of 'blindsight' discriminatory abilities in its absence are conceptually or metaphysically impossible. For more details, see Siewert (1998: chs. 3 and 4).

how it is pictured or represented to be in this image (map, diagram)'. Whether we use words or images here, we may say that, if both are representations, and have representational content, we are specifying differences among experiences by attributing to them representational contents.

Now consider the following four claims.

(a) All differences in representational content of visual experience are, in principle, expressible by means of language or images.

(b) The phenomenal character of some of our experiences differs in ways we have reason to think cannot be specified by attributing distinct representational contents to the experiences.

(c) Nonetheless, in virtue of having such phenomenal character, some experience is assessable as illusory, or (by contrast) as correct or accurate—and thus has intentionality.

(d) The character of some of our experience that is intentional, but eludes representational specification, is such that, necessarily, one has this sort of experience only if one has appropriate sensorimotor skills.

If we can understand and support (a)–(d), we will have one way of rendering more precise and defending the idea of sensorimotor intentionality, vaguely indicated above in Section 1, and a way of addressing some of the problems identified for Merleau-Ponty's views in Section 2.

I will not say too much about thesis (a). Here I will stipulate that in-principle-expressibility in the form of language or images is constitutive of the notion of visual representational content, and that the notion of a visual representation is the notion of something with content thus expressible. Admittedly, the use of 'representation' is somewhat up for grabs. And the notions of content, and of expressibility in language or images, themselves need elucidation. But I hope it is clear that I understand such expressibility as subject to broad construal, so as to include the 'sentence-like' and 'image-like' forms of representation that are hypothesized to inhabit our brains. If you use the term 'visual representation' more widely than I do here, then you can simply interpret my remarks to apply only to my stipulated sense. It will then be a further question whether the concerns I raise ultimately apply to visual representation in your sense.

In the rest of this section I will say a little to explain (b), and why one might think there are differences in the character of experience that cannot be tied to differences in representational content. For current purposes, it is important to do this in a way that does not suggest that these are 'non-intentional', purely 'qualitative' differences, since I want to set the stage for (c)—the claim that experience has intentionality in virtue of having such character.

Consider now the difference between the way something you are looking *at*—and focusing your attention *on*—looks to you, and the way *what surrounds it* looks to you (which you are attending to less). One may note a difference in the phenomenal character of the experience here. Further, one may note that the way the 'less-attended-to' looks is not homogenous. What surrounds what you are looking at does not look all the same (as would a uniformly lit and unvariegated expanse of color), and normally the way the less-attended-to surroundings look to you is often—almost constantly—changing.

One is hard-pressed to *say* what all the relevant differences in ways of looking *are*, by plugging some sentence into a locution of the form 'It looks to me as if...'. In other words, it is difficult, on the basis of first-person thought, to specify precisely the differences in phenomenal character of which one is aware, by attributing verbally expressible contents to the experience. If one tries to specify, in a verbalized, content-attributing thought, the differences among the ways in which the relatively unattended background looks (at a time, over time), one will be tempted to shift one's attention to what lies in the unattended background of the (formerly focal) object. But the verbal specification one then gives will be based on experience one has after redirecting attention. And this—first-person reflection itself tells us—does not have the very same phenomenal character as the experience one had of that region when one attended less to it. That is to say, the effort to specify the character of the less attentive experience by attributing content to it invites a redirection of attention that risks *assimilating* the prior experience *to*—and not *distinguishing* it *from*—a more attentive experience that differs from it in phenomenal character. Further examination will, I believe, reveal this difficulty is not a superficial one.

Consider an example offered by Merleau-Ponty, meant to contrast the normal direction of visual attention with the use of cinematic close-up.

When, in a film, the camera is trained on an object and moves nearer to it to give a close-up view, we can *remember* that we are being shown the ashtray or an actor's hand, but we do not actually identify it...In normal vision, on the other hand, I direct my gaze upon a sector of the landscape, which comes to life and is disclosed, while the other objects recede into the periphery and become dormant, while, however, not ceasing to be there.[19]

For Merleau-Ponty, this contrast between, on the one hand, the normal visual identification of a thing (as a hand, or an ashtray) through the direction of attention to what had lain in the perceptual 'horizon', and, on the other, the use of close-up in film to zoom in on an object, highlights something generally distinctive about the operation of visual attention and the nature of the perceptual horizon. He says that the film, unlike normal vision, 'has no horizons'. Without trying to explain the notion of horizon generally, or just what it means to say that a film has no horizon, I think we can glean some insights that will help to make the case that there are experiential differences not specifiable through attributions of representational content.

A key suggestion I take from the passage above is this. In the cinematic case invoked, when we see the ashtray (for example) in a close-up, we remember that what now looks to us like an ashtray *was* what looked to us like an ashtray a moment before, only then seen in less detail, now more. But this is unlike the process of normal visual identification. In such a case, I turn my attention to an object that had formerly been in the less attended but still visually apparent surroundings of what I was looking at, so as to identify it, to see it *as* some F (an ashtray, a hand). But I do not remember its

[19] Merleau-Ponty (p. 78).

having looked to me as if there was an ashtray (or whatever) *before* directing my attention there. As near as I can remember, it did not look to me as if there was an F, until I turned my attention there. At least this is often what happens. (This will perhaps be clearest if you think of entering a room for the first time, and looking around at what is there.) I take it that this is commonplace: you turn your attention to look at what formerly lay merely in the visually apparent surroundings of what you *were* looking at. And, in doing so, you attend to what *was* unidentified—what as yet did not look to you as if it was an F—and *then* you do identify it as an F, and it then looks to you as if it is an F.

How are we to specify the character of what we might call the *pre-identification* experience of the visual background? One might acknowledge that, if I am (at t_2) visually identifying (and not *re*-identifying) something as an ashtray, which had been in the visually apparent surroundings at t_1, then at t_1 it did not look to me as if there was an ashtray there. More generally, if I am visually identifying it as an F, it did not look to me as it was an F, prior to the identification, while it lay in the experiential background. Still, one might propose, there was *some G*, such that it looked to me as if it was a G, before I directed enough attention to it to see it as an F. My claim here is otherwise. There is often much lying in the relatively unattended visual background (the 'horizon') that we can (for some F), through directing attention, identify as an F, even though prior to this there was no G we can remember, such that it then looked to us as if there was a G just there.

Perhaps this merely reveals a faulty memory: even if I cannot recall it, before visually identifying what lies in the surroundings as an F, there always is in fact some G, such that it looks to one as if it's a G. But the problem is not just that this hypothesizes *ad hoc* lapses in experiential memory (though that is bad enough). It also fails as a way of representationally specifying differences in the character of experience. It seems that, for any G we care to propose for the role of what we visually identified the marginally viewed F *as*, prior to identifying it *as an F*, there will still be a discernible difference in character between this experience and the experience one has of something as a G when one is looking *at* it. So, suppose prior to its looking to you as if there's an ashtray, someone suggests that it looked to you as if there was (e.g.) a roundish thing there (in the then-unattended surroundings). And suppose, for the sake of the argument, we granted this suggestion (though otherwise I would not). Still, there would be a difference between the character of *that* experience 'as of a roundish thing', and the character of a similarly describable experience typically had when you are looking *right at* a roundish thing. And *this* difference in the character of experience is evidently not captured.

The general point is this. There is a difference in character between the inattentive experience of the visually apparent surroundings of what you are looking at, and the attentive experience of what you are looking at. And we cannot successfully specify this difference by employing, in the former case, some predicate to say what something in the background looks to you to be, or what it looked to you as if it was. Nor can we rightly say, for some G, that it looked G to you. For, either such would-be specifications of the character of experience will just be false (for it did not begin to look to you this way until you paid more attention), or else they will leave the character of the experience in question undifferentiated from that of the (more attentive) experience that occurs when one does look *at* something in the relevant area. Thus we have reason to think that there are differences in the phenomenal character of visual experiences, even when these cannot be specified by attributing verbally expressible content.

But perhaps those elusive differences can be captured by attributing to experience a *different sort* of representational content—the sort expressed not in words, but in *images*. How would this work for the kind of cases I've been discussing? Suppose one tried to create an image of how the less attended-to surroundings looked to one, prior to one's visual identification of what was there. One might, as with the close-up/ zooming-in technique, try to do this by making what lay in the background first take up *less*, then gradually *more* room in one's depiction. But this is a non-starter. For clearly there are cases where you turn your attention to what lay in the visual apparent background, though there is no temptation to suppose that the newly attended-to item in some sense *takes up more room in your visual field* (as there might be, in a situation where you attended to an object by moving nearer to get a better look).

So let's pursue a different suggestion. We may make relatively higher or lower resolution images—blurrier or sharper images—and propose that the relevant differences in the character of experience of some area can be captured by the right contrast between the contents of lower and higher resolution images of it. Now it is true of course that when one looks at what had been visually apparent but unattended-to, one has in some sense a clearer, less blurry experience of what is there, and generally vision has greater acuity when one is looking at something than when one is not. But this alone doesn't show that the character distinguishing relatively less attentive experience can be specified by attributing to it the content of some relatively low resolution image.

Suppose you are, for a few moments, looking at a book lying on a table, surrounded by other books, papers, and various household clutter. Your gaze shifts from the book to a glass on the table and then to a pen. As you looked at each of these things, you attended more to them than you had just before, and some of the area *around* the things looked some way to you, even though a good part of this area contained nothing that you then looked at and attended to nearly as much as you did to the book, the glass, and the pen—when you did this. As this little episode (or some similar one) occurs, the phenomenal character of your visual experience is changing, and you can be aware of this. As your gaze shifts, there are changes, both in how *what you're looking at* looks, and in how *what you're not looking at* looks. Can these changes in experiential character be specified by attributing to your experience the content of an image that varies in degree of resolution?

Imagine the task of making a film that creates such an image for some brief episode of visual experience, of the kind just illustrated. In making this image you have unlimited ability to fine-tune what parts of the area filmed are represented with just what degree of resolution and when, so as to correspond to the change in the character of your experience as you shifted your attention and looked at different things. You can also alter the framing of the shot, supposing that you can, by doing this, make an image whose edges will correspond to the changing limits of your 'field' of visual experience, as you shift your gaze from one thing to the next.

Many possible films would be quite hopeless candidates. They clearly would not furnish an image whose content would allow you to specify the changes in character of your experience. But consider those that are at least in the neighborhood of getting it right, if any are. Would there be any way in principle of narrowing their range so as to find the image that faithfully tracks the shifts in your attention by changes in resolution and framing? Just which of various possible levels of resolution will match how the area around the book appeared to you when you were looking at the book and then shifted your gaze to the glass? I think it's clear that one should not employ such a low degree of resolution that the image dissolves into a uniform undifferentiated blur. And clearly it would be wrong to raise the resolution very close to the level of the image that corresponds to the book when you are looking right at it. But where in between these extremes do we stop? And how exactly are we to choose among various ways of framing the shot to get the one which matches the 'boundaries' of the visual field?[20] It seems that there would be many different ways of altering the resolution of the image and its boundaries, such that you would have no more warrant for thinking *one* of these corresponded to the change in character of your experience than another did. However, if change in the character of your visual experience while you were looking—now at this, now at that, now at the other thing—is specifiable by attributing to your experience content expressible in images of varying degrees of resolution, then all of the candidates can't be right.

Similar problems of indeterminacy would afflict attempts to find the right character-specifying image content, not by varying the resolution of the image ('blurring it') but just by leaving 'gaps' or 'holes' in what it represents about the environment, much as a picture (without being blurry) might simply lack information about certain aspects of the objects' spatial configuration and relationships. For there will, it seems, be many ways to impoverish the information the image contains about the relevant section of the subject's environment, each with as good (or bad) a claim to provide the character-specifying content of one's visual experience of the less attended portions of the area visually apparent to one. And it won't do simply to say that the representational content of the visual experience is poor, sparse, or gappy. For this won't provide a representational specification of the differences in character among different inattentive visual experiences.[21]

---

[20] Merleau-Ponty (p. 6) discusses the problem of drawing the 'boundaries' of the visual field. Noë, Pessoa, and Thompson (1999) also raise this issue (with reference to Merleau-Ponty).

[21] One might think the challenge I am raising here could be met in principle. Suppose we could arrange for subjects repeatedly to have experiences with precisely the same character as the target for which we seek some character-specifying representational content. Then we could alter the stimulus conditions in various ways and ask subjects whether they can tell the difference in what they are experiencing, and what kinds of differences they can report. Perhaps, in something like this manner, we could narrow down the choice of image-content, so as to find the right degree and sort of representational poverty to attribute to the original target experience.

But problems arise. For one, there probably would still be changes in one's experience of what one is not looking at, which one could report as changes, without being able to say in exactly what respect what one experienced changed. And it's not clear that merely by getting subjective sameness/differences judgments we will be able to assign some specific image content to the experience of what we are not looking at. Furthermore, how are we, even in theory, to get suitable repetitions of the same type experience? For consider: are the subjects supposed to be able to remember previous trials in which they had experiences of ostensibly the same type? If they do, then this will affect how well they

Maybe we will imagine that the problem of specifying experiential character by representational content stems from reliance on subjective reports, and we will look for some way of determining the correct character-specifying content for the experience without this, by looking at what is going on in the subject's brain. However, that would appear to help us to decide the case only if this very sort of problem had already been solved on previous occasions, where the findings had been put into correspondence with observations of the brain that would (only then) permit one to 'read' people's 'visual images' off images of their brains. And it would seem that establishing the original correlations would need the very reliance on subjective reports that brain scans were enlisted to avoid.

Is all this *merely* a problem of inadequate evidence? This would be the right attitude to take, only if we had reason to be confident that one of the possible candidate images *must* be the right character-specifying one, even if we can't tell *which* one is. But there is nothing that guarantees that there *is* an image whose content will express the changes in the character of your visual experience as attention shifts. In the absence of a convincing reason to think that some such image must do the job, we should take a high degree of indeterminacy in matching image to experiential character as reason to think that no image does.

The basic problem here is how to specify representationally (in either words or images) the change in phenomenal character that occurs when you look at what lies in an area that had already just looked some way to you. Let's label this 'the problem of attentive difference'. It seems that there are changes in the phenomenal character of spatial experience that we have reason to believe elude such specification.[22]

are able to distinguish what they are experiencing in subsequent trials. That is, they will become better able to distinguish what they are experiencing. But then this will probably also interfere with the goal of repeating experiences that are of the same type as the original target of content attribution. For as memory aids one's ability to attend to differences in the stimulus array, the experiences themselves change in character. At the very least, there is no reason to be confident that the purported 'repetitions' really would instantiate the same phenomenal character. For increased attention to the same visual stimuli does at least sometimes change the way they look to one on subsequent occasions— even if the direction of one's gaze is the same. And memory of past trials will enable one to attend more to the stimuli in question over time.

Suppose then that we imagine there is some way of erasing all memory of previous trials and any effect this might have on subsequent discriminations. But even then the worry arises that the subjects' trying to notice differences between the 'repeated' experience, and experiences that vary from it in stimulus conditions will affect the character of the would-be repetitions so as to make them fail as authentic reproductions of the target. Further, we will now not be able to rely on subjects' reports to determine whether we're succeeding in reproducing the character of the original, since *ex hypothesi*, they don't remember their previous experiences. And, on top of that, there is no reason to think that by producing contrived episodes of experience purified of the effects of recent memory, one will produce an experience of the same character as the original experience that occurred in a different, natural context. The general problem here is that we don't seem to have a way of determining what about the context of the original, target experience needs to be duplicated in order to get subsequent experiences that are genuinely the same in character. But without this, there seems to be no way to use repetitions and varying stimulus conditions to narrow down assignment of content, and remove the indeterminacy we first encountered in considering natural, ordinary circumstances.

[22] Compare Merleau-Ponty (p. 35): 'To pay attention is not merely to elucidate pre-existing data, it is to bring about a new articulation of them by taking them as figures. . . . [A]ttention is neither an association of images, nor the return to itself of thought already in control of its objects, but the active constitution of a new object which makes explicit and articulate what was until then presented as no more than an indeterminate horizon.'

Here I do assume we ordinarily have visual experience of areas in which there is nothing we are then focusing our attention on. This might seem disputable. For it has sometimes been denied—by philosophers and psychologists—that we have visual experience of anything but what we focus attention on.[23] And they have claimed that empirical evidence explodes some allegedly common-sense impression that we visually represent in uniform detail all of the area that visually appears to us—that looks some way to us—during a given time. This then, in turn, is taken to show that visual experience is not rich—as we naively think—but poor, sparse, and gappy.[24] I have argued elsewhere that the evidence does not warrant restricting visual experience to the focus of attention, and it is a mistake to attribute to common sense such an exaggerated idea of the detail of the visual experience of our surroundings. (In any case, any such notion is easily corrected by a little clear-headed first-person reflection.)[25] Here I have maintained that what is evident to first-person or phenomenological reflection on visual appearance is neither some uniformly detailed visual representation of space, nor a radically impoverished one, but rather an experience whose changes in phenomenal character resist being specified in a correlatively rich (or poor) representation. The experimental research that allegedly shows the poverty of consciousness actually shows this, only if we assume that differences in experiential character are no richer than what may be reflected in attributing representational content to experience. But the data in question, taken together with phenomenological reflection, should instead make us doubt that very assumption. If changes in experience are not captured by differences in descriptions or images, perhaps this reveals not the poverty of experience, but the poverty of theories that require us to conceptualize experience as internal sentences or images.

4

I have argued that we can recognize differences in phenomenal character without thinking of them as representational differences. The challenge now is to argue that experience has intentionality in virtue of its phenomenal character, even in such cases. Here I will assume that an experience has intentionality in virtue of its phenomenal character, if in virtue of having it, there are conditions under which the experience would be *illusory* (incorrect, inaccurate).[26] I want to extend the discussion now to cases where shifts in visual attention enable us to recognize visual illusions—occasions where, through attending more to what we had previously not had 'a good enough look at', we find that we were subject, however fleetingly, to a form of visual illusion.

Merleau-Ponty offers an example of this in his description of a visual experience had while walking on a path, illuminated in patches by the sunlight (maybe coming

---

[23] Noë (2002), Mack and Rock (1998).   [24] Dennett (1991).   [25] Siewert (2002).
[26] By saying that it is 'in virtue of' its phenomenal character that an experience is assessable as illusory or correct, I mean to say that, given its possession of this character, there is nothing that need be added to the experience that has the status of an *interpretation* for its illusoriness or correctness to follow—in the sense in which an interpretation *does* need to be added to a *verbal utterance* or an *image*, if anything is to follow regarding whether it correctly or incorrectly represents something. (See Siewert 1998: ch 5.)

through overhanging trees).[27] First it looks to you as if there is a stone on the path ahead. But, on a closer look, this appears only to be a more brightly illuminated area of the path—more brightly illuminated on account of the way the sunlight comes down through the foliage. Thus the way it *first* looked to you was revealed as incorrect by how it *subsequently* looked to you. Another example mentioned by Merleau-Ponty is pertinent. A ship has run aground in the sand before a forest. When first you look in its direction (what turn out to be its) masts appear as more trees in the forest. But as you look a little more, the masts appear to stand out from the trees in the background, and to belong to the ship.[28] In such a case, you can recognize that the way it first looked to you was wrong.

If we are alert, we can, I think, recognize similar illusions in our own experience. Once, when leaving a building, what turned out to be part of a bicycle frame looked to me momentarily as if it was a part of the bike rack to which it was locked. As I looked a little more, the spatial layout of the bike and rack appeared to me discernibly different— and *what* was a part of *what*, and how the bike-frame and rack were spatially related, then appeared to me correctly. In another case, an orange cord that first (inaccurately) looked to me as if it was lying on the pavement ahead then—when I got a better look—appeared to me (correctly) to be pulled tight a little above the surface. Similarly, illusions of motion sometimes arise naturally, and are exposed as such with a little more attention. Once, in the evening after a rain, light from passing cars reflected on the water in a gutter made it (wrongly) look to me as if the water was moving. Then it appeared to me as if (and then I saw that), actually, patterns of light were changing on water that was still.

Such cases of visual illusion differ from many of those familiar from drawings in psychology textbooks (where figures appear larger or smaller than they are, or curved when actually straight). In these we cannot recognize the illusion just by looking harder—by getting a better look. We need to make a measurement against some standard, or to remove or hide lines or figures that give rise to the illusion. In the kind of case just illustrated, however, the illusions become recognizable without such strategies, through awareness of relevant changes in the character of one's experience, as one attends better or more closely to what one sees. Even in the 'textbook' cases awareness of phenomenal character has a part in exposing the illusion. The figures appear not to bend, grow, or shrink as one measures them or alters the auxiliary lines or figures— and this is crucial in revealing the illusions. However, let's focus now on illusions of the kind illustrated earlier, which are recognizable as such just by getting a better look at something. These I'll call 'phenomenally corrigible illusions'.

Notice that, with these, the character of the earlier, less attentive visual experience that is exposed as illusory also resists representational specification in the ways previously

[27] Merleau-Ponty's description (p. 346): 'If on a sunken path, I think I can see, some distance away, a broad, flat stone on the ground, which is in reality a patch of sunlight, I cannot say that I ever see the flat stone in the sense in which I am to see, as I draw nearer, the patch of sunlight. The flat stone, like all things at a distance, appears only in a field of confused structure in which connections are not yet clearly articulated.'

[28] His description: 'If I walk along a shore towards a ship which has run aground, and the . . . masts merge into the forest bordering on the sand dune' (p. 20).

considered. It is difficult to say what distinguishes that phenomenal character from others from which it is subjectively discernible, by attributing to the experience verbal or image content. One can, as above, say 'It looked to me as if there was a stone on the path'; or 'as if there were just more trees there'; or 'as if an orange cord was lying on the ground'. But such content attributions would not suffice to distinguish the character of the experience from that of other, more attentive experiences. I described the way the path ahead first (less attentively) looked, by saying 'It looks to you as if there is a stone on the path ahead'. But this way of describing the experience might apply equally well to another experience that differed markedly from it in phenomenal character: for example, an experience had when standing nearer some area on the path where there actually is a stone, and getting a good look at it.

An attempt to attribute the content of an image to the experience would seem to run up against the same problem. Any image rich enough to be a plausible candidate could serve at least equally well as an image of what was seen when one looked more attentively at something, though the difference in experiential character is subjectively discernible. In order to give the image the content of a false representation of the relevant configuration and relative spatial distribution of objects and their surfaces, one must put in enough detail to remove ambiguities that would leave its content indistinguishable from a *correct* representation of the scene (e.g. we need to make it definitely an image of a cord *lying on the ground*, not suspended above it). And such an image will as well express the content attributable to the visual experience of a better (more attentive) look at a cord (or trees, or a bike rack, or what-have-you). An image might, for example, represent a specific part of one bike frame as merging into a specific part of the bike rack—but the way the frame looked to me continuous with the rack when I experienced the illusion was not that definite and specific. The resultant image would express as well or better the content attributable to a more attentive, sustained look at a bike rack and frame that really *were* melded together at the relevant point. But the character of that experience would be different.

Here it seems we have an experience (the earlier less attentive look at the path up ahead, and of the bike rack at first glance, and so on) whose phenomenal character makes it assessable as illusory, as inaccurate, though it eludes representational specification. Thus we can, in a sense, affirm that some experience is intentional in virtue of having the phenomenal character it does, even if we do not regard it as representationally specifiable.[29]

5

So far so good, perhaps. But how does any of this shed light on what is essentially 'motor' about the kind of intentionality exhibited by such experience? To get to this, I need first to return to the idea—emphasized earlier in the discussion of Merleau-Ponty—that,

---

[29] My point is not that it would be false to attribute to the relatively inattentive experience the content 'as of a stone'. The point is just that this does not specify its character, so as to differentiate it from the character of other more attentive experience. We may say that both 'have' the content expressed by these words. But what it is for the experience to have the content is not in each case just the same.

as we perceive, we in some sense 'anticipate' how we will further experience things. The examples of phenomenally corrigible illusions may work to illustrate this idea. In each case—the stone on the path, the masts on the ship, the bike and bike rack, etc.— an earlier experience is recognized as illusory, because later (as one got a better look at what was being experienced) it did not look quite as one had *expected* or *anticipated* it would look. I will assume that this way of talking is in *some* sense correct; you can judge your experience to have been illusory only because later experience was 'not as expected'. The question is: in what sense is this so? What is the nature of this sensory expectation whose frustration enables us to judge when we have been subject to visual illusion?

We need to clarify a few points. First, if one has expectations of experience that are frustrated when one discovers a phenomenally corrigible illusion, one also has expectations that are *fulfilled*, as the accuracy of one's experience is confirmed.[30] Second, *what* one expects, experience-wise, is somehow contingent on what one *does*. In cases where my experience turns out 'as expected', it won't be true that I expected experience to be as it was, willy-nilly, *regardless of what I did*. For there are many ways of having acted differently such that, had I acted in *those* ways without having the experience in question, my experience would not have violated expectations. We can say this while leaving open for now in what *way* one's expectations of further experience depend on motor activity. But (third) we can say at least this much: the relevant activity is the sort needed to get a 'better look' at something, or more generally, to sense things better or more fully. Our capacity for such activity is the sort of *motor* skill whose exercise is needed if one is to have *sense-experience* enabling one to make phenomenally based assessments of the accuracy of one's experience. For this reason it is appropriate to call these *sensorimotor* skills. And I propose that we label that sort of expectation whose frustration enables one to discover visual illusion, and whose fulfillment allows one to confirm one's experience as correct, a 'sensorimotor *anticipation*'.

Now, whatever such 'anticipations' amount to, they need to be distinguished from representation of the following sort. On my birthday you hand me a package wrapped in shiny paper tied up with ribbons. There is some way I believe it will look, if I open it up. In particular, I believe that it will look like there is something inside. In a sense then, I *expect* it will look as if there's something inside, when I open it up to get a better look. But now suppose this expectation is disappointed: when I open the package, I find nothing inside. However, frustration of *this* kind of expectation (unlike that in the cases of the stone on the path, the bike rack, etc.) does nothing to show that the initial appearance of the package to me was somehow illusory—nothing to impugn the accuracy of my visual experience.

---

[30] Of the ship illusion, Merleau-Ponty (p. 20) writes: 'there will be a moment when these details [the masts] suddenly become part of the ship and indissolubly fused with it. As I approached I did not perceive the resemblances or proximities which finally came together to form a continuous picture of the upper part of the ship. I merely felt that the look of the object was on the point of altering, that something was imminent in the tension, as a storm is imminent in the storm clouds. Suddenly the sight before me was recast in a manner satisfying to my vague expectation. Only afterwards did I recognize, as justifications for the change, the resemblance and contiguity of what I call "stimuli" . . .'.

In what does the difference lie? Apparently it lies in the fact that, in the birthday case, there is a way it *looks* to me that I can distinguish from a *belief* of the form: if I do such and such, then it will look thus and so to me, which belief I hold because of how it now looks to me. I can distinguish a manner of visual appearance from a belief of the sort I hold on account of it, because I can conceive of its still looking to me in this manner, even if I did not hold this belief. The belief/expectation is in a certain way *optional* relative to the appearance. It was, if you like, an interpretation of the way things are, based on how it appeared to me, and not part of the appearance itself. Where my expectation of how it will appear to me consists in an 'appearance detachable' representation of this nature, disappointment of the expectation will not be illusion-revealing.

But perhaps sensorimotor anticipations are still representations of how it will look to me if I do certain things. It's just that they are not 'detachable', but an inseparable *part of* the appearances themselves. If so, then maybe the problem of attentive difference has an answer after all. Maybe we *can* specify the character of experience by attributing representational content to it, provided we employ content expressible in the form of certain 'sensorimotor conditionals': 'It looks to me as if it *will* look to me thus and so, *if* I do such and such'.[31]

Will this work? We need to ask how we can identify the relevant sensorimotor conditionals. How do I determine how to fill in the 'thus and so's' and 'such and suches' of the conditionals? It seems to me that I have no way of identifying how it looks to me as if it *will* look, *if* I do certain things, and what those 'certain things' are, other than the following. I actually *do* what I am disposed to do to get a better look at something, and take doing *that* as an illustration of the kind of activity that belongs in the antecedent of the conditional, and the resultant experience (if I am not surprised by it) as an instance of the sort of experience that should be covered by the consequent. I can attribute such content to the experience only in this manner, retrospectively: I act in accordance with my sensorimotor anticipations and project some identification of the results back into the past experience as content.

Now, if I identify the sort of activity that is to figure in the antecedent of the conditional only by providing myself with an example ('if, for instance, I do, *this*'), then that will give me no conception of the *other* movements that would have satisfied my prior anticipations equally well. Nor will such exemplification give me a conception of the *additional sensory consequents* ('then it will look *this* way') to be paired with those motor antecedents. So—the exemplars I furnish for myself give me no basis for the generalization needed to give the relevant content to the conditional. The only evident means by which I can warrant attributing to my prior experience the content of a conditional, so as to construe my sensorimotor anticipations as representations, will not enable me to capture the *range* of circumstances that would constitute my sensorimotor history turning out either 'as anticipated' or 'contrary to what I anticipated'. Thus if my anticipations are construed in this way, the representational content alleged to distinguish them will be inaccessible.

[31] Susanna Siegel (unpublished) argues that the character of visual experience is to be understood partly by attributing to it the content of what I call a sensorimotor conditional—though her view does not go as far with this as the view I discuss here.

There is this further problem with determining the content of the sensory consequent. When I try to get a better look at something, I may well recognize the resultant experience as 'not contrary' to what I anticipated. But that experience, in all its specificity of character, I will also recognize as nothing I *positively anticipated*. I can't say I already expected it to look just *this* way. The way it turns out to look always goes beyond anything I anticipated. So this means by which I try to access the purported content of my earlier anticipation will use an illustrative experience whose content will not match any I might reasonably think belongs to the relevant sensory consequents of those conditionals I am using it to identify. I conclude that we cannot solve the problem of attentive difference by trying to specify differences in character through attributing to experience the content of sensorimotor conditionals.

But how then are we to construe sensorimotor anticipation, if we do not see it as the representation of sensorimotor conditionals? We may be tempted at this point to junk the idea of sensorimotor anticipation altogether. But there is a better alternative. Consider first that, even if we have no way of representing to ourselves what patterns of movements we can or do execute in the course of exercising our sensorimotor skills, even if we have no right to think these representations lie hidden in the character of our experience, still we unquestionably do have and exercise the relevant skills. There is at least that much to work with. Now, instead of supposing that your sensorimotor anticipation is a representation of what experience you will have, contingent on what motor activity you engage in, try supposing that *such activity itself*, and your shifting dispositions to engage in it, constitute your anticipation of further experience. That is to say, sensorimotor anticipation can be found in motor activity *anticipatory of* further experience.

Think here of the anticipatory movements you make in reaching for something—a glass, a doorknob, a pen. The movements are appropriate to the size, shape, and location of these things—they are the right movements to make for getting a hold of them. But the movements are also appropriate to the way the size, shape, and location of the things will feel to you, once your hand has completed its trajectory. For if they were not, you would not say they were the right movements for getting to the glass, the doorknob, or what-have-you.[32] And, if they were not, you could say your movements anticipated a rather different sort of experience than what actually occurred.

I suggest we think similarly of the cases of visual illusion that led me to discuss sensorimotor anticipation. That is, when you look at the path ahead, and it looks to you as if there's a stone there, then as you continue to cast your gaze up that way, how you actually move and become more likely (or prepared or set) to move your eyes and your body as a whole anticipates the experience of a stone on the path up there.[33] We might interpret this to mean: these movements and tendencies to move are among those suitable for enabling you to have experience by which you could confirm the

[32] Compare Merleau-Ponty (p. 119): 'From the outset the grasping movement is magically at its completion; it can begin only by anticipating its end, since to disallow taking hold is sufficient to inhibit the action.'

[33] Merleau-Ponty (p. 346) describes it this way: 'I see the illusory stone in the sense that my whole perceptual and motor field endows the bright spot with the significance "stone on the path". And already I prepare to feel under my foot this smooth, firm surface.'

accuracy of your previous experience of the path up ahead. (Of course you may not then be *intending* to confirm anything.) Thus when the accuracy of your later experience turns out to be incompatible with that of previous appearance, it turns out too that your sensorimotor activity and dispositions anticipated experience *other* than what you came to have; hence your experience was not 'as anticipated'. In that sense then, your sensorimotor anticipations can be frustrated or disappointed.[34]

On this way of construing sensorimotor anticipation, you need not represent to yourself (or in your brain) the execution of a certain motor program, and some further course of experience conditional on it. The anticipation of experience can be found in the way you move and are ready to move, and in the fact that such patterns of movement constitute the exercise of sensorimotor skills of the kind suitable to give you that experience by which you could assess the accuracy of previous experience. As long as the problem of attentive difference persists this seems the most plausible construal of the idea that, as in cases of phenomenally corrigible illusions, experience is *not* 'as expected', or, as commonly occurs, experience *is* 'as expected'.

With this background, we can finally address the key question of sensorimotor intentionality. That is the question of whether differences in the character of visual experience comprising the contrasts between more and less attentive experience can be separated from our sensorimotor skills. More specifically: are differences in the way it looks to you when you look *more* attentively at what you *had* looked at *less* attentively separable from possession of the sort of sensorimotor skills whose exercise enables you to assess the accuracy of your experience?

So: consider these changes in the character of experience that occur when you look more attentively at what you had looked at less. Is there a way to conceive of such a shift occurring, but *without* a change in what or how much you were visually attending to something—a change in what you were looking at or how much? Perhaps you could drive a conceptual wedge between *attending* and *the attentiveness character* of experience, if you could specify differences in the latter by attributing representational content to experience. For perhaps we can think of differences occurring in what experience represents something to be, without this constituting a change in what one is visually attending to and looking at. However, if the relevant differences in the character of visual experience stubbornly resist representational capture, then it becomes very unclear how to conceive of them just occurring on their own, without any *attending* to and *looking at* going on. How can we even consider *these* differences without conceiving of them as differences that occur *when one is attending more to what one had attended less*, and *when one looks more at what one had looked at less*? It seems we have no way of conceptualizing the kind of difference in question, if we deprive ourselves of such concepts for getting at them.

[34] Merleau-Ponty (p. 395) contrasts hallucination with perception by saying that in the latter, '[m]y perception brings into co-existence an indefinite number of perceptual chains which, if followed up, would confirm it in all respects and accord with it. My eyes and my hand know that any actual change of place would produce a sensible response entirely according to my expectation, and I can feel swarming beneath my gaze the countless mass of more detailed perceptions that I anticipate, and on which I already have a hold. I am, therefore, conscious of perceiving a setting which "tolerates" nothing more than is written or foreshadowed in my perception, and I am in present communication with a consummate fullness.'

Now, if we have no cognitive purchase on these differences in phenomenal character independent of changes in the activity of visual attention involved in looking at something, then we must ask ourselves what such activity consists in. Again, we have left behind the idea that it consists in forming mental representations with varying content. Evidently all that's left for this attending to be is the exercise of visuo-motor abilities—by, e.g., moving, or at least trying to move, one's eyes or head. And those are sensorimotor abilities of the kind whose exercise is appropriate to confirming or disconfirming the accuracy of one's experience. The moral is: once we've given up trying to solve the problem of attentive difference, or as long as it remains unsolved, our means of cognitive access to the difference in question leaves us no room to think of these as merely contingently and instrumentally related to the exercise of sensorimotor skills. If we can find no way of capturing the relevant differences in experiential character so as to separate them from such activity of attending, we regard these changes in character in a way that links them necessarily with the exercise of sensorimotor skills. I don't know how to show that it would be *impossible* to find an alternative way to conceive of just such changes in experiential character, without at all conceiving of them in terms of the exercise of sensorimotor skills. But the prospects of finding that don't seem particularly good.

6

Let me now sum up my phenomenological case for sensorimotor intentionality. The phenomenal character of visual experience commonly and pervasively exhibits differences—differences between less and more attentive visual experience—that resist specification by attributing distinct representational contents to experience. When one considers a given case of less attentive experience, and various candidate representational specifications of its character, first-person reflection will lead one to conclude either: the content of the sentence or image is simply not correctly attributed to the experience in question; or it would be attributable with equal or greater right to a second, more attentive experience of different character; or there is no way to decide among various representational contents which of them really specifies the character of the experience, and no reason to think one of these must.

However, even where this 'problem of attentive difference' remains, we have reason to regard the phenomenal character of the experience in question as intentional. For in virtue of having such character, an experience is assessable as illusory or correct. Examples showing this are found when we consider a class of naturally occurring illusions, discoverable as such by doing what is required to perceive better or more fully what first presented an illusory appearance—phenomenally corrigible illusions. In such cases, it will in some sense be correct to say that, upon getting a better look, it did not look to one *as expected*. These reveal that when it appears to one a certain way, one has expectations of some sort concerning how it will look, upon doing what is required to get a *better* look. Their frustration is required for one to recognize one's phenomenally corrigible illusions *as* illusions, and their fulfillment enables one to confirm the accuracy of one's experience. These anticipations are not representations of sensorimotor conditionals, detachable from appearances. For the frustration of such belief/expectation would not give one grounds to judge that the relevant appearances were illusory. Furthermore, we would be unjustified in regarding sensorimotor anticipations as representations of sensorimotor conditionals that are *built into* the sensory appearance itself. For relevant 'if-then' propositions are identifiable only retrospectively, through the exercise of those sensorimotor capacities required to confirm or disconfirm the accuracy of one's experience. And when one tries, in such a manner, to find the relevant conditionals, one finds experience too specific to provide the right sensory consequents, and no basis on which to generalize to an appropriate range of antecedent/consequent pairings.

The most plausible alternative is to see sensorimotor anticipation as lying in the exercise of and disposition to exercise sensorimotor skills. That is, *in doing and being prepared to do* what is suitable for getting a better look, I *anticipate* how it will look to me upon doing this. Doing and being prepared to do this is not a *consequence* or *result* of my anticipation of further visual appearances; it *constitutes* such anticipation.

But now, how is the experiential character of the attentive difference related to these sensorimotor skills? So long as the problem of attentive difference remains, certain changes in the character of visual experience are conceivable only as changes in visual attend*ing*, constituted by exercising sensorimotor skills of the kind needed for phenomenally based assessments of experiential accuracy. So there is reason to accept a constitutive, necessary connection between the exercise of these skills and the kind of intentional phenomenal character of visual experience that pervades conscious mental life. And this is to say: we have sensorimotor intentionality.

That, in outline, is the argument I propose. While I cannot now examine in just what ways it may contribute to or depart from its inspirational sources in the phenomenological tradition, it suggests a few ways of interpreting some of Merleau-Ponty's puzzling notions I pointed out in Section 2. First, we now have some way of clarifying how we could, as he proposes, conceive of a consciousness of place that is intentional, without thinking of it as a mental representation. There is a consciousness of place that is intentional, even if it is not representational, because even where the phenomenal character of visual experience resists specification by attributing the content of words or images to it (and in that sense is not and cannot be made 'explicit'), the experience is assessable as illusory or correct in virtue of this character—and experience thus assessable surely has intentionality. Second, we can say something about what makes this sensori*motor* intentionality. For the differences in experiential character at issue constitute the exercise of visual attention, and such changes in how one visually attends, if they do not consist in differences in how one represents (pictures, describes) the world, are inseparable from the exercise of certain sensorimotor skills—specifically, those that constitute our knowledge of how to get a better look at things. Third, and relatedly, I have found a place for something resembling Merleau-Ponty's talk of 'anticipation'. For I have proposed there is a sense in which, in perceiving, we 'anticipate' further experience upon further motor activity, not by representing to ourselves what experience will ensue if we do this or that, but by engaging and becoming ready to engage the motor skills suitable for making available experience by which one could confirm the correctness of ongoing and past experience. That sort of confirmatory experience is the experience 'anticipated'—the experience towards which our acts are 'directed' or 'project themselves'—even if we do not in those acts represent or 'posit' it (or what the anticipated experience is of) as an object.

Of course, much more remains to be done to reconnect my proposals with Merleau-Ponty. One would need to see how to integrate it with what he says about the perception of one's own body, 'orientated space', and the varieties of consciousness of place he claims are revealed by clinical and experimental results.[35] Also, I think, it would be interesting to examine (either in connection with Merleau-Ponty or independently of this) the relationship of the sort of view I've been proposing to Husserl's and Gurwitsch's views on perception. I should note too that, to take these ideas further, it would be important to consider explicitly where they diverge or converge with the contemporary sensorimotor theories of perception to which I alluded at the outset. And, of course, it would be important to take into account relevant aspects of the enormous amount of experimental research that has been done on visual attention.

I cannot undertake those projects here. But I will close by briefly considering two large concerns one might raise for the position I am staking out, which I think I need to say at least a little about. The first concern is this. Does this conception of sensorimotor intentionality give us a way of dealing with the issue that opened this essay— the issue, namely, of what distinguishes sensory experience from judgment? One might suppose that, even before we get to the idea that the character of sensory experience is essentially linked to sensorimotor skills, the mere notion that its character is intentional without being representational is enough to yield the contrast with judgment. For, whatever we want to say about the character of sensory experience, the character of judgment, we might plausibly suppose, surely does not elude specification by verbally expressible contents. However, there is reason to be cautious. For we should not dismiss out of hand the idea that some analogue of the relatively less attended background we find in the case of visual appearance can be found also in the case of linguistically expressible 'conceptual' thought. That is, when you are thinking about something, you are cognitively attending *more* to what you had cognitively attended to *less*, but which lay, in some sense, in the 'vicinity' or background of your verbally expressed thought. Also, maybe the background or context to our explicit thoughts or judgments resists capture in some set of propositions stored in the head, much as does what is visually less attended-to. Perhaps it is properly understood only relative to cognitive skills and their exercise, somehow analogous to sensorimotor skills. Conceptual thought then has its 'horizons' no less than does visual experience.[36] So, I suspect we would be on better ground if we propose that what is special about the intentionality of perception lies in its constitutive link with sensorimotor skills. Even if there is some cognitive analogue of this—'exploring' and 'knowing your way

---

[35] For a discussion of these, see Bermudez (2005).

[36] Merleau-Ponty (p. 146): 'Although Schneider's trouble affects motility and thought as well as perception, the fact remains that what it damages, particularly in the domain of thought, is his power of apprehending simultaneous wholes . . . It is then in some sense mental space and practical space which are destroyed or impaired'. Merleau-Ponty thinks this impairment in 'mental space' is revealed in the pervasive difficulties Schneider has in understanding stories and analogies, and initiating and sustaining conversation.

around' in thought—still, the skills involved there are (e.g.) skills of inference and analogy, not *motor* skills whose activity enables us to confirm assessments for accuracy of intentionality directed at particular places and spatial configurations.

This last point—about the 'motor' part of 'sensorimotor'—leads to the second concern. Are the sensorimotor skills I deem essential to the visual experience of attending necessarily possessed only by someone *actually embodied* in such a way that their exercise consists in real movements of eyes, head, and so on? Or would it not be enough to have all the sensorimotor skills required for the experience of visual attention, merely to have a 'virtual' body, and a 'virtual' world? Here we might conjure up the usual philosophical scenarios invoking the possibility of total hallucination—experience type identical to our own in phenomenal character, though radically incorrect about the position and movement of the subject's body and the shape and position of things in his or her actual surroundings: a 'brain in a vat' scenario, for example. It seems to me that you could interpret my talk of sensorimotor skills so as to leave it open that their merely *virtual* activation, in merely *seeming to oneself to move in relevant fashion*, would be sufficient for their 'exercise'.

But even if we cannot show that brain in a vat scenarios are impossible, limits to their intelligibility may be found when we ask whether we could rationally regard such a situation as our own. What do we regard our situation to be? Whatever else, we take it to be a situation in which we *look for*, *reach for*, or *handle* things (by 'handling' I mean, e.g., grasping, lifting, carrying, pulling, pushing, turning, or holding something). In taking ourselves to do this, we arguably manifest belief in things that have an indefinitely large potential not only to be revealed by what we do, but to be or become *hidden* from us. (One can look only for what isn't yet apparent; one can reach only for something that will exist; one can handle only what one can keep hold of—and one can *keep* hold of only what can *escape*.) Perhaps we could, consistently with this, conceive of ourselves as merely virtually embodied, in a virtual world, only if we took ourselves merely to be trying to make it *appear to ourselves in certain ways, by appearing to ourselves to move in such and such a fashion*. However, we could adopt that attitude, only provided that we could represent to ourselves just *what* ways of appearing we are trying to bring about by means of what apparent movements. But if we could do that, we could construe our sensorimotor anticipations representationally, in ways that, if my earlier proposals are correct, are unavailable to us. Then, perhaps, we have no way to make what we are doing intelligible to ourselves while also thinking we experience a merely virtual world.[37] If, in this way, we cannot rationally think of ourselves as having a merely virtual world, we need not worry about qualifying our understanding of sensorimotor skills so that it would apply to merely virtually embodied subjects.

[37] Compare Merleau-Ponty (p. 401): 'To ask oneself whether the world is real is to fail to understand what one is asking, since the world is not the sum of things which might always be called into question, but the inexhaustible reservoir from which things are drawn.' As I understand this, the world is not a 'sum which may always be called into question' because it is not something, our understanding of which can be expressed in a representation whose content could then serve as the content of a doubt. It is the 'inexhaustible reservoir' because it is that which, by indefinitely various fulfillment of our sensorimotor anticipations, allows us to 'draw things' to us in perception—i.e. perceive them better.

In these last remarks I am obviously only sketching a line of thought. And, I have to acknowledge, the argument of the essay as a whole, if it is to be fully satisfying, needs to be set in the context of a broader and deeper theory. I would like to think that's possible. But I would be content if a response to the ideas offered here helped clarify and stimulate debate on emerging and intriguing sensorimotor approaches to perception.[38]

REFERENCES

Bermudez, J.-L. (2005) 'The Phenomenology of Bodily Awareness' (this volume).

Clark, A. (1997) *Being There* (Cambridge, Mass.: MIT Press).

Dennett, D. (1991) *Consciousness Explained* (Boston: Little, Brown & Co.).

Dreyfus, H. (1992) *What Computers Still Can't Do: A Critque of Artificial Reason* (Cambridge, MA: MIT Press).

—— (2001) 'The Primacy of Phenomenology over Logical Analysis', *Philosophical Topics* 27/2 (Fall 1999).

—— (2002a) *Thinking in Action: On the Internet*, rev. 2nd edn. London: Routledge & Kegan Paul.

—— (2002b) 'Intelligence without Representation: Merleau-Ponty's Critique of Mental Representation', *Phenomenology and the Cognitive Sciences* 1/4: 367–83.

Gibson, J. J. (1979) *The Ecological Approach to Vision* (New York: Houghton Miflin).

Gunther, Y. (2002) *Essays on Nonconceptual Content* (Cambridge, Mass.: MIT Press).

Gurwitsch, A. (1964) *The Field of Consciousness* (Pittsburgh, Pa: Duquesne University Press).

Hurley, S. (1998) *Consciousness in Action* (Cambridge, Mass.: Harvard University Press).

Hurley, S. and Noë, A. (2003) 'Neural Plasticity and Consciousness', *Biology and Philosophy* 18: 131–68.

Kelly, S. (2004) 'Seeing Things in Merleau-Ponty', in Taylor Carman and Mark Hansen (eds.), *The Cambridge Companion to Merleau-Ponty*. (Cambridge: Cambridge University Press).

Merleau-Ponty, M. (1945/2002) *Phenomenology of Perception*, trans. Colin Smith (London: Routledge & Kegan Paul).

Mack, A. and Rock, I. (1998) *Inattentional Blindness* (Cambridge, Mass.: MIT Press).

Milner, A. D. and Goodale, M. A. (1995) *The Visual Brain in Action* (Oxford: Oxford University Press).

Noë, A. (ed.) (2002) *Is the Visual World a Grand Illusion?* Special issue of *Journal of Consciousness Studies* 9/5–6.

Noë, A. (2004) *Action in Perception* (Cambridge, Mass.: MIT Press).

Noë, A., Pessoa, L., and Thompson, E. (1999) 'Perceptual Completion: A Case Study in Phenomenology and Cognitive Science', in J. Petitot, F. Varela, B. Pachoud, and J.-L. Roy (eds.), *Naturalizing Phenomenology*. (Stanford: Stanford University Press).

Noë, A., Pessoa, L., and Thompson, E. (2000) 'Beyond the Grand Illusion: What Change Blindness really Teaches us about Vision', *Visual Cognition* 7 (1/2/3): 93–106.

O'Regan, J. K. and Noë, A. (2001) 'A Sensorimotor Account of Vision and Visual Consciousness', *Behavioral and Brain Sciences* 24/5: 883–917.

[38] For their helpful comments, criticisms and suggestions on earlier drafts of this essay I would like to thank Hubert Dreyfus, David W. Smith, Amie Thomasson, and an anonymous referee for Oxford University Press.

Siegel, Susanna. (unpublished) 'Subject and Object in the Contents of Visual Experience'.
Siewert, C. (1998) *The Significance of Consciousness* (Princeton: Princeton University Press).
——— (2002) 'Is Visual Consciousness Rich or Poor?' in Noë (2002).
Smith, D. W. and MacIntyre, R. (1982) *Husserl and Intentionality* (Dordrecht: Reidel).
Tye, M. (1995) *Ten Problems of Consciousness* (Cambridge, Mass.: MIT Press).
——— (2003) *Consciousness, Color and Content* (Cambridge, Mass.: MIT Press).

14

The Phenomenology of Bodily Awareness

José Luis Bermúdez

Abstract: This essay explores the dialectic between discussions of bodily awareness in the phenomenological tradition and in contemporary philosophy of mind and scientific psychology. It shows, with particular reference to Merleau-Ponty's *Phenomenology of Perception*, how phenomenological insights into bodily awareness and its role in agency can be developed and illuminated by research into somatic proprioception and motor control. The essay presents a taxonomy of different types and levels of bodily awareness and presents a model of the spatiality of bodily awareness that explains some of the fundamental differences that Merleau-Ponty identified between our experience of our bodies and our experience of non-bodily objects. The key to these differences is that bodily locations are given on a non-Cartesian frame of reference. The final section shows how this way of thinking about the phenomenology of bodily awareness has interesting and fruitful connections with current thinking about motor control.

1. INTRODUCTION

As embodied subjects we are aware of our bodies in distinctive ways. One source of this distinctiveness is that we have ways of finding out about our own bodies that we do not have about any other physical objects in the world. There are distinctive information channels that allow us directly to monitor both the body's homeostatic states and its spatial properties. Some of these information channels are conscious and others unconscious. They all contribute, however, to a distinctive type of experience, viz. the experience of oneself as an embodied agent. It is this distinctive type of experience that I call the phenomenology of bodily awareness. The phenomenology of bodily awareness has an important role to play in self-consciousness. It is, moreover, of critical importance in generating and controlling action.

Bodily awareness is a complex phenomenon that has received attention from a number of different theoretical and experimental approaches. It of course has intricate and highly developed physical underpinnings that are relatively well understood. Physiologists and neurophysiologists have devoted considerable attention to understanding the

This essay has been greatly improved by comments from David Smith, Amie Thomasson, and an anonymous reviewer for Oxford University Press. A much shorter version of the central sections was published as Bermúdez (2004).

mechanisms of *proprioception* (awareness of limb position and bodily configuration) and *somatosensation* (bodily sensation).[1] We have a good understanding of how bodily sensations originate in specialized receptors distributed across the surface of the skin and within the deep tissues. Some of these receptors are sensitive to skin and body temperature. Others are pain detectors (*nociceptors*). There are receptors specialized for mechanic stimuli of various kinds, such as pressure and vibration. Information about muscle stretch comes from muscle spindles. Other receptors monitor stresses and forces at the joints and in the tendons. Information from all of these receptors and nerve endings is carried by the spinal cord to the brain along three different pathways. One pathway carries information stemming from *discriminative touch* (which is a label for a complex set of tactile ways of finding out about the shape and texture of physical objects).[2] Another carries information about pain and temperature. The third carries proprioceptive information. Each of these pathways ends up at a different brain area. The discriminative touch pathway travels to the cerebral cortex while the propriocept-ive pathway terminates in the cerebellum. The properties of these brain areas have been well studied. We know, for example, that tactile information is processed in the somatosensory cortex, which is located in the parietal lobe. The somatosensory cortex is *somatotopically* organized, with specific regions representing specific parts of the body. The cortical space assigned to information from each bodily region is a function of the fineness of tactile discrimination within that region (which is itself of course a function of the number of receptors there). Neuropsychologists, neuro-imagers, and computational neuroscientists have made considerable progress in understanding how somatosensory and proprioceptive information is processed in the brain and how that processing can be disturbed by brain injury.

Explanations of the physiological underpinnings of bodily awareness can only at best form part of an understanding of the distinctiveness of the experience of embodiment—of what I earlier termed the phenomenology of bodily awareness. The gap between an understanding of the mechanisms underlying experience and the distinctive character of that experience has been much stressed in contemporary philosophy—many would think excessively so. Moving beyond physiology, bodily awareness has been approached from a number of perspectives. From the scientific point of view, much light has emerged from the study of patients with various forms of disorders of bodily awareness, such as *deafferentation* (where patients lose the ability to feel peripheral sensations) and *autotopagnosia* (where patients lose the ability to recognize and point to body parts). The verbal reports from patients suffering from neuropathies such as these can be very instructive in plotting the phenomenology of normal bodily awareness, precisely because of the insight they provide into what bodily awareness is like when certain central elements of normal bodily awareness are absent or distorted. So too can experimental exploration of the implications of abnormal bodily awareness for different types of motor behavior and deliberative action. As we will see further below, attention to the neuropathological data allows us to make considerable progress towards a taxonomy of the different components of bodily awareness.

---

[1] For a very helpful introduction see Part 3 of Roberts (2002).
[2] See Hsiao et al. (2002) for a useful tutorial on the neural basis of discriminative touch.

From a philosophical point of view, there has been a resurgence of interest in the phenomenon of bodily awareness within the analytic tradition.[3] In many ways this is an extension of analytical philosophers' preoccupation with pain as a paradigmatic mental state. It is natural to compare and contrast the metaphysics and epistemology of pain with, say, the metaphysics and epistemology of bodily awareness. Many of the issues that arise mesh naturally with established concerns within the analytic tradition. So, for example, philosophers have explored whether the information about the body yielded by the various mechanisms of bodily awareness has the same type of *privileged* status that many theorists grant to the information about our own mental states that we derive from introspection. There are, moreover, longstanding debates about the role of bodily continuity in personal identity to which one might expect thinking about bodily awareness to be highly relevant. Many philosophers, beginning with Locke, have argued that psychological continuity (in the form of memories and other diachronic mental states) is what really matters for personal identity, so that bodily continuity is neither necessary nor sufficient for securing personal identity. The plausibility of this line of argument is likely to rest, at least partially, upon the centrality that one accords to awareness of one's own body in underwriting one's sense of self. More generally, just as analytical philosophers have moved towards recognition that the mind is embedded within a social and physical context, and hence that we have to take social and environmental factors into account in thinking about the nature and content of mental states, so too are they coming to realize that we have to consider cognition and self-consciousness within an embodied context.

However, despite this resurgence of interest within the analytical tradition, the experiential dimension of bodily awareness has been most extensively explored within the phenomenological tradition.[4] The most comprehensive treatment is to be found in Part One of Merleau-Ponty's *Phenomenology of Perception* (Merleau-Ponty 1962). One particularly interesting feature of Merleau-Ponty's work in this area is how deeply informed it is by a detailed knowledge of current research in neuropsychology and neurophysiology at the time he was writing. Although the scientific study of bodily awareness has made huge advances since he was writing in the 1940s, the interface that he opened up between our understanding of experience, on the one hand, and our understanding of the mechanisms underlying that experience continues to be vitally important. And it remains the case that no subsequent author has explored this interface with anything like Merleau-Ponty's depth and insight.

The problem that I will be addressing in this essay can be understood in terms of two of the different strands that we find in Merleau-Ponty's rich exploration of the phenomenology of bodily awareness. From a phenomenological point of view Merleau-Ponty explores in very insightful ways our distinctive ways of finding out

[3] Early work includes Armstrong (1962), which is a book-length treatment of bodily sensation, and Anscombe's short paper of the same year on sensations of position (Anscombe 1962), which proved very influential. Brian O'Shaughnessy's two-volume *The Will* (O'Shaughnessy 1980) marked the beginning of more recent work in this area. For a representative sample, see the philosophical essays in Bermúdez et al. (1995), together with Cassam (1997) and Bermúdez (1998).

[4] My talking of the analytical and phenomenological traditions as distinct should be understood in purely sociological terms. As should become clear, my interest in this essay is with issues that arise at the intersection of cognitive science, phenomenology, and analytical philosophy of mind.

about, and acting through, our bodies—the ways in which, as he puts it, 'the body is the vehicle of being-in-the-world' (p. 82). His project here is phenomenological in the non-technical sense of the word. That is to say, he is concerned with characterizing agency and bodily awareness from the perspective of the experiencing subject. The distinction between first-person and third-person perspectives is useful at this point. Merleau-Ponty does not present matters quite in these terms, but it is one component of how he understands the distinction between the *for-itself* and the *in-itself*—a distinction which goes back at least as far as Hegel's *Phenomenology of Spirit*, although Merleau-Ponty's usage is no doubt more closely tied to Sartre's use of the distinction in *Being and Nothingness*. From a first-person perspective we experience the body *qua* for-itself, via the ways that it structures and gives meaning to our engagements with the physical world. From a third-person perspective, in contrast, we treat the body *qua* in-itself, as a complex of muscles, bones and nerves that enters into causal interactions with other objects and that can in principle be studied and understood as one object among others, albeit a distinctive and highly complex object.[5]

The general contours of the distinction that Merleau-Ponty is making between the in-itself and the for-itself should be congenial to many theorists working within analytical philosophy of mind, although they would probably have some difficulty with how it is formulated. The basic idea that we cannot understand human agency in the same way that we understand causal interactions between non-animate physical objects has been widely canvassed within the analytical tradition. One obvious point of contact is with theorists writing in the Wittgensteinian tradition, particularly those such as Anscombe, Taylor, and Kenny who argued that the reasons for which people act should not be understood in causal terms.[6] But there are points of contact with theorists who accept that reasons can be causes. The distinction that some have tried to make between agent causation and event causation is very much in the spirit of Merleau-Ponty's distinction.[7] So too is the approach of Davidson's anomalous monism, which is based upon a sharp distinction between the law-governed domain of the physical and the norm-governed realm of the psychological.[8]

There are two aspects of Merleau-Ponty's approach to agency and bodily experience, however, that analytical philosophers are likely to find unpalatable. The first is its susceptibility to an interpretation that draws strong metaphysical conclusions from the phenomenological distinction between the for-itself and the in-itself. Merleau-Ponty frequently writes as if the experienced body in some sense stands outside the physical world. He draws a distinction between the phenomenal body and the objective body

---

[5] Merleau-Ponty emphatically distinguishes himself from those who construe the in-itself/for-itself distinction in terms of a distinction between the physiological, on the one hand, and pure consciousness, on the other. As emerges very clearly in his discussion of the patient Schneider (see further below), Merleau-Ponty understands the for-itself in terms of what he calls motor intentionality, a complex theoretical notion that is intended to overcome standard construals of the gap between the realm of the physiological and the realm of consciousness. As he cautions the reader on p. 124, 'As long as the body is defined in terms of existence in-itself, it functions uniformly like a mechanism, and as long as the mind is defined in terms of pure existence for-itself, it knows only objects arrayed before it'.   [6] See, for example, Anscombe (1957), Taylor (1964), and Kenny (1963).

[7] For agent causation see Chisholm (1976) and O'Connor (2000).

[8] See the essays in Davidson (1980), particularly 'Mental Events' and 'Philosophy as Psychology'.

that can be interpreted in a manner incompatible with any ontological position that, in the last analysis, treats the body as simply a highly developed biochemical object that stands apart from other objects in the world only in virtue of its complexity and organization.[9] It is unclear, to this reader at least, where Merleau-Ponty draws the line between phenomenology and ontology in *Phenomenology of Perception*, but he often writes in a distinctly idealist vein, saying for example that 'the constitution of our body as object' is a 'crucial moment in the genesis of the objective world'. This dimension of his thinking might seem to place the experienced body outside the physical world in a way that is incompatible with even the weakest form of philosophical naturalism.

Even if we do not take Merleau-Ponty to be committed to such a drastic ontological position, and instead see him as primarily exploring a distinction between two ways of experiencing the body,[10] he develops his views in a way that has significant repercussions for how we think about explanation—repercussions that philosophers of mind in the analytic tradition are unlikely to find congenial. As we will see in more detail in the next section, Merleau-Ponty is more than happy to draw the conclusion that the explanatory power of scientific investigation is severely constrained by the distinction between the phenomenal body and the objective body (which is a special case of his overall distinction between the phenomenal world and the objective world).[11] The phenomenal body, Merleau-Ponty thinks, cannot be elucidated scientifically. Science can only inform us about the objective body.

The aim of this essay is to offer a way of doing justice to the phenomenological insights of Merleau-Ponty's thinking about bodily awareness and its role in agency without following him in the limitations he places upon the explanatory power of the scientific study of the body. I shall discuss one central feature of bodily awareness in a way that tries to respect the points that Merleau-Ponty stressed about the distinctive phenomenology of the experienced body. This feature is what Merleau-Ponty terms the 'spatiality' of the body, which he discusses in the lengthy third chapter of Part One of *Phenomenology of Perception*, 'The Spatiality of One's Own Body and Motility'. There are, I shall argue, some very fundamental differences between how we experience the spatiality of our own bodies and how we experience the spatiality of non-bodily physical objects. Bodily space, I shall argue, is represented in a fundamentally different way from the space within which we perceive and act upon non-bodily physical objects. I will stress that we need to understand the spatiality of bodily awareness in terms of a non-Cartesian frame of reference, in contrast to the Cartesian frames of reference that structure our perception of, and interactions with, non-bodily physical

---

[9] There are, of course, a number of philosophers who reject philosophical naturalism, particularly with respect to the qualitative features of experience. But no one has ever suggested that this rejection should have any consequences for how we think about the ontology of the body.

[10] For a clear interpretation of Merleau-Ponty along these lines see Priest (1998: ch. 4).

[11] Merleau-Ponty's views on the relation between the phenomenal world and the objective world are instructively summarized in the following passage from Dillon (1988), 'whereas the objective world is an ideal variant of the phenomenal world. It is an end posited by thought troubled by its own partiality. It is the name for a universal validity that once was conceived through the symbols of divinity and now is conceived through the optimistic projections of science. Objectivity is a responsibility we assume; to take it as a character of the real is to collapse time, ignore ambiguity, and presume a vantage that does not exist.'

objects. This basic distinction between two different types of frame of reference goes a long way, I shall suggest, towards accommodating what Merleau-Ponty correctly sees as the distinctiveness of the spatiality of our own bodies. And yet it is, of course, a distinction between two ways of representing space, rather than between two types of space—a distinction at the level of Fregean sense rather than Fregean reference. The fact that we experience our own bodies in terms of a non-Cartesian reference frame is perfectly compatible with our bodies being ontologically on a par with objects that we experience in terms of a Cartesian reference frame. Moreover, and this is the key methodological point, there is nothing about this distinction between two different frames of reference that stands in the way of our taking a third-person perspective on how bodily awareness feeds into and controls motor behavior and intentional action. I shall make good this claim in the final section by illustrating how this approach to the experienced spatiality of somatic proprioception can be integrated with contemporary work on the psychology of motor control.

2. MERLEAU-PONTY ON BODILY AWARENESS AND THE BODY

The general tenor of Merleau-Ponty's thinking about our experience as embodied agents is given by his concise comment that 'The outline of my body is a frontier which ordinary spatial relations to do not cross' (Merleau-Ponty 1962: 98). There is, he claims, a very fundamental discontinuity between the experienced spatiality of the physical world and the experienced spatiality of the body—more precisely, of the lived body, of the body as we might experience it from the inside. The body is not an object—or, more precisely, the lived body, the experienced body, cannot be understood as an object on a par with other objects in the external world.

In presenting Merleau-Ponty's analysis of the phenomenology of bodily experience I will focus on his discussion of the patient Schneider in the long chapter entitled 'The Spatiality of One's Own Body and Motility'. He is discussing a patient suffering from what he terms *psychic blindness*—the essence of the disorder being an inability to carry out what he (Merleau-Ponty) calls abstract movements, such as moving his arms and legs to order, naming and pointing to body-parts, when his eyes are shut. He points out that there are certain movements that this patient is perfectly capable of making. Some of these are what we might call body-relative reactions. Here is an example.

A patient of the kind discussed above, when stung by a mosquito, does not need to look for the place where he has been stung. He finds it straight away, because for him there is no question of locating it in relation to axes of coordinates in objective space, but of reaching with his phenomenal hand a certain painful spot on his phenomenal body, and because between the hand as a scratching potentiality and the place stung as a spot to be scratched a directly experienced relationship is presented in the natural system of one's own body. (Merleau-Ponty 1965/1968: 105–6)

Here the distinction between the epistemological and the metaphysical strands in Merleau-Ponty's thinking comes across very clearly. The epistemological point that he makes about the experience of localizing a sensation on the body seems exactly right. When one performs a simple body-relative action such as scratching a mosquito sting there is indeed no question of locating the sting on some sort of objective coordinate system, working out where one's hand is on the same coordinate system, and then plotting a path between the two locations. The locations of both hand and sting are given in body-relative space (and I shall have more to say later about how this should be understood).

Merleau-Ponty uses these points about the phenomenology of bodily awareness to draw an explicit distinction between 'objective space' and 'the natural system of one's own body'. The following passage is instructive:

The whole operation takes place in the domain of the phenomenal; it does not run through the objective world, and only the spectator, who lends his objective representation of the living body to the acting subject, can believe that the sting is perceived, that the hand moves in object-ive space, and consequently find it odd that the same subject can fail in experiments requiring him to point things out. (Merleau-Ponty 1962: 106)

These basic ideas then get generalized into a global distinction between the phenom-enal body and the objective body. A few lines further on he writes: 'It is never our objective body that we move, but our phenomenal body, and there is no mystery in that, since our body, as the potentiality of this or that part of the world, surges towards objects to be grasped and perceives them' (Merleau-Ponty 1962: 106). The distinction between the phenomenal body and the objective body plays an important role in *Phenomenology of Perception*. The phenomenal body is supposed to play a founda-tional role in the very constitution of the objective world. Here is a representative passage:

The body is not one more among external objects. It is neither tangible nor visible in so far as it is that which sees and touches. The body, therefore, is not one more among external objects, with the peculiarity of always being there. If it is permanent, the permanence is absolute and is the ground for the relative permanence of disappearing objects, real objects. The presence and absence of external objects are only variations within a field of primordial presence, a perceptual domain over which my body exercises power. Not only is the permanence of my body not a par-ticular case of the permanence of external objects in the world, but the second cannot be under-stood except through the first: not only is the perspective of my body not a particular case of that of objects, but furthermore the presentation of objects in perspective cannot be understood except through the resistance of my body to all variations in perspective. (Merleau-Ponty 1962: 92)

I am not a Merleau-Ponty scholar and I do not want to make any strong claims about what is going on here. What I would like to stress, however, is a conditional claim, namely, that *if* we accept Merleau-Ponty's distinction between the phenomenal body and the objective body at face value, then it looks as if there will be very little scope for scientific study of the interesting and important aspects of bodily experience. Science, whether cognitive science, empirical psychology, or neurophysiology, can only inform us about the objective body. It can have nothing to say about the phenomenal body.

It is clear that Merleau-Ponty himself accepted this implication of the distinction between the phenomenal body and the objective body. That the distinction imposes limits on what we can learn from physiology and psychology is clearly stated in the first two chapters of Part One. In Chapter 1, 'The Body as Object and Mechanistic Physiology', Merleau-Ponty argues with some power that the physiological study of the body intrinsically involves an objectification of something that is fundamentally non-objective. To study the physiology of the body is to treat the *for-itself* as an *in-itself*—to try to reduce the distinctive functioning of the body to mechanical causation of the type that governs interactions between non-bodily physical objects. As Merleau-Ponty brings out in discussing the phenomena of *phantom limb* and *anosognosia* (a patient's refusal to accept the reality of their illness and deficits), the physiological treatment of neuropsychological disorders imposes upon us the burden of explaining how 'the psychic determining factors and the physiological conditions gear into each other' (p. 77)—an explanatory burden that he thinks it impossible to discharge. If we are to understand the phenomenology of bodily awareness, Merleau-Ponty concludes, there is little to be gained from studying the physiology of the body.

In Chapter 2, 'The Experience of the Body and Classical Psychology', Merleau-Ponty takes a related but somewhat different tack. Although classical psychology, no less than classical physiology, is committed to treating the body as objective, he argues that it itself points us towards the inadequacy of the objectifying perspective. It is somewhat unclear what he means by 'classical psychology', but the points he wants to extract are clear enough. Within psychology we find descriptions of the body and of the role of the body in action that are, he thinks, simply incompatible with the idea that the body is just an object in the world among other objects. As far as this essay is concerned one particularly interesting example Merleau-Ponty gives is the contrast drawn by 'classical psychology' between ordinary perception of the movement of extra-bodily physical objects and kinaesthetic perception of bodily movement. The contrast is between the global perception of bodily movement yielded by kinaesthesis, on the one hand, and the successive perception of the movement of ordinary objects. Whereas we simply feel the body move, we perceive the movement of non-bodily objects by comparing their different positions at different times. The contrast is crude, according to Merleau-Ponty, but contains a germ of truth:

What they were expressing, badly it is true, by 'kinaesthetic sensation' was the originality of the movements which I perform with my body: they directly anticipate the final situation, for my intention initiates a movement through space merely to obtain the objective initially given at the starting-point; there is as it were a germ of a movement which only secondarily develops into an objective movement. I move external objects with the aid of my body, which takes hold of them in one place and shifts them to another. But my body itself I move directly, I do not find it at one point of objective space and transfer it to another. I have no need to look for it, it is already with me.   (p. 94)

Nonetheless, Merleau-Ponty thinks, psychologists have failed to carry through their insights into the phenomenology of our experience of our own bodies. And what this means, of course, is that we can learn relatively little about the phenomenology of the body from empirical psychology—all we can learn, really, is the inadequacy of the objectifying approach of psychologists.

This pessimism about the possibility of learning from physiology and psychology might seem to be in tension with Merleau-Ponty's interdisciplinary focus, and his constant appeal to neuropsychological case studies. However, the appearance is deceptive. What Merleau-Ponty is objecting to is the idea that we can understand the phenomenology of bodily awareness by studying the mechanisms that make the associated experiences possible—or, to put it in different terms, that we can study a first-person phenomenon through physiological and psychological mechanisms that are only susceptible to a third-person approach. But this is not in any sense incompatible with the thought that we can learn about the first-person phenomenon of bodily awareness by looking at the behavior of subjects in whom those mechanisms are not functioning properly—and indeed at how those subjects describe their experience of the world. It is mechanistic explanation of bodily awareness that Merleau-Ponty opposes, rather than scientific investigation *per se*.

Nonetheless, although Merleau-Ponty's position is perfectly consistent one can certainly wonder whether it is desirable. The price seems high. It is difficult when reading Merleau-Ponty not to be convinced in very general terms that there must be some sort of distinction between two ways of thinking about the body—between those two approaches that he connects with the distinction between the *for-itself* and the *in-itself*. But should we follow him in concluding that there can be no dialogue between these two approaches; that there is nothing to be learned about the body *qua* for-itself by exploring the body *qua* in-itself? It is natural to wonder whether there might not be a way of doing justice to at least some of those features of bodily awareness that led Merleau-Ponty to make such a sharp distinction between the for-itself and the in-itself within a theoretical perspective that treats the body as ontologically on a par with non-bodily objects.

3. TYPES AND LEVELS OF BODILY AWARENESS

Let us look again at the crucial passage where Merleau-Ponty first begins to draw metaphysical conclusions from the phenomenology of bodily awareness.

The whole operation takes place in the domain of the phenomenal; it does not run through the objective world, and only the spectator, who lends his objective representation of the living body to the acting subject, can believe that the sting is perceived, that the hand moves in object-ive space, and consequently find it odd that the same subject can fail in experiments requiring him to point things out. (Merleau-Ponty 1965/1968: 106)

The crucial claims here are both negative. The first is the denial that we should view Schneider's awareness of his own body as awareness of an object (viz. the objective body), while the second is the denial that we should view Schneider's reaching behavior as taking place in objective space. Only thus, Merleau-Ponty appears to be arguing, can we make sense of Schneider's simultaneous ability to respond to stimuli on his own body and inability to point on command to locations on his own body.

This argument is not, as it stands, very persuasive. It seems plausible that there is a number of different information systems and neural circuits involved in our awareness of our own bodies, and one would expect it to be occasionally the case that some of these systems and circuits are damaged while others are preserved. Indeed theorists concerned to distinguish different types of neural system frequently place considerable weight on the *dissociations* between different abilities and skills revealed by differential preservation in neuropathologies.[12] From this perspective the points that Merleau-Ponty notes about Schneider are far better viewed as evidence for a distinction between two different ways of processing information about the body than as evidence for an ontological distinction between the objective body and the phenomenal body. To put the point in terms employed earlier, we can locate the distinction at the level of sense rather than the level of reference.

Of course, adopting this strategy only makes sense within the context of a general taxonomy of different types of bodily awareness—a taxonomy motivated by reflection on a wider range of cases and factors than those that are at issue here. In the remainder of this section I will make some remarks in this direction before returning to Merleau-Ponty's analysis of Schneider.

We can begin with a general distinction between high-level and low-level representations of the body. High-level representations of the body feed directly into central cognitive/affective processes, while low-level representations of the body feed directly into action. The distinction here is *not* between personal and subpersonal or between conscious and unconscious. Both low-level and high-level representations of the body function at the personal level and are usually conscious. The distinction will become clearer, however, with some examples.

Within the general category of high-level representations of the body we can distinguish at least four different types of representation or bodies of information:

> *Conceptual representations of the body* (the set of beliefs we all have about the structure and nature of our body: how the body fits together, the functions of particular body-parts, their approximate locations and the sort of things that can go wrong with them).
> *Semantic knowledge of the names of body-parts* (knowledge that interfaces with non-semantic ways of identifying events in the body to allow us to give verbal reports of what is going on in our bodies).
> *Affective representations of the body* (representations of the body associated with emotional responses to the body).
> *Homeostatic representations of the body* (representations of the body relative to basic criteria of self-regulation and self-preservation).

Conceptual representations of the body are the least interesting, both philosophically and scientifically. There seems little reason to think that such conceptual representations will be any different in kind from the set of common-sense beliefs that we all have about the physical and social world. Homeostatic bodily representations present a number of interesting issues, but these are best considered in the context of the lower-level mechanisms that give rise to them. From the point of view of bodily awareness it is more interesting to consider how the body is represented in the mechanisms

---

[12] See Shallice 1988 for an influential textbook promoting this approach.

that give rise to the experience of pain than it is to consider the judgment that one is in pain.

The remaining two types of higher-level representation are more interesting. There are identifiable pathologies specific to both semantic and affective representations of the body. The pathologies associated with affective representations of the body are familiar. Bulimia and anorexia are good examples—forms of emotional response based on distorted representations of the body. There are also identifiable pathologies associated with semantic representations of the body. Patients with *autotopagnosia* have difficulty in naming body-parts or pointing to body-parts identified by name or by the application of some stimulus, either on their own bodies or on a schematic diagram of the body. The problems here are not *purely* semantic. Semantic representation of the body is not simply a matter of knowing the names of body-parts. Although superficially similar deficits can be found in some aphasic patients (Semenza and Goodglass 1985), autotopagnosic patients do not have a localized word-category deficit. They lack a particular way of representing bodily locations, as we see from the fact that the problem carries across to pointing to body-parts identified by the application of a stimulus.

Turning to lower-level representations of the body, here too we find a range of phenomena and associated information channels that need to be distinguished. The first is information about the structure and limits of the body. This type of body-relative information has a number of distinctive pathologies. The best-known example is the phenomenon of phantom limb found in many patients with amputated limbs, as well as some with *amelia*, the congenital absence of limbs (Melzack 1992). This first category of body-relative information performs two tasks. First, it is responsible for the felt location of sensations. Sensations are referred to specific body-parts in virtue of a body of information about the structure of the body. Second, the same body of information informs the motor system about the body-parts that are available to be employed in action.

This type of body-relative information should be distinguished from semantic representations of the body. In deafferented patients these types of information are dissociated in both directions. Deafferented patients have lost peripheral sensations in certain parts of the body. Jacques Paillard's patient GL suffers from almost complete deafferentation from the mouth down, although she retains some sensitivity to thermal stimuli. If a thermal stimulus is delivered to a point on her arm that she is prevented from seeing then, although she is unable to point to the location of the stimulus on her body, she is able to identify the location verbally and on a schematic body diagram. In my terms, she possesses semantic information without body-relative information. The dissociation also holds in the opposite direction. Another of Paillard's patients had a parietal lesion that resulted in central deafferentation of the forearm. Although she could not verbally identify and report on a tactile stimulus delivered to her deafferented hand in a blindfolded condition she was able to point to the location of the stimulus (Paillard et al. 1983).[13]

---

[13] Unlike the very similar and well-documented phenomenon of blindsight (Weiskrantz 1986) there was no need to apply a forced-choice paradigm. The dissociation here may well be between an

There is a second type of lower-level representation of the body. This is a moment-to-moment representation of the spatial position of the various parts of the body. This moment-to-moment representation of bodily position is essential for the initiation and control of action, and needs to be constantly updated by feedback from moving limbs. This representation has been called the *short-term body-image* by Brian O'Shaughnessy (O'Shaughnessy 1995), but the name is misleading, suggesting that there is a single way in which the disposition of body-parts is represented, whereas in fact the spatial location of any given body-part can be coded in three different and independent ways.

The first type of coding is relative to objects in the distal environment. Consider a simple action, like reaching one's hand out for an object. The success of this action depends upon an accurate computation of the trajectory from the initial position of the hand to the position of the relevant object.[14] This requires the position of the hand and the position of the object to be computed relative to the same frame of reference. I shall call this *object-relative spatial coding*. It is most likely that object-relative spatial coding takes place on an egocentric frame of reference—that is to say, a frame of reference whose origin is some body-part. The reason for calling this type of coding object-relative is that it deals primarily with the spatial relations between body-parts and objects in the distal environment.

But many actions are directed towards the body rather than to objects independent of the body. Some of these actions are voluntary, as when I clasp my head in my hands in horror. Some are involuntary, as when I scratch an itch. Many more are somewhere between the two, as when I cross my legs or rub my eyes. Clearly, the possibility of any of these sorts of action rests upon information about the location of the body-parts in question relative to each other. We can call this sort of information *body-internal spatial coding*. It is information about the moment-by-moment position of body-parts relative to each other.

Body-internal spatial coding is required, not just for body-directed action, but also for many types of action directed towards objects in the distal environment. Psychological studies of action often concentrate on very simple actions, such as grasping objects with one hand. But the vast majority of actions require the coordination of several body-parts. When I play volleyball, for example, I need to know not just where each of my hands is relative to the ball as it comes over the net, but also where each of my hands is relative to the other hand. Both body-internal and object-relative spatial coding is required.

A third type of information about the moment-to-moment disposition of the body is just as important for the initiation and control of action as the first two. This is

action-based representation of the body and an objective representation of the body (compare Cole and Paillard 1995). An action-based representation of the body represents body location in a way that feeds directly into action, whether that action is body-directed or world-directed. It is this that is lost in GL, but preserved in the patient with the deafferented forearm. In what I am calling an objective representation of the body, on the other hand, the body does not feature purely as a potentiality for action, but rather as a physical object whose parts stand in certain determinate relations to each other.

[14] This will be discussed further in the final section.

information about the orientation of the body as a whole in objective space, primarily involving information about the orientation of the body with respect to supporting surfaces and to the gravitational field. This information comes from the calibration of information from a number of sources. The three principal sources of orientational information are vision, the vestibular system in the inner ear, and the proprioceptive/kinaesthetic system (at least two of which must be properly functioning for orientational information to be accurate). I shall call this *orientational coding*.

If the taxonomy I have offered is correct then there seem to be the following principal types of information about the body:

High-level
- Beliefs about the structure and nature of body-parts
- Semantic localization (enabling verbal report)
- Affective representations of the body

Low-level
- Representation of the structure and limits of body (enabling localization of sensation and specifying range of body-parts available for action)
- Representation of the moment-to-moment disposition of body-parts
  —Object-relative spatial-coding
  —Body-internal spatial coding
  —Orientational spatial coding

Let us return, then, to Merleau-Ponty's Schneider. What Merleau-Ponty finds so striking in Schneider is his inability to point on command to locations on his own body, when this is taken in the context of his residual abilities to respond to stimuli on his body by grasping and other body-directed behaviors. The following passage contains a very clear statement of the reasoning that leads him to the conclusion that we cannot understand the distinction between pointing and grasping in physiological terms.

If the grasping action or the concrete movement is guaranteed by some factual connection between each point on the skin and the motor muscles that guide the hand, it is difficult to see why the same nerve circuit communicating a scarcely different movement to the same muscles should not guarantee the gesture of *Zeigen* [pointing] as it does the movement of *Greifen* [grasping]. Between the mosquito which pricks the skin and the ruler which the doctor presses on the same spot, the physical difference is not great enough to explain why the grasping movement is possible, but the act of pointing impossible. The two 'stimuli' are really distinguishable only if we take into account their affective value or biological meaning, and the two responses cease to merge into one another only if we consider the *Zeigen* and the *Greifen* as two ways of relating to the object and two types of being in the world. But this is precisely what cannot be done once we have reduced the living body to the condition of an object.   (p. 123)

Without denying the insights that emerge from the existential analysis to which Merleau-Ponty subsequently turns, the argument here is far from persuasive. Merleau-Ponty may well be right that there is little physical difference between the mosquito bite and the touch of a ruler (although this is far from obvious), but this is the wrong place to look for an explanation of why one type of movement is possible, but not the other. It seems far more plausible, particularly in the light of the taxonomy above, to seek an explanation in terms of the different representations of the body that the two types of movement respectively involve. So, for example, we might wonder whether Schneider's difficulty in pointing is not, at least in part, best identified as a deficit in high-level bodily representations—as a problem in the mechanisms that underwrite explicit localization. It might also be the case that there are two fundamentally different forms of coding of moment-to-moment body-parts in play in the two movements. Sensations such as mosquito bites are experienced within the boundaries of the body, in such a way that the movement of scratching the bite requires body-relative spatial coding, as opposed to the touch of a ruler which might be thought to require object-relative spatial coding. This would mean that pointing, unlike grasping, would require calibration of different forms of information about the location of body-parts.[15]

The point here is not that we should interpret Schneider's pathology in one or both of these ways. Rather, the claim is that careful distinctions between different types and levels of information about the body offer a greater number of potential resources for understanding what is going on in Schneider's curious pattern of body-related motor behavior than Merleau-Ponty considers. In place of the simple distinction between the objective body and the phenomenal body it makes sense to consider more complex distinctions between different ways of representing the objective body. Quite apart from avoiding metaphysical difficulties with Merleau-Ponty's notion of the phenomenal body, this approach is likely to give a more nuanced way of tackling the phenomenology of bodily awareness.

4. THE SPATIALITY OF BODILY AWARENESS

It remains the case, however, that the finer-grained analysis of different types of information about the body proposed in the previous section does not yet do justice to Merleau-Ponty's deeper motivation for the distinction between the phenomenal body and the objective body—viz. his insistence that the spatiality of the body is fundamentally different from the spatiality of the objective world. I turn to this claim in this section, where I offer a way of thinking about how we represent bodily space that distinguishes it sharply from our representation of 'body-external' space.

Almost all existing discussions of the spatiality of proprioception have presupposed that exteroceptive perception, proprioception, and the intentions controlling basic bodily actions must all have spatial contents coded on comparable frames of reference (where a frame of reference allows locations to be identified relative to axes centered on an object). This is an obvious assumption, given that action clearly requires integrating motor intentions and commands with perceptual information and proprioceptive information. Since the spatial locations of perceived objects and objects featuring in

---

[15] There are interesting parallels between Schneider and Jacques Paillard's patient with the deafferented forearm discussed earlier.

the contents of intentions are given relative to axes whose origin lies in the body—in an *egocentric frame of reference*—it is natural to suggest that the axes that determine particular proprioceptive frames of reference are centered on particular body-parts, just as are the axes determining the frames of reference for perceptual content and basic intentions. The picture that emerges, therefore, is of a number of different representations of space, within each of which we find representations both of bodily and of non-bodily location. So, for example, we might imagine reaching behavior to be controlled by an egocentric frame of reference centered at some location on the hand—a frame of reference relative to which both bodily location (such as the mosquito bite on my arm) and non-bodily location (such as the cup on the table) can be identified.[16]

Despite its appealing economy, however, this account is ultimately unacceptable, because of a fundamental disanalogy between the *bodily space* of proprioception and the egocentric space of perception and action. In the case of vision or exteroceptive touch there is a perceptual field bounded in a way that determines a particular point as its origin. Since the visual field is essentially the solid angle of light picked up by the visual system the origin of the visual field is the apex of that solid angle. Similarly, the origin of the frame of reference for exploratory touch could be a point in the center of the palm of the relevant hand. But our awareness of our own bodies is not like this at all. It is not clear what possible reason there could be for offering one part of the body as the origin of the proprioceptive frame of reference.

There are certain spatial notions that are not applicable to somatic proprioception. For any two objects that are visually perceived it makes obvious sense to ask both of the following questions:

(a) Which of these two objects is further away?
(b) Do these objects lie in the same direction?

The possibility of asking and answering these questions is closely bound up with the fact that visual perception has an origin-based frame of reference. Question (a) basically asks whether a line between the origin and one object would be longer or shorter than a corresponding line between the origin and the other object. Question (b) is just the question whether, if a line were drawn from the origin to the object that is furthest away, it would pass through the nearer object.

Neither question makes sense with respect to proprioception. One cannot ask whether this proprioceptively detected hand movement is farther away than this itch, nor whether this pain is in the same direction as that pain. What I am really asking when I ask which of two objects is further away is which of the two objects is further away from me, and a similar tacit self-reference is included when I ask whether two objects are in the same direction. But through somatic proprioception one learns about events taking place within the confines of the body, and there is no privileged part of the body that counts as *me* for the purpose of discussing the spatial relations they bear to each other.

---

[16] The remainder of this section draws upon Bermúdez (1998: ch. 6).

In order to get a firmer grip on the distinctiveness of the frame of reference of bodily awareness one need only contrast the bodily experience of normal subjects with that of completely deafferented subjects, such as Jonathan Cole's patient IW. The moment-to-moment information about their bodies that deafferented patients possess is almost exclusively derived from vision. Their awareness of their own body is continuous with their experience of the extra-bodily world. They are aware of their bodies only from the same third-person person perspective that they have on non-bodily physical objects. The frame of reference for their bodily awareness does indeed have an origin—the eyes—and for this reason both of the two questions mentioned make perfect sense. But this is not at all the way in which we experience our bodies *from a first-person perspective*.

The conclusion to draw from this is that the spatial content of bodily awareness cannot be specified within a Cartesian frame of reference that takes the form of axes centered on an origin. But then how is it to be specified?

We can start from the basic thought that an account of the spatiality of bodily awareness must provide criteria for sameness of place. In the case of somatic proprioception this means criteria for sameness of bodily location. But there are several different types of criteria for sameness of bodily location. Consider the following two situations:

i. I have a pain at a point in my right ankle when I am standing up and my right foot is resting on the ground in front of me.
ii. I have a pain at the same point in my ankle when I am sitting down and my right ankle is resting on my left knee.

According to one set of criteria the pain is in the same bodily location in (i) and (ii)—that is to say, it is at a given point in my right ankle. According to another set of criteria, however, the pain is in different bodily locations in (i) and (ii), because my ankle has moved relative to other body-parts. Let me term these *A-location* and *B-location* respectively. Note, moreover, that B-location is independent of the actual location of the pain in 'objective space'. The B-location of the pain in (ii) would be the same if I happened to be sitting in the same posture five feet to the left.

Both A-location and B-location need to be specified relative to a frame of reference. In thinking about this we need to bear in mind that the human body has both moveable and (relatively) immoveable body-parts. On a large scale the human body can be viewed as an immoveable torso to which are appended moveable limbs—the head, arms, and legs. Within the moveable limbs there are small-scale body-parts that can be directly moved in response to the will (such as the fingers, the toes, and the lower jaw) and others that cannot (such as the base of the skull). A joint is a body-part that affords the possibility of moving a further body-part, such as the neck, the elbow, or the ankle. In the human body, the relatively immoveable torso is linked by joints to five moveable limbs (the head, two legs, and two arms), each of which is further segmented by means of further joints. These joints provide the fixed points in terms of which the particular A-location and B-location of individual body-parts at a time can be given.

A particular bodily A-location is given relative to the joints that bound the body-part within which it is located. A particular point in the forearm is specified relative to the elbow and the wrist. It will be the point that lies on the surface of the skin at such-and-such a distance and direction from the wrist and such-and-such a distance and direction from the elbow. This mode of determining A-location secures the defining feature of A-location, which is that a given point within a given body-part will have the same A-location irrespective of how the body as a whole moves, or of how the relevant body-part moves relative to other body-parts. The A-location of a given point within a given body-part will remain constant in both those movements, because neither of those movements will bring about any changes in its distance and direction from the relevant joints.

The general model for identifying B-locations is as follows. A particular constant A-location is determined relative to the joints that bound the body-part within which it falls. That A-location will either fall within the (relatively) immoveable torso or it will fall within a moveable limb. If it falls within the (relatively) immoveable torso then its B-location will also be fixed relative to the joints that bound the torso (neck, shoulders, and leg sockets)—that is to say, A-location and B-location will coincide. If, however, that A-location falls within a moveable limb, then its B-location will be fixed recursively relative to the joints that lie between it and the immoveable torso. The B-location will be specified in terms of the angles of the joints that lie between it and the immovable torso. Some of these joint angles will be rotational (as with the elbow joint, for example). Others will be translational (as with the middle finger joint).

This way of specifying A-location and B-location seems to capture certain important elements in the phenomenology of bodily awareness.

- We do not experience peripheral body parts in isolation, but rather as attached to other body-parts. Part of what it is to experience my hand as being located at a certain place is to experience that disposition of arm-segments in virtue of which it is at that place.

- It is part of the phenomenology of bodily awareness that sensations are always experienced within the limits of the body. This is exactly what one would expect given the coding in terms of A-location and B-location. There are no points in (non-pathological) body-space that do not fall within the body.

- Although B-location is specified recursively in terms of the series of joint angles between a given A-location and the immovable torso, the torso does not function as the origin of a Cartesian frame of reference.

To return, then, to Merleau-Ponty, my proposal is that a due recognition of the distinctive frame of reference relative to which proprioception and somatosensations are located can do justice to many of his insights about the phenomenology of bodily awareness. Moreover, and this is the important point when it comes to skepticism about Merleau-Ponty's distinction between the objective body and the phenomenal body, the distinctiveness of bodily awareness is being accommodated at the level of sense rather than the level of reference—in terms of how we represent the body. There is no temptation to postulate a phenomenal body that stands apart from the objective body. The fact that we experience our own bodies in terms of a non-Cartesian reference frame does not in any sense rule out our bodies being ontologically on a par with objects that we experience in terms of a Cartesian reference frame. Nor does it preclude our studying bodily experience from the third-person, scientific perspective. Indeed, as I shall try to bring out in the next section, a proper understanding of the reference frame governing bodily awareness opens up a number of exciting possibilities for the scientific study of bodily awareness.

5. THE SPATIALITY OF BODILY AWARENESS AND THE CONTROL OF ACTION

The previous section offered a way of thinking about the spatiality of bodily awareness as fundamentally different from the spatial content of visual and other forms of exteroceptive awareness. One obvious question that this raises is how proprioceptive content features in the control of action, given that action requires the contribution and integration of proprioceptive and exteroceptive awareness. What I will try to do in this final section is explain how the account I have offered of the spatial content of somatic proprioception fits in with some influential current thinking about motor control. This will go some way towards substantiating my earlier comments about the possibility of incorporating the distinctive phenomenology of bodily awareness within a 'third-person' perspective on agency.

Any planned motor movement directed towards an extra-bodily object requires two basic types of information:

1. Information about the position of the target relative to the body.
2. Information about the starting position of the relevant limb (the hand in the case of a reaching movement).

The first question to ask is how this position information is coded. Recent work, based on the study of trajectory errors and the velocity profiles of hand movements, suggests that the first type of information is coded in extrinsic coordinates in a frame of reference centered on the hand (Ghez et al. 2000). Intended reaching movements are coded, roughly speaking, in terms of their goal and end-point, rather than the means by which that end-point is to be achieved. This coding involves hand-centered vectors, rather than the complex muscle forces and joint torques required for the action to be successfully carried out. One source of evidence for this is that hand movements directed at extra-bodily targets have constant kinematic profiles, remaining straight and showing bell-shaped velocity curves with predictable acceleration at the beginning of the movement and deceleration as the target is approached (Morasso 1981). These kinematic profiles do not seem to be correlated with joint movements. There is considerable debate about whether the frame of reference on which target position is coded is egocentric or allocentric (Jeannerod 1997), but there is relatively little dispute that the coordinates are extrinsic rather than intrinsic (but see Uno et al. 1989 who suggest that the kinematic profiles observed by Morasso are consistent with the mini-mization of overall joint torque).

Turning to the second type of information, information about the starting position of limbs, the thrust of this essay has been that awareness of the body derived from somatic proprioception and somatosensation is not coded on either an object-centered or a body-centered frame of reference. The coordinates on which the location of body-parts is coded are intrinsic rather than extrinsic. This leads us to an obvious second question: how is this type of bodily awareness involved in the control of action? The experienced spatiality of the body, as I have analyzed it, is closely bound up with awareness of the body's possibilities for action. The body presents itself phenomenologically as segmented into body-parts separated by joints because these are the natural units for movement. But what we need to know are the details of the contribution that somatic proprioception makes to the initiation and control of action.

If the spatial dimension of proprioception and somatosensation is as I have described it, somatic proprioception clearly cannot provide information about the position of the relevant limb that will be *sufficient* to fix the initial position of the movement vector. Somatic proprioception and somatosensation provide informa-tion about how limbs are distributed, but this information will not suffice to fix the starting-position of the hand in a way that allows immediate computation of the movement vector required to reach the target. There is no immediate way of computing the trajectory between the location of a limb given in terms of A-location and B-location, and a target location given in terms of extrinsic coordinates. As Merleau-Ponty puts it in a passage cited earlier, 'the outline of my body is a frontier which ordinary spatial relations do not cross' (1962: 98). To put things somewhat more prosaically, acting effectively upon the world requires some sort of translation between two fundamentally different coordinate frames. The translation required for the calculation of the movement vector will involve integrating information derived from the various mechanisms of bodily awareness with visually derived infor-mation. This yields a testable prediction, namely, that subjects who are prevented from seeing their hands before making a reaching movement to a visible target should not be capable of making accurate movements. And this in fact is what experimenters have found (Ghez et al. 1995). The fact that information derived from bodily aware-ness is not sufficient to guide and control action is powerful evidence that there is no single spatial coordinate system that encompasses both bodily awareness and external perception.

Does the specific proposal that the coordinate system of bodily awareness should be understood in terms of A-location and B-location (as distinct from the general proposal that the spatiality of the body is fundamentally different from the spatiality of the perceived world) link up in any interesting ways with the empirical study of action?

Many researchers into motor control currently think that we need to distinguish the kinematics of motor control from the dynamics of motor control (Bizzi and Mussa-Ivaldi 2000). Movements are planned in purely kinematic terms, as a sequence of positions in peri-personal space that the hand will successively occupy during the performance of the movement. Clearly, however, the actual execution of the movement depends upon these extrinsically specified feedforward motor commands being implemented by intrinsically specified muscle forces, joint angles, joint torque, and so forth. The transition from extrinsically specified coordinates to intrinsically specified coordinates comes when the nervous system computes the dynamical implementation of the kinematically specified goal. Various proposals have been made about how this computation is achieved.[17] One traditional assumption is that this is a process of reverse engineering, so that the calculation of the muscle forces and joint angles required to implement the movement is achieved by working backwards from the trajectory of the end-point. There are obvious problems of computational tractability here. The problem does not have a unique solution, and in any case there are likely to be considerable difficulties in factoring in biomechanical factors due to fatigue and other variables. Accordingly it has been suggested that the translation into intrinsic coordinates does not depend upon the solution of complex inverse-dynamic and inverse-computations but instead involves translating the targeted endpoint into a series of equilibrium positions (Feldman 1986). The basic thought here is that muscles and reflexes work as springs in ways that allow effector limbs to be treated as mass-spring systems that have adjustable equilibria. Motor planning, on this model, involves determining the equilibrium positions for the relevant effector limbs.

Whether the inverse-dynamic approach or the equilibrium approach is correct, it is precisely at this point that proprioceptively derived information about the distribution of body-parts becomes crucial. The frame of reference of the intrinsic coordinates in which joint angles and equilibrium positions are coded seems much closer to the frame of reference of proprioceptive bodily awareness as I have characterized it than it is to the Cartesian frames of reference on which movement endpoints are coded. This provides a good explanation of why proprioceptive and somatosensory feedback is able to play such an integral part in the smooth performance and correction of actions, as indeed in the development of internal models of limb dynamics. The feedforward commands directed at the hand are recursively structured in much the same way as proprioceptive feedback from the hand and intervening body-segments. Motor commands to the hand need to specify appropriate angles for the shoulder, the elbow, and the wrist. Proprioceptive feedback about the (B)-location of the hand will equally specify the relevant joint angles. Comparison is straightforward. The crucial role of bodily awareness in the initiation and control of action comes at the point of transition between kinematic plan and dynamic instruction, as well as later on in the execution of the movement. What makes it possible for somatic proprioception to perform this role is that the awareness of the body it provides is coded on a frame of reference that maps straightforwardly onto the internal model of limb dynamics that specifies the body's potentialities for movement.

---

[17] For introductory surveys see Brown and Rosenbaum (2002) and Wolpert and Ghahramani (2002).

6. CONCLUSION

Let me draw the threads of the argument together. I began by considering two of the central themes in Merleau-Ponty's discussion of the body in *Phenomenology of Perception*. The first theme stresses the distinctiveness of how we experience our own bodies, and in particular the phenomenological differences between our awareness of the spatiality of our own bodies and our awareness of the spatiality of the extra-bodily physical world. This theme is predominantly phenomenological. The second theme has to do with the relation between the phenomenological investigation of bodily awareness and the scientific study of the body. This second theme emerges particularly in Merleau-Ponty's development of the distinction between the objective body and the phenomenal body—between the body as a physical mass of bone, muscles, and nerves and the body as it is lived and experienced. As we saw, Merleau-Ponty develops this distinction in a way that places our first-person experience of our bodies and of our actions outside the domain of third-person physiology and scientific psychology.

The principal aim of this essay has been to try to accommodate the insights behind the first theme in *Phenomenology of Perception* in a way that keeps the body and bodily awareness 'within the world', and hence without following Merleau-Ponty in the conclusions he draws from the distinction between the phenomenal body and the objective body. It is true that our experience of our own bodies and of our own agency has a number of very distinctive features that sets it apart from our experience of non-bodily objects. But these differences can, I suggested, be illuminated by thinking about the physiological and psychological mechanisms and information sources that underlie them. As we saw in the context of Merleau-Ponty's discussion of Schneider, careful distinctions between different types of body-relative information and different ways of representing the body show promise for dealing with the puzzles and problems that led Merleau-Ponty to the distinction between phenomenal body and objective body. More importantly, I proposed a way of thinking about the spatiality of bodily awareness that goes a considerable way to explaining the fundamental differences that Merleau-Ponty identified between our experience of our bodies and our experience of non-bodily objects. The key to these differences is that bodily locations are given on a non-Cartesian frame of reference. As brought out in the final section, this way of thinking about the phenomenology of bodily awareness has interesting and fruitful connections with current thinking about motor control.

REFERENCES

Anscombe, E. (1957) *Intention* (Ithaca, NY: Cornell University Press).
—— (1962) 'On Sensations of Position', *Analysis* 22: 55–8.
Armstrong, D. M. (1962) *Bodily Sensations* (London: Routledge & Kegan Paul).
Bermúdez, J. L. (1998) *The Paradox of Self-Consciousness* (Cambridge, Mass.: MIT Press).

Bermúdez, J. L. (2004) 'The Phenomenology of Bodily Awareness. *Theoria et Historia Scientiarum*', *International Journal for Interdisciplinary Studies*, 7: 43–52.

Bermúdez, J., Marcel, A. J., and Eilan, N. (eds.) (1995) *The Body and the Self* (Cambridge, Mass.: MIT Press).

Bizzi, E. (2000) 'Motor Control', in Wilson and Keil (1999).

Bizzi, E. and Mussa-Ivaldi, F. A. (2000) 'Toward a Neurobiology of Coordinate Transformations', in Gazzaniga (2000).

Brand, M. and Walton, D. (eds.) (1976) *Action Theory* (Dordrecht: Reidel).

Brown, L. E. and Rosenbaum, D. A. (2002) 'Motor Control: Models', in Nadel (2002).

Cassam, Q. (1997) *Self and World* (Oxford: Oxford University Press).

Chisholm, R. (1976) 'The Agent as Cause', in Brand and Walton (1976).

Cole, J. and Paillard, J. (1995) 'Living without Touch and Information about Body Position and Movement', in Bermúdez et al. (1995).

Davidson, D. (1980) *Essays on Actions and Events* (Oxford: Oxford University Press).

Dillon, M. C. (1988) *Merleau-Ponty's Ontology* (Bloomington: Indiana University Press).

Feldman, A. G. (1986) 'Once More on the Equilibrium-point Hypothesis (lambda model) for Motor Control', *Journal of Motor Behavior* 18: 17–54.

Gazzaniga, M. S. (ed.) (2000) *The New Cognitive Neurosciences* (Cambridge, Mass.: MIT Press).

Ghez, C., Gordon, J., and Ghilardi, M. F. (1995) 'Impairments of Reaching Movements in Patients without Proprioception II: Effects of Visual Information on Accuracy', *Journal of Neurophysiology* 73: 36–372.

Hsiao, S. S., Yoshioka, T., and Johnson, K. O. (2002) 'Somesthesis, Neural Basis Of', in Nadel (2002).

Kenny, A. (1963) *Action, Emotion and Will* (London: Routledge & Kegan Paul).

Jeannerod, M. (1997) *The Cognitive Neuroscience of Action* (Oxford: Blackwell).

Melzack, R. (1992) 'Phantom Limbs', *Scientific American* 266: 120–6.

Merleau-Ponty, M. (1962) *The Phenomenology of Perception* (London: Routledge & Kegan Paul).

Morasso, P. (1981) Spatial Control of Arm Movements, *Experimental Brain Research* 42: 223–7.

Nadel, L. (ed.) (2002) *Macmillan Encyclopedia of Cognitive Science* (London: Macmillan).

O'Connor, T. (2000) *Persons and Causes* (Oxford: Oxford University Press).

O'Shaughnessy, B. (1980) *The Will: A Dual Aspect Theory* (Cambridge: Cambridge University Press).

—— (1995) 'Proprioception and the Body Image', in Bermúdez et al. (1995).

Paillard, J., Michel, F., and Stelmach, G. (1983) 'Localization without Content: A Tactile Analogue of Blindsight', *Archives of Neurology* 40: 548–51.

Priest, G. (1998) *Merleau-Ponty* (London: Routledge).

Roberts, D. (2002) *Signals and Perception: The Fundamentals of Human Sensation* (Basingstoke: Palgrave Macmillan).

Semenza, C. and Goodglass, H. (1985) 'Localization of Body Parts in Brain Injured Subjects', *Neuropsychologica* 23: 161–75.

Shallice, T. (1988) *From Neuropsychology to Mental Structure* (Cambridge: Cambridge University Press).

Taylor, C. (1964) *The Explanation of Behaviour* (London: Routledge & Kegan Paul).

Uno, Y., Kawato, M., and Suzuki, R. (1989) 'Formation and Control of Optimal Trajectory in Human Multi-joint Arm Movement: Minimum Joint-torque Model', *Biological Cybernetics* 61: 89–101.

Weiskrantz, L. (1986) *Blindsight: A Case Study and Implications* (Oxford: Oxford University Press).

Wilson, R. A. and Keil, F. C. (1999) *The MIT Encyclopedia of the Cognitive Sciences* (Cambridge, MA: MIT Press).

Wolpert, D. and Ghahramani, Z. (2002) 'Motor Learning Models', in Nadel (2002).

Index